STANDARD LEVEL
HIGHER LEVEL

**PEARSON BACCALAUREATE**

# English B
## Student Book

PAT JANNING • PATRICIA MERTIN

Supporting every learner across the IB continuum

Published by Pearson Education Limited, Edinburgh Gate, Harlow, Essex, CM20 2JE.

www.pearsonglobalschools.com

Text © Pearson Education Limited 2014

Edited by Nicole Elliot
Designed and typeset by Astwood Design and Cobalt id
Project managed by Cambridge Publishing Management Limited
Cover design by Pearson Education Limited
Cover image © Bridget Davey Photography

The rights of Pat Janning and Patricia Mertin to be identified as authors of this work have been asserted by them in accordance with the Copyright, Designs and Patents Act 1988.

First published 2014

17 16 15 14
IMP 10 9 8 7 6 5 4 3 2 1

**British Library Cataloguing in Publication Data**
A catalogue record for this book is available from the British Library

ISBN 978 1 447 94413 3
eBook only ISBN 978 1 447 94417 1

**Copyright notice**
All rights reserved. No part of this publication may be reproduced in any form or by any means (including photocopying or storing it in any medium by electronic means and whether or not transiently or incidentally to some other use of this publication) without the written permission of the copyright owner, except in accordance with the provisions of the Copyright, Designs and Patents Act 1988 or under the terms of a licence issued by the Copyright Licensing Agency, Saffron House, 6–10 Kirby Street, London EC1N 8TS (www.cla.co.uk). Applications for the copyright owner's written permission should be addressed to the publisher.

Printed in Italy by Lego S.p.A

**Websites**
Pearson Education Limited is not responsible for the content of any external internet sites. It is essential for tutors to preview each website before using it in class so as to ensure that the URL is still accurate, relevant and appropriate. We suggest that tutors bookmark useful websites and consider enabling students to access them through the school/college intranet.

**Acknowledgements**
Every effort has been made to contact copyright holders of material reproduced in this book. Any omissions will be rectified in subsequent printings if notice is given to the publishers.

The assessment criteria have been reproduced from IBO documents. Our thanks go to the International Baccalaureate Organization for permission to reproduce its intellectual copyright.

The material has been developed independently by the publisher and the content is in no way connected with or endorsed by the International Baccalaureate (IB). International Baccalaureate® is a registered trademark of the International Baccalaureate Organization.

The publisher would like to thank the following for their kind permission to reproduce their photographs:

(Key: b-bottom; c-centre; l-left; r-right; t-top)

**123RF.com:** Alexander HAA1/4bert 344, Andrfei Krauchuk 37cr, belchonock 332tl, Burak Cakmak 332br, Carsten Reisinger 346b, chris willemsen 292, Dmitriy Shpilko 334-335b, Dmytro Pauk 222, 223, Fedor Selivanov 26, Felix Pergande 342, greatandlittle 44, Heinz Leitner 259, Jacek Chabraszewski 240, Jakub Cejpek 324cl, jantra suktaworn 42, Jeff Crow 291, Jit Lim 284, joannawnuk 350cr, Kamaga 240-241b, kzenon 307, lattesmile 332cl, miss_j 260, nataliia 349, Olga Dmitrieva 243, Rancz Andrei 378-379t, 387t, robodread 293tr, 293bl, 294, 295, Ruth Black 341b, Saergii Koval 281, serg_v 226, subbotina 332bl, 333t, Thanida Nianpradit 321l, Vera Kuttelvaserova Stuchelova 216, yanlev 241cl; **2014 Ryan's Well Foundation, all rights reserved:** 13tc, 13tr, 13bl, 14t, 14c, 14b, 15t, 15b; **Adriaan van der Bergh:** 161; **Alamy Images:** age fotostock Spain, S.J. 56, age fotostock Spain, S.L. 61, CBW 69, david donohue 140, eye35.pix 6, Fabienne Fossez 74, Image Republic Inc 10-11, Janine Wiedel Photolibrary 105, Jeff Morgan 253, Jeffrey Blakler 221, Martyn Evans 154, MBI 165, Melba Photo Agency 328, Oliver Pumfrey 313, Olivier Asselin 168, Steve Bloom Images 18, Tim Graham 94tr, United Archives GmbH 315, Uwe Skrzypczak 17t, Wayne HUTCHINSON 1/b, ZUMA Press, Inc 298bl, 299; **Bahamas Tourist Office:** Terrance Strachan 347; **Bernd-Michael Mertin:** 285; **Klaas Gettner:** 351; **(c) Telegraph Media Group:** 357; Corbis: Christie's Images 397r, Lemage 66, Thinkstock 29; **Creative Commons http://creativecommons.org:** Eric Gjerde 218, Peter Tittenberger 170; **Digital Vision:** Rob van Petten 118; **DK Images:** Dave King 336, Dorling Kindersley 81br, 323b, Gary Ombler 156, Linda Whitwam 238b, Lloyd Park 300, Peter Anderson 224, Ram Rahman 271bl; **Fotolia.com:** africa 34, ahmety34 398c, Bablo 215, Christian Kipka 398br, Frank Boston 331, giadophoto 398bl, Intellistudies 84br, Kaktus2536 79, Kowalewski 40, Maksim Kostenko 176, Marcel Schauer 268, Monkey Business 54, T.Michel 398tl, V.R.Murralinath 83; **Fullwood Ltd. Ellesmere:** www.fullwood.com with permission 377tc; **Getty Images:** Darryl Leniuk 323t, David Roth 160, Gary Burke 144, Hagen Hopkins/Stringer 341t, Hiroko Masuike/Stringer 353, Ian McKinnell 194, LatitudeStock - TTL 326, Laurence Dutton 92, LEMAIRE StAphane/hemis.fr 70-71, Lester Lefkowitz 24, Matt Cardy/Stringer 289, Maximilian Stock Ltd 366, Michael Blann 250, Warwick Lister-Kaye 329; **GNU Free Documentation License: Wikipedia:** 32, 94bl, 359t, 373, 374; **Illustrated London News Picture Library:** Ingram Publishing/Alamy 67tr, 67br, Ingram Publishing/Alamy 67tr, 67br; **iStockphoto:** 101dalmatians 43, 298tl, 298br, amphotora 128, Antagain 219, Artpilot 330, chuyu 37b, ClarkandCompany 211br, DavorLovincic 63, ewastudio 20, GlobalStock 191, klikk 8, lisegagne 35, livecal 388-399, Meinzahn 81bl, Mi 372, MistikaS 304, monkybusinessimage 201, nale 302, omersukrugoksu 345, omersukrugoksy 283, onfilm 256, oqlpo 361, Purdue9394 230, Raycat 354, s-c-s 210-211, Sezeryadigar 113, STILLFX 108, stocknshares 338, Tolga_TEZCAN 85, 86, 287, 288r, Vertigo3d 197, 198, 199, VisualCommunications 286; **Jupiterimages:** Polka Dot 97; **Leeds Teaching Hospitals NHS Trust with permission:** 355; **Leonora Saunders:** with permission from Leonora Saunders http://www.leonorasaunders.co.uk 98, 99, 100, 101, 103, with permission from Leonora Saunders http://www.leonorasaunders.co.uk 98, 99, 100, 101, 103, with permission from Leonora Saunders http://www.leonorasaunders.co.uk 98, 99, 100, 101, 103, with permission from Leonora Saunders http://www.leonorasaunders.co.uk 98, 99, 100, 101, 103, with permission from Leonora Saunders http://www.leonorasaunders.co.uk 98, 99, 100, 101, 103; **National Archives and Records Administration (NARA):** 47; **Pearson Education Ltd:** Naki Kouyioumtzis 130, Sozaijiten 244cl; **Penguin Books Ltd:** (Stockett,K) 52, (T.C.Boyle), The Tortilla Curtain by T. Coraghessan Boyle, copyright 1995 T. Coraghessan Boyle. Used by permission of Viking Penguin, a division of Penguin Group (USA) LLC 60; **PhotoDisc:** Andrew Ward/

Life File 320; **photos8.com:** 149; **Rough Guides:** Chloe Roberts 310, Chris Christoforo 306b, Jean-Christophe Godet 401, Martin Richardson 271tl, Nelson Hancock 68t; **Shutterstock.com:** 1000 Words 217t, Africa Studio 350b, Aletia 110, Ammit Jack 296, amybbb 238t, Andrjuss 45, Angela Waye 172, Anneka 195, bikeriderlondon 271tc, 311, 402tc, BMCL 265t, Boris15 68b, Clive Chilvers 266, CREATISTA 115, 368tl, 400tr, Danny E Hooks 337tr, Denis Radovanovic 244b, djem 314, Dmitry Kalinovsky XV, 293, dotshock 244t, DVARG 48-49, Elena Dijour 263, erandamx 2, Ewa Studio 402tr, Georgios Kollidas 94cl, grafvision 142, Grandpa 246, Gyva Fotografija 335t, Herbert Kratky 288, Hurst Photo 337tl, igor kisselev 30, James Steidl 196, jan kranendonk 272, JASPERIMAGE 321, Jayakumar 84c, Joe Gough 255, Johan Larson 400tl, John Wollwerth 237, Jorg Hackemann 84tr, joshya 363, kavring 397l, Kevin Day 319, Kevin Renes 367cr, Kiev. Victor 147, 261, Kozorez Vladislav 364, lancu Cristian 399, Lichtmeister 187, lightpoet 163, lightwavemedia 178, Margot Petroski 370t, Marisa estivill 382-383, MilanB 398tr, Monkey Business Images 120, 232, 235, 370b, mrmichaelangelo 324t, Nathalie Speliers Ufermann 94br, netsuthep 217b, oliveromg 333b, ollyy 369, ombaert Patrick 265b, Orhan Cam 271br, Paolo Bona 324b, pavalena 346t, Peter Weber 402tl, PHOTOCREO Michal Bednarek 370tc, Photosani 290, picturepartners 228, Poznyakov 125, PT Images 400cl, Rob Marmion 164, romakoma 400cr, Sheftsoff 400bl, Sofarina79. 271tr, spirit of america 88, steve estvanik 84l, Syda Productions 368tr, Thomas M Perkins 59, Tsekhmister 359b, wavebreakmedia 370bc, 400br, wong yu liang 350t, Zoltan Katona 94l; **Universidad Politecnica de Madrid:** 377tl; **Vision Robotics Corporation:** copyright 2004, all rights reserved 375, 377tc; **www.hotsmartwatch.com:** with permission 185

**Cover images:** *Front:* **Bridget Davey**

All other images © Pearson Education

We are grateful to the following for permission to reproduce copyright material:

**Photographs and illustrations**

Photographs on pages 14-15 Ryan and Jimmy meeting for the first time, Ryan at his first well at Angolo Primary School, Ryan assisting a child, Uganda, Ryan with Ugandan children, Ryan at a well in Uganda, Pen-pals, now brothers, Ryan and Jimmy, © 2014 Ryan's Well Foundation, all rights reserved; Book cover on page 52 from *The Help*, Penguin Books (Stockett, K); Book cover on page 60 from *The Tortilla Curtain* Penguin Books (T. C. Boyle), The Tortilla Curtain by T. Coraghessan Boyle, copyright © 1995 T. Coraghessan Boyle. Used by permission of Viking Penguin, a division of Penguin Group (USA) LLC; Photographs on pages 98-103 Katie Gillard, Fran Wilkins, Rachel Martin, Caroline Lake, Charlotte Harbottle, with permission from Leonora Saunders http://www.leonorasaunders.co.uk/ ; Photograph on page 161 with permission from Adriaan van der Bergh; Photograph on page 185, HOT Smart Watch with permission from www.hotsmartwatch.com; Photograph on page 355 from UK''s first hand transplant patient describes progress *The Telegraph*, 09/02/2013, Leeds Teaching Hospitals NHS Trust with permission; Photograph on page 357 from Ears and noses could be grown in lab, *The Telegraph* 02/03/2014 (Knapton, S), copyright © Telegraph Media Group Limited; Illustration on page 377 The farmer of the future? The fruit picking Orange Harvester, provided by Vision Robotics Corporation © copyright 2004 Vision Robotics Corporation, all rights reserved; Illustration on page 377 Merlin Robotic Milker, Fullwood Ltd. Ellesmere www.fullwood.com with permission; Illustration on page 377 Rosphere Milker, with permission from Universidad Politécnica de Madrid.

**Text**

Extract on page 3 adapted from Food Waste facts, United Nations with permission; Article on page 6 adapted from Homelessness, hunger climbing in U.S. cities, mayors' survey *L A Times*, 11/12/2013 (Matt Pearce); Article on page 20 from Food-share database to end supermarket waste: Stores boost links with charities to help the hungry hungry, *Mail Online* 03/07/2012, © Daily Mail 2012; Link on page 20 from http://www.dailymail.co.uk/news/article-2168018/Food-share-database-end-supermarket-waste-Stores-boost-links-charities-help-hungry.html#ixzz2eJJqupUB, © Daily Mail 2012; Article on pages 10–11 adapted from A clean water crisis, with permission from National Geographic Magazine; Extract on page 13,14,15 adapted from Ryan's well foundation mission, © 2014 Ryan's Well Foundation, all rights reserved; Article on page 25 adapted from History of Wind Energy from http://www1.eere.energy.gov/wind/wind_history.html U.S. Department of Energy, Source: U.S. Energy Information Administration (2014); Article on page 28 adapted from Why I don't think wind costs the earth *Daily Express*, 11/08/2012 (Smith, M), RenewableUK with permission; Article on page 31 adapted from Wind farms are useless, says Duke of Edinburgh *Daily Telegraph*, 19/11/2011 (Wynne-Jones, J), copyright © Telegraph Media Group Limited; Article on page 34 adapted from International Energy Agency, © 2014 OECD/IEA, www.iea.org/topics/energypoverty; Article on page 35 adapted from International Energy Agency (IEA), © 2014 OECD/IEA www.iea.org/topics/energypoverty; Article on page 36 adapted from Wind farms are robbing Britain of its porpoise Wild Notebook column, *The Times*, 27/07/2013 (Barnes,S), © The Times 2013; Article on page 54 adapted from The Cost of a T-Shirt *The Times London Leader*, 11/05/2013, © The Times 2013; Article on page 41 adapted from Ethics are soon forgotten when faced with a five pound dress, *Independent*, 25/04/2013 (Hamilton, C),© The Independent 2013; Article on page 44 adapted from Fight Slavery Now, with permission from Avra Cohen, Co-organizer, Fight Slavery Now! http://www.FightSlaveryNow.Org; Article on page 52 adapted from A review of the novel 'The Help' by Kathryn Stockett, *The Guardian*, 14/01/2012 (NewYorkGirl), Guardian News and Media Ltd; Extract on page 60, 61 adapted from *The Tortilla Curtain*, Chapter on illegal immigration, Penguin Books (Boyle, TC 1995) pp. 101–102, ; Article on page 63, 64 adapted from An illegal immigrant's story – From arriving a slave to working on checkout at Tesco, *Daily Mirror*, 01/02/2014 (Wynne Jones, R); Article on page 70, 71 adapted from Stuck between two worlds, life of an Illegal Immigrant in Australia, Artespresso, Zhou M, 12/06/2014, with permission from Mingyue Zhou; Extract on pageS 75, 76, 77, 78, 79 from Malala Yousafzai's speech *The Guardian*, 12/07/2013, with permission from Curtis Brown Agency Ltd; Extract on page 82 from *Witness in the Night* Simon & Schuster (Desa, K 2012) p.67, Simon & Schuster UK Ltd; Extract on page 83 from *Witness in the Night*, Simon & Schuster (Desai, K 2012) p.83, Simon & Schuster UK Ltd; Article on page 85,86 adapted from Education for all in fiction, *The Guardian: Books Blog*, 04/09/2013, © Guardian News and Media Ltd 2013; Article on page 95,96 from Today, girls, it's double maths – in Mandarin, *Sunday Times*, 28/07/2013 (Griffiths, S), © Sunday Times 2013; Article on page 105 adapted from International Women's Day, copyright 2014 Aurora Ventures; Article on pages 98, 99, 101, 102, 103 from Meet the women doing 'men's work' *The Guardian*, 26/04/2013 (Claffey, D), © Guardian News and Media Ltd 2013; Article on page 100 adapted from Rachel Martin, black cab driver, with permission from Eve Katie Sprange; Article on page 109, 110 from Father's Day: The changing face of fatherhood *The Independent*, 17/06/2013 (Moorhead, J), © The Independent 2013; Article on page 113 from Helicopter parents creating a generation incapable of accepting failure, *Daily Telegraph*, 30/08/2013 (Dixon,H), copyright © Telegraph Media Group Limited 2013; Article on page 115, 116 from Mistakes 'Helicopter Parents' Make That Prevent Their Children From Growing Up by Michael S. Broder, Ph.D. Michael S. Broder, Ph.D. is a

iii

psychologist and bestselling author. He conducts seminars, talks, and presentations to professional as well as lay audiences worldwide His latest book is Stage Climbing: The Shortest Path to Your Highest Potential; Article on page 125 from Changing face of childhood *The Telegraph*, 16/02/2013 (Bingham,J), copyright © Telegraph Media Group Limited 2013; Article on pages 118, 119 from The Educating Parent www.homeschoolaustralia.com Paine. B 04/08/2013, with permission from Beverley Paine; Extract on page 119 from *How Children Learn* Penguin Books (Holt, J), How Children Learn by John Holt (Copyright © John Holt, 1964) reprinted by permission of A.M. Heath & Co Ltd.; Article on page 120,121 from The changing role of grandparents © 2013 Age Concern New Zealand Inc; Article on page 129, 130 from The English Language, © British Library Board; Article on page 133, 134 from The history of the English language in 100 places, *The Telegraph*, 27/10/2013 (Copping, J), copyright © Telegraph Media Group Limited; Article on page 136, 137 from Why your mother tongue is important *Huffington Post*, 23/04/2013 (Kumar, R), with permission from the author Rohit Kumar; Extracts on pages 139, 140 from *Lost in Translation* Michael O'Mara Books Limited www.mombooks.com, (Coker, C) from the chapter on the English Language; Article on page 156, 157 from How has advertising changed? Johnson, A GetSmarter. GetSmarter is a premier online education company that partners with prestigious universities and leading organisations to offer a variety of online courses and education solutions; Article on page 145 from Message to Advertisers It's the year of newspapers, 20/06/2013 Raitt,S, Suzanne Raitt with permission; Article on page 147, 148 from What does advertising do?, 31/08/2010, Markman.A, Psychology Today, with permission from Professor Art Markman; Article on pages 149,150,151 from Sold on Language, Sedivy, J, Psychology Today, 20/11/2007, with permission from Dr Julie Sedivy; Article on pages 152,153,154 from Highly Disturbing Trends in Junk Food Advertising to Children, Gottesdiener, L, 29/11/2012, Laura Gottesdiener with permission; Interview on pages 161, 162 from An Interview with an international school technology teacher, with permission from Adriaan van der Bergh; Article on pages 170, 171 from The Hole-in-the-Wall Project HiWEL, The Hole-in-the-Wall Project with permission; Article on pages 172, 173, 174 from *Flattening Classrooms, Engaging Minds*, Pearson (Lindsay and Davis), Lindsay, Julie; Davis, Vicki, Flattening classrooms, engaging minds: move to global collaboration one step at a time 1st, © 2013. Printed and Electronically reproduced by permission of Pearson Education, Inc., Upper Saddle River, New Jersey; Quote on page 175 from Dr Eric Brunsell 03/05/2009, in an email to the NetGenEd project. Dr Eric Brunsell with permission; Article on pages 180,181,182 from 40 years of the mobile phone, *Daily Express*, 03/04/2013 (Lee, A), Daily Express 2013; Article on pages 184,185 from Talk to the hand: HOT watch turns your palm into a mobile phone Fincher, J, 06/08/2013, with permission from Gizmag.com and Jonathan Fincher; Article on pages 190,191 from The future of mobile phones: A remote control for your life *The Independent*, 14/05/2007 (Webb, W), © The Independent 2013; Article on page 187 from Balancing Act: Wellington technology consultant Tilmann Steinmetz has found the perfect way to maintain a good work/life balance - turn your phone off. *Fairfax NZ News*, 17/07/2013 (Cowlishaw, S.), © Fairfaz NZ/Dominion Post; Article on pages 197, 198, 199 from The Influence of Mass Media Mass media is one of the farthest reaching… and take it forward!, Kulkarni, 16/01/2010, www.buzzle.com, Arjun Kulkarni/Buzzle.com; Article on page 201, 202 from How Does Social Media Affect the Way We Communicate?, 01/06/2013, ITViz Multimedia, Australia; http://itviz.com/2013/06/how-does-social-media-affect-the-way-we-communicate/; Article on page 210 from Cyber bullying, *Daily Mail*, 21/10/2013 (Edwards, A), © Daily Mail; Article on page 205 from Tips for dealing with cyberbullying, with permission from The BeatBullying (BB) Group; Extract on page 206, 207 from *Alone Together*, Basic Books (Sherry Turkle 211) pp.172--174, copyright © Oct 2, 2012 Sherry Turkle. Reprinted by permission of Basic Books, a member of the Perseus Books Group; Article on page 215, 216 from Girl Meets Bug: Edible Insects: the Eco-Logical Alternative, Daniella Martin, author of 'Edible: An Adventure Into the World of Eating Insects and the Last Great Hope to Save the Planet'; Article on pages 217, 218, 219 from The Observers, Bermúdez Liévano, A, with permission from Andrés Bermúdez Liévano; Article on pages 220, 221 from Try not to be sick: Rentokil launches pop-up 'pestaurant' with pigeon, worms and ants on the menu, *The Independent*, 15/08/2013 (Saul, H), © The Independent ; Article on pages 222, 223 from Why do you need to eat vegetables every day?, The George Mateljan Foundation. World's Healthiest Foods. Available at: http://whfoods.org/ Accessed on (20/03/2014); Article on pages 226, 227 from Why Do People Become Vegetarians? © The Nemours Foundation/KidsHealth. Reprinted with permission; Article on page 228 from Seaweed as a Food Source, Freelance Commentaries with permission; Article on pages 231, 232 from Text Messaging to Improve Teen Health, *Psych Central: University of Arizona Journal of Nutrition Education and Behavior*. (Nauert, R), Reprinted from Journal of Nutrition Education and Behavior, Volume: 45, Issue: 1, Hingle, M et al, Texting for Health: The Use of Participatory Methods to Develop Healthy Lifestyle Messages for Teens Copyright (2012), with permission from Elsevier; Article on pages 234, 235 from Healthy eating for teens, http://www.nhs.uk/Livewell/Goodfood/Pages/healthy-eating-teens.aspx, NHS Choices, © Crown Copyright 2013 Department of Health; Article on pages 237, 238 from Third of primary school children 'cannot swim', *The Telegraph* 17/05/2012 (Paton,G), copyright © Telegraph Media Group Limited; Article on pages 240, 241 from Too much sport 'may be bad for teens' health, *Medical News Today* (Whiteman, H), www.medicalnewstoday.com; Article on pages 243, 244 from Why team sports really do improve grades, *Daily Mail* 24/05/2013 (Harris, S), © Daily Mail 2013 with permission; Article on pages 246,247 from I wasted so many years dieting, trying to be sexier and worrying about the size of my thighs, *The Times Magazine*, 01/06/2013 (Reid, M); Poetry on page 251 from *The Wicked World* anthology, Puffin Books (Zephaniah, B 2000), reprinted with permission from Penguin Books Ltd; Extract on page 255 from Global Citizens – Make an Impact!, Heritage Learning with permission; Article on page 257 from Europe's most exotic city? It's Manchester! *Daily Mail*, 16/12/2012 (Fagge, N), © Daily Mail 2013 with permission; Article on page 260 from What exactly is a curry?, Cookthink.com, with permission; Article on pages 261, 262 from Spitalfields, London. Cultural diversity is not a new thing in London's East End, Spitalfields E1 with permission; Article on pages 263, 264, 265 from Visit Brick Lane, London. An app for tourists, Design Revolutions; Article on pages 272, 273 from UNESCO declares French cuisine 'world intangible heritage', *The Telegraph*, 16/11/2010 (Samuel, H),copyright © Telegraph Media Group Limited 2010; Article on pages 280, 281 from Robin Cook's chicken tikka masala speech, *The Guardian*, 19/04/2001 (Cook, R), Copyright Guardian News & Media Ltd 2001; Article on page 291 from Sydney Harbour Bridge – Climb it!, RedBalloon with permission; Extract on pages 293, 294 from What is Paintball? Moore, G 22/09/2013, SocialPaintball.com; Extract on pages 294, 295 from 'Paintball and a Child's Mental Health' Moore, G 09/07/2013, SocialPaintball.com; Article on pages 298, 299 from Ryan Doyle: one of the most well-known parkour stars in the UK, Red Bull with permission; Article on pages 298, 299 from Ryan Doyle: biography, World Freerunning Parkour Federation (WFPF) with permission; Article on pages 300, 301 from Pure Adrenaline -Bungee Jumping, www.bungeejumpsscotland.co.uk; Link on page 301 from http://www.bungeejumpsscotland.co.uk/page/bungee#sthash.ALp4uaYA.dpuf, with permission from www.bungeejumpsscotland.co.uk; Extract on pages 302, 303 from Bungy jumping Down Under: Two men put New Zealand on the adventure tourism map, http://www.bungy.co.nz; Extract on page 305 adapted from Taking Part: The National Survey of Culture, Leisure and Sport, Jan–Dec 2010 Statistical Release, March 2011, Department for Culture, Media and Sport, www.culture.gov.uk, Open Government Licence v2.0 © Crown Copyright; Article on page 307 from Men have more leisure time than women, says new report *The Telegraph*, 09/03/2010 (Roberts, L), copyright © Telegraph

Media Group Limited; Article on pages 308, 309, 310 from How 'cheap' leisure pursuits can hit your wallet *The Telegraph*, 14/06/2014 (Gorst-Williams, J), copyright © Telegraph Media Group Limited; Extract on page 310 from Longman Dictionary of Contemporary English, Pearson Education Limited; Article on pages 314, 315 from Great novels can change your life...and your brain *The Telegraph*, 06/01/2014 (Knapton, S), copyright © Telegraph Media Group Limited; Extract on page 317 adapted from Exploring your world – the River Thames, The Southern and South East England Tourist Board, Visit Thames Marketing Partnership; Extract on page 318 adapted from Free things to do beside the River Thames, The Southern and South East England Tourist Board, Visit Thames Marketing Partnership; Poetry on page 319 from A poem about the River Thames Tamasá Reaches, Jenyth Worsley © May 2003; Article on page 320 from Safety from flooding Environment Agency 2013; Article on pages 323, 324 from New Zealand: Sports and leisure 20/12/2012, The Encyclopedia of New Zealand www.teara.govt.nz with permission; Extract on pages 327,328 from New Zealand: The Maori Maori Tourism Limited; Extract on pages 330, 331 from St. Nicholas to Santa: The Surprising Origins of Mr. Claus, *National Geographic* (Handwerk, B), Brian Handwerk/National Geographic Creative; Extract on pages 340, 341 from Hogmanay Customs, May Cropley (Scotland's Enchanting Kingdom.com) with permission; Extract on pages 346, 347 from The Bahamas , The Bahamas Tourist Office UK; Extract on pages 350, 351 from AfternoonTea.co.uk with permission; Article on page 355, 356 from UK's first hand transplant patient describes progress *The Telegraph*, 09/02/2013, copyright © Telegraph Media Group Limited; Article on page 357 from Ears and noses could be grown in lab, *The Telegraph* 02/03/2014 (Knapton, S), copyright © Telegraph Media Group Limited 2013; Extract on page 361 from *Blurb from Pig-Heart Boy*, Ernst Klett Publications (Blackman, M); Extract on pages 361, 362 from *Pig-Heart Boy*, Ernst Klett Publications (Blackman, M) pp.63–4; Extract on page 263 from Be an organ donor, Reprinted with permission from National Kidney Foundation Inc.; Article on page 364 from An organ is sold every hour, WHO warns: Brutal black market on the rise again thanks to diseases of affluence *The Mail* 28/05/2012 (Gayle, D), Mail Online ; Article on page 367 from Descent of man: how texting stops us walking tall, *The Telegraph*, 23/01/2014 (Knapton, S), copyright © Telegraph Media Group Limited 2014; Extract on page 369 from The effects of technology on children, © British Chiropractic Association; Link on page 369 www.Chiropractic-uk.co.uk/straightenup, © British Chiropractic Association Extract on page 370 from Ergonomic Tips for Students Who Use Notebook Computers, Jacobs, K, with permission from Professor Karen Jacobs; Article on pages 372, 373 from Robots in the Home: What Might They Do? from Don Norman's website, jnd.org: 'Robots in the Home: What Might They Do?' http://tinyurl.com/ HomeRobots Copyright 2007–2012 © Donald A. Norman. All rights reserved; Extract on page 374 from Alone Together Basic Books (Turkle, S) pp.105–6, From *Alone Together* by Sherry Turkle, copyright © 2012. Reprinted by permission of Basic Books, a member of The Perseus Books Group; Article on page 375 from Agriculture shock: How robot farmers will take over our fields *Metro*, 23/09/2013, © Metro 2013 ; Blurb on page 379 from *The Book Thief*, Random House Children's Books/Alfred A. Knopf (Zusak,M), Blurb, copyright © 2005 by Alfred A. Knopf, an imprint of Random House Children's; Books; from THE BOOK THIEF by Markus Zusak. Used by permission of Alfred A. Knopf, an imprint of Random House Children's Books, a division of Random House LLC. All rights reserved.; Extract on page 379 from *Unique*, Oxford University Press 'Rollercoasters' (Allen-Gray, A); Extract on page 380 from Penguin Active Reading Teacher Support Programme, Pearson Education 2008, Blurb from *About a Boy* by Nick Hornby, Penguin Books, Pearson Education, Pearson Education Limited; Extract on pages 381, 382, 383, 384 from *Short story We Walked on Water*, Granta (Robertson, E), with permission from Curtis Brown UK Ltd; Article on page 390 from Global warming pause 'may last for another decade', scientists suggest, *The Telegraph*, 21/08/2014 (Gosden, E), copyright © Telegraph Media Group Limited 2014; Article on page 389 from Over £200 million boost for renewables, Department of Energy & Climate Change 24/07/2014; Article on page 391 from Prince Charles: climate change is the greatest challenge facing humanity, *The Telegraph*, 22/09/2014 (Gosden, E), copyright © Telegraph Media Group Limited 2014; Extract on page 391 from Shared interests key to friendship, *Telegraph*, 01/12/2010 (Alleyne, R), copyright © Telegraph Media Group Limited 2010; Article on page 392,393 from How Facebook makes you distrusting and miserable, *The Telegraph*, 01/09/2014 (Sparkes, M), copyright © Telegraph Media Group Limited 2014; Extract on page 393 from Facebook friends are virtual, finds Oxford University study, *Telegraph*, 24/01/2014 (Adams, S), copyright © Telegraph Media Group Limited 2014; Quote on page 398 from Ruth Fulton Benedict From Patterns of Culture, The Science of Custom, reprinted by permission of Mary Catherine Bateson; Quote on page 401 from Albert Einstein, from interview with G. S. Viereck, 'What life means to Einstein', Saturday Evening Post, October 26, 1929, with permission: The Albert Einstein Archives, The Hebrew University of Jerusalem; Extract on page 401 from Definition of Faith, Longman Dictionary of Contemporary English, Pearson Education Limited; Article on pages 403, 404 from Teetering on the Footbridge, June 27, 2006, Wray Herbert APS Association Phsychological Science

# Contents

Introduction ........................................................................... x

How to use your enhanced eBook ............................. xiv

**CORE: GLOBAL ISSUES**

## 01 Food and water
| | | |
|---|---|---|
| **1.1** | Food waste | 3 |
| **1.2** | Food shortages | 6 |
| **1.3** | Water, water, everywhere | 10 |
| **1.4** | Ryan's Well | 13 |

## 02 Wind farms
| | | |
|---|---|---|
| **2.1** | Wind energy | 25 |
| **2.2** | The cost of wind farms | 28 |
| **2.3** | Perspectives on wind farms | 31 |

## 03 Slave labour
| | | |
|---|---|---|
| **3.1** | Cheap products | 41 |
| **3.2** | Slave labour | 44 |
| **3.3** | The story of a slave | 46 |
| **3.4** | *The Help* | 52 |

## 04 Undocumented immigration
| | | |
|---|---|---|
| **4.1** | Undocumented immigration | 57 |
| **4.2** | Undocumented immigration in the UK | 63 |
| **4.3** | Well-known immigrants | 66 |

**CORE: SOCIAL RELATIONSHIPS**

## 05 Education for all
| | | |
|---|---|---|
| **5.1** | Malala Yousafzai | 75 |
| **5.2** | *Witness the Night* | 81 |
| **5.3** | Education for all in fiction | 85 |

## 06 Women's achievements in the 21st century
| | | |
|---|---|---|
| **6.1** | Famous female achievers | 93 |
| **6.2** | Girls in school | 95 |
| **6.3** | Meet the women doing 'men's work' | 98 |

## 07 The family
| | | |
|---|---|---|
| **7.1** | The changing face of fatherhood | 109 |
| **7.2** | Helicopter parents | 113 |
| **7.3** | Home schooling | 118 |
| **7.4** | Grandparents | 120 |

## 08 The English language
| | | |
|---|---|---|
| **8.1** | English as a global language | 129 |
| **8.2** | The history of English | 133 |
| **8.3** | The mother tongue | 136 |
| **8.4** | Lost in translation | 139 |

**CORE: MEDIA AND COMMUNICATION**

## 09 Advertising
| | | |
|---|---|---|
| **9.1** | Advertising in the 21st century | 145 |
| **9.2** | The effects of advertising | 147 |
| **9.3** | The power of language | 149 |
| **9.4** | Advertising and children | 152 |

## 10 Technology in education
| | | |
|---|---|---|
| **10.1** | Laptops in the classroom | 161 |
| **10.2** | Technology in education around the world | 168 |

## 11 Mobile phones
| | | |
|---|---|---|
| **11.1** | Mobile phones and manners | 177 |
| **11.2** | The history of mobile phones | 180 |
| **11.3** | Mobile phones in the future | 184 |
| **11.4** | Mobile phones and stress | 187 |

## 12 Mass media and social media
| | | |
|---|---|---|
| **12.1** | Mass media and social media | 195 |
| **12.2** | Mass media today | 197 |
| **12.3** | The effects of social media | 201 |
| **12.4** | Social media and the family | 206 |

**OPTIONS: HEALTH**

## 13 Alternative food supplies
| | | |
|---|---|---|
| **13.1** | Edible insects | 215 |
| **13.2** | The future is vegetarian! | 222 |
| **13.3** | Anyone for seaweed? | 228 |

# Contents

## 14 Teenage health
- **14.1** Teenage health issues — 231
- **14.2** Young people and sport — 237
- **14.3** What really matters in life — 246

**OPTIONS: CULTURAL DIVERSITY**

## 15 Multicultural Great Britain
- **15.1** The making of a nation — 251
- **15.2** Cultural diversity — 255
- **15.3** Manchester, UK — 256
- **15.4** Colourful London — 261

## 16 The role of culture in our lives
- **16.1** What is culture? — 269
- **16.2** Celebrating cultural diversity — 272
- **16.3** Personal comments on cultural diversity — 275
- **16.4** A political view of cultural diversity — 280
- **16.5** An example of cultural diversity in action — 282

**OPTIONS: LEISURE**

## 17 The changing face of leisure
- **17.1** Adventure sports — 287
- **17.2** Three athletes talk about what motivates them — 289
- **17.3** An unusual place to go climbing — 291
- **17.4** Paintball – more than just a game of tag? — 293
- **17.5** An exhilarating activity for those who don't mind getting wet — 296
- **17.6** Parkour — 298
- **17.7** Bungee jumping — 300

## 18 How we spend our free time
- **18.1** What role does leisure play in our lives? — 305
- **18.2** Reflections on leisure — 306
- **18.3** The cost of leisure — 308
- **18.4** Active leisure — 317
- **18.5** Leisure activities around the world — 321

**OPTIONS: CUSTOMS AND TRADITIONS**

## 19 Customs and traditions around the English-speaking world
- **19.1** New Zealand: Maori — 327
- **19.2** The traditions of Christmas — 330
- **19.3** The traditions of Valentine's Day — 332
- **19.4** Superstitions — 334

## 20 Commonwealth customs and traditions
- **20.1** An introduction to the Commonwealth — 339
- **20.2** Customs and traditions of some Commonwealth countries — 341
- **20.3** England — 349

**OPTIONS: SCIENCE AND TECHNOLOGY**

## 21 Repairing the body
- **21.1** Transplanting a limb — 355
- **21.2** Tissue engineering — 357
- **21.3** Xenotransplantation — 359
- **21.4** The gift of life — 363

## 22 Technology and mankind
- **22.1** Technology and mankind — 367
- **22.2** Robots — 372

## 23 Written Assignment: Higher Level — 378
## 24 Written Assignment: Standard Level — 387

Theory of Knowledge — 397

Index — 405

# Introduction

## IB English B Standard and Higher Level – SL/HL

Welcome to this new English B textbook, which will accompany you for the next two years while you are studying English B for the IB Diploma. The book is divided into several sections, which address the Core themes, the Options themes and the Written Assignment tasks.

The Core chapters, 1–12, deal with Global Issues, Social Relationships, and Media and Communication. Each section has a number of related texts together with the kind of exercises you will meet in Paper One, as well as additional tasks to practise written and oral skills.

The Options chapters, 13–22, cover Health, Cultural Diversity, Leisure, Customs and Traditions, and Science and Technology, with the sort of exercises you will find in Paper Two. For more practice we have also included comprehension questions, vocabulary items and tasks to practise written and oral skills.

## Chapters 23 and 24

These chapters are concerned with the Written Assignment (SL/HL). For Standard Level there are texts which have a common theme and offer you the opportunity to practise cross-reading. You can then choose your own text type to complete the written assignment. The other chapters in the book also have several sections which discuss a related theme and so can be used for additional Written Assignment practice.

For Higher Level there are excerpts from literature and suggestions on how to choose the written task based on the text. In addition, teachers can look in the Teacher's Guide for suggestions and further literature related to the chapter themes. Stimuli for the Higher Level Personal Response can be found throughout the book.

## Chapter 25

This chapter offers a chance for you to become accustomed to the ideas, expressions and ways of thinking required for Theory of Knowledge (TOK). Using the texts and suggestions in the book, you will be able to start discussing some of the ideas in your English B class, so that you will feel more confident in your regular TOK class.

## Oral work

Throughout the book there are suggestions for interactive oral activities, such as discussions, presentations and debates. Visual stimuli are also included as practice material for the Individual Oral with the final examination component in mind.

## Chapters are divided into activities as follows:

### General comprehension

1. What is the definition of *modern energy services*?
2. What effect does the lack of access to energy sources have on the economic development of a country?
3. What is the goal of the organisation World Energy Outlook in collecting information on energy poverty?

**General comprehension:** General questions to get into a text and familiarise yourself with it.

### Zoom in on grammar

**Complex sentences**

Write your own complex sentences using *although* or *despite*.

1. I do not speak good French. People understand me.
2. My mother is on a business trip. We have a cooked dinner every evening.
3. It is pouring with rain. I have hockey training.
4. Playing squash is an unusual hobby. I know five people who play squash.

**Zoom in on grammar:** Grammar explanations or reminders.

### Grammar in context

**Complex sentences**

Look again carefully at the text and notice in particular the verbs, adverbs and conditional sentences and how they are used. Note the interesting sentence structures and try to imitate these structures in your own writing.

**Grammar in context:** Activities and exercises aimed at reusing a grammar point covered in a specific context.

### Text handling

Explain the following words and phrases in your own words.

1. our only source (paragraph 2)
2. abducted (paragraph 3)
3. adjusting to (paragraph 5)

**Text handling:** Exercises designed to familiarise you with the different types of questions you may encounter in any exam paper.

### Written work

Write an email to the writer of the text, either agreeing or disagreeing with the article and justifying your thoughts. Write between 250 and 400 words.

**Written work:** These activities provide writing practice based on the different topics and themes in each chapter.

### Individual oral activity

Research the geography, history or present situation in Rwanda. Use the information you find to make a three to four minute presentation to your class or group. Be ready to answer any question the other students may have.

**Individual oral activity:** These boxes contain activities suitable for practising the skills needed in the Individual Oral Assessment.

# Introduction

### Interactive oral activity

The above texts tell you something about energy poverty. Research this theme yourself and find out further information about some of the issues. Make notes and prepare yourself for a group discussion.

In groups of three or four discuss the contrasting issues of energy poverty in developing countries and environmental protection in developed countries.

Be prepared to report the results of your discussion to the class.

**Interactive oral activity:**
These boxes contain activities suitable for practising the skills needed in the interactive Oral Assessment.

### Creativity, action and service

Creativity, action and service (CAS) involves students in a range of activities alongside their academic studies throughout the Diploma Programme. *Creativity* encourages students to engage in the arts and creative thinking. *Action* seeks to develop a healthy lifestyle through physical activity. *Service* in the community offers a vehicle for a different kind of learning with a practical value. The three strands of CAS enhance students' personal and interpersonal development through experiential learning and enable journeys of self-discovery.

**Creativity, action and service:**
A few Creativity, action and service activities appear when appropriate, as this is an integral part of your IB course.

### Intercultural activity

The text above mentions suffragettes and the right to vote. Research three or four countries around the world to find out if women have the right to vote, and if they have, when it was granted to them. Make bullet points and then with a partner compare your findings and discuss the information that you found. Was there anything that surprised you? Anything that made you want to know more? Anything that made you want to ask questions/find answers?

Women and men have not always had the right to vote for the same length of time in history. What do you think the reasons for this were?

**Intercultural activity:**
Opportunities for you to compare your experiences based on your own cultural background, with the chance to share your ideas in discussion.

### Exam hints

**Remember:**
- Use bullet points only when you present.
- Do not learn the presentation off by heart.
- Look at your audience and talk to them.
- Make your presentation lively and interesting by using a good range of vocabulary and sentence structures.
- Look closely at the rubric, which is used to grade oral presentations, and aim to meet the criteria.

**Exam hints:**
These give hints on how to approach questions, and suggest approaches that examiners like to see. They also identify common pitfalls to understanding and omissions made in answering questions.

### Hotlinks

Hotlink boxes can be found throughout each chapter, indicating that there are weblinks available for further study. To access these links go to www.pearsonhotlinks.com and enter the ISBN or title of this book. Here you can find links to related background material that will help to deepen your interest in and understanding of the topic.

To learn more about Ryan, go to www.pearsonhotlinks.com, enter the title or ISBN of this book and click on Chapter 17.

### Interesting fact

These give background information that will add to your wider knowledge of the topic and make links with other topics and subjects. Aspects such as historic notes on particular topics are included here.

> The boat race described in this poem is an annual rowing competition on the River Thames between Oxford and Cambridge Universities. The first race was in 1829. The course is 4.2 miles (6.8 km).

### Theory of Knowledge

These stimulate consideration of knowledge issues as they arise in context. Each box contains open questions to trigger critical thinking and discussion.

> Texting and tweeting: How are language and emotion influenced by tweeting and texting? To what extent can these be positive or negative?

### Hints for success

These give hints on how to approach questions, and suggest approaches that examiners like to see. They also identify common pitfalls in understanding, and omissions made in answering questions.

> Before you start to write, collect your ideas about this quote. Decide on the position you will take and which text type will be most suitable for your arguments. Be sure to organise your ideas into paragraphs and have a strong opening statement and clear conclusion.

### Cultural facts

These boxes give you cultural information that enriches the content of the text.

> In the past, families sat down to watch TV together, but now with modern devices family members often watch different programmes in different rooms.

## eBook

The eBook version of this book can be accessed online by following the instructions on the inside of the front cover. Details on how to get the most out of your eBook are given on the next page.

For teachers, there is also an accompanying Teacher's Guide that can be downloaded from www.pearsonglobalschools.com/englishbteacherguide. This includes teaching ideas and answers to the questions in this book.

**Improving your skills**

To improve your fluency and accuracy in English we recommend that you:

- make a point of being an active learner
- read and re-read the texts so that your own language and your range of active vocabulary grow
- read and research around the themes studied independently
- keep a vocabulary book, with sections for each topic so that the specific vocabulary related to the themes continues to develop
- take every opportunity to discuss the topics so that you become more confident when speaking and your oral fluency and accuracy develop.

# How to use your enhanced eBook

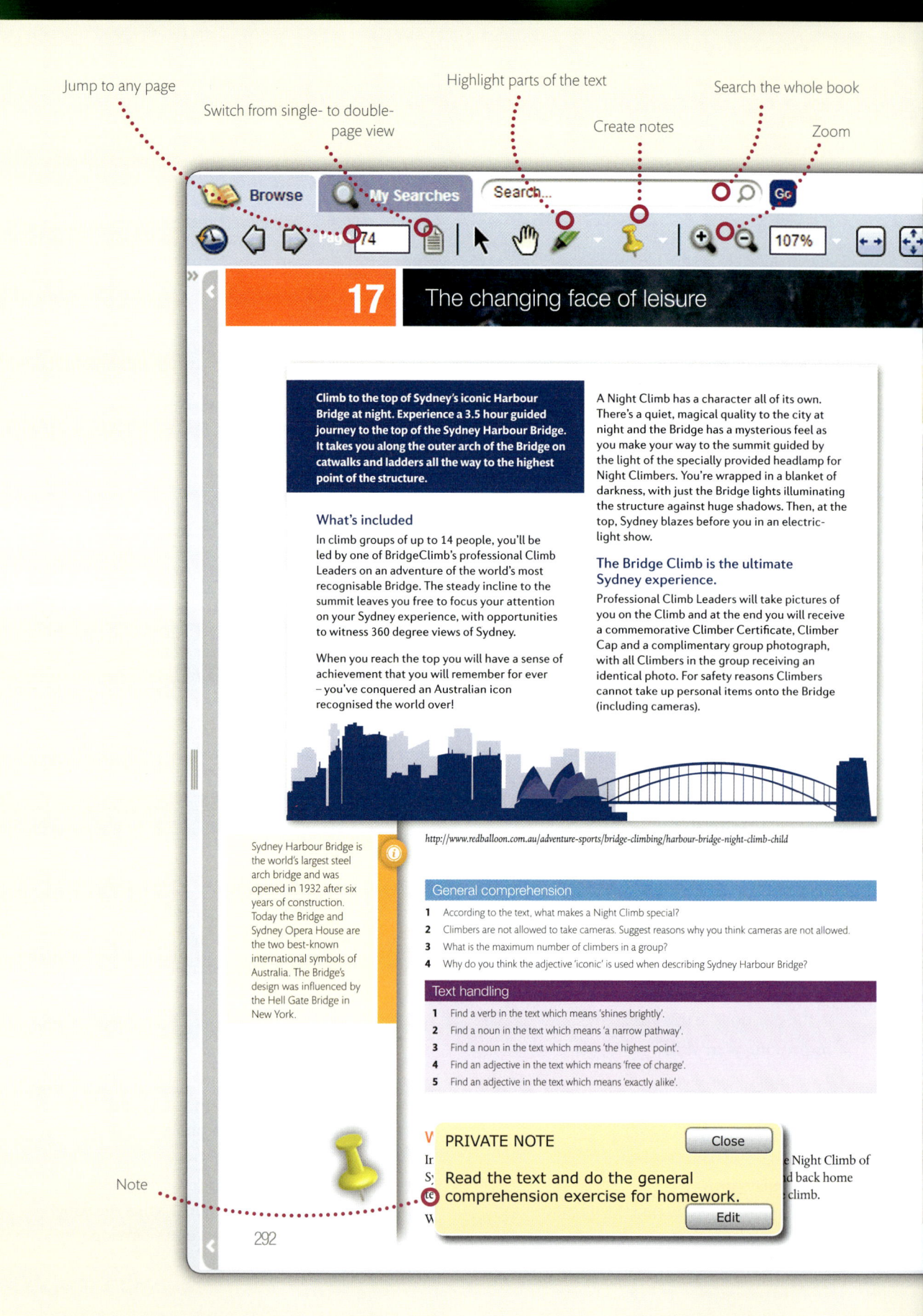

Jump to any page

Switch from single- to double-page view

Highlight parts of the text

Create notes

Search the whole book

Zoom

## 17 The changing face of leisure

**Climb to the top of Sydney's iconic Harbour Bridge at night. Experience a 3.5 hour guided journey to the top of the Sydney Harbour Bridge. It takes you along the outer arch of the Bridge on catwalks and ladders all the way to the highest point of the structure.**

### What's included

In climb groups of up to 14 people, you'll be led by one of BridgeClimb's professional Climb Leaders on an adventure of the world's most recognisable Bridge. The steady incline to the summit leaves you free to focus your attention on your Sydney experience, with opportunities to witness 360 degree views of Sydney.

When you reach the top you will have a sense of achievement that you will remember for ever – you've conquered an Australian icon recognised the world over!

A Night Climb has a character all of its own. There's a quiet, magical quality to the city at night and the Bridge has a mysterious feel as you make your way to the summit guided by the light of the specially provided headlamp for Night Climbers. You're wrapped in a blanket of darkness, with just the Bridge lights illuminating the structure against huge shadows. Then, at the top, Sydney blazes before you in an electric-light show.

### The Bridge Climb is the ultimate Sydney experience.

Professional Climb Leaders will take pictures of you on the Climb and at the end you will receive a commemorative Climber Certificate, Climber Cap and a complimentary group photograph, with all Climbers in the group receiving an identical photo. For safety reasons Climbers cannot take up personal items onto the Bridge (including cameras).

Sydney Harbour Bridge is the world's largest steel arch bridge and was opened in 1932 after six years of construction. Today the Bridge and Sydney Opera House are the two best-known international symbols of Australia. The Bridge's design was influenced by the Hell Gate Bridge in New York.

*http://www.redballoon.com.au/adventure-sports/bridge-climbing/harbour-bridge-night-climb-child*

### General comprehension

1. According to the text, what makes a Night Climb special?
2. Climbers are not allowed to take cameras. Suggest reasons why you think cameras are not allowed.
3. What is the maximum number of climbers in a group?
4. Why do you think the adjective 'iconic' is used when describing Sydney Harbour Bridge?

### Text handling

1. Find a verb in the text which means 'shines brightly'.
2. Find a noun in the text which means 'a narrow pathway'.
3. Find a noun in the text which means 'the highest point'.
4. Find an adjective in the text which means 'free of charge'.
5. Find an adjective in the text which means 'exactly alike'.

**PRIVATE NOTE** — Close

Read the text and do the general comprehension exercise for homework.

Edit

Note

Create a bookmark

Switch to whiteboard view

## 17.4 Paintball – more than just a game of tag?

Text 17.4.1 What is paintball?

http://socialpaintball.com/2013/09/22/what-is-paintball/

**This is such a simple question, but not an easy one to answer. Let me, as a parent, explain to you, a parent, about paintball**

In its basic form, paintball is a game of tag using balls made with gelatin shells filled with water-soluble dye. The "paintballs" are fired by a gun using compressed gas, but the team sport of paintball is a lot more complex.

That's right; I just used the words team, sport and paintball together.

Surprised?

Let's look at how paintball is played. I will get into the various forms of paintball further into the article, but they all have a few things in common.

There is a set of rules for the field of play, such as: keeping your mask on, the field's boundaries, not over-shooting someone, and when you are tagged by a paintball you are out, along with other similar guidelines.

There are referees on the field to ensure that these rules are followed.

There is an objective to the game. That is right: we are not just running around on a field shooting each other. It could be 'tag all the players on the other team', 'capture the flag', 'touch the other team's bunker', 'rescue a down pilot' or a number of other scenarios. We are about teams.

### Types of paintball
I am going to break down paintball into two game types: speedball and woodsball.

*Woodsball*
Woodsball, also known as Rec Ball, is the original form of paintball and is mainly played outside in a natural or semi-built-up environment. For most new parents to paintball, this is usually the first view you have of a paintball field.

Types of field include indoor fields and fields built up with multi-storey buildings and vehicles. Some fields in Europe are composed of entire villages.

Versions of Rec Ball include Tactical-Milsim paintball, which uses tactical or simulated military (milsim) gear, game play and objectives; and big game scenarios which can take place over a few days on large fields.

*Speedball*
Speedball is played on level fields of grass or artificial turf. These fields look like a small soccer field. The bunkers are air-filled and made out of fabric. Speedball fields are mainly found outdoors, but can also be found indoors.

# 01 Food and water

**Opposite** A young man using a traditional method of fishing in Sri Lanka.

## Objectives
- To practise the active and passive voices
- To review complex sentence structures
- To practise the text type of a blog
- To develop persuasive language skills
- To consider the importance of water in our lives

# 1.1 Food waste

## Text 1.1.1 Food waste facts

Read the text and make notes as you read of the key facts which you find surprising.

The impact of food waste is not just financial. Environmentally, food waste leads to wasteful use of chemicals such as fertilizers and pesticides; more fuel used for transportation; and more rotting food, creating more methane – one of the most harmful greenhouse gases that contributes to climate change. Methane is 23 times more potent than $CO_2$ as a greenhouse gas. The vast amount of food going to landfills makes a significant contribution to global warming.

> **Roughly one third of the food produced in the world for human consumption every year – approximately 1.3 billion tonnes – gets lost or wasted.**

Every year, consumers in rich countries waste almost as much food (222 million tonnes) as the entire net food production of sub-Saharan Africa (230 million tonnes).

> **The amount of food lost or wasted every year is equivalent to more than half of the world's annual cereals crop (2.3 billion tonnes in 2009/2010).**

Food loss and waste also amount to a major squandering of resources, including water, land, energy, labour and capital, and needlessly produce greenhouse gas emissions, contributing to global warming and climate change.

> In developing countries food waste and losses occur mainly at early stages of the food value chain and can be traced back to financial, managerial and technical constraints in harvesting techniques as well as storage and cooling facilities. Thus, a strengthening of the supply chain through the support of farmers and investments in infrastructure and transportation, as well as in an expansion of the food and packaging industry could help to reduce the amount of food loss and waste.

# 01 Food and water

As this is an American text, some spellings are slightly different – for example, 'behavior' (not 'behaviour') and 'industrialized' (not 'industrialised').

In medium- and high-income countries food is wasted and lost mainly at later stages in the supply chain. Differing from the situation in developing countries, the behavior of consumers plays a huge part in industrialized countries. Moreover, the study identified a lacking coordination between actors in the supply chain as a contributing factor. Farmer–buyer agreements can be helpful to increase the level of coordination. Additionally, raising awareness among industries, retailers and consumers as well as finding beneficial uses for food that is presently thrown away are useful measures to decrease the amount of losses and waste.

> In the United States 30% of all food, worth US$48.3 billion (€32.5 billion), is thrown away each year. It is estimated that about half of the water used to produce this food also goes to waste, since agriculture is the largest human use of water. (Jones, 2004 cited in Lundqvist *et al.*, 2008)

United Kingdom households waste an estimated 6.7 million tonnes of food every year, around one third of the 21.7 million tonnes purchased. This means that approximately 32% of all food purchased per year is not eaten. Most of this (5.9 million tonnes or 88%) is currently collected by local authorities. Most of the waste (4.1 million tonnes or 61%) is avoidable and the food could have been eaten had it been better managed (WRAP, 2008; Knight and Davis, 2007).

> In the USA, organic waste is the second highest component of landfills, which are the largest source of methane emissions.

Global Food Losses and Food Waste – *FAO, 2011*; The environmental crisis: The environment's role in averting future food crisis – *UNEP, 2009*

## General comprehension

1. Discuss the facts you found surprising and what you have learnt from the text with your group. Brainstorm some ways to help solve the problem – think globally, act locally.

   Then prepare a short group presentation for the rest of the class on this topic, based on the ways you have found to help solve the problem of food wastage.

2. True or false? Justify your answer with a relevant brief quotation from the text.
   a) Global warming is solely caused by food waste.
   b) The causes of food waste in developing countries differ from the causes in medium- to high-income countries.
   c) Improvement in the packaging industry could help reduce food waste in medium- to high-income countries.
   d) The largest human use of water is in agriculture.
   e) One third of the food bought in the UK is wasted.

## Text handling

1. Find words in the text which have the same meaning as the following words. They are in the order of the words you need to find in the text.
   a) powerful
   b) huge
   c) the same as
   d) wasting
   e) followed back
   f) advantageous

2. Explain, in your own words, why the impact of food waste is not just financial. What other effects does it have? Write between 100 and 200 words.

## Zoom in on grammar

### Passive and active sentences

Look at these two sentences.

1. Every year, consumers in rich countries *waste* almost as much food as the entire food production of sub-Saharan Africa.
2. Every year, almost as much food *is wasted* by consumers in rich countries as the entire food production of sub-Saharan Africa.

The first sentence tells us clearly about the consumers and what they do. The second sentence tells us clearly about the food and what happens to it. Both sentences have the same meaning, but the focus is different. In the active sentence (1), the focus is on consumers and their actions. In the passive sentence (2), the focus is on the food and what happened to it – the food did nothing; it was passive. In these sentences we do not always clearly state who carried out the action.

We can change active sentences to passive sentences in order to change the focus from *who did something* to *what happened to something or someone*.

The passive is formed by *to be* plus a past participle.

## Grammar in context

### Passive and active sentences

Change these passive sentences to the active; the first example has been done for you.

1. In medium- and high-income countries food is wasted (by consumers).
   *Consumers in medium- and high-income countries waste food.*
2. In the United States 30% of all food is thrown away each year (by consumers).
3. Approximately 32% of all food purchased per year is not eaten (by consumers).

Now change these active sentences to the passive.

4. Consumers often buy too much food.
5. Companies waste too much fuel on transportation.
6. Rotting food causes climate change.
7. Climate change makes the lives of humans more difficult.
8. Climate change causes many floods and storms.
9. Everyone can help to reduce the causes of climate change.

# Written work

Write a blog about this topic, expressing your concern and encouraging others to become involved in reducing the waste of food worldwide. Include aspects of the IB Learner Profile which you feel need to be encouraged and developed more in individuals. Write between 250 and 400 words.

# 01 Food and Water

> Discuss the ethical and moral implications of food wastage from different perspectives, for example, the mother of a poor family, a professional couple, a restaurant. Take on different roles; think about the issues from that point of view and be ready to defend your opinions and actions. Use the facts from the text to support your arguments.
>
> **TOK**

### Hints for writing a blog

Before you start, decide:

- **why** you are writing
- **what** you want to say
- **which** facts to include from the text.

And think about **who** you are writing to.

Organise your ideas into paragraphs with key information plus supporting details. Decide what action you would like your readers to take. Have a strong heading and a good finish to your blog.

## 1.2 Food shortages

### Text 1.2.1 Homelessness and hunger climbing in US cities, mayors' survey reveals

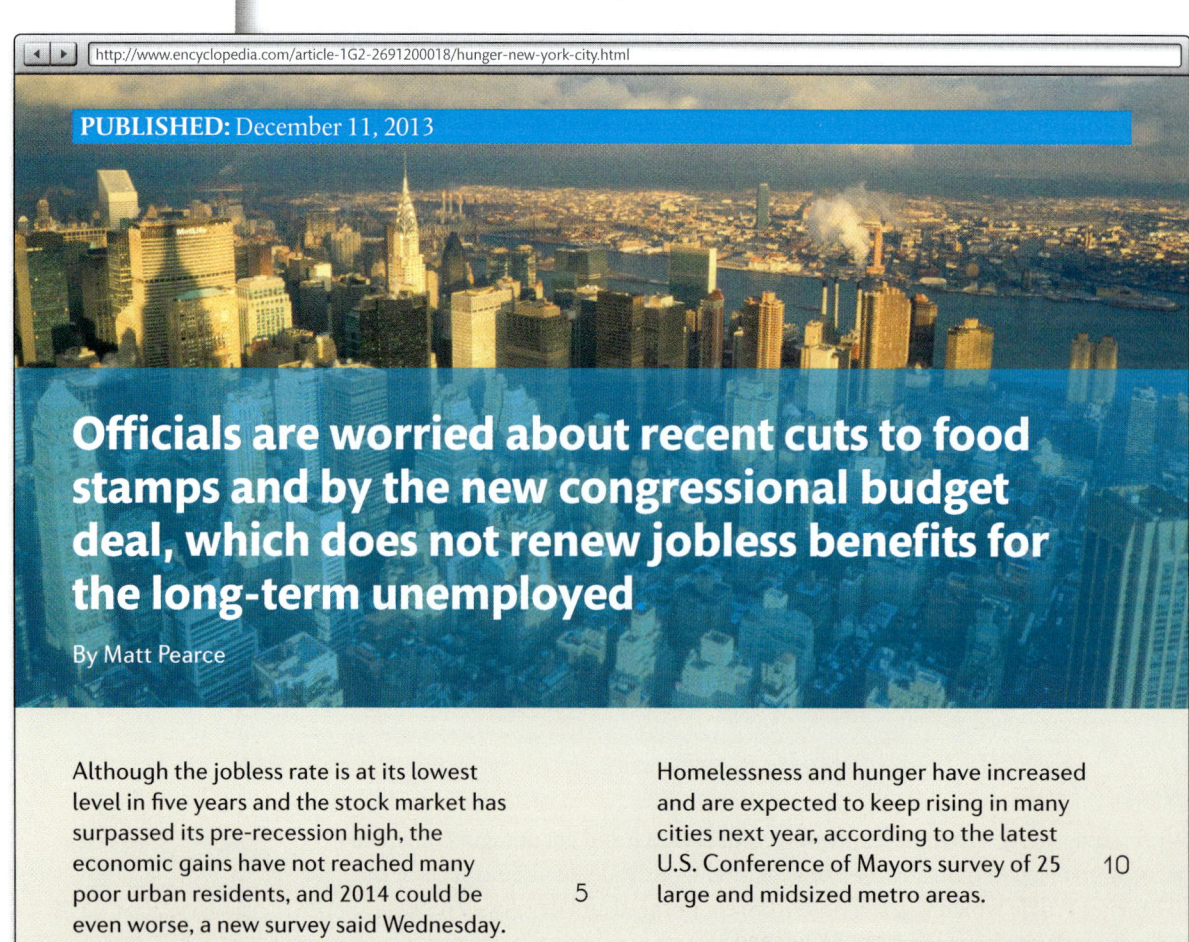

http://www.encyclopedia.com/article-1G2-2691200018/hunger-new-york-city.html

**PUBLISHED:** December 11, 2013

## Officials are worried about recent cuts to food stamps and by the new congressional budget deal, which does not renew jobless benefits for the long-term unemployed

By Matt Pearce

Although the jobless rate is at its lowest level in five years and the stock market has surpassed its pre-recession high, the economic gains have not reached many poor urban residents, and 2014 could be even worse, a new survey said Wednesday. 5

Homelessness and hunger have increased and are expected to keep rising in many cities next year, according to the latest U.S. Conference of Mayors survey of 25 large and midsized metro areas. 10

http://www.encyclopedia.com/article-1G2-2691200018/hunger-new-york-city.html

Last year's national poverty rate of 15% is still near the Great Recession's high of 15.1%, according to U.S. Census figures.

"We anticipated that problems related to unemployment and the slow national recovery would be reflected in the survey cities, and they were," Santa Barbara Mayor Helene Schneider, a co-chair for the group's task force on hunger and homelessness, told reporters in a conference call. Officials involved in the urban survey said they were worried about recent cuts to food stamps and by the new congressional budget deal, which does not renew jobless benefits for the long-term unemployed. Those extended benefits will expire after Christmas.

> Food stamps are vouchers given to people in need to buy food in supermarkets and other food shops. The name was changed in 2008 to SNAP – Supplemental Nutrition Assistance Program.

"Despite the budget problems we all face, every level of government has got to focus its resources on solving these problems," Schneider said.

The 25 surveyed cities, which include Los Angeles, Santa Barbara, Dallas, Chicago, Philadelphia and Washington, reported a 3% increase in overall homelessness, and half of the cities expected the number of homeless families to rise in 2014. On an average night, more than 20,000 people sleep on Los Angeles' streets, and almost 2,000 of them are families or children living on their own, the city reported. Homelessness has increased 26% in Los Angeles since last year, and 16% of L.A.'s homeless were turned away for housing help.

Chicago reported an 11.4% increase in the number of homeless families since last year, with requests for emergency food assistance up 6%. City pantries had to reduce the amount of food they gave to the hungry. And homeless shelters were increasing the number of people allowed to sleep in a room to meet rising demand.

Officials around the country cited a lack of affordable housing as a factor in persistent homelessness. Nineteen percent of the cities' homeless adults had jobs, including 22% of those in San Francisco, according to the survey.

"The housing market is such, particularly over the last few years, that shelter is taking a large chunk of what money they have," said Paul Ong, director of the Center for the Study of Inequality at UCLA's Luskin School of Public Affairs. He added that median earnings for Americans had increased just 5% between 2007 and 2012, but that rents had risen 12%.

The result is a squeeze, he said. "You can't pay for shelter and you end up being homeless. Or if you continue to live in the apartment, you have less available to you in terms of food, so you end up relying on other sources of food for your family."

One bright spot in the survey: A wide majority of the cities said they had made gains in getting veterans off the streets and into housing. National veteran homelessness rates plunged by 24% between 2010 and 2013, according to the U.S. Department of Housing and Urban Development. "We've seen success across the country," said Laura Green Zeilinger, deputy director of the U.S. Interagency Council on Homelessness, citing a federal plan to end veteran homelessness by 2015. "Now we must invest in solutions in staying that course."

Some of the 2013 hunger stats were grim: Twenty-one percent of people needing emergency food assistance didn't get it, and all but four of the 25 surveyed cities reported an increased need. The exceptions were Santa Barbara; Nashville; Plano, Texas; and St. Paul, Minn. Overall, demand for food assistance rose 7%, and all but one of the cities—Dallas— expected demand to increase in 2014.

"The hungry and homeless issue continues to be with us," said Tom Cochran, chief

# 01 Food and Water

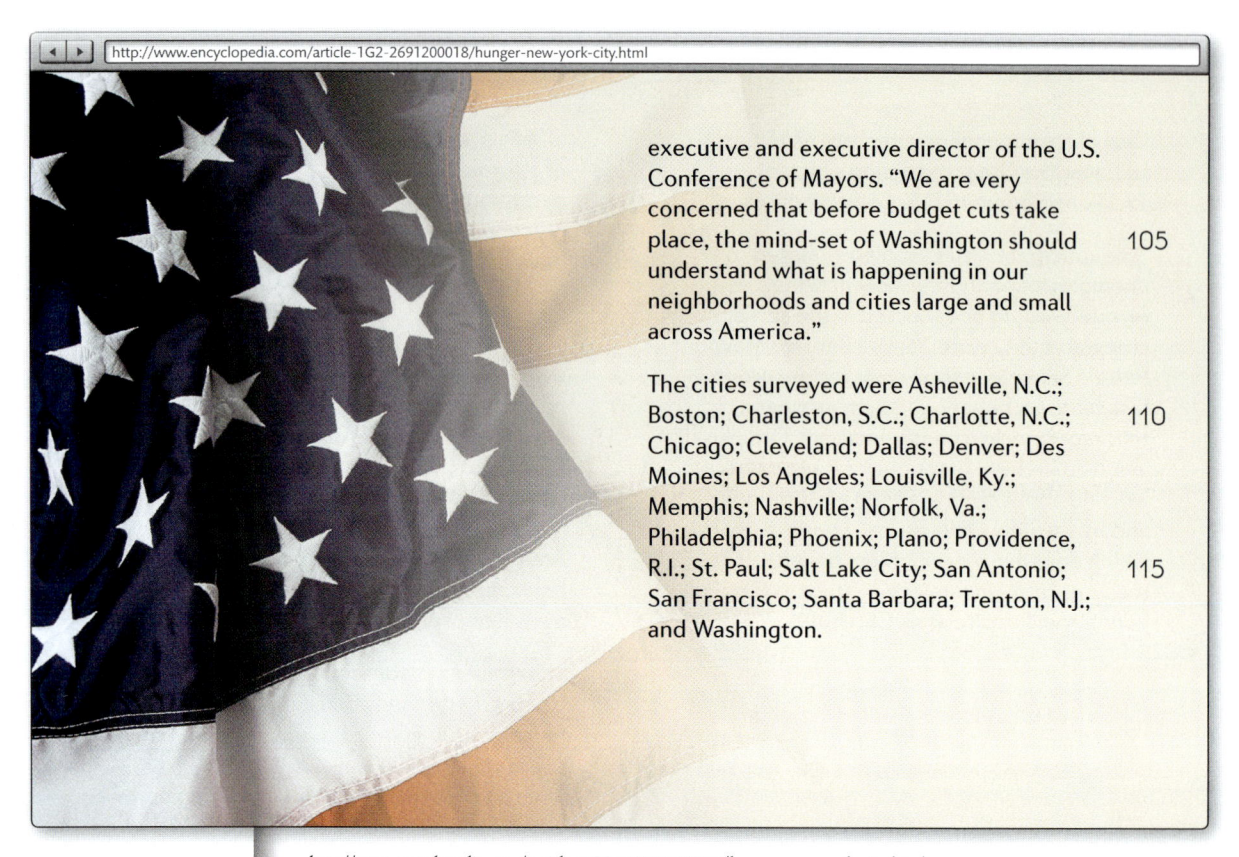

executive and executive director of the U.S. Conference of Mayors. "We are very concerned that before budget cuts take place, the mind-set of Washington should understand what is happening in our neighborhoods and cities large and small across America."

The cities surveyed were Asheville, N.C.; Boston; Charleston, S.C.; Charlotte, N.C.; Chicago; Cleveland; Dallas; Denver; Des Moines; Los Angeles; Louisville, Ky.; Memphis; Nashville; Norfolk, Va.; Philadelphia; Phoenix; Plano; Providence, R.I.; St. Paul; Salt Lake City; San Antonio; San Francisco; Santa Barbara; Trenton, N.J.; and Washington.

*http://www.encyclopedia.com/article-1G2-2691200018/hunger-new-york-city.html*

### General comprehension

1. According to the article, written in December 2013, what will be the situation in 2014?
2. Is the increase in the number of homeless people caused by an increase in the jobless rate?
3. What is causing officials the most worry?
4. What is the percentage increase in homelessness in the surveyed cities?
5. Are you shocked by the number of people who sleep on the streets in Los Angeles? Who are these people?
6. How are city pantries trying to cope with the problem of increasing numbers of homeless people?
7. What changes have been made in homeless shelters because of greater numbers of people in need?
8. What is one reason for homelessness according to the article?
9. Why have rising rents caused a problem?
10. What is the good news mentioned in the article?

## Text handling

1. The phrase '(the stock market) has surpassed' (line 2) means
   a) has been left behind
   b) has improved
   c) has been greater than
   d) has slowed

2. The phrase 'is taking a large chunk' (line 61) means
   a) is giving away
   b) is ignoring
   c) is using up
   d) is sharing

3. The phrase 'one bright spot' (line 76) means
   a) a beam of light
   b) one positive factor
   c) a spotlight
   d) good weather

4. The word 'urban' (line 5) means
   a) smooth
   b) unemployed
   c) related to a town or city
   d) ineffective

5. The word 'anticipated' (line 15) means
   a) thought about
   b) expected
   c) realised
   d) were surprised

6. The word 'pantries' (line 49) means
   a) underwear
   b) out of breath
   c) a place where food is kept
   d) a kind of cake

7. The word 'persistent' (line 56) means
   a) difficult to avoid
   b) unexpected
   c) continuing for a long time
   d) sweating

8. The word 'grim' (line 90) means
   a) smiling
   b) very serious
   c) unfortunate
   d) unchanging

## Zoom in on grammar

### Complex sentences

Re-read these two sentences.

1. Although the jobless rate is at its lowest level in five years and the stock market has surpassed its pre-recession high, the economic gains have not reached many poor urban residents.
2. Despite the budget problems we all face, every level of government has got to focus its resources on solving these problems.

Both sentences are complex sentences. Using complex sentences will enrich your written and spoken work.

Sentences 1 and 2 could be turned around:

1. Economic gains have not reached many poor urban residents, although the jobless rate is at its lowest level in five years and the stock market has surpassed its pre-recession high.
2. Every level of government has got to focus its resources on solving these problems, despite the budget problems we all face.

Or re-phrased simply:

1. The jobless rate is at its lowest level in five years and the stock market has surpassed its pre-recession high, <u>but</u> the economic gains have not reached many poor urban residents.
2. Every level of government has got to focus its resources on solving these problems, even with the budget problems we all face.

## Grammar in context

### Complex sentences

Write your own complex sentences using *although* or *despite*.

1. I do not speak good French. People understand me.
2. My mother is on a business trip. We have a cooked dinner every evening.
3. It is pouring with rain. I have hockey training.
4. Playing squash is an unusual hobby. I know five people who play squash.

# 01 Food and Water

### Individual oral activity (for students who study Economics)

Give a short presentation to the class or a group on some of the terms used in the text which are familiar to you from your study of Economics. Try to explain them in a way which is appropriate for students with little knowledge of the topic.

### Written work

Possibly this report has given you insights into life in the USA which are shocking for you. Write a reflection on the article in the form of a diary, a blog or an email to a friend. Write between 250 and 400 words.

## 1.3 Water, water, everywhere

### Text 1.3.1 A clean water crisis

# Water is life

The water you drink today has likely been around in one form or another since dinosaurs roamed the earth, hundreds of millions of years ago. While the amount of freshwater on the planet has remained fairly constant over time—continually recycled through the atmosphere and back into our cups—the population has exploded. This means that every year competition for a clean, copious supply of water for drinking, cooking, bathing, and sustaining life intensifies. Water scarcity is an abstract concept to many and a stark reality for others. It is the result of myriad environmental, political, economic, and social forces.

Freshwater makes up a very small fraction of all water on the planet. While nearly 70 percent of the world is covered by water, only 2.5 percent of it is fresh. The rest is saline and ocean-based. Even then, just 1 percent of our freshwater is easily accessible, with much of it trapped in glaciers and snowfields.
In essence, only 0.025 percent of the planet's water is available to fuel and feed its 6.8 billion people.
Due to geography, climate, engineering, regulation, and competition for resources, some regions seem relatively flush with freshwater, while others face drought and debilitating

pollution. In much of the developing world, clean water is either hard to come by or a commodity that requires laborious work or significant currency to obtain.

Wherever they are, people need water to survive. Not only is the human body 60 percent water, but the resource is also essential for producing food, clothing, and computers, moving our waste stream, and keeping us and the environment healthy. Unfortunately, humans have proved to be inefficient water users. (The average hamburger takes 2,400 liters, or 630 gallons, of water to produce, and many water-intensive crops, such as cotton, are grown in arid regions.)

According to the United Nations, water use has grown at more than twice the rate of population increase in the last century. By 2025, an estimated 1.8 billion people will live in areas plagued by water scarcity, with two-thirds of the world's population living in water-stressed regions as a result of use, growth, and climate change.

The challenge we face now is how to effectively conserve, manage, and distribute the water we have.

National Geographic's Freshwater Web site encourages you to explore the local stories and global trends defining the world's water crisis. Learn where freshwater resources exist; how they are used; and how climate, technology, policy, and people play a role in both creating obstacles and finding solutions. Peruse the site to learn how you can make a difference by reducing your water footprint and getting involved with local and global water conservation and advocacy efforts.

To access the website mentioned in the text, go to www.pearsonhotlinks.com, enter the title or ISBN of this book and click on Chapter 1.

http://environment.nationalgeographic.com/environment/freshwater/freshwater-crisis/

## Text handling

1   Find words in the text which can be meaningfully replaced by the vocabulary below. The words are in the order of their occurrence in the text.

   a) wandered
   b) plentiful
   c) maintaining life
   d) very many
   e) shortage of rainwater
   f) weakening
   g) product
   h) take a look at
   i) support

# 01 Food and Water

## Text handling

**2** Try to explain the following expressions, as they are used in the text, in your own words.
   a) since dinosaurs roamed the earth
   b) the population has exploded
   c) in essence
   d) to fuel and feed
   e) seem relatively flush with water
   f) water-intensive crops

**3** True or false? Justify your answer with a relevant brief quotation from the text.
   a) The water you drink today is very old.
   b) The amount of freshwater on the planet has grown in our time.
   c) For some people, water scarcity is normal.
   d) In the developing world, water is often scarce.
   e) Humans are expert water users.

**4** According to the text it takes 2,400 litres of water, or 630 US gallons, to produce the average hamburger. Do you believe this? Do some additional research to find information about the amount of water needed to produce meat on the dinner table. Does this justify becoming vegetarian? Collect your information for a class debate. Your teacher will tell you more.

**5** Explore your water footprint on the internet. There are a number of sites, including one from *National Geographic*, which let you check your water footprint and give you ideas on how you can reduce it. Share your findings with the class.

## Zoom in on grammar

**Sentence structure**

> *Not only* is the human body 60 percent water, *but* the resource is *also* essential for producing food, clothing, and computers.

If there are two equal ideas in a sentence, they can be listed using *not only… but also* or using *both… and*:

> Water is *both* 60 percent of the human body *and* essential for producing food, clothing, and computers.

## Grammar in context

**Sentence structure**

Make sentences using both forms – *not only… but also* and *both… and* – using the following prompts:
1. We have maths and science homework.
2. Water is needed to feed and fuel the Earth's population.
3. Many people lack enough water due to population growth and climate change.

## Written work

Write an article for the school magazine to inform your fellow students about the water crisis. You need to explain the link between water use and meat production, and offer suggestions which will help everyone reduce their water consumption. Use ideas from the text and from your research. Write between 250 and 400 words.

## Exam hints

**Tips for writing an article**
- Remember to use an attention-grabbing headline (and subheadings) – you want people to read your article.
- Have a strong opening sentence and a strong conclusion.
- Draw your readers in to your argument.
- Organise your ideas into paragraphs with a clear main idea in each.

## 1.4 Ryan's Well

### Text 1.4.1 Ryan's Well project

http://environment.nationalgeographic.com/environment/freshwater/freshwater-crisis/

# Ryan's Well
## FOUNDATION

The Ryan's Well Foundation is a family of people committed to delivering access to safe water and sanitation as an essential way to improve the lives of people in the developing world. We empower citizens of all ages to take action and effect change in the world. We have two goals – BUILD and EMPOWER.

### Build: *Water, sanitation and hygiene projects*

Our BUILD program supports water, sanitation, and hygiene education projects in partnership with local non-governmental and community-based organizations in developing countries. Our current focus is to the communities of West Africa (Burkina Faso, Ghana, and Togo), East Africa (Kenya and Uganda), and Haiti.

### Empower: *Get involved and make a difference*

Ryan's story has been compelling not just for his actions against the global water and sanitation crisis, but for all grassroots action. It continues to motivate people of all ages – youth in particular – to take action and effect positive change in the world.

Our EMPOWER program consists of:

- Youth in Action – This program educates students about the need to conserve water and to understand the importance of safe water and sanitation. This elementary and secondary curriculum helps to inspire students to find where their 'puzzle' piece fits in our world and take action.

- Getting Involved – School groups, community groups, individuals and other dedicated Ambassadors of the Foundation are encouraged to organize their own fundraising activities, help raise awareness, and share our story, thereby making a difference in their own way.

- Social Media – In addition to the Ryan's Well blog and monthly email updates, we have increased our social networking presence. Be sure to follow us to read all the latest and stay in touch!

http://www.ryanswell.ca/about-us/mission.aspx

# 01 Food and Water

### General comprehension

**1** Identify the following and explain the answers in your own words.
   a) Who is involved in the project?
   b) Who do they want to help?
   c) How do they want to help?
   d) Who do they want to get involved?

**2** Explain what is meant in this context by the key words *Build* and *Empower*.

Now read about Ryan in the text below.

## Text 1.4.2 Ryan's story

*My story is really very simple. One day in January 1998, I was sitting in my Grade One classroom. My teacher, Mrs. Prest, explained that people were sick and some were even dying because they didn't have clean water. She told us that some people walked for hours in Africa and sometimes it was just to get dirty water.*

*All I had to do was take ten steps from my classroom to get to the drinking fountain and I had clean water. Before that day in school, I figured everyone lived like me. When I found out this wasn't the case, I decided I had to do something about it. So, I went home and begged my mom and dad to help. After a few days, they told me I could do extra chores to earn the $70 I thought would build a well. I thought that's all it would take to solve the world's water problem. I worked for four months to earn my first $70. Then I learned that it was actually going to cost $2,000 to build a well in a place like Uganda. I also learned that the problem was way bigger than I realized.*

*I started speaking to service clubs, to school classes, to anyone who would listen to my story so that I could raise money for my first well at Angolo Primary School in Uganda. That's how my little Grade One project became the Ryan's Well Foundation.*

*I am now a fourth year student at the University of King's College in Halifax on the east coast of Canada. I am studying international development and political science but remain involved with the Foundation as a speaker and Board member. I speak around the world on water issues and on the importance of making a difference no matter who you are or how old you are.*

*My work would not happen without the support of my family and friends. My Ugandan pen pal, Jimmy Akana, who I met on my first trip to Uganda, is now a member of our family. Jimmy is an inspiration because he works hard and has a positive outlook. He always has a great big smile.*

*My advice to anyone is that in order to make a positive change in the world, you need to find something you are passionate about and then you need to take steps to act. For me, the issue is water and sanitation.*

*Water is essential to all life. I hope my story is a reminder that we can all make a difference – it applies to each and every one of us.*

Ryan

http://www.ryanswell.ca/aboutus/ryans-story.aspx

## General comprehension

Think carefully and then answer each question in a separate paragraph.

1. What is your reaction to the text written by Ryan? What surprises you most?.
2. What do you think was the key factor in all the work Ryan has undertaken? Was it his personality? His family? The issue? What drove him to do what he did?
3. Thinking about the IB Learner Profile, which characteristics do you think Ryan displays?.

## Creativity, action, service

1. Suggest some ways in which supporting Ryan's Well could be a CAS project. Do some research online to find more information to share with your CAS adviser, or friends, in an email. Write an email of 100–120 words giving the key information.
2. Complete the following sentence beginnings that Ryan used in his text, to make them personal for you.
   a) One day I was sitting in my Grade One classroom...
   b) My advice to anyone is...
   c) For me, the issue is...

**TOK** To what extent do we have a responsibility to help people in third world countries?

Now read the story of Jimmy, Ryan's friend.

## Text 1.4.3 Jimmy's story

In 1999, my class at Angolo Primary School in Uganda started writing to a Grade One class from Canada. My pen pal was Ryan. I was fascinated by Ryan's life in Canada and he asked what life was like for me in my village.

Life was very different for me in Uganda. Every night, I walked eight kilometres carrying a small container to collect water. I had to go back and back again to fill the pot we used at home for cooking and washing. I usually got up at midnight to do this so I could still go to school in the morning. The water I collected was not clean; it looked like chocolate – but it was our only source before Ryan's well was built.

In 2003, my village was facing many problems as a result of the Lord's Resistance Army (LRA) – a rebel group looking to overthrow our government. I was abducted by the LRA but thankfully managed to escape and find my friend Tom Omach – a project coordinator for Ryan's Well. It took some time – and lots of paperwork – but eventually I came to Canada to live with Ryan and his family.

I love being a part of this incredible family and in 2007 I received my Canadian citizenship and graduated from high school!

It has been interesting adjusting to life in Canada – a new language, a new culture, cold weather! – but I couldn't be happier. I like to help the Foundation when I can – volunteering at the office or joining Ryan for presentations about the need for clean water and the work of the Foundation. We have fun talking with school kids about our stories and how they can help other kids around the world.

In the spring of 2012, I graduated from St. Francis Xavier University in Nova Scotia, Canada!

*Jimmy*

http://www.ryanswell.ca/aboutus/jimmys-story.aspx

15

# 01 Food and Water

## General comprehension

Answer each question in a separate paragraph.

1. What is your reaction to the text written by Jimmy? What surprises you most?
2. How different was Jimmy's life from yours or Ryan's? List the three most important points.
3. Thinking about the IB Learner Profile, which characteristics do you think Jimmy displays?

## Text handling

Explain the following words and phrases in your own words.

1. our only source (paragraph 2)
2. abducted (paragraph 3)
3. adjusting to (paragraph 5)

## Written work (SL)

Write a letter to a younger relative or friend telling them about Ryan and the work he has done, how he started, what inspired him and your personal reaction to it. Plan your work before you start to write. Think about the main ideas that you want to share and organise them carefully. Write between 250 and 400 words.

## Written work (HL)

**Personal response**

'Give a man a fish and you feed him for a day. Teach him to catch fish and you feed him for a lifetime.'

Write a personal response based on the stimulus and justify it. Choose any text type you have worked on in class. Write between 150 and 250 words.

## Exam hints

**Before you write**

- Decide what it is you want to say – do you agree or disagree? Can you link this to the unit topic? Be clear about your goal before you start to write.
- Decide on the most suitable genre for your text.
- Make an outline. Check you have all the points you want to make and that you have a clear, coherent argument.

And then write your text.

Text 1.4.4 Kenya and Ryan's Well

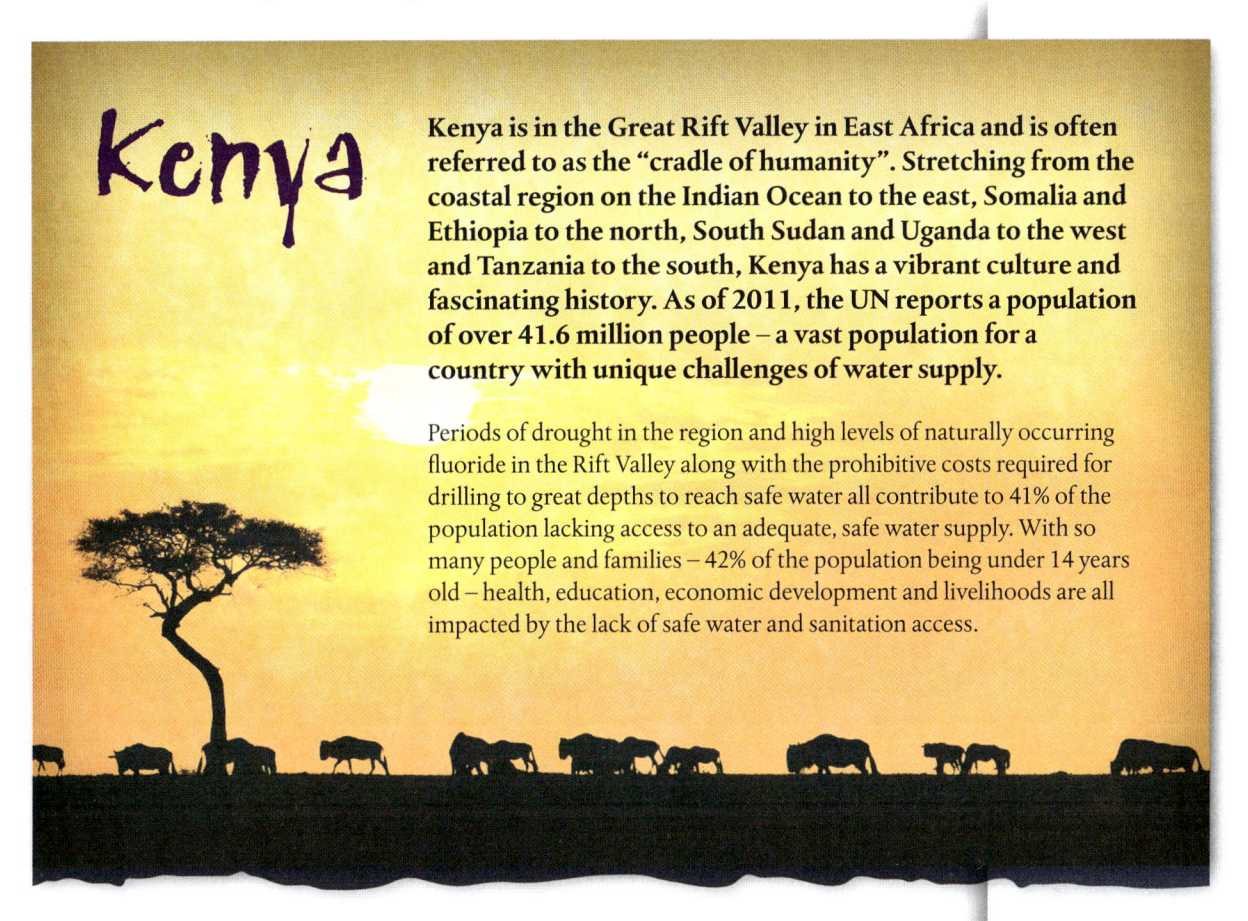

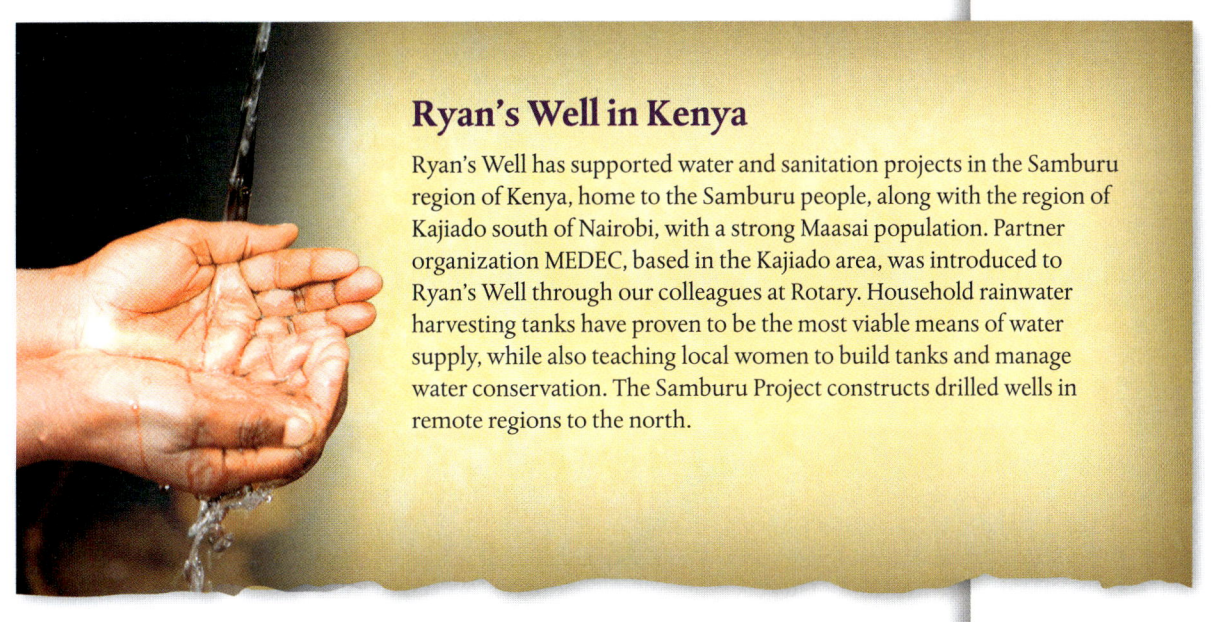

# Kenya

Kenya is in the Great Rift Valley in East Africa and is often referred to as the "cradle of humanity". Stretching from the coastal region on the Indian Ocean to the east, Somalia and Ethiopia to the north, South Sudan and Uganda to the west and Tanzania to the south, Kenya has a vibrant culture and fascinating history. As of 2011, the UN reports a population of over 41.6 million people – a vast population for a country with unique challenges of water supply.

Periods of drought in the region and high levels of naturally occurring fluoride in the Rift Valley along with the prohibitive costs required for drilling to great depths to reach safe water all contribute to 41% of the population lacking access to an adequate, safe water supply. With so many people and families – 42% of the population being under 14 years old – health, education, economic development and livelihoods are all impacted by the lack of safe water and sanitation access.

## Ryan's Well in Kenya

Ryan's Well has supported water and sanitation projects in the Samburu region of Kenya, home to the Samburu people, along with the region of Kajiado south of Nairobi, with a strong Maasai population. Partner organization MEDEC, based in the Kajiado area, was introduced to Ryan's Well through our colleagues at Rotary. Household rainwater harvesting tanks have proven to be the most viable means of water supply, while also teaching local women to build tanks and manage water conservation. The Samburu Project constructs drilled wells in remote regions to the north.

http://www.ryanswell.ca/projects/where-we-work/kenya.aspx

## 01 Food and Water

# Kenya – Rainwater Harvesting 2012/13

### Kajiado County

Project Partner: Maasai Environment Development Consortium (MEDEC)

The Kajiado region of Kenya, south of Nairobi in the Great Rift Valley, faces serious challenges with water supply. Rainwater harvesting is a viable option for household water supplies in this region. Ryan's Well is now building on the experience and success of earlier partnership projects with MEDEC, which resulted in over 100 household tanks being constructed.

Maasai communities in the Kajiado region are adapting to new realities of daily life. Traditionally pastoralists, the livelihood of the Maasai people is inextricably linked to the availability of land, water and pasture. Changing climatic conditions in the region have had an impact on these traditions and limited development and education opportunities.

With the goal of continued support for household water supply as a means of improving livelihoods, Ryan's Well and MEDEC continue to work together with common interest groups in the region. This collaboration seeks to effectively and efficiently address these problems, step by step, and focus on improving opportunities for women and girls.

### Activities (revised 25-Jan-2013)

- Construction of 50 household rainwater harvesting tanks. Originally 25 tanks were planned and this goal has been increased!

- Development of a detailed monitoring tool to improve maintenance of tanks

- Household water usage assessment and education on best practices for management of household water supplies

- Training of women's common interest groups for design and construction of rainwater harvesting tanks.

## Updates

*18-March-2013* To date, the first 10 rainwater tanks (10,000 litres each) have been constructed. A meeting was held in order to identify vulnerable populations including households of elderly, ill, orphaned or widowed people. These groups have the least means to collect their own water and face many struggles each day. Fifty such households were identified to have rainwater tanks constructed.

In the first four days of the project, 12 schools were visited to mobilize teachers, students and communities around the WASH (water, sanitation and hygiene) program that was beginning. Workshop training sessions were held to share knowledge about the linkages between health and safe water, hygiene and sanitation. Our partners at MEDEC have put into use much of the information shared at the Community Health Promotion Workshop in November 2012.

http://www.ryanswell.ca/projects/where-we-work/kenya.aspx

### General comprehension

1. Why do you think Kenya is referred to as 'the cradle of humanity'?
2. Why does the country suffer from a unique shortage of water?
3. What particular problems do they have in their population?
4. What does 'rainwater harvesting' mean?
5. How does this project improve opportunities for girls and women?

### Text handling

Which of the words in the text could be meaningfully replaced by each of the following? The words are in the order they appear in the text.

1. severe water shortage
2. workable
3. built
4. people who live on the land and keep animals
5. inseparably

### Written work

Now that you have read and researched about the achievements of Ryan, write a reflective diary entry about your impressions. Try to make links to the IB Learner Profile. Write between 300 and 400 words.

# 01 Food and Water

## Exam practice

## Food sharing in the UK

Supermarkets and sandwich chains could soon share surplus food with families struggling in the economic downturn.

Under a proposal backed by the government, retailers would log details of products approaching the end of their shelf-life on a database.

Charities, who are increasingly working with families who cannot afford to feed themselves, would use the information to arrange pick-ups of food and other unsold products set aside during the week by stores.

Charities would then put together parcels or cook meals using the surplus food and distribute it to the needy.

Britain has seen an explosion in demand for food banks and food parcels amid the biggest squeeze on living standards in 60 years.

The government is putting pressure on food giants to back the scheme, which is designed to both cut food waste and help those in need.

Environment Secretary Caroline Spelman is bringing together supermarkets, retail industry leaders and food charities at a summit in London today to ensure food goes into kitchens rather than landfill.

She said: 'Preventing food waste protects the environment, helps communities and makes good business sense.

'Charities and retailers are already working together to make great use of surplus food and I'm hosting the roundtable today to look at new ways to make the system work even better.'

The nation's biggest stores, including Tesco, Asda, Sainsbury's, Morrisons, the Co-op, M&S and Boots, will take part. The charities FareShare and FoodCycle, which were set up to tackle food poverty, will also be present.

FareShare collects surplus from the food and drink industry and redistributes it to around 700 charities including the Salvation Army and homeless shelters.

The charities it supplies are also increasingly working with families living in food poverty.

The group wants supermarkets to provide food at each of its 18 outlets which would be picked up on a rota basis by local charities.

FoodCycle has called for the creation of a database so that food can be shared more effectively.

The charity uses professional kitchens to produce free meals in 14 locations across the country and is currently in partnership with Sainsbury's and Waitrose, as well as smaller grocers and markets.

Other retailers have been reluctant to back its work because they are worried about being sued if people fall ill as a result of eating surplus food.

The charities are supporting the introduction of a so-called Good Samaritan law, which exists in the US and ensures firms providing food in good faith are exempt from legal action.

The British Retail Consortium said its members already give excess food to charities but said discussions on improving communication between charities and retailers will be held.

It said the scheme should apply to all food retailers and could involve sandwich chains.

It comes as Waitrose announced a commitment to donate surplus food from all branches to charities by the end of this year. In the future, making donations to charities will be its preferred option for any unsold food that is still fit for consumption.

*http://www.dailymail.co.uk/news/article-2168018/Food-share-database-end-supermarket-waste-Stores-boost-links-charities-help-hungry.html#ixzz2eJJqupUB*

## Exercises

Answer the following questions.

1 Why has there been an increase in demand for food banks and food parcels recently?

..................................................................................................

2 The government is supporting the scheme, which will bring two benefits. What are they?

..................................................................................................

3 What three reasons does the Environment Secretary give for preventing food waste?

..................................................................................................

4 What does FareShare do?

..................................................................................................

5 What does FoodCycle do that is different from FareShare?

..................................................................................................

6 Why are some retailers concerned about the project?

..................................................................................................

7 How would the Good Samaritan law help them?

..................................................................................................

**TOK** To what extent do we have a responsibility to help poorer people in our own countries? How is this different from helping people in other countries?

# 01 Food and Water

**8** Do you know the story of the Good Samaritan? If not, do some research to help you understand this reference.

.....................................................................................................................................

**9** How is being green becoming a way of life?

.....................................................................................................................................

Explain the following expressions in your own words.

**10** to boost links

.....................................................................................................................................

**11** sandwich chains

.....................................................................................................................................

**12** an explosion in demand

.....................................................................................................................................

**13** the needy

.....................................................................................................................................

**14** to donate surplus food

.....................................................................................................................................

**15** fit for consumption

.....................................................................................................................................

Based on the information in the text, match the first part of the sentence with the appropriate ending on the right. Write the appropriate letter in the box below. An example has been provided.

**Example:** The charities it supplies are also increasingly... **B**

**16** The group wants supermarkets to...

**17** FoodCycle has called for...

**18** The charity uses professional kitchens to...

**19** It said the scheme should apply to all food retailers and...

**20** Supermarkets and sandwich chains could soon...

22

**A** ... share surplus food with families struggling in the economic downturn.

**B** ... working with families living in food poverty.

**C** ... the creation of a database so that food can be shared more effectively.

**D** ... produce free meals in 14 locations across the country.

**E** ... could involve sandwich chains.

**F** ... provide food at each of its 18 outlets.

## Further exercises

### Zoom in on grammar

**The + adjective**

The + adjective can be used to talk about groups of people.

For example: *the poor, the needy, the lonely, the old, the young, the wealthy*.

The meaning is the same as *poor people, needy people*, etc.

### Grammar in context

**Reference pronouns**

Explain the meaning of the word *it* in the following sentences.

1. FareShare collects surplus from the food and drink industry and redistributes *it* to around 700 charities including the Salvation Army and homeless shelters.
2. The charities *it* supplies are also increasingly working with families living in food poverty.
3. The charity uses professional kitchens to produce free meals in 14 locations across the country and is currently in partnership with Sainsbury's and Waitrose, as well as smaller grocers and markets. Other retailers have been reluctant to back *its* work because they are worried about being sued if people fall ill as a result of eating surplus food.

## Written work

Based on the information in the newspaper article, write a blog article commending the supermarkets for the work they are doing for the poor. People generally write blogs because they feel strongly about an issue or have ideas they want to share. What would be your reason for writing the blog? What do you want to share with the reader? Write between 250 and 300 words.

# 02 Wind farms

## Objectives

- To speak about the needs for alternative energy sources
- To discuss the advantages and disadvantages of wind farms
- To discuss the controversial aspects of wind energy
- To analyse vocabulary and meaning in context
- To practise writing a formal letter
- To revise the use of 'have to' in the sense of 'must'
- To practise using reported speech

**Opposite** A wind farm with a large number of turbines.

**TOK** To what extent do birds and animals have rights? Discuss the ethical and moral implications of setting up wind farms in areas where it is known that migratory birds will be affected.

# 2.1 Wind energy

## Text 2.1.1 The history of wind energy

**Since early recorded history, people have been harnessing the energy of the wind. Wind energy propelled boats along the Nile River as early as 5000 BC. By 200 BC, simple windmills in China were pumping water, while vertical-axis windmills with woven reed sails were grinding grain in Persia and the Middle East.**

Early in the twentieth century, windmills were commonly used across the Great Plains to pump water and to generate electricity.

New ways of using the energy of the wind eventually spread around the world. By the 11th century, people in the Middle East were using windmills extensively for food production; returning merchants and crusaders carried this idea back to Europe. The Dutch refined the windmill and adapted it for draining lakes and marshes in the Rhine River Delta. When settlers took this technology to the New World in the late 19th century, they began using windmills to pump water for farms and ranches, and later, to generate electricity for homes and industry.

Industrialization, first in Europe and later in America, led to a gradual decline in the use of windmills. The steam engine replaced European water-pumping windmills. In the 1930s, the Rural Electrification Administration's programs brought inexpensive electric power to most rural areas in the United States.

However, industrialization also sparked the development of larger windmills to generate electricity. Commonly called wind turbines, these machines appeared in Denmark as early as 1890. In the 1940s the largest wind turbine of the time began operating on a Vermont hilltop known as Grandpa's Knob. This turbine, rated at 1.25 megawatts in winds of about 30 mph, fed electric power to the local utility network for several months during World War II.

The popularity of using the energy in the wind has always fluctuated with the price of fossil

## 02 Wind farms

fuels. When fuel prices fell after World War II, interest in wind turbines waned. But when the price of oil skyrocketed in the 1970s, so did worldwide interest in wind turbine generators.

The wind turbine technology R&D [= Research and Development] that followed the oil embargoes of the 1970s refined old ideas and introduced new ways of converting wind energy into useful power. Many of these approaches have been demonstrated in "wind farms" or wind power plants – groups of turbines that feed electricity into the utility grid – in the United States and Europe.

Today, the lessons learned from more than a decade of operating wind power plants, along with continuing R&D, have made wind-generated electricity very close in cost to the power from conventional utility generation in some locations. Wind energy is the world's fastest-growing energy source and will power industry, businesses and homes with clean, renewable electricity for many years to come.

*http://www1.eere.energy.gov/wind/wind_history.html*

### Text handling

Match the beginnings of the following sentences with the suitable endings.

1. People have harnessed the energy of the wind...
2. In the 20th century...
3. Draining water from lakes and marshes...
4. The process of industrialisation started...
5. Large windmills, used for generating electricity...
6. The world's fastest growing energy source...

A ...has been an aim of the Dutch in using windmills for many years.
B ...is currently wind energy.
C ...windmills were used to provide energy.
D ...were called turbines as early as the 1890s.
E ...in Europe and later developed in America.
F ...for over 5,000 years.

### Interactive oral activity

Before you start reading about wind farms today, share some ideas with other students about the issue of energy sources. Wind farms are not welcomed by everybody. In small groups, discuss reasons why people might be against energy produced from wind.

Are there plans to find alternative sources of energy in your culture?

Think about why many countries are discussing ways to find alternative sources of energy.

## Text 2.1.2 What exactly is a wind farm?

A wind farm is the name given to a collection of wind turbines installed in open countryside or at sea with the aim of capturing wind energy and converting it into electricity. The wind turbine itself looks like a tall pole, on average 200m high, topped by three blades that rotate like a propeller, making the turbine look much like a futuristic windmill. The reason for the height is simple: winds are stronger the higher they are from the ground.

As wind results from atmospheric changes in temperature and pressure which is triggered by the sun, wind energy is another form of solar power. It is the function of the turbine to capture the wind and create kinetic energy which can then be converted into electricity.

### What are the benefits of wind power?

The most significant benefit of wind power is the fact that it is non-polluting and renewable: an advantage that makes those who are worried about the demise of fossil fuels clap their hands with joy. The electricity produced by one turbine is sufficient to generate enough electricity for a complete household. Also, for many people the idea of producing affordable electricity without generating greenhouse gases or toxic waste regardless of the time of day, or year, makes any arguments against wind power seem minor. Add to that the bonus of not contributing to global warming, and wind energy seems to be the answer to the Earth's energy crisis.

### Are there any disadvantages?

Few studies have been carried out to determine the effect of wind turbines on birds or animals, but one of the more obvious effects is on migratory birds which follow regular flight paths and become victims of the turbine propellers. Wind turbines near residential areas have been the cause of numerous complaints, not scientifically confirmed, that turbines are a health hazard and cause headaches, insomnia, palpitations and various other physical disturbances.

As to the beauty or ugliness of the wind turbines, that remains a topic for debate. Opinions vary; for some people they are elegant, modern sculptures, and for others they are clumsy constructions defacing the landscape.

### General comprehension

1. In the first sentence of the text, what is the meaning of 'open countryside'?
2. According to the text, why is wind energy a form of solar power?
3. What is the biggest attraction of wind energy for those seeking alternatives to fossil fuels?
4. List four aspects of wind energy that make it attractive.
5. Have studies been carried out to show the effects of wind turbines on migratory birds?
6. Is public opinion in agreement about the beauty of wind turbines?

# 02 Wind farms

### Text handling

It is important to develop strategies for analysing new words and working out what they mean. To do this you must look at the sentence before and after the one that has the new word in it. This is called 'examining the context', and a lot of this is intelligent guesswork. Try it!

1. Without using a dictionary say what you think the following words mean by examining the context.
   a) kinetic energy
   b) demise of fossil fuels
   c) migratory birds
   d) victims of the turbine propellers
   e) residential areas

2. Find words in the text which are similar in meaning to the following:
   a) set up
   b) changing
   c) coal, petroleum or gas
   d) enough
   e) find out
   f) subject
   g) sleeplessness
   h) spoiling

### Individual oral activity

Choose one of these issues and then see what information you can find from websites. Organise your research findings and think how you want to present them to your class.

- The effects of wind turbines on migratory birds.
- The effects of wind turbines on people who live near them.
- The need for energy forms that are not derived from fossil fuels.

Your teacher will tell you how much preparation time you have.

## 2.2 The cost of wind farms

### Text 2.2.1 Why I don't think wind costs the Earth

http://www.express.co.uk

# Britain is the windiest country in Europe so let's use it to the full

by Maf Smith – Deputy Chief Executive, Renewable UK

We have enough wind energy to supply nearly five million households all year round. We already get five per cent of our electricity from wind turbines – we're on course to get 25 per cent of it by 2020. Turbines don't need much wind to start turning, that's why they generate electricity for at least 80 per cent of the time.

We want to keep electricity bills as low as possible. So we have to stop importing massive amounts of expensive fossil fuels from abroad as we have no control over how much they cost. We know exactly how much wind costs: just 2p per household per day – that's according to independent regulator Ofgem [Office of Gas and Electricity Markets, a government body].

Nearly 12,000 people work in the UK's wind energy industry. That number is set to increase to nearly 90,000 by 2021.

Independent opinion polls by Ipsos MORI [one of the largest market research organisations in the UK] show two thirds of us want more wind power, and 57 per cent have no problem with the visual impact of wind turbines on the landscape.

There are many myths peddled about wind energy, often by those with a vested interest in spreading untruths. The fact is that modern wind turbines aren't noisy. Try standing right under one and hear how quiet they are. No doctors who are experts in the field believe that wind turbines affect people's health. There's no peer-reviewed evidence to support any such claims. And there's no direct evidence that they affect house prices, in fact the Royal Institute of Chartered Surveyors says they don't.

This reliable source of power is providing us with a secure supply of energy and jobs while cutting carbon emissions – so wind doesn't cost the Earth.

Daily Express, *Saturday August 11 2012*

## General comprehension

1. What is the author's aim in this article?
2. Find four positive aspects of wind energy mentioned in the text.
3. The author mentions three official organisations that support his argument. List the three groups mentioned.
4. What do you think is the author's strongest argument for wind energy? Give reasons for your choice.
5. What does the author mean when he says 'wind doesn't cost the Earth'?

## Text handling

Match the words from the text on the left with the correct definitions on the right.

| | | | |
|---|---|---|---|
| 1 | to generate (line 6) | A | to try to get people to believe something |
| 2 | a poll (line 20) | B | to reduce |
| 3 | a myth (line 26) | C | a person of the same age or position |
| 4 | to peddle (line 26) | D | to produce |
| 5 | vested interest (line 27) | E | a strong personal interest resulting in private gain |
| 6 | peer (line 33) | F | a story that is not based on truth |
| 7 | to cut (line 40) | G | a survey among a group of people |

## 02 Wind farms

**Above** A group of people protesting against wind farms.

### Zoom in on grammar

**Must and have to**

Look at this sentence from the above text:

'So we *have to* stop importing massive amounts of fossil fuels from abroad....'

In this sentence, 'have to' is used in the sense of 'must'.

We use 'must (do)' and 'have to (do)' to say that it is necessary to do something. Often it does not matter which you use:

I'm hungry; I *must / have to* eat something.

There is sometimes a difference. We use 'must' to express a speaker's own feelings:

I *must* wash my hair this evening.

However, with 'have to' the speaker is expressing facts:

Mr Brown cannot come to the meeting; he *has to* meet a customer.

The past tense of 'must' is 'had to':

Mr Brown couldn't come to the meeting because he *had to* meet a customer.

The negative forms are, however, completely different:

- 'mustn't' means that it is necessary not to do something:

  You *mustn't* plagiarise in academic texts of any kind.

  You *mustn't* leave the restaurant before you have paid the bill.

- 'don't have to' means you have an option to do something or not:

  I *don't have to* get up early on Saturday but I usually do.

  We *don't have to* walk to school but it's good for our fitness.

### Text handling

In each of the following phrases, say what the underlined word is referring to.

1. we're on course to get 25 per cent of <u>it</u> by 2020 (line 4) ...........................................
2. we have no control over how much <u>they</u> cost (line 11) ...........................................
3. Try standing right under <u>one</u> (line 29) ...........................................
4. <u>they</u> affect house prices (line 35) ...........................................

### Written work (HL/SL)

Based on the information you have gained from looking at websites in preparation for your oral activity, and arguments you have heard from other students, complete the following written assignment.

Write a letter to Maf Smith, the Deputy Chief Executive of the trade association Renewable UK, and express your agreement or disagreement with his views in the newspaper article. Your letter will have at least 200 words.

**Points to remember:**

- Your letter will be written in formal English. Use Maf Smith's full name in the opening address.
- At the beginning, give your reason for writing the letter.
- Use a paragraph for each new point.
- Use phrases to make your letter flow. For example: *I would also like to say, Another point I would like to make, Further to this.*

- Finish with a concluding sentence, maybe a general statement of your hope for the future development of wind power.
- Use the phrase *Yours sincerely* to finish the letter and put your full name at the end. (Do not begin the letter by saying your name.)

> Formal letters addressed to a person by name, for example, *Dear Mr Smith*, are finished with the words *Yours sincerely*.
>
> However, if the person's name is not known, the letter will start like this: *Dear Sir*, or *Dear Madam*, or even *Dear Sir or Madam*, and will finish with the words *Yours faithfully*.

## 2.3 Perspectives on wind farms

### Text 2.3.1 Wind farms are useless, says Duke of Edinburgh

# The Duke of Edinburgh has made a fierce attack on wind farms, describing them as "absolutely useless"

by Jonathan Wynne-Jones

**In a withering assault on the onshore wind turbine industry, the Duke said the farms were "a disgrace".**

He also criticised the industry's reliance on subsidies from electricity customers, claimed wind farms would "never work" and accused people who support them of believing in a "fairy tale".

The Duke's comments will be seized upon by the burgeoning lobby who say wind farms are ruining the countryside and forcing up energy bills.

Criticism of their effect on the environment has mounted, with *The Sunday Telegraph* disclosing today that turbines are being switched off during strong winds following complaints about their noise.

The Duke's views are politically charged, as they put him at odds with the Government's policy significantly to increase the amount of electricity generated by wind turbines.

The country has 3,421 turbines – 2,941 of them onshore – with another 4,500 expected to be built under plans for wind power to play a more important role in providing Britain's energy.

Chris Huhne, the Energy Secretary, last month called opponents of the plans "curmudgeons and fault-finders" and described turbines as "elegant" and "beautiful".

The Duke's attack on the turbines, believed to be the first public insight into his views on the matter, came in a conversation with the managing director of a leading wind farm company.

When Esbjorn Wilmar, of Infinergy, which builds and operates turbines, introduced himself to the Duke at a reception in London, he found himself on the end of an outspoken attack on his industry.

"He said they were absolutely useless, completely reliant on subsidies and an absolute disgrace," said Mr Wilmar. "I was surprised by his very frank views."

Mr Wilmar said his attempts to argue that onshore wind farms were one of the most cost-effective forms of renewable energy received a fierce response from the Duke.

## 02 Wind farms

"He said, 'You don't believe in fairy tales do you?'" said Mr Wilmar. "He said that they would never work as they need back-up capacity."

One of the main arguments of the anti-wind farm lobby is that because turbines do not produce electricity without wind, there is still a need for other ways to generate power.

Their proponents argue that it is possible to build "pump storage" schemes, which would use excess energy from wind power to pump water into reservoirs to generate further electricity in times of high demand and low supply.

It emerged last year that electricity customers are paying an average of £90 a year to subsidise wind farms and other forms of renewable energy as part of a government scheme to meet carbon-reduction targets.

Mr Wilmar said one of the main reasons the Duke thought onshore wind farms to be "a very bad idea" was their reliance on such subsidies.

The generous financial incentives being offered to green energy developers have led landowners to look to build wind farms on their estates, including the Duke of Gloucester, the Queen's cousin.

Prince Philip, however, said he would never consider allowing his land to be used for turbines, which can be up to 410ft tall, and he bemoaned their impact on the countryside.

Mr Wilmar said: "I suggested to him to put them on his estate, and he said, 'You stay away from my estate, young man'.

"He said he thought that they're not nice at all for the landscape."

The Duke's comments echo complaints made by his son, the Prince of Wales, who has refused to have any built on Duchy of Cornwall land.

Yet a turbine will be erected opposite the Castle of Mey in Caithness, where he stays for a week every August, if a farmer succeeds in gaining planning permission from Highland Council.

While they are opposed to onshore wind farms, the Royal family stands to earn millions of pounds from those placed offshore.

Last year, the Crown Estate, the £7billion land and property portfolio, approved an increase in the number of sites around the coast of England. The Crown Estate owns almost all of the seabed off Britain's 7,700-mile coastline.

Mr Wilmar claims that onshore turbines are less reliant on subsidies and more cost-effective than those built in the sea. "If you go offshore it costs you twice as much as being on-shore because you have to lay foundations in the sea," he said. "It's very expensive for very obvious reasons."

Two-thirds of the country's wind turbines are owned by foreign companies, which are estimated to reap £500 million a year in subsidies.

A spokesman for the Duke said that Buckingham Palace would not comment about a private conversation.

http://www.telegraph.co.uk/news/uknews/prince-philip/8901985/Wind-farms-are-useless-says-Prince-Philip.html

**Opposite** A photograph of Prince Philip, The Duke of Edinburgh, husband to Queen Elizabeth II.

## General comprehension

1. What is Prince Philip's opinion of wind farms?
2. Who was Prince Philip talking to when he made these comments, and what is that person's job?
3. Which group of people will be delighted by Prince Philip's comments?
4. According to the text, what is the main argument of the anti-wind farm lobby against?
5. What is the attitude of the Prince of Wales to wind turbines?
6. Although the Royal Family is against wind turbines, they will earn money from any that are in use. What is the reason for this?
7. According to the text, who owns the majority of the wind turbines in the UK?

## Text handling

1. The words below are synonyms for words in the text. Can you find the words in the text?
    a) attack
    b) financial aid
    c) growing
    d) in opposition to
    e) openly honest
    f) supporters
    g) put up

2. What do the underlined words refer to?
    a) He also criticised the industry's reliance on subsidies from electricity customers, claimed wind farms would "never work" and accused people who support <u>them</u> of believing in a "fairy tale".
    b) Mr Wilmar said one of the main reasons the Duke thought onshore wind farms to be "a very bad idea" was <u>their</u> reliance on such subsidies.
    c) Mr Wilmar said: "I suggested to him to put <u>them</u> on his estate, and he said, 'You stay away from my estate, young man'."

## Zoom in on grammar

**Reported and direct speech**

Direct speech is when the speaker's words are presented to the reader between inverted commas:

   He said, "You stay away from my estate, young man".

Reported speech is when the words are 'reported':

   Prince Philip told the young man to stay away from his estate.

In reported speech, the words are introduced by phrases like 'he said' or 'the man shouted'.

## Grammar in context

**Examples of the use of reported speech**

- The teacher said he was disappointed with the test results.
  This reports the teacher's words: 'I am disappointed with the test results.'
- My mother asked if I would tidy my room that morning.
  This reports the mother's question: 'Will you tidy your room this morning?'

Notice that in the reported speech the verb takes a past form: 'your room' becomes 'my room' and 'this morning' becomes 'that morning'.

1. Can you find two examples of reported speech in the text about Prince Philip's attitude to wind farms?
2. Can you work out what the spoken words were?

33

## 02 Wind farms

> For more information on energy poverty, go to www.pearsonhotlinks.com, enter the title or ISBN of this book and click on Chapter 2.

### Written work

You have read the article in the newspaper about Prince Philip's reaction to wind farms but you know that in many countries there is an urgent need to provide reliable energy. Using the information and statistics that you find in the two websites suggested here, write a letter to the editor of the *Telegraph* newspaper supporting wind energy in countries where there is energy poverty. Write between 400 and 450 words.

### Text 2.3.2 International Energy Agency: the other side of the energy discussion

## blog

## energy poverty

Energy poverty is a lack of access to modern energy services. These services are defined as household access to electricity and clean cooking facilities (e.g. fuels and stoves that do not cause air pollution in houses).

Modern energy services are crucial to human well-being and to a country's economic development; and yet globally over 1.3 billion people are without access to electricity and 2.6 billion people are without clean cooking facilities. More than 95% of these people are either in sub-Saharan African or developing Asia and 84% are in rural areas.

The lack of access to modern energy services is a serious hindrance to economic and social development, and must be overcome if the UN Millennium Development Goals are to be achieved.

For a decade, the World Energy Outlook (WEO) has highlighted the crucial role that energy access plays in a country's development. During this time, it has developed its own databases on energy access, and published several substantive analytical reports on different elements of this issue. In order to inform the debate about how to overcome energy poverty, the IEA flagship publication has provided energy-poverty data, quantitative analysis and projections for energy use in developing countries. The WEO evaluates energy poverty in the global energy context to inform [the] OECD [Organisation for Economic Co-operation and Development], governments, industry, the private sector and financial institutions.

http://www.iea.org/topics/energypoverty/

Text 2.3.3 Modern energy for all

# The facts about energy poverty

Despite the availability of technical solutions, two in every five people still rely on wood, charcoal or animal waste to cook their food and one in five people lack electricity.

Each year, 2 million people die from diseases caused by indoor smoke – more than deaths from malaria.

An estimated 1 billion people use health services without electricity.

Over 291 million children go to primary schools without access to any electricity.

Almost 50% of vaccines in developing countries are ruined due to poor cold chain services.

In Uganda only 1% of rural outpatient clinics are connected to the electricity grid.

To reach universal energy access by 2030, 55% of additional electricity generated for households will need to be through mini- and off-grid solutions.

Four out of five health facilities in Rwanda offer antenatal care, but only 17% of those have examination lights which allow a proper pelvic examination.

http://practicalaction.org/totalenergyaccess

# 02 Wind farms

### General comprehension

1 What is the definition of *modern energy services*?
2 What effect does the lack of access to energy sources have on the economic development in a country?
3 What is the goal of the organisation World Energy Outlook in collecting information on energy poverty?

### Interactive oral activity

The above texts tell you something about energy poverty. Research this theme yourself and find out further information about some of the issues. Make notes and prepare yourself for a group discussion.

In groups of three or four discuss the contrasting issues of energy poverty in developing countries and environmental protection in developed countries.

Be prepared to report the results of your discussion to the class.

## Exam practice

# Wind farms are robbing Britain of its porpoise

*The title of the article by Simon Barnes is a play on the pronunciation of the word 'purpose'. The two words 'purpose' and 'porpoise' are linked humorously – try saying them. Although in formal English there is a difference in pronunciation, they can sometimes sound similar when spoken by people with regional accents.*

*The headlines in English-language newspapers can be very difficult to understand. Words are often used in unusual ways and headlines are rarely complete sentences. As in the following article, puns are very popular. A pun is a word or phrase that exploits possible double meaning in words, often for humorous effect.*

1 The thinking person's television comes in two forms, summer and winter. It's elemental; in winter the wise person stares at fire and thinks deep thoughts or, better still, just goes beyond thoughts altogether and just sits. In summer it's water. It's a fact that you can stare at water without boredom for longer then you can stare at anything else on the planet. The sea commands us to keep an eye on it; don't let it out of your sight, not for a moment, because it's got a lot more moving about to do.

2 Sea-staring is a profound experience; there's so much of it and you can't often see what lives in it. It's impossible to take a long look at the sea – superficially the least human-affected place on Earth – without wondering about the planet we live on. Binoculars help. Shift your gaze to a good mile out and with luck you'll pick out a gannet or two; startlingly white, cruciform, black tips to their wings. In some places you'll be rewarded with the head of a seal, an air-breather like ourselves, but quite unafraid of the forbidding sea. And there are other, still greater prizes.

3 If you tell someone that your plan is to sit and stare at the sea, he may well ask: "With what porpoise?" It is the question of the Mock Turtle in *Alice*, invariably asked when he hears that fish are going on a journey. Any session of sea-staring is richer if you have a porpoise. So let me tell you that today (27 July) is the start of the annual National Whale and Dolphin Watch, organised by Sea Watch Foundation, old friends of this column. There are two good reasons for this annual watch. The first is that it's jolly good fun. People who had no idea that such wonderful creatures could be seen with their feet still firmly on

our island have a chance to enrich their lives. They will see the world (especially the wet bits) for ever in a slightly different way. I remember the delight of finding harbour porpoises off the coast of Cornwall. They are creatures of great modesty and charm. Not showy-offy like dolphins and lacking the self-conscious grandeur of the big whales. Porpoises are one of the sea's more subtle pleasures.

**4** The second reason for the watch is that the information helps to build up a picture of the habits and numbers of the whales and dolphins that use our coastal waters. Once armed with that information we can do something about protecting them. Or we could if the Government would listen. The European Commission's Habitats Directive places the harbour porpoise on a special annex requiring special areas of conservation. Most countries have been surveying and designating appropriate sites. Almost uniquely the UK is not among them. Our own nation says "Let the porpoises go hang": Our Government is determinedly anti-porpoise.

**5** It's about wind farms. The Government is mad on them. Offshore wind farms are the answer to everything and nothing must get in their way. And wind farming can affect porpoises; the din of the pile-driving during construction is horribly disturbing and affects their echolocation talents.

**6** The Government response is a knee-jerk opposition to anything to do with marine conservation. This polarises the debate on traditional lines, developers versus conservationists. It's an old story and we all know the way it turns out.

Peter Evans, the director of Sea Watch, has another view: "The idea that a marine protected area precludes any human activity is a misconception," he says. "If only developers, environmentalists and politicians all realised that one doesn't preclude the other, we would have much less resistance to the establishment of large areas recognised as important for marine life."

**7** Our relationship with the sea has never been wholly exploitative. There is always fascination and love to go with the "what's in it for me?" attitude. We need to approach marine conservation with larger minds – if we don't, our seas will die. Stick to entrenched positions and we lose our porpoises. And I'm not sure I really want to live in a country that lacks a porpoise in life.

*Simon Barnes in his 'Wild Notebook' column, The Times, Saturday July 27 2013*

## 02 Wind farms

### Exercises

Answer the following questions.

1   Match the headings below with the paragraphs in the text. Write the appropriate number in the box below. NOTE: There are more options than paragraphs. An example has been provided.

**Example:** Seasonal changes ☐ 1

| | | |
|---|---|---|
| **A** | A porpoise in life | ☐ |
| **B** | Fascination with the sea | ☐ |
| **C** | The prize of the sea | ☐ |
| **D** | Marine protected areas | ☐ |
| **E** | National Whale and Dolphin Watch | ☐ |
| **F** | UK porpoise sites | ☐ |
| **G** | Watching porpoises and turtles | ☐ |
| **H** | The Government's obsession | ☐ |
| **I** | What you'll see | ☐ |
| **J** | The dying seas | ☐ |
| **K** | Conflicting interests | ☐ |
| **L** | Protecting inhabitants of coastal areas | ☐ |

2   Which of these words best describes the writer's feeling when he stares at the sea around the UK? ☐

| | | | | |
|---|---|---|---|---|
| **A** | worried | | **C** | disappointed |
| **B** | inspired | | **D** | interested |

38

**3** Match the words from the text with the synonyms on the right. Write the appropriate letter in the box below.

| I | cruciform | | A | magnificence |
|---|---|---|---|---|
| II | forbidding | | B | cross-shaped |
| III | annual | | C | very |
| IV | grandeur | | D | hostile |
| V | preclude | | E | equipped |
| VI | armed | | F | yearly |
| VII | jolly | | G | exclude |

## Further exercises

### General comprehension

1. What does the author mean when he compares summer and winter to television?
2. What is the event that takes place annually on the 27th July?
3. Name four large sea creatures that the author delights in seeing when he watches the sea.
4. What is the British Government's attitude to the porpoises around the coast?
5. Is the British Government's attitude to wind farms a positive or negative one?
6. What injuries do wind farms cause to porpoises?
7. According to the text there are traditionally two standpoints on the environment: the standpoint of the developer on the one hand, and the standpoint of the conservationist on the other. Explain these two standpoints.
8. Identify the sentence in the text that refers to a character from *Alice in Wonderland* by Lewis Carroll.

### Interactive oral activity

In pairs, prepare arguments for or against wind farms. Decide in advance how many pairs of students in your class will be for and how many will be against. With your partner, decide on the arguments you will use and make some notes.

Remember to concentrate only on the one aspect and be persuasive. You must be strongly in support of your side of the argument.

Take time to explore some websites to find more information and images about wind farms.

After an agreed amount of preparation time, get together with another pair who have the opposite opinion and carry out a discussion using the points you have prepared.

You should aim to keep your discussion going for at least ten minutes.

# 03 Slave labour

## Objectives

- To practise writing in various registers: a formal letter, a semi-formal blog
- To develop persuasive language skills
- To practise interactive oral skills
- To practise using the gerund
- To revise the use of verbs that change their meaning when they take either a *to*-infinitive or an *-ing* form
- To revise prepositions of time
- To revise the use of 'would' to remember things that often happened in the past

**Opposite** Spools of thread at a weaving mill.

> The nickname that Primark fans give to the store, 'Primani', is a reference to the Italian fashion house Armani. Armani designs and manufactures top-quality goods and is a highly successful and well-known company in the fashion world.

# 3.1 Cheap products

### Text 3.1.1 Ethics are soon forgotten when you're faced with a five-pound dress

## Primark shoppers say they are attracted by the price and style of clothing, not its quality or origins, writes Chloe Hamilton

The fashion equivalent of fast food, Primark has created a new breed of shopper: who considers its discount clothing so addictively cheap and disposable that they hoard items with little concern if they need or want them.

At Primark's flagship branch in Oxford Street, central London, Hannah Rose, 21, is shopping with her friend for a trip to the US with Camp America. Hannah admits she doesn't bother taking clothes back to the store if she doesn't like them after she gets home. "If it's only 2 pounds there's no point, I'll just shove it to the back of my wardrobe," she says.

While Primark has become increasingly popular for its prices, many customers know its range of T-shirts, shoes, skirts and jeans are inexpensive largely thanks to the low cost of sourcing them in less-developed countries.

Primark bosses said they were "shocked and saddened" by the collapse of a factory in Bangladesh, after confirming that one of its suppliers occupied the second floor of the eight-storey building. The company has been dogged by rumours that it uses child labour since 2008, when it axed three suppliers in India for passing work to unapproved sub-contractors who used under-age workers. It has also confirmed that it does not use child labour now.

But what effect this has upon shoppers, even those who have been suspicious of the ethics surrounding cheap clothes, is minimal when they are faced with a five-pound dress. Primark's parent company said like-for-like sales rose by seven per cent in the 24 weeks to the start of March, a performance it describes as "exceptionally strong". […]

# 03  Slave labour

Traditionally, Primark shoppers buy in bulk, leaving the shop laden with clothes, shoes and accessories. The brand, dubbed "Primani" by its fans, doesn't have a website as it believes its low-cost, high-volume business model wouldn't be an attraction online. But competition on the high street means more shops are driving their costs down by using factories in developing countries to make cheap clothes quickly.

Primark claims it can take as little as six weeks for catwalk styles to appear in the shops – and that doesn't just attract teenagers. "It's cheap and there's a lot of variety for young people" says Claire O'Brien, 53. "I think it should be investigated. They were paying (the Bangladeshi workers) their wages but it doesn't necessarily mean Primark were negligent."

Rabih Galach, 35, a banker, says Primark is good value for money. "We have disasters all over the world every day. I'm from Lebanon and I hear about Palestine and Syria every day. I can sympathise, but it won't stop me buying from there."

Full version at http://www.independent.co.uk/life-style/fashion/news/despite-the-factory-collapse-in-bangladesh-ethics-are-soon-forgotten-when-faced-with-a-5-dress-8588858.html

## General comprehension

1. What kind of product is Primark compared to and what does this mean?
2. What is Hannah Rose's attitude to buying clothes at the London store?
3. Quote the phrase that tells the reader that Primark cancelled its contracts with some producers in India.
4. What was the reason for cancelling the contracts with the suppliers?
5. According to the text, how concerned are shoppers if they hear that the clothes they are buying were produced by slave labour?
6. What reason does the company Primark give for not having a website?
7. How many weeks does it take for catwalk styles to appear in Primark shops?

## Text handling

1. Find a word in the text that has the same meaning as the following.
   a) designed to use and then throw away
   b) most important
   c) push
   d) clothes cupboard
   e) producing
   f) troubled
   g) large quantities
   h) designer clothes shown at a presentation

2. Match the words from the text on the left with the correct definition on the right.

   | | | | |
   |---|---|---|---|
   | I | discount | A | comparison of same time periods |
   | II | shove | B | large quantity |
   | III | dogged by | C | loaded with |
   | IV | like-for-like | D | push |
   | V | bulk | E | cheap |
   | VI | laden | F | followed by bad luck |

## Zoom in on grammar

### The verb 'stop'

The verb 'stop' changes its meaning depending on whether it is followed by the *to*-infinitive or the *-ing* form.

In the final sentence Rabih Galach says 'it won't stop me buying from there'.

Look at these two examples.

1  **The customers stopped *buying* cheap T-shirts after the fire.**

   'Stop doing something' means to end an action, to finish doing it.

2  **The workers *stopped* to take a break.**

   'Stop to do something' means to stop what you are doing so that you can do something else.

## Grammar in context

### The verb 'stop'

Put in the correct form of the verb in brackets after 'stop' in the following sentences.

1  The driver of the car stopped _____ (take a break).
2  I was late and didn't stop _____ (check) I had all my things for school.
3  Stop _____ (play) with your phone and focus on the lesson.
4  We wanted to stop _____ (buy) some groceries on the way home.
5  If I had more self discipline I would stop _____ (smoke).
6  In the traffic the driver behind me didn't stop _____ (flash) his lights until I switched off my indicator.
7  A man walking along the street stopped _____ (talk) to us.

## Interactive oral activity

In this discussion you are asked to consider the text about cheap products through the TOK lens. We know that in TOK there are four ways of knowing: perception, emotion, reason and language. In your discussion, focus on the ethical issues and explore the question of how ethical it is to produce these cheap products. There is also the ethical aspect from the consumer's point of view. Before the discussion begins you should prepare some ideas – to do this it may be helpful to get together with a partner and collect your ideas.

# Written work

Your local newspaper has printed an article about a shop that is selling cheap T-shirts made in Bangladesh. The newspaper has a page where readers' opinions are published and you decide to express your opinion in a letter to the editor. Before you begin, you must decide what opinion you want to express.

The register of the letter will be formal, and as you don't know the editor's name, your letter will begin 'Dear Sir or Madam' and end with the words 'Yours faithfully', before you sign your name. Write between 250 and 300 words.

# 03 Slave labour

> The text 'Products of labour abuse' is written in American English. This is clear when we examine the spelling of the words *labor*, *jewelry* and *clamor*. In British English they are written *labour*, *jewellery* and *clamour*.

## 3.2 Slave labour

### Text 3.2.1 Products of labour abuse

http://www.fightslaverynow.wordpress.com

You check your email over morning coffee, stirring in just a bit of sugar. As you put on a fresh cotton shirt, you're planning a special dinner for someone close to you. You need to prepare that shrimp dish with saffron rice before they arrive. You hope they'll like your gifts of chocolates and gold jewelry. The balloon decorations are in place. You make a cell phone call before you get ready to drive to the market.

You've now been slapped in the face with slavery over a dozen times before you even leave your driveway! Coffee, sugar, rice, and cotton are commodities that, depending on their place of origin, may likely have been produced with slave labor or child labor. Luxury items like chocolate, saffron, and gold are frequently tainted by slavery. Much seafood, especially shrimp, is harvested by children under abusive conditions beyond belief. Cell phones and computers depend on a rare metal called tantalum extracted from the ore coltan, which is mined in the Democratic Republic of the Congo using slave labor. Gold is dug in deep pits by children scratching the earth with crude tools. Even your festive balloons may have been produced by child slaves laboring intensively in chemically hazardous environments for hardly enough to live. As you close that car door, would you ever suspect that the rubber in its tires was tapped by slave laborers in Liberia, or that the steel may derive from pig iron mined by slaves deep in the Amazon jungle where they are watched over by taskmasters with guns?

## The list of products is long and surprising

The Trafficking Victims Protection Reauthorization Acts of 2005 and 2008 required the Department of Labor to compile and publish a list of products produced by child labor or forced labor, and the countries where these abuses were prevalent. After much foot-dragging, and in response to public clamor from the abolitionist community, the list was finally unveiled in 2009 by the new administration.

122 goods in 58 countries were produced with a significant incidence of forced labor, child labor, or both. Child labor abuse seems the most prevalent worldwide.

The most common goods having a significant incidence of forced and/or child labor in agriculture: cocoa, coffee, cotton, rice, sugarcane, and tobacco. In manufacturing: bricks, garments, carpets, and footwear. In mined/quarried goods: gold, diamonds and coal.

http://www.fightslaverynow.wordpress.com

### General comprehension

1. Make a list of the products mentioned in the text that are manufactured using slave labour.
2. According to the text, how many of these slave labourers are children?
3. What is the name of the ore mined in the Democratic Republic of Congo and used to produce the metal tantalum?
4. What word in the text is used to describe a primitive, simple tool?
5. In the text the American Department of Labor is accused of 'foot-dragging' in its work on publishing a list of products produced using child labour. What does this phrase mean?
6. The Department of Labor published a list of countries and products involving slave labour after 'clamor from the abolitionist community'. Explain the meaning of this phrase.
7. What word used in the text means 'items of clothing'?

### Text handling

Find the following words in the text and examine the context. Then give synonyms (word or phrase) for them.

1. gifts
2. slapped in the face
3. commodities
4. tainted
5. crude tools
6. hazardous
7. foot-dragging
8. clamor

## Written work

Imagine that at your school you have had a guest speaker from an organisation called Stop Slavery Now. The speaker talked to your class about cheap products and slave labour, giving you detailed information about the situation in the textile factories in Pakistan and Bangladesh and the conditions the workers there have to endure.

Write a personal blog entry in which you reflect on your reactions to the guest speaker and your feelings about the situation of the workers. Write between 300 and 400 words.

See Chapter 1 for guidance on writing a blog.

# 03 Slave labour

**Some points to think about when you are preparing your blog**

Remember that a blog entry is like a website: it is read electronically and is often in the style of a newspaper or magazine article. It will be written in a formal or semi-formal register. A blog invites reactions and comments from other readers. In your blog you may want to consider some of the points below.

- The reason you have chosen to write this blog.
- Your thoughts about the speaker: was he/she persuasive, interesting, dynamic, well informed and committed?
- What you have learnt about countries and products connected to slave labour.
- How much you think this issue should affect our shopping habits.
- Whether you want to propose any action that should be taken.

### Individual oral activity

Do you think you or your family buy products that are produced using slave labour? Explore the website www.slaveryfootprint.org to find out how many slaves work for you.

Find other sites that give you information. Organise the results of your search and prepare a three- or four-minute presentation to give to your class or to a group within your class. Link your presentation to the knowledge you have gained from your reading and the opinions you have formed.

## 3.3 The story of a slave

### Text 3.3.1 Frederick Douglass: biography

> To read about modern day slave labour using children, read *Iqbal* by Francesco d'Adamo. It is based on the lives of child slaves making carpets in Pakistan.

For us the majority of slaves are people without names. Not that they were never given a name, but we never learn their names and never get a chance to hear them tell their story. Their lives remain an untold tragedy.

However, the life of one slave, Frederick Douglass, is well documented and his story and his fame stand for the millions whose lives remain anonymous.

Frederick Douglass was born into slavery in the United States of America at the beginning of the 19th century. His date of birth is not known because details of the parentage of slaves were not recorded. At the age of 12 Frederick Douglass was sold to the slave owner Hugh Ald, whose wife taught Douglass to read and write. These skills would vault him to national celebrity years later.

In the year 1838 Frederick Douglass escaped from his slave owners and travelled to New York where he was supported by the abolitionist

David Ruggles. Douglass became a vociferous supporter of the abolition of slavery and gave passionate speeches at abolitionist meetings. The journalist William Lloyd Garrison encouraged Frederick Douglass to write down his experiences as a slave. His autobiography *Narrative of the Life of Frederick Douglass, an American Slave* was published in 1845, became a bestseller in the United States and was translated into several European languages.

Frederick Douglass became famous; his writings and the talks he gave were inspirational and won many supporters for the abolition of slavery. President Abraham Lincoln and Frederick Douglass had long discussions about slavery. In 1863 President Lincoln's Emancipation Proclamation declared the freedom of slaves in Confederate territory.

Frederick Douglass died in 1895.

**Above** Frederick Douglass.

## General comprehension

1. Explain the meaning of the sentence 'Their lives remain an untold tragedy'.
2. Frederick Douglass was literate, an unusual ability for a slave. How did he become literate?
3. What event made it possible for Frederick Douglass to become a speaker at abolitionist meetings?
4. What influence did Frederick Douglass have on achieving freedom for slaves in Confederate territory?

## Text handling

Match the words from the text on the left with the corresponding definitions on the right. There are more words on the right than you need.

| | | | |
|---|---|---|---|
| 1 | anonymous | A | a person in favour of slavery |
| 2 | parentage | B | loud and articulate |
| 3 | vault | C | a supporter of the ending of slavery |
| 4 | vociferous | D | having no name |
| 5 | abolitionist | E | to achieve something in a short time |
| | | F | angry |
| | | G | family origins |
| | | H | to jump over something |

47

## 3.3.2 From *Narrative of the Life of Frederick Douglass, an American Slave* by Frederick Douglass

### CHAPTER 1

I was born in Tuckahoe, near Hillsborough, and about twelve miles from Easton, in Talbot county, Maryland. I have no accurate knowledge of my age, never having seen an authentic record containing it. By far the larger part of the slaves know as little of their ages as horses know of theirs, and it is the wish of most masters within my knowledge to keep their slaves thus ignorant. I do not remember to have ever met a slave who could tell of his birthday. They seldom came nearer to it than planting-time, cherry-time, spring-time, or fall-time. A want of information concerning my own was a source of unhappiness to me even during childhood. The white children could tell their ages. I could not tell why I ought to be deprived of the same privilege. I was not allowed to make any inquiries of my master concerning it. He deemed all such inquiries on the part of a slave improper and impertinent, and evidence of a restless spirit. The nearest estimate I can give makes me now between twenty-seven and twenty-eight years of age. I come to this, from hearing my master say, some time during 1835, I was about seventeen years old.

My mother was named Harriet Bailey. She was the daughter of Isaac and Betsy Bailey, both colored and quite dark. My mother was of a darker complexion than either my grandmother or grandfather.

My father was a white man. He was admitted to be such by any I ever heard speak of my parentage. The opinion was also whispered that my master was my father, but of the correctness of this opinion, I know nothing; the means of knowing was withheld from me. My mother and I were separated when I was but an infant – before I knew her as my mother. It is a common custom, in the part of Maryland from which I ran away, to part children from their mothers at a very early age. Frequently, before the child has reached its twelfth month, its mother is taken from it, and hired out at some farm a considerable distance off, and the child is placed under the care of an old woman, too old for field labor. For what this separation is done, I do not know, unless it be to hinder the development of the child's affection towards its mother, and to blunt and destroy the natural affection of the mother for the child. This is the inevitable result.

I never saw my mother, to know her as such, more than four or five times in my life; and each of those times was very short in duration, and at night. She was hired by Mr Stewart, who lived about twelve miles from my home. She made her journeys to see me in the night, travelling the whole distance on foot, after the performance of her day's work. She was a field hand, and a whipping is the penalty for not being in the field at sunrise, unless a slave has special permission from his or her master to the contrary – a permission which they seldom get, and one that gives to him that gives it the proud name of being a kind master. I do not recollect ever seeing my mother by the light of day. She was with me in the night. She would lie down with me, and get me to sleep, but long before I waked she was gone. Very little communication ever took place between us. Death soon ended what little we could have while she lived, and with it her hardships and suffering. She died when I was about seven years old, on one of my master's farms, near Lee's Mill. I was not allowed to be present during her illness, at her death or burial. She was gone long before I knew any thing about it. Never having enjoyed, to any considerable extent, her soothing presence, her tender and watchful care, I received the tidings of her death with much the same emotions I should have probably felt at the death of a stranger.

*From* Narrative of the Life of Frederick Douglass, an American Slave, *published by Penguin Books*

# 03 Slave labour

## General comprehension

1. According to the text, what is the reason for slaves not knowing when they were born?
2. 'I never knew my mother, to know her as such.' Explain the meaning of the words 'as such'.
3. Frederick Douglass describes his grandparents as 'colored'. What does he mean by this?
4. What is the impression created in the first paragraphs of this book about the life of a slave?

## Text handling

Examine the following statements and say if they are true or false according to the text.
Give a brief justification by quoting from the text.

1. Frederick Douglass suffered as a child from not knowing when he was born.
2. Frederick's master considered questions about his birth to be appropriate.
3. Death was a relief for Frederick's mother.
4. Frederick did not go to his mother's funeral.

## Zoom in on grammar

**'Would'**

We use *would* when we look back on the past and remember things that happened repeatedly. Look at this sentence from the excerpt in which Frederick Douglass is talking about his mother:

*She would lie down with me and get me to sleep.*

The word *would* shows that this action happened in the past on more than one occasion.

## Grammar in context

**'Would'**

1. These sentences are about things that often happened in the past. Use the word *would* with one of these verbs: help / be / take.
   a) The cinema today is nearly always empty but I remember a few years ago it _____ crowded every night.
   b) When she went out, my grandmother _____ always _____ an umbrella with her whether it was raining or not.
   c) When I was a child I _____ my father wash the car every Saturday.

2. Now make your own examples by completing the sentences.
   a) In the 1960s people...
   b) I walk to school now, but when we lived in California...
   c) When my brother was 5 years old...

## Zoom in on grammar

**Prepositions of time**

- For days of the week – *on* Monday, *on* Tuesday, etc
- For months – *in* January, *in* February, but *on* 26th January, *on* 12th May
- For years – *in* 2012, *in* 1066
- For the time – *at* 3pm, *at* 6 o'clock, *at* a quarter past 5.

## Grammar in context

**Prepositions of time**

Fill in the correct prepositions:
1. I left the house _____ 5 a.m.
2. President Abraham Lincoln issued the Emancipation Proclamation _____ 1st January 1863.
3. The Rana Plaza factory in Bangladesh collapsed _____ April 2013.
4. I always go swimming _____ 5pm _____ Monday.
5. Frederick Douglass escaped from slavery _____ 1838.
6. I am completing this exercise _____ the year 20??.

## Zoom in on grammar

**The gerund**

Look at the following sentence from Text 3.2.1:

'You check your email over morning coffee, *stirring* in just a bit of sugar.'

The gerund shows the reader that the activity 'to stir' is happening at the same time as the activity 'to check'. This example could be re-written as follows:

'You check your email over morning coffee while you stir in just a bit of sugar.'

Be careful though: while the gerund is a verb in the *-ing* form, not all verbs + *-ing* are gerunds! Compare these two sentences:
1. The student is *studying* for the final exams.
2. *Studying* is essential for success.

In the first sentence, 'studying' is the participle of the verb and not the gerund form; in the second sentence, 'studying' is the subject of the sentence and the gerund. It is used as a noun.

## Grammar in context

**The gerund**

Join these sentences using a gerund (*-ing* verb).
1. She ran down the road. She shouted for help and looked desperately for someone who could help her.
2. The band played a march that drowned out all other sounds. It made conversation impossible.
3. Tim drove down the High Street. He laughed and waved to his friends who were waiting at the bus stop.

# Written work (HL)

Read the following text:

> 'Slavery was abolished 150 years ago, right? While it is true that slavery is illegal almost everywhere on earth, the fact is there are more slaves today than there ever were.'
>
> Robert Alan Silverstein

Give a personal response to the stimulus and justify it. Write a speech or mini essay in/using 150–250 words.

## Exam hints

Think about the following questions when you are planning your personal response.
- What is your first reaction to the statement?
- Will you write from only one standpoint, or will you present a balanced answer?
- What facts will you use to support your ideas?
- Who is your audience?
- What words or phrases will you use to make sure your text flows smoothly from one point to the next?

For more information on Robert Alan Silverstein, go to www.pearsonhotlinks.com, enter the title or ISBN of this book and click on Chapter 3.

## 3.4 The Help

Text 3.4.1 A review of the novel *The Help* by Kathryn Stockett

http://www.theguardian.com/childrens-books-site/2012/jan/14/review-the-help-kathryn-stockett

# "Jackson, Mississippi, 1962. Black maids raise white children, but aren't trusted not to steal the silver" is the first line that you read on the blurb of The Help and this rings true not only in the book but in history too.

*The Help* is an unforgettable story told from the viewpoints of three very unforgettable women: Aibileen, raising her seventeenth white child; Minny, forever losing jobs due to her sassy tongue; and Miss Skeeter, an aspiring writer who has been raised by black maids all her life.

When Skeeter gets the opportunity of a lifetime to become a published author, she of course takes it but in order for this to happen, she has to write about things that people need to read about.

In a time when even talking to a black person was shunned, these three women team up on a project that will put them all at risk in an attempt to change the minds of the Jackson residents. What follows was, for me, a rollercoaster ride of emotion, as we hear stories of cruelty and humiliation but also those of tenderness.

This book has characters in it that you are meant to empathise with and those, of course, whom you are meant to dislike. The way in which Stockett has written about her characters is so believable that I didn't find myself thinking 'no-one would have said or done that.' As I was reading this book, it didn't cross my mind at all that it was fiction because everything Kathryn Stockett wrote about seemed thoroughly believable, particularly coming from such different characters.

It is told in alternating viewpoints from the three main characters, so we get to see from both sides of the story in this book; from the League ladies such as the truly venomous Miss Hilly, to the maids who work for them and basically raise their children single handedly.

It's hard for me to fault this book, except I feel that Skeeter did not quite understand the danger she was putting the maids in to help her write the book, as there was much more risk for black maids to tell stories about their employers than it was for Skeeter to write them. However, the characters were well built and the plot was very intriguing. It's definitely a hard subject to write about and we see that from both Kathryn Stockett's and Skeeter's writing. *The Help* changed the lives of the women in the book and I feel as if somehow it changed my life too. *The Help* really is a special book and I encourage anyone and everyone to check it out.

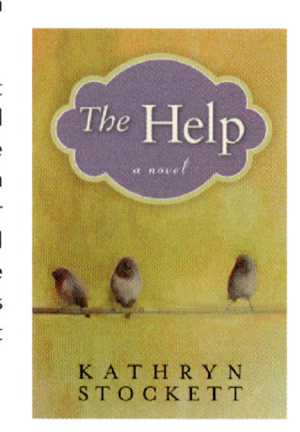

http://www.theguardian.com/childrens-books-site/2012/jan/14/review-the-help-kathryn-stockett

## General comprehension

1 List the narrators in the novel and the roles they play.
2 The use of three narrators enables the reader to gain insight into the situation in a special way. Can you explain how this makes the story successful?
3 From your previous knowledge, can you describe how the social situation in the USA has changed since 1962?

## Text handling

Here are four words from the text. Of the four possible meanings offered for each one, which is the most accurate according to the text?

1 sassy
   a) loud
   b) foreign
   c) cheeky
   d) heavily accented

2 shunned
   a) banned
   b) avoided
   c) punished
   d) forbidden

3 venomous
   a) friendly
   b) helpful
   c) poisonous
   d) sly

4 intriguing
   a) fascinating
   b) complicated
   c) intense
   d) disturbing

## Exam hints

There are a number of points to notice about writing a book review. Read the tips below.

- Write in the present tense.
- Include a brief summary of the events in the story.
- Avoid saying 'I think…'.
- Give an opinion of the story.
- Give a recommendation to readers.

# Written work

Consider one of the books you have read in your Diploma course and write a review of it. Follow the tips given above and write the review in 300–400 words.

# 03 Slave labour

## Exam practice

## The cost of a T-shirt

*Textile workers in Bangladesh deserve better protection from their employers*

It is brutally apparent that the garment factories employing millions of workers in Bangladesh are unsafe. Seventeen days ago a building collapsed, killing more than 1,000 people. More recently, a fire in another claimed a further eight lives.

Health-and-safety legislation in the Western world is often mocked, yet the enforcement of tight controls means that industrial accidents have become mercifully rare. However, in the developing economies of Asia and Africa scenes of carnage at the workplace are all too frequent.

Many of the cheap clothes sold on British high streets are made in Bangladesh. The temptation to blame bargain-hunting consumers for the poor pay and conditions endured by textile workers in Dhaka is clear, yet should be resisted. As the Trades Union Congress (TUC) pointed out yesterday, using figures from unions in Bangladesh, wages account for only a fraction of the retail price of clothing originating in Bangladesh. Pay rates could be doubled, says the TUC, while adding a negligible amount to the cost of a T-shirt.

It is not often this newspaper is in agreement with the TUC but on this issue their argument is persuasive. British people want cheap clothes, but surely not at the cost of the life of the person who makes them.

Shoppers should make this view plain to the many retailers and suppliers currently profiting from using grossly underpaid workers labouring long hours in factories that can turn into death-traps in an instant. The responsibility for ensuring the fair remuneration and safety of those workers lies with their employers and the authorities in Bangladesh. It is a responsibility that both parties appear to have shirked.

> TUC is the abbreviation for the Trades Union Congress – an umbrella organisation of all trade unions in the UK.

The Times, *London Leader, May 11 2013*

## Exercises

Answer the following questions.

**1** What does the collapse of the building in Bangladesh tell you about health-and-safety regulations in that country?

..........................................................................................................

**2** According to the text, should consumers looking for cheap clothes be blamed for the situation of the textile workers in Bangladesh?

..........................................................................................................

**3** Match the words from the text with the synonyms on the right. Write the appropriate letter in the box below.

**Example:** apparent   **B**

| I | mocked | | A | extremely |
| II | carnage | | B | clear |
| III | retailers | | C | slaughter |
| IV | negligible | | D | avoided |
| V | grossly | | E | minimal |
| VI | shirked | | F | laughed at |
| | | | G | shop owners |

## Further exercises

### Interactive oral activity

In groups of three, discuss what you think the main idea is that is expressed in this text. Read the text again, then talk about the following points.

- Express your own opinions about slave labour and the clothes you buy with the other students in your group. You thought about some of these points when you wrote the answers to the 'General comprehension' exercises.
- Some people think it is better to have a hard job than no job at all. What is your opinion about this?
- Discuss the factors that influence your choices when you buy clothes in the country you live in. Do you think as a consumer you can change anything?

When you give an opinion always give reasons for your thinking. Before the discussion you must take time to prepare some thoughts and arguments. Planning what you want to say is a vital part of any oral work.

It is important that each member of the group has a chance to express opinions and thoughts. You must also be prepared to report back to the other groups in the class at the end of your discussion.

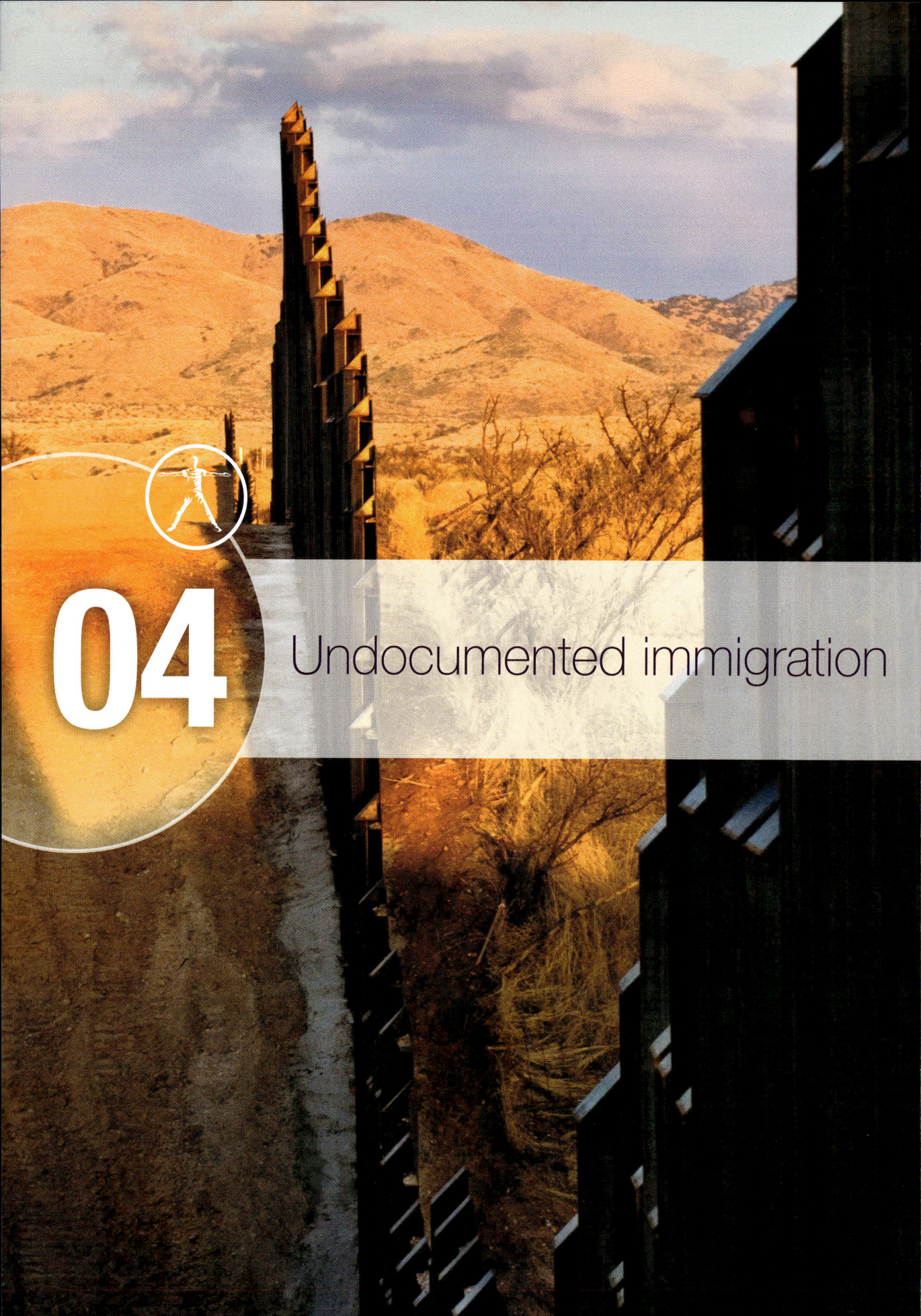

# 04 Undocumented immigration

## Objectives

- To speak about the topic of immigration
- To explore idioms used in context
- To revise the meaning of 'ought to'
- To revise the use of the past continuous
- To practise asking and answering general comprehension questions
- To practise giving an oral presentation on a given topic

**Opposite** The fence that runs along the border between Mexico and the USA.

# 4.1 Undocumented immigration

## Text 4.1.1 Undocumented immigration

**1** Migration defines the movement of people from one country or region to settle permanently somewhere else. Immigration defines movement into a country or region. Throughout history groups of people have seldom stayed in one place permanently, but have moved around to find areas more suited to their needs. Today, immigration has become a political issue and is the cause of controversial and heated debate in many countries in the world. The reasons motivating this movement of people are manifold: religious persecution, the search for economic prosperity, escape from man-made disasters such as war and armed conflict, or from natural disasters such as famine or earthquake. The countries attracting the highest numbers of immigrants – both legally and illegally – are often the wealthy, developed countries that appear to offer a safe environment, opportunities to find work, or simply hope of a better life. Australia, the USA and Canada, parts of Europe, and South West Asia are examples of the places that attract immigrants. But some people simply need to escape – according to the UNHCR, in 2012 more than 45 million people left their native countries due to war alone. The majority of these were from the Third World.

**2** One of the perceived problems of immigration in the prosperous countries are the so-called 'illegal immigrants' – those people entering a county without authorization or staying longer than previous authorization had allowed. The accuracy of any statistics on undocumented immigration is impossible to ascertain because, by definition, anyone illegally entering a country is not registered. Estimates given by countries vary, but the figures given are frequently over the million mark. Despite the reasons motivating immigration being understandable, there is nevertheless a great deal of animosity shown by large numbers of the 'native' population, frequently associated with the fiscal side of the problem. Undocumented immigrants to developed countries are often successful in finding work because they are willing to accept lower wages than native-born workers – sometimes below the minimum wage stipulated by that country, and assuming employers are willing to exploit workers in this way. Knowing that a person has illegally entered a country makes it easier to put pressure on them to accept lower wages. This is often seen as a situation that reduces the numbers of jobs available offering regular wages – to the detriment of the native jobseekers. Proponents of stricter immigration laws often cite foreigners taking 'their' jobs. In addition, illegal aliens may be perceived to be a drain on government resources for health and education. There are also many people who fear that a large population of illegal aliens will pose a threat to the national security of a country, giving terrorist elements an opportunity to establish themselves within its borders.

**3** It is interesting that not all groups of immigrants, legal or illegal, are necessarily considered undesirable. For example, in the USA, where there is a heated debate in progress about the situation of undocumented immigration and the consequences for the country, the influx of millions of European

57

# 04 Undocumented immigration

immigrants throughout the past two centuries, starting with the Pilgrim Fathers, has contributed to the creation of the nation as it exists today. In the 19th and 20th centuries, many Europeans were attracted to the USA by promises of liberty and the hope of economic prosperity. The abject poverty caused by the potato famine in Ireland, and later the rise of fascism pre-World War II, drove millions away from their homelands. These groups of people settled in America and today are accepted as being an integral part of the country. The attitude of many to undocumented immigration in the USA seems to reflect a kind of cultural amnesia, with the once proudly proclaimed idea of America as a 'melting pot' conveniently forgotten.

UNHCR is the acronym for the United Nations High Commissioner for Refugees.

## General comprehension

1. According to the text, what are the major causes of migration today?
2. Read the text again and decide on appropriate headings for each paragraph. Then compare your headings with a partner and choose the best one for each section together.
3. What is the meaning of 'cultural amnesia' in paragraph 3?
4. Consider the immigrants who enter a country illegally. What do you think could be some of the day-to-day problems that confront them? Make a list of possible situations.
5. In the text it says that immigrants often do the jobs that are poorly paid. What kind of jobs do you think they could be? Make a list of suggestions with a partner.
6. According to the text, what caused migration to the USA in the 20th century?

## Text handling

Match the words from the text on the left with an appropriate synonym on the right so that the meaning in the text is maintained.

| 1 | influx | A | scarcity |
| 2 | prosperity | B | financial |
| 3 | famine | C | wealth |
| 4 | abject | D | foreigners |
| 5 | aliens | E | hopeless |
| 6 | cite | F | inflow |
| 7 | proponents | G | quote |
| 8 | fiscal | H | memory loss |
| 9 | detriment | I | supporters |
| 10 | amnesia | J | disadvantage |

## Written work

Work with a partner. First research some countries with high numbers of immigrants and identify why they are there and where they are from. Present your findings in the form of a speech that you will deliver to the class. You will need to give an introduction to the subject of migration. The written text should be 500–600 words long.

# Text 4.1.2 Concerns about illegal immigration

Prosperous countries such as Australia, the USA, the UK, the Netherlands and Germany will always attract immigrants in search of a better life. The proper immigration channels often pose insurmountable problems for those hoping to get a chance to enter one of these countries and this can lead to undocumented immigration.

For the inhabitants of the countries targeted by the immigrants there is also concern, even fear. It is a concern about a lowering of the quality of life or a threat to an established order.

Read these quotations from people expressing their opinions on undocumented immigration in the city of Birmingham, UK.

"I work as a refuse collector. I don't want these illegals coming in and taking my job."

"I'm worried about diseases like Ebola, Dengue Fever and TB. Those illegal immigrants increase the risks of us getting those diseases here, don't they?"

"These people have a totally different lifestyle. I've heard they keep chickens in the house."

"It's not fair that these illegal immigrants are getting free health care and school."

"These illegals are everywhere – they're pushing down the wages."

"This country is too small for all these people – there are millions of immigrants being brought in every year – it's scary."

## Text handling

Find words in the text with a similar meaning to those given below.
1. wealthy
2. procedure
3. impossible to overcome
4. worry
5. verbalising

## Written work (HL)

Read the quotations again and summarise the ideas expressed there. To what extent do you think the comments are based on fact or opinion? What influences are at work in society that stimulates people to express these ideas? Do not exceed 250 words.

## Interactive oral activity

Prepare for a group discussion about ways of dealing with illegal immigration.

Think about these points:
- What is your opinion? Decide if you are more sympathetic to the situation of the immigrants or to the government that needs to find a solution to the economic and legal issues.
- Consider some points you would like to make and find examples of relevant situations.
- Research some websites and see if you can find comments from immigrants – both legally and illegally in the country – that you can use in the discussion.
- Think about positive and negative aspects of immigration.

Organising your group discussion:
- Do not have too many people in your group – four is a good number.
- Choose one person to be a facilitator and keep the discussion flowing, making sure everyone gets a chance to speak.
- At the end of the discussion, report to the rest of your class what points you brought up and any decisions you made. Choose another person (not the facilitator) to do this.

**TOK**

Consider the situation of undocumented immigration into a country. In discussions about undocumented or illegal immigration, the word 'fair' is frequently heard. People say, for example, 'it's not fair to the workers who pay taxes', or 'it's not fair to keep people out who just want a better lifestyle'.

What does 'fair' mean in this context?

## 4.1.3 *The Tortilla Curtain* by T.C. Boyle: an extract

Delaney and Kyra are a white American couple living in California near the Mexican border with their six-year-old son Jordan. One day Delaney runs down a poor Mexican with his car and gives him money to compensate for the man's serious injuries. However, he soon feels he did not behave correctly. Some time later Delaney meets his friend Jack Jardine in the supermarket. They start talking:

"Did you know that the U.S. accepted more immigrants last year than all the other countries of the world combined – and that half of them settled in California? And that's legal immigrants, people with skills, money, education. The ones coming in through the Tortilla Curtain down there, those are the ones that are killing us. They're peasants, my friend. No education, no resources, no skills – all they've got to offer is a strong back, and the irony is we need fewer and fewer strong backs every day because we've got robotics and computers and farm machinery that can do the labor of a hundred men at a fraction of the cost." He dropped his hand in dismissal. "It's old news."

Delaney set the milk down on the floor. He was in a hurry, dinner on the stove, Jordan in the car, Kyra about to walk in the door, but in the heat of the moment he forgot all about it. "I can't believe you," he said, and he couldn't seem to control his free arm, waving it in an expanding loop. "Do you realize what you're saying? Immigrants are the lifeblood of this country – we're a nation of immigrants – and neither of us would be standing here today if it wasn't."

"Clichés. There's a point of saturation. Besides which, the Jardines fought in the Revolutionary War – you could hardly call us immigrants."

"Everybody's an immigrant from somewhere. My grandfather came over from Bremen and my grandmother was Irish – does that make me any less a citizen than the Jardines?"

A woman with frosted hair and a face drawn tight as a drum skin ducked between them for a jar of olives. Jack worked a little grit into his voice: "That's not the point. Times have changed, my friend. Radically. Do you have any idea what these people are costing us, and not just in terms of crime, but in real tax dollars for social services? No? Well, you ought to. You must have seen that thing in the Times a couple weeks ago, about the San Diego study?"

**Below** *The Tortilla Curtain* by T.C. Boyle is published by Penguin Books.

Delaney shook his head. He felt his stomach sink.

"Look, Delaney," Jack went on, cool, reasonable, his voice in full song now, It's a simple equation, so much in, so much out. The illegals in San Diego County contributed seventy million in tax revenues and at the same time they used up two hundred and forty million in services – welfare, emergency care, schooling and the like. You want to pay for that? And for the crime that comes with it? You want another crazy Mexican throwing himself under your wheels hoping for an insurance payoff? Or worse, you want one of them behind the wheel bearing down on you, no insurance, no brakes, no nothing?"

Delaney was trying to organize his thoughts. He wanted to tell Jack that he was wrong, that everyone deserved a chance in life and that the Mexicans would assimilate just like the Poles, Italians, Germans, Irish and Chinese and that besides which we'd stolen California from them in the first place, but he didn't get the chance. […]

And then they were moving in the direction of the cash registers – all three of them, as a group – and Jack, the conciliatory Jack, Jack the politician, Jack the soother of gripes, grievances and hurts real or imaginary, put an arm over Delaney's shoulder and warbled his sweetest notes: "Listen, Delaney, I know how you feel, and I agree with you. It's not easy for me either – it's nothing less than rethinking your whole life, who you are and what you believe in. And trust me: when we get control of the border again – if we get control of it – I'll be the first to advocate taking that gate down. But don't kid yourself: it's not going to happen anytime soon."

The Tortilla Curtain by T.C. Boyle, Penguin Books, 1995

## General comprehension

1. What is the meaning of the phrase 'we're a nation of immigrants'?
2. Delaney and Jack have different opinions about the Mexican immigrants. What are the two points of view?
3. Jack says about the immigrants, 'all they've got to offer is a strong back'. What exactly is he referring to?
4. What do you understand by the phrase 'we'd stolen California from them'?

## Text handling

Explain the meaning of these idiomatic phrases from the text.
1. 'immigrants are the lifeblood of this country' (line 23)
2. 'a face drawn tight as a drum skin' (line 33)
3. 'Jack worked a little grit into his voice' (line 35)

---

Idiomatic language is the name given to a group of words that are used in an unexpected context to give a clearer and stronger idea of a person or situation. They are usually specific to one language and cannot be translated word for word (though related languages may share the same idiom). The title of the book, The Tortilla Curtain, is an example of an idiom. The 'curtain' refers to the border between the USA and Mexico, and 'tortilla' is a Mexican thin pancake made from corn meal. In this way the two ideas of the border and the country of Mexico are combined.

# 04 Undocumented immigration

### Zoom in on grammar

**Using 'ought to'**

We use *should* and *ought to* to say what is the best thing or the right thing to do. There is no difference in the meaning:

> You don't look well, perhaps you *should* see a doctor.
>
> It is my aunt's birthday next week; I *ought to* send her a birthday card.

### Grammar in context

**Using 'ought to'**

Find an example of the use of 'ought to' in the excerpt from *The Tortilla Curtain*.

## Written work

The USA is only one example of a country with a large number of undocumented immigrants. Do some research about the situation in other countries: make some notes and collect examples of other countries with immigration concerns.

Have a look at other websites and find out what problems the immigrants themselves face. Note: Undocumented immigrants are often referred to as 'illegal immigrants', a term that is frequently criticised because it implies that a person is 'illegal' when in fact this is not possible – only the immigration can be illegal.

Present the results of your research in the form of an information flyer about undocumented immigration.

### Exam hints

**Tips for creating an effective flyer**

- Plan the information and layout you want to use.
- Use bold headlines and subheadings.
- Use powerful, descriptive language.
- Keep one main idea for each paragraph.
- Make your flyer attractive and colourful to encourage others to read it.
- Remember that a flyer contains both text and bullet points and may include illustrations.
- Remember that in the exam your flyer will not include illustrations.

### Individual oral activity

Preparation time: You will have 15 minutes to prepare your presentation. In this time you need to organise your ideas and plan the sequence of what you will talk about. Examine the photograph opposite and consider the following points – these will form the basis of your presentation.

- What do you see in the picture?
- Reflect on the photograph in connection with the theme of undocumented immigration and what you have read about.
- What aspects of illegal immigration do you want to focus on?
- Make connections to the situation in various countries.

Your presentation will last three or four minutes, and then your teacher and the other students will follow up with some comments and questions referring to what you have presented.

**Left** Here today, gone tomorrow. Consider the consequences of this sort of work for a street vendor and his family.

**TOK** To what extent should we as consumers consider the origins of the products we buy? How much responsibility do you think the individual has in this context?

## 4.2 Undocumented immigration in the UK

### Text 4.2.1 An illegal immigrant's story

# From arriving a slave to working on the till at Tesco

Ruth Asmah was working on the till at Tesco when the letter came from her bosses. It said: "Please bring your passport to work on the next shift for an immigration check". Ruth immediately went home and started packing her two-year-old daughter's few belongings into plastic bags. "I don't have a passport," she says. "I knew I would be deported. I had to leave my job, and with no job I couldn't pay my rent, so we would lose our home. We went to a charity but they couldn't help us. We couldn't go to social services in case the authorities caught up with us. We would have been homeless without the kindness of a friend."

Ruth and her young daughter Dyanna (not their real names) are illegal immigrants. Since Ruth was trafficked from Ghana at the age of 14 by her aunt, who abandoned her to work as a domestic slave, she has lived beneath the radar of British life without any official documentation. "This is how you live when you are undocumented," she tells me. "You are constantly moving. I don't take anything – no benefits, not even free school meals for Dyanna."

## 04 Undocumented immigration

Just two of an estimated 660,000 undocumented people living in the UK, Ruth and Dyanna's life without papers is one of fear, poverty and broken dreams. There is no access to the welfare state. Ruth has a national insurance number lent to her by a friend and now works in a fast-food chain. A tall, shy young woman, her uniform name badge says "Sheila" and she has to remember to answer to it. Otherwise, Ruth and Dyanna live law-abiding lives in a Lancashire suburb, going to church, living quietly. Ruth tries to give Dyanna a normal childhood but they regularly move house to evade the authorities, vulnerable to the whims and abuses of landlords who ask no questions. "Moving is a part of me now," she says.

With no access to benefits that could top up their income, even child benefit, sometimes Ruth and Dyanna are malnourished. Ruth recently had to turn down a new and better-paid job because again she would need to provide her passport. Soon they may not even be able to see a doctor if they are sick. The Government wants patients to have to prove their immigration status. It's already hard for them to be registered with a GP because they don't have proof of address.

"I understand why people want to send me home," Ruth says quietly, sitting in a faded roadside cafe in Manchester. "They say Britain is full up. If I was a British person I would be worried too." Ruth didn't choose to come to the UK. She was trafficked here by her aunt, who brought her in on a visitor's visa when she was 14. She believed she was coming on holiday, but instead the aunt left her with a family who used her as a domestic slave. Passed from family to family in and around London, she didn't know her papers were not in order and naively trusted the aunt to come back for her. "In Ghana, I lived by the seaside with my grandmother," she says. "We used to sell peppers and kerosene door to door, simple things. We had food to eat. I lived in a compound. But my grandmother died when I was 14 and my auntie took me to London saying that we were going for a holiday." In England, Ruth yearned to go to school like the children she looked after but she just had to cook, clean and be an unpaid nanny. "It was very hard work," she says. She had nowhere of her own. She slept on the floor in the children's room and ate their leftovers. "I would like to ask my aunt why she did it." Her eyes fill with tears. "So many things I have to block out of my mind."

Still, Ruth dreamed of becoming British. When she was 20 she ran away to live with a friend in Manchester. At the local church she fell in love with an undocumented Ghanaian man called Thomas. They moved in together and had a child. But then Thomas was arrested and deported. When Ruth traced him in Ghana, she found out he was married. "After that I stopped getting in touch with my family," she says. "I was too ashamed."

Dyanna is now five years old and has started school. "She has very good school reports," Ruth says. Her face grows animated. "Dyanna is good at music. They say she is very friendly, she participates in everything. They really miss her when she's not there because she brings everybody together." She doesn't think Dyanna would survive in the Ghana she came from. "I'm scared to take her," she says. "If I was on my own I could fend for myself. But I have no qualifications and I wouldn't be able to afford the school fees. She doesn't speak Ga – the language. I have no family there now. She is so happy here at school."

Meanwhile, she has fallen in love with misty, rainy Manchester. "It is so beautiful here. I have a lot of friends. I feel like I belong to Manchester. This is my home."

http://www.mirror.co.uk/news/real-life-stories/illegal-immigrants-story—arriving-3099790#ixzz31oNK99DE

## General comprehension

1. What was the reason Ruth Asmah left her job at the supermarket Tesco?
2. How did Ruth arrive in England?
3. What are the daily consequences of being an undocumented immigrant for Ruth and her daughter?
4. What does Ruth feel about the negative attitude towards undocumented immigrants expressed by some British people?
5. What role does the Church play in Ruth's life?
6. What is Ruth's feeling about living in England?

## Text handling

Match the words from the text on the left with the correct definitions according to the text on the right.

| | | | |
|---|---|---|---|
| 1 | till | A | easily hurt |
| 2 | deported | B | underfed |
| 3 | charity | C | frightened |
| 4 | suburb | D | cash register |
| 5 | vulnerable | E | colourless |
| 6 | landlord | F | a child carer |
| 7 | malnourished | G | removed from the country |
| 8 | faded | H | outer part of a city |
| 9 | nanny | I | an organisation that helps people in need |
| 10 | scared | J | a person who lets a place to live |

## Zoom in on grammar

**The past continuous**

This verb tense is used to show that at a time in the past someone was in the middle of an action.

   I *was reading* all Saturday afternoon.
   When the phone rang he *was watching* television.

It is used with action verbs and not with states (examples of state verbs are *be, believe, belong, contain, hate, know, like, love, mean, prefer, remember, understand*).

In the above text there is an example of the past continuous in the first paragraph:

   Ruth Asmah *was working* on the till at Tesco when the letter came from her bosses.

## Grammar in context

**The past continuous**

What can you say in these situations? Make a sentence using the past continuous to show that the activity lasted a long time.

   **Example:** You had to work on your lab report for science yesterday. You spent two hours on it.
   *I was working on my lab report for two hours yesterday.*

1. Your mother had to write emails on Monday. It went on all day.
2. You went on a hike with the school. It rained all day.
3. You had to do homework on Saturday. You worked until late in the evening.
4. Your brother had to practise his violin. He played all day.

# 04 Undocumented immigration

### Written work (SL)

Imagine that you are in the country where you are living now but you are an undocumented immigrant. Write a diary entry about some of the difficulties you experience and how you feel about living outside the law. Describe your family situation and the conditions you live in.

Your diary entry should be between 350 and 400 words.

## 4.3 Well-known immigrants

### Text 4.3.1 Well-known immigrants' stories

The situation of undocumented immigrants is a controversial one. However, in many developed countries in the world immigrants have been welcomed and invited into the country legally. They have gone on to become integrated members of the community and in many cases have become well-known, even famous. Read the following texts about six iconic figures – it is not always common knowledge that they were immigrants.

### Hans Holbein (c.1497–1543)

Hans Holbein was born in Germany and travelled to England looking for work in 1526. He was already an accomplished artist, someone today we would describe as an 'all-round talent', not only painting portraits, but also illustrating books, and designing jewellery and furniture.

Holbein was extraordinarily skilled, and it is said that he was responsible for bringing the Renaissance to England. Achieving fame and the patronage of King Henry VIII, his impact on cultural life was outstanding, and today he is considered a truly great British artist.

## Alexander Graham Bell (1847–1922)

In 1870, the Bell family migrated to Canada from Scotland for health reasons, after two of Alexander's siblings had died of tuberculosis.

In 1882 Alexander Bell became an American citizen. He was a scientist, engineer, and entrepreneur, and achieved success in a number of fields. However, around the world he is best known in association with the word 'telephone'.

He was the first person to make capital from the telephone – an invention actually developed by a colleague of his, but Bell gained the patent rights and consequently world fame.

## Sigmund Freud (1856–1939)

Austrian-born Sigmund Freud was a psychiatrist and neurologist, but is best known as the father of psychoanalysis and one of the greatest thinkers of the 20th century.

In 1930 he was awarded the Goethe Prize for his contributions to philosophy. At that time the prize was considered the greatest scientific and literary distinction in the German-speaking world.

He contributed many words to the English language that are now commonly used, for example: 'complex', 'inhibition', 'neurosis' and 'psychosis'.

However, his Jewish heritage meant that he was subject to Nazi persecution following Hitler's rise to power, forcing him to seek refuge in England in 1938.

# 04 Undocumented immigration

## Levi Strauss (1829–1902)

The Strauss family migrated to America from Germany in 1847 for economic reasons, following the death of the father.

There were already other members of the family in America who were working in the textile trade and it was the textile trade that made Levi Strauss successful and later famous.

Together with a brother and brother-in-law he founded a company making tough clothing and tents for the gold-diggers who flocked to America in the mid-1800s.

Today the name Levi Strauss is so closely connected with jeans that the word has become synonymous for a style of trousers.

The word 'jeans' originates from the name given to sailors from the city of Genoa in Italy, and became synonymous with the material originally used for making hard-wearing workmen's trousers, which was later used by Levi Strauss.

## John F. Kennedy (1917–1963)

The initial in his name stands for 'Fitzgerald'. In the 19th century, two families left Ireland to escape the devastating effects of the potato famine: they were the Fitzgerald family and the Kennedy family. Through marriage, the two families came together and worked hard to establish a life in their newly adopted country.

The 19th-century Fitzgeralds and Kennedys worked as labourers and coopers. It was slow progress through the decades, but their fortunes improved and family members became clerks, tavern owners, retailers and eventually politicians, culminating in John F. Kennedy becoming the 35th president of the United States of America in 1961.

Although he was born in the United States of America, John F. Kennedy was always proud of his Irish ancestry.

### Jung Chang (1952– )

Jung Chang moved to England from China to further her education in 1978. She studied linguistics at the University of York, receiving her PhD in 1982. She was the first person from the People's Republic of China to be awarded a doctorate from a British university.

As a writer, she published *Wild Swans* in 1993 – a novel describing the lives and experiences of three generations of Chinese women: her grandmother, her mother, and herself.

*Wild Swans* sold 10 million copies worldwide and made her a celebrity, although the work was not published in her home country.

### Text handling

**1** Read the six texts above and fill in the chart with the requested information.

| Name | Country of origin | Country migrated to | Reason for migration | Achievements |
|------|-------------------|---------------------|----------------------|--------------|
|      |                   |                     |                      |              |

**2** Research other well-known figures who were immigrants to the country they were successful in. Write a brief text (not exceeding 100 words) about each of them.

### Interactive oral activity

**1** Together with a partner imagine you are able to interview the people mentioned in the above texts. Work out the questions you would like to ask them and then role-play the interview. Be prepared to share your live interview with the class.

**2** Form groups of three and prepare to discuss the positive aspects of immigration. Use examples from your own experience and focus on the question: 'How is a country enriched by immigration?'. Your discussion should be sustained for about ten minutes. Be prepared to summarize the results of your discussion and share your ideas with the class.

# 04 Undocumented immigration

### Interactive oral activity

Form groups of three and prepare to discuss the positive aspects of allowing immigrants into a country. Use examples from your own country. How is a country enriched by immigrants?

Spend between five and ten minutes on your discussion and be prepared to share with the group the outcomes of your discussion and answer any questions.

## Exam practice

## Stuck between two worlds: The life of an illegal immigrant in Australia

by Mingyue Zhou, June 12, 2013

*This feature article is based on an interview with a Chinese illegal immigrant who has been living in Australia for the past 17 years.*

When Jack (assumed name) left his village home on the east coast of China, he had little idea that he would never see his wife and three young daughters again for the next seventeen years. But at that moment, it seemed going overseas with whatever cost would ensure the family's financial security for years to come, like many other villagers did before him.

Jack came from Fujian (or Hokkien) Province of China. He has been living in Australia since 1996. Not speaking a word of English, he nevertheless made a living by working hard labour in construction. Although he managed to send back enough money to support his wife and raise three daughters, he has never seen them for the past seventeen years. Officially he is not accounted for as an Australian citizen or resident. Jack is an illegal immigrant, or "black citizen" in Chinese.

The illegal immigrants are unlawful non-citizens who don't have a legal visa or their visa have expired or voided. According to the Department of Immigration and Citizenship (DIAC) website, "As at 30 June 2012, it was estimated that 60 900 people were unlawfully in Australia." Another document released in Nov. 2011 showed, plane arrivals from China (8070), United States (5080), Malaysia (4200) and Britain (3610) are the top four countries where illegal immigrants came from. But Jack believes the actual figures are much bigger than these.

Jack came from a small fishing village on the China's southeast coast. Sandwiched between high mountains and sea, traditionally the villagers made a living solely on fishing for hundreds of years. But slowly as the fishing resources depleted, people started to go overseas to make money. Some did successfully and came back with incredible fortune and stories. Going overseas has become a deep-rooted tradition in these economically disadvantageous areas.

But for Jack and his wife, there was something else. Like all other young couples living in the countryside, they always wanted a son. In Chinese countryside in the 90s, where little social welfare system ever existed, the traditional belief was that a son would take care of his parents when they get old. Unfortunately Jack and his wife had three daughters in a row.

Driven to despair, Jack decided to go to Australia to make a living. In the early spring of 1986, he arrived in Australia using a fake South Korean passport under a temporary working visa. In the first three years after he arrived, he worked hard labours in Melbourne, switched jobs between Chinese restaurants, supermarket delivery and a tofu factory. During those days, he worked 14 hours every day and earned about $500 a week. Apart from paying for meals and accommodation, he sent back around half of his income to his wife and daughters. In the 90s, the average annual household income in his town was just around 2000RMB, or $300. The money he sent back home would have provided his family a comfortable life.

After three years in Melbourne, he came to Sydney to work in the construction. From six in the morning till six in the afternoon, six to seven days a week, and in constant contact with hazardous materials, building a house is hard labour but pays well. Jack started with $360 per week, but eventually out-performed other co-workers and earned as much as $300 a day after obtaining a license in gyprock plastering.

But contradictory to the DIAC's finding, that illegal workers take away job opportunities and evaded tax, Jack said illegal immigrants are working those jobs that most Aussies don't want, and as high as 80% of illegal immigrants he knows of have Tax File Number and have paid tax for many years, because without a TFN, they cannot find a well-paying job in the long term. Jack said he himself has paid no less than $100,000 in the past seventeen years working in Australia.

"Australia has a high living standard. This leads to a lot of dirty and hard labour jobs difficult to be filled, if without these cheap labourers... A lot of illegal immigrants work in gyprock, tiling and painting, all of which have health risks because of close contact with hazardous chemicals," he said, "Illegal immigrants have worked on 70% of houses in Australia. The property prices would have been unaffordable without them." Jack believed the Australian Government has purposefully kept quiet on this fact.

http://artsespresso.com/2013/06/12/stuck-between-two-worlds-life-of-an-illegal-immigrant-in-australia/

# 04 Undocumented immigration

### Exercises

Answer the following questions.

**1** According to the text, what was the tradition in Jack's home town that motivated the people to move illegally overseas?

.......................................................................................................................................

**2** Name four kinds of work that Jack has been involved in during his time in Australia.

.......................................................................................................................................

**3** What does Jack imply about the attitude of the Australian government towards the numbers of undocumented immigrants working in the construction industry?

.......................................................................................................................................

**4** Match the words from the text with the synonyms on the right. Write the appropriate letter in the box below. Note: There are more options than you need.

| I | assumed name | ☐ | A | positioned |
| II | construction | ☐ | B | given |
| III | sandwiched | ☐ | C | name at birth |
| IV | fortune | ☐ | D | building industry |
| V | in a row | ☐ | E | land and house |
| VI | accommodation | ☐ | F | false name |
| VII | provided | ☐ | G | a place to live |
| VIII | hazardous | ☐ | H | dangerous |
| XI | findings | ☐ | I | successively |
| X | property | ☐ | J | wealth |
| | | | K | research results |
| | | | L | in a line |
| | | | M | complicated |

**5** True or false? Justify your answer with a relevant brief quotation from the text. An example has been provided.

**Example:** Jack came from one of China's heavily populated regions.
False – he came from 'his village home'.

**A** Jack's ability to speak a little English made it possible for him to get his first job.

..................................................................................................................

**B** The reason Jack decided to work overseas was because fish stocks were no longer sufficient to provide a living.

..................................................................................................................

**C** Jack entered Australia without a passport.

..................................................................................................................

**D** Illegal immigrants do not pay tax.

..................................................................................................................

**E** The work of illegal immigrants in the construction industry made it possible for Australians to buy a house of their own.

..................................................................................................................

**F** The Australian government intentionally ignores the role played by illegal immigrants in making house-buying financially possible.

..................................................................................................................

## Further exercises

### Written work

You have read the Australian article online and have seen that it is a blog and that readers are invited to post comments. You decide to express your opinion about Jack's situation and that of his family and post a blog entry with your comments and opinions. Write around 250 words.

Before you write your blog you need to think about how you feel about Jack's situation and then plan what you want to say. The best way to do this planning is to make some notes in bullet-point form or a mind map. You may want to get together with a partner and discuss this first to work out some ideas.

# 05 Education for all

## Objectives

- To revise the structure of a speech
- To examine rhetorical devices used in a speech
- To compare word forms: verbs, nouns and adjectives
- To practise a number of complex sentence structures
- To discuss issues related to education for all

**Opposite** We share the globe, yet human lives and values differ greatly. Is this fair?

# 5.1 Malala Yousafzai

Text 5.1.1 The first part of Malala Yousafzai's speech at the United Nations, July 12 2013

In the name of God, The Most Beneficient, The Most Merciful.

Honourable UN Secretary General Mr Ban Ki-moon,

Respected President General Assembly Vuk Jeremic,

Honourable UN envoy for Global education Mr Gordon Brown,

Respected elders and my dear brothers and sisters;

Today, it is an honour for me to be speaking again after a long time. Being here with such honourable people is a great moment in my life.

I don't know where to begin my speech. I don't know what people would be expecting me to say. But first of all, thank you to God for whom we all are equal and thank you to every person who has prayed for my fast recovery and a new life. I cannot believe how much love people have shown me. I have received thousands of good wish cards and gifts from all over the world. Thank you to all of them. Thank you to the children whose innocent words encouraged me. Thank you to my elders whose prayers strengthened me.

I would like to thank my nurses, doctors and all of the staff of the hospitals in Pakistan and the UK and the UAE government who have helped me get better and recover my strength. I fully support Mr Ban Ki-moon the Secretary-General in his Global Education First Initiative and the work of the UN Special Envoy Mr Gordon Brown. And I thank them both for the leadership they continue to give. They continue to inspire all of us to action.

Dear brothers and sisters, do remember one thing. Malala day is not my day. Today is the day of every woman, every boy and every girl who have raised their voice for their rights. There are hundreds of Human rights activists and social workers who are not only speaking for human rights, but who are struggling to achieve their goals of education, peace and equality. Thousands of people have been killed by the terrorists and millions have been injured. I am just one of them.

So here I stand... one girl among many.

I speak – not for myself, but for all girls and boys.

75

# 05 Education for all

I raise up my voice – not so that I can shout, but so that those without a voice can be heard.

Those who have fought for their rights:

> Their right to live in peace.
>
> Their right to be treated with dignity.
>
> Their right to equality of opportunity.
>
> Their right to be educated.

Dear Friends, on the 9th of October 2012, the Taliban shot me on the left side of my forehead. They shot my friends too. They thought that the bullets would silence us. But they failed. And then, out of that silence came, thousands of voices. The terrorists thought that they would change our aims and stop our ambitions but nothing changed in my life except this: Weakness, fear and hopelessness died. Strength, power and courage was born. I am the same Malala. My ambitions are the same. My hopes are the same. My dreams are the same.

Dear sisters and brothers, I am not against anyone. Neither am I here to speak in terms of personal revenge against the Taliban or any other terrorists group. I am here to speak up for the right of education of every child. I want education for the sons and the daughters of all the extremists especially the Taliban.

I do not even hate the Talib who shot me. Even if there is a gun in my hand and he stands in front of me. I would not shoot him. This is the compassion that I have learnt from Muhammad-the prophet of mercy, Jesus Christ and Lord Buddha. This is the legacy of change that I have inherited from Martin Luther King, Nelson Mandela and Muhammad Ali Jinnah. This is the philosophy of non-violence that I have learnt from Gandhi Jee, Bacha Khan and Mother Teresa. And this is the forgiveness that I have learnt from my mother and father. This is what my soul is telling me, be peaceful and love everyone.

https://secure.aworldatschool.org/page/content/the-text-of-malala-yousafzais-speech-at-thee-united-nations

In 2014, aged 17, Malala was awarded the Nobel Peace Prize jointly with Kailash Stayarthi from India for risking their lives to fight for children's rights. Malala was in a chemistry class at school in Birmingham UK when she heard the news.

### General comprehension

1. At first Malala says she is unsure how to begin her speech. How does she begin?
2. What happened to Malala?
3. How has she learnt to forgive?
4. What have you learnt about Malala from her speech? Write a paragraph describing who she is and what happened to her. Add any other information you think is important from the text.

### Interactive oral activity

Which of the IB Profile traits do you think Malala displays? Discuss this with your group and be ready to share your opinions and support them with examples from the text.

### Text handling

1. Re-read the speech and make notes of those features used which show it is a speech and not a written text.
2. Did you notice the rhetorical devices she used? Make a list of those you have found.
3. Vocabulary – check you understand the meanings of these words from the text.
    a) revenge
    b) compassion
    c) legacy.
4. Are there any other unfamiliar words? Make a list of your own and find the correct meanings.

### Individual oral activity

Malala refers to a number of famous people in her speech. Choose one of these famous people to research. Make bullet points about their life and achievements to use in a short talk to the class. Be sure to explain why Malala referred to them.

## Text 5.1.2 Malala's speech continued

**Dear sisters and brothers, we realise the importance of light when we see darkness. We realise the importance of our voice when we are silenced. In the same way, when we were in Swat, the north of Pakistan, we realised the importance of pens and books when we saw the guns.**

**The wise saying, "The pen is mightier than sword" was true. The extremists are afraid of books and pens. The power of education frightens them. They are afraid of women. The power of the voice of women frightens them. And that is why they killed 14 innocent medical students in the recent attack in Quetta. And that is why they killed many female teachers and polio workers in Khyber Pukhtoon Khwa and FATA. That is why they are blasting schools every day. Because they were and they are afraid of change, afraid of the equality that we will bring into our society.**

**I remember that there was a boy in our school who was asked by a journalist, "Why are the Taliban against education?" He answered very simply. By pointing to his book he said, "A Talib doesn't know what is written inside this book." They think that God is a tiny, little conservative being who would send girls to the hell just because of going to school. The terrorists are misusing the name of Islam and Pashtun society for their own personal benefits. Pakistan is peace-loving democratic country. Pashtuns want education for their daughters and sons. And Islam is a religion of peace, humanity and brotherhood. Islam says that it is not only each child's right to get education, rather it is their duty and responsibility.**

**Honourable Secretary General, peace is necessary for education. In many parts of the world especially Pakistan and Afghanistan;**

Pashtuns are an ethnic group who mainly live in Afghanistan and Pakistan.

## 05 Education for all

terrorism, wars and conflicts stop children going to their schools. We are really tired of these wars. Women and children are suffering in many parts of the world in many ways. In India, innocent and poor children are victims of child labour. Many schools have been destroyed in Nigeria. People in Afghanistan have been affected by the hurdles of extremism for decades. Young girls have to do domestic child labour and are forced to get married at early age. Poverty, ignorance, injustice, racism and the deprivation of basic rights are the main problems faced by both men and women.

Dear fellows, today I am focusing on women's rights and girls' education because they are suffering the most. There was a time when women social activists asked men to stand up for their rights. But, this time, we will do it by ourselves. I am not telling men to step away from speaking for women's rights rather I am focusing on women to be independent to fight for themselves.

Dear sisters and brothers, now it's time to speak up.

So today, we call upon the world leaders to change their strategic policies in favour of peace and prosperity.

We call upon the world leaders that all the peace deals must protect women and children's rights. A deal that goes against the dignity of women and their rights is unacceptable.

We call upon all governments to ensure free compulsory education for every child all over the world.

We call upon all governments to fight against terrorism and violence, to protect children from brutality and harm.

We call upon the developed nations to support the expansion of educational opportunities for girls in the developing world.

We call upon all communities to be tolerant – to reject prejudice based on cast, creed, sect, religion or gender. To ensure freedom and equality for women so that they can flourish. We cannot all succeed when half of us are held back.

We call upon our sisters around the world to be brave – to embrace the strength within themselves and realise their full potential.

Dear brothers and sisters, we want schools and education for every child's bright future. We will continue our journey to our destination of peace and education for everyone. No one can stop us. We will speak for our rights and

we will bring change through our voice. We must believe in the power
and the strength of our words. Our words can change the world.  65

Because we are all together, united for the cause of education. And if
we want to achieve our goal, then let us empower ourselves with the
weapon of knowledge and let us shield ourselves with unity and
togetherness.

Dear brothers and sisters, we must not forget that millions of people  70
are suffering from poverty, injustice and ignorance. We must not forget
that millions of children are out of schools. We must not forget that our
sisters and brothers are waiting for a bright peaceful future.

So let us wage a global struggle against illiteracy, poverty and
terrorism and let us pick up our books and pens. They are our most  75
powerful weapons.

One child, one teacher, one pen and one book can change the world.

Education is the only solution. Education first.

https://secure.aworldatschool.org/page/content/the-text-of-malala-yousafzais-speech-at-thee-united-nations

### General comprehension

1. Who and what do the extremists fear?
2. How did the boy answer the journalist's questions to explain why the Taliban are against education?
3. Why does Malala focus on women's rights and girls' education? What are the other issues?
4. Do women want the help of men to stand up for their rights?
5. How can the pen be mightier than the sword?
6. Discuss these questions in your group or with a partner.
    a) Do you know how old Malala was when she made this speech? Find out when she was born.
    b) Re-read the speech and add any examples of new rhetorical devices you have found to the previous list.
    c) Can you identify places in the whole speech where Malala uses the three main principles of a speech, which originate from the work of Plato and Aristotle?
    Logos – logical ideas, appealing to reason
    Pathos – emotional appeal
    Ethos – appeal to the common core ideas of a community.
    d) Read the speech once more and mark or make a note of the relevant sections.
    e) Malala calls upon different groups to take action in the final part of her speech (lines 44–60). Choose one of those statements and expand and support her idea in an additional paragraph. How can these groups take action?

# 05 Education for all

## Text handling

Match the words from the text with the definitions on the right.

1 poverty
2 ignorance
3 injustice
4 racism
5 deprivation
6 prejudice
7 illiteracy

A lack of something you need
B lack of knowledge
C state of not knowing how to read or write
D belief that some races are inferior to others
E situation of being poor
F unreasonable dislike of or preference for something
G unfairness or lack of justice

## Zoom in on grammar

### Adjective–noun and verb–noun

In advanced English, many words which may be familiar to you as adjectives or verbs are also used as nouns. For example:

| ADJECTIVE | NOUN | VERB | NOUN |
|---|---|---|---|
| beautiful | beauty | to collect | collection |
| reliable | reliability | to attract | attraction |
| independent | independence | to consume | consumption |

## Grammar in context

### Abstract nouns

The words in the *Text handling* list above are all abstract nouns. Use either the adjective or verb from each word to form your own sentences. If you are not sure, use a dictionary to check your words.

**Example:** poverty (N) – poor (ADJ): Many people living in Pakistan are poor.

1 ignorance
2 injustice
3 racism
4 deprivation
5 prejudice
6 illiteracy.

## Zoom in on grammar

### Sentence structure

Malala uses an interesting sentence construction at the beginning of the second half of her speech:

> We realise the importance of light when we see darkness.
> We realise the importance of our voice when we are silenced.
> We realised the importance of pens and books when we saw the guns.

These sentences are used to emphasise the importance of something by contrasting it with an opposite. The idea is that you only appreciate something when you do not have it, or when you experience something that is opposite to it.

---

**TOK:** To what extent do you think education is the only solution? Could there be others?

## Grammar in context

**Sentence structure**

Use these sentence starters to create the same style of sentences.

1. We only know the importance of education when...
2. You only value your family when...
3. We only appreciate comfort when...
4. You only miss your friends when...
5. We only understand the problems of others when...

### Written work (HL)

Malala closes her speech with the words 'Education is the only solution'. Write a thoughtful response and justify it. Use the text type which you feel is most appropriate. Write between: 150 and 250 words.

> Before you start to write, collect your ideas about this quote. Decide on the position you will take and which text type will be most suitable for your arguments. Be sure to organise your ideas into paragraphs and have a strong opening statement and clear conclusion.

# 5.2 Witness the Night

## Text 5.2.1 Excerpt from *Witness the Night* by Kishwar Desai

Kishwar Desai was a journalist, but her anger about violence used against girls and women in Indian society led her to become a novelist. Her first novel, *Witness the Night*, won the Costa First Novel Award 2010. It tells the story of a 14-year-old girl accused of murdering her family, and describes the inequality of males and females in society. Each chapter begins with the diary of the young girl, Gurga, reflecting her thoughts and feelings, and then continues as the story is told by an 'unconventional' social worker, Simran Singh, who is trying to discover if Gurga is really guilty or not. Gurga's reflections about the lives of girls, school and education show the situation of many girls in India.

**Left** Families in times of change.

# 05 Education for all

## Gurga's diary, 12/09/07

*Being a girl is not easy. There are few comforts that you are born with or can achieve. I know, they dress you in frocks and put ribbons in your hair, bangles on your arms, anklets on your feet, teach you to sing and dance and bake cakes, but what about the Inside-you? The Outside-you can smile and cut vegetables and sit with legs crossed and say 'namaste auntie' ["I bow to you, Auntie" in Hindi] but the Inside-you is always angry and looking out of the window and wanting to run with the Boys.*

*The Boys did not have to go to convent school; they went to a proper co-educational boarding school where they learnt to smoke and drink, but my sister and I had to be 'got ready for marriage'. My sister was, I think, cleverer than the Boys. She was a good business woman, too. She could look at the stocks and shares in the business programme on television and tell us which ones were going to go up, and which were not. She would study the trends over a few weeks and then make a complicated chart and my father would then invest in the shares. But who got the shares? Not she. They were all put in the names of the Boys. Nothing ever came to my sister because she, like me, was paraya dhan. Amla explained the concept of paraya dhan to me. It meant basically that girls were wealth, but not wealth that belonged to you, but to someone else, i.e., the husband. The man who would come one day, with a lot of music and dance, and take the wealth away. From what I could gather, this would happen quite soon, because girls were like horses, the young fillies were easier to manage than the older ones. And the younger they were, the more they were in demand.*

Witness the Night *by Kishwar Desai, published by Simon & Schuster 2012*

### General comprehension

1. What does the author mean by 'There are few comforts that you are born with or can achieve'?
2. Why do you think the author capitalises 'the Boys'?
3. What does the author mean by 'Inside-you' and 'Outside-you'? Do you have an Inside- and Outside-you?
4. Why didn't the Boys have to go to convent school?
5. What did the Boys learn at the co-educational school, according to Gurga?
6. Why does Gurga think her sister is cleverer than the Boys?
7. Why does she compare girls to horses?
8. In the final sentence of this extract, Gurga uses the parallel structure 'the more… , the more…'. Explain the sentence in your own words without using this parallel structure.

### Grammar in context

**Reference pronouns**

Examine the following sentences from the text and state who or what the underlined reference pronouns refer to in each case.

1. Being a girl is not easy. There are few comforts that <u>you</u> are born with or can achieve.
2. I know, <u>they</u> dress you in frocks and put ribbons in <u>your</u> hair.
3. The Boys did not have to go to convent school; <u>they</u> went to a proper co-educational boarding school.
4. <u>She</u> was a good business woman, too.
5. <u>She</u> could look at the stocks and shares in the business programme on television and tell <u>us</u> <u>which</u> ones were going to go up, and which were not.
6. <u>It</u> meant basically that girls were wealth, but not wealth that belonged to <u>you</u>.
7. From what I could gather, <u>this</u> would happen quite soon.

## Zoom in on grammar

**Sentence structure: 'the more... , the more...'**

This structure is used to show that a change in one thing leads to a change in another. This structure is used in the text:

> And the younger they were, the more they were in demand.

Some other examples of this are:

> The more I work, the better my grades are.
> The longer we wait, the angrier we become.

## Grammar in context

**Sentence structure**

Write sentences of your own using this structure. Here are some example sentence prompts.

1. The longer... , the better...
2. The older... , the easier...
3. The sooner... , the more....

## Text 5.2.2 Excerpt from *Witness the Night* by Kishwar Desai

### Gurga's diary, 13/09/07

*Sometimes I think I could live like this for ever. In limbo, I speak only when spoken to. Eat when food is placed before me. Drag myself around since the weight of my body has become unbearable. After all, what is the difference between being here and being outside? I could go to school, I suppose, but learn what? Some of the girls in school like to talk about doing things and joining a profession, but I know that all those are pipe dreams; ultimately they will all get married, and then have children and be forced to stay at home (or go to the club every night, like my mother used to until she found religion might help her have a baby boy). But basically do whatever the Darling Husband says. This is what my mother told Sharda and me, that we should stop feeling sorry for ourselves – because that is what happened to all girls. Not just us. And then we Would Grow To Like It.*

Witness the Night *by Kishwar Desai, published by Simon & Schuster 2012*

## General comprehension

1. Why do you think the author uses extremely short sentences in the first part of the diary?
2. How does Gurga feel in this excerpt?
3. What is the difference between her life and the lives of girls who go to school?
4. What will their lives be like in the future?
5. Who does Gurga think will decide what happens in their lives?

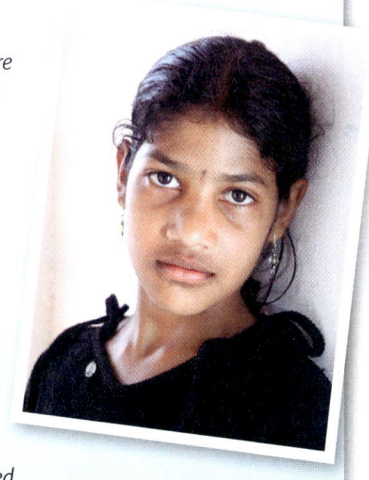

83

# 05 Education for all

## Text handling

1. Explain the following expressions in your own words.
   a) in limbo
   b) pipe dreams
   c) to be forced to stay at home
   d) to find religion
   e) would grow to like it.

2. True or false? Justify your answer with a relevant brief quotation from the text.
   a) Gurga moves around quite easily.
   b) Gurga wants to go to school to learn for her future.
   c) The girls can determine their own lives when they are married.
   d) Gurga's mother understands her problem and is sorry for her.

## Interactive oral activity

In your group discuss the following questions.
- How do these two extracts from the novel relate to the speech made by Malala?
- Can you see connections?
- Will the changes Malala asks for help girls like Gurga?
- Do you think education is the only answer?

Before beginning the discussion, re-read the texts carefully and make notes that will help you contribute to the discussion and develop your thinking.

## Interactive oral activity

In groups of three students, choose one of the photos and create a conversation that the people in the picture might have about school and their lives.

## Written work

Write a diary entry reflecting your thoughts after reading the two excerpts from *Witness the Night*. Write between 200 and 300 words.

## 5.3 Education for all in fiction

Text 5.3.1 Fictional bad girls are back with a vengeance

http://www.theguardian.com/books/booksblog/2013/sep/04/fictional-bad-girls-are-back

**Violent, sexual and even murderous, today's teen antiheroines have a rich literary lineage dating back to Angela Brazil**

It's 1913, and Angela Brazil's 10th boarding school story has just been published. By now, Brazil is well on her way to earning her later reputation as boarding school story grand dame. Her books, depicting all-female micro-societies controlled by teenage girls, have redefined the genre; for the first time in British fiction, their friendships, feelings, fears and frustrations take centre stage.

Unlike those in the fiction for young women that preceded Brazil's books – usually emphasising moral instruction and traditional gender roles – her characters are authentic and multi-dimensional. And with a focus on courage and independent spirit over physical appearance, class or other circumstantial factors, the books' true heroines are the ones bold enough to break the rules.

They sneak out at night, they take matters into their own hands; they're defiant, playful and irrepressible. And despite attempts to control them by archetypal authority figures such as parents and teachers, they never do as they're told. Today, their hijinks can be read as kitsch nostalgia; at the time the books were published, they were far more radical.

Beyond the pages of Brazil's books, the exciting possibilities they depicted remained distant. Although the suffrage movement was gaining momentum, access to education was inconsistent across the UK, especially for working class women, and there was widespread panic about the perceived decline in girls' morals. This is documented in detail in Carol Dyhouse's brilliant book *Girl Trouble*, which charts the media fascination and fear surrounding young women's progress towards equality throughout the last century (and echoed in Laurie Penny's latest, *Cybersexism*, which explores the way girls' online behaviour is controlled by a cultural paranoia of predators). Things were shifting, but slowly – and girls were definitely still discouraged from subversive "bad" behaviour.

Fast-forward a century, and girls are still the subject of endless ideological battles. Young women's thoughts, bodies and actions are controlled, pressured and policed at every turn, by a wider array of agendas and influences than ever before.

## 05 Education for all

From the early 1900s many boys and girls attended school in England between the ages of 5 and 11. The majority continued until they were 14 years old.

The word *suffrage* means the right to vote. The word *suffragette* was used to describe women who were demanding the right to vote. This word was first used in a British newspaper in 1908. Women were not allowed to vote until 1918, when the right was granted to women who were over 30 years old and owned or were renting property worth at least five British pounds per year or who were married to someone who did. In July 1928 a law was passed allowing all women in the UK to vote.

So maybe it's no wonder that the bad girl is back with a vengeance, giving contemporary fiction lovebites, bruises and a shoplifted bottle of super-strength cider to drink down the park. More than a century since Brazil's first book, and almost seven decades since Enid Blyton's first tale of Malory Towers, the fictional bad girl has gone to the dark side, getting into more extreme scrapes than ever before.

It's a natural evolution that's led from classroom mayhem to today's violent, sexual and at times even murderous teen antiheroines. Jenn Ashworth's *Cold Light*, for instance, is the chilling account of cruel, beautiful 14-year-old Chloe, found dead in a frozen lake with her much older, forbidden boyfriend in what seems like a Valentine's Day suicide pact – until another body is found nearby. *Weirdo*, by Cathi Unsworth, charts a private investigator's inquiries into the long-cold case of 15-year-old Corinne Woodrow, convicted amid media frenzy for murdering a classmate. And Anais Hendricks, the fierce, funny 15-year-old survivor who narrates Jenni Fagan's critically acclaimed debut *The Panopticon*, tells her tale from a detention centre for chronic young offenders, accused of putting a police officer in a coma after being found with matching blood on her school uniform.

The fictional bad girl is getting badder in the US, too – from the joyriding, activism and extortion of girl gang members in Joyce Carol Oates' *Foxfire* to the "young and out for glory" Sacred Heart Sluts in Colleen Curran's controversial Catholic schoolgirls novel *Whores on the Hill*, and the manipulative, malicious little madams in Gillian Flynn's *Sharp Objects*. (Flynn's world-conquering *Gone Girl* is about a rule-breaking adult, but the title itself has kicked off a whole publishing trend very much informed by what society expects and disapproves of in young women.)

Just as the rise of the now-classic boarding school story and its spunky, independent leading ladies corresponded to significant social and political changes further afield, such as the suffrage movement and educational reforms, so too today's bad girls mirror our wider cultural conflicts, issues, frustrations and fears.

It's tough being a teenage girl in the modern world, and – with on- and offline surveillance at an all-time high in real life and in fiction – the ones fighting the system provoke the most extreme emotions. Most bad girls are a combination of instigator and underdog, demanding recognition, respect, empathy and awe, and winning over readers with ease.

The best of this fictional breed are rebels with a cause, fighting for themselves and those they care about, against impossible odds. The bad girl represents the rebellious rule-breaker we all want to be, but with scars to show her fallibility and demonstrate the damage done to young women by today's society. Despite the bruises and broken hearts, her rebelliousness and resilience is intoxicating, and suggests she will endure for another century or more.

Have you got a favourite fictional bad girl? Which rebellious literary heroines would you want to raise hell with, and which ones deserve detention?

http://www.theguardian.com/books/booksblog/2013/sep/04/fictional-bad-girls-are-back

## General comprehension

1. What did Angela Brazil's boarding school novels describe for the first time in fiction?
2. How did they differ from books written about girls and/or education previously?
3. Were all girls able to receive education in Britain at that time?
4. According to the author, which problems do girls and young women in Britain face now?
5. How is the fictional bad girl in the 21st century different from her predecessor?
6. Which of the new novels described in the text would you like to read and why?
7. How did/do girls portrayed in fiction reflect society –
    a) In the early 20th century
    b) In the early 21st century?
8. Why isn't it easy being a teenage girl in Britain in the 21st century?
9. Who or what does the 'bad girl' represent?
10. How do the problems of girls in Britain in the 21st century compare to those of the girls in the other countries you have read about? What message would you give the British girls?

## Text handling

1. Match the given words with the meaning most suitable for the text

    | | | | |
    |---|---|---|---|
    | I | depicting | A | not approved by everyone |
    | II | radical | B | refusing to obey |
    | III | archetypal | C | chaos |
    | IV | mayhem | D | showing |
    | V | defiant | E | extreme |
    | VI | irrepressible | F | weakness |
    | VII | fallibility | G | lively and energetic |
    | VIII | controversial | H | typical |

2. True or false? Justify your answer with a relevant brief quotation from the text.
    a) Angela Brazil was the first author to depict girls realistically.
    b) Her characters always do as they are told.
    c) The author of the text believes that bad girls in stories now get into less trouble than those of the past.
    d) In American fiction the heroines are getting worse.

## Written work (HL)

'There are two powers in the world; one is the sword and the other is the pen. There is a great competition and rivalry between the two. There is a third power stronger than both, that of the women.'

Muhammad Ali Jinnah

Write a personal response and justify it. Use any genre you have studied in class. Write between 150 and 250 words.

Think and plan before you begin to write:
- Do you agree with the quote?
- What is your opinion? Make a list of key points which you want to include.
- Is your argument balanced, stating both sides, or do you have a definite opinion which you want to share?
- Remember to organise your writing in clear paragraphs.
- Have a strong beginning and ending.

## Written work (SL)

Imagine you had been born in a different country, or even at a different time. Write a diary entry where you reflect on how different your life could have been and how you would have coped with it.

Plan the entry carefully; remember that a diary is a personal reflection to be read only by you, so it can be in fairly informal language. Write between 150 and 250 words.

## Exam practice

# The importance of education

We often hear about speeches made by Barack Obama during his many public appearances as President of the United States of America. However, did you know that his wife, Michelle Obama, is also a very accomplished speaker?

One of the topics close to her heart is the education of all young people. This summer she travelled to Senegal, South Africa, and Tanzania with the President. In each country she spoke to children and students in school, vocational training centres, and clinics, and she consistently emphasised the importance of education and how education can improve not only the lives of individuals but also the progress and well-being of the whole continent. Education, she emphasised, has the power to transform lives.

She said, 'Don't ever forget that by investing in your education you are doing the very best thing you can do, not just for yourselves, but for your children and your grandchildren. And you're also doing the very best thing you can do for your country.'

Across the world, over 57 million children of primary school age do not go to school, which is a very serious problem. Of these children, more than 50 per cent live in sub-Saharan Africa, where over 30 million children are not in any form of education. This number has remained static for the past five years. So many children are not receiving an education and probably never will: they will never learn to read, write, or even add up and subtract – those basic skills that all children should learn when they are still at primary school. This deficit needs to be addressed.

The standard of education in Africa is also inconsistent. This means that the education a child receives can depend on their ethnic group, social class, gender, and if they live in a rural or urban district. These inequalities persist in the quality of that education, if indeed they get any at all. The Center of Universal Education's Africa Learning Barometer shows that despite having had four years of primary school education, half of the children will still not have gained basic maths or reading skills. In South Africa, almost 34 per cent of children have not learned these skills, with the figure in rural areas an even more shocking 48 per cent. And for the poorest children the situation is worse still: their lack of educational opportunities means that 54 per cent of them never learn the fundamentals of numeracy and literacy.

Another challenge is to ensure that girls also gain an education. In Africa, education is often considered more important for boys than girls. As a result, even if they have had a primary school education, it is not easy for girls to continue on to secondary school or beyond. Michelle Obama had already spoken about this issue in a speech in 2011 to the Young African Women's Leaders Forum, and in Africa she repeated yet again that girls' education is 'a transformative investment and the best a government can do to foster economic growth and stability'.

President Obama also spoke about the importance of educational achievement during an address in Johannesburg in which he introduced an exciting new programme investing in the future of Africa – The Washington Fellowship for Young African Leaders. Through this initiative, he said, young African leaders will be 'trained and mentored to gain the skills and connections they need to accelerate their own career trajectories and contribute more robustly to strengthening democratic institutions, spurring economic growth, and enhancing peace and security in Africa.'

However, despite all the talk, the fact is that financial support for the development of education in Africa has not been increased by the USA. In fact, US foreign aid for global education has been reduced. In addition, the UNESCO Institute for Statistics shows that six of the ten major countries that provide financial aid for basic education have reduced their support. This has had a dramatic effect, not least in sub-Saharan Africa where it equates to a 7 per cent decrease in financial support. This deficit is having a major impact on people's lives.

We still have to remember though, as Michelle Obama reiterated, 'Mandela's most important quote, of the millions of things he has said, is that education is probably the most powerful weapon for change.' Let's hope that the governments of the world remember that and help to foster education for all.

## Exercises

Answer the following questions.

1. Which issue did Michelle Obama emphasise above all?

   ..................................................................................

2. Who was she addressing?

   ..................................................................................

3. Who benefits from education according to Michelle Obama?

   ..................................................................................

4. How does the author of the text explain the unequal educational opportunities in parts of Africa?

   ..................................................................................

5. Which group did President Obama address?

   ..................................................................................

6. What was his topic?

   ..................................................................................

**TOK** To what extent does the rest of the world have an ethical responsibility to support developing countries?

**05 Education for all**

**7** What is the situation regarding global support for education in Africa, according to the text?

..................................................................................................................................

**8** True or false? Justify your answer with a relevant brief quotation from the text.

**A** Michelle Obama was speaking to a cross-section of society, so her message was heard by all.

..................................................................................................................................

**B** The number of children not in school in sub-Saharan Africa is increasing steadily.

..................................................................................................................................

**C** All children can read and write after four years of school in Africa.

..................................................................................................................................

**D** US foreign aid to global education is growing.

..................................................................................................................................

**E** Michelle Obama believes that girls' education is a transformative investment and the best one a government can make.

..................................................................................................................................

**9** Match the words from the text with the synonyms on the right. Write the appropriate letter in the box below.

| | | | | |
|---|---|---|---|---|
| I | consistently | ☐ | A | restate |
| II | transform | ☐ | B | continue |
| III | urgent | ☐ | C | constantly |
| IV | deficit | ☐ | D | change for the better |
| V | persist | ☐ | E | pressing |
| VI | reiterate | ☐ | F | lack |

## Further exercises

### Zoom in on grammar

**Complex sentences: 'despite'**

*Despite* and *in spite of* are followed by a noun phrase or an *-ing* form.
  Despite the rain, we went for a walk.
  Despite being fired, we went for a walk.
  In spite of his hunger, he refused to eat his dinner.
  In spite of being hungry, he refused to eat his dinner.

## Grammar in context

**Complex sentences: 'despite'**

Re-read the text and locate two complex sentences which use 'despite'.

Based on what you have read, construct sentences of your own with the following openers.

1. Despite the money which has been spent on education in Africa...
2. Despite spending four years in school...
3. Despite the publicity given to the situation in Africa...
4. Despite reading about the situation in the press...

## Zoom in on grammar

**Complex sentences: 'during' and 'while'**

*During* and *while* are sometimes confused by students. After *during* we use a noun or noun phrase:

During lunch / during the night / during the war / during the maths class

However, with *while* we use a verb phrase in the continuous form:

While we were eating lunch / while we were sleeping / while they were speaking

## Grammar in context

**Complex sentences: 'during' and 'while'**

Put *during* or *while* in each of the following sentences.

1. _____ Michelle Obama's speech, students were making notes.
2. The students chatted about the article they had read _____ the teacher was writing the homework on the board.
3. _____ Marie was doing her homework, the phone rang three times.
4. Although she was distracted by the phone, Marie was determined not to stop and chat _____ her study time.

## Interactive oral activity

Discuss the article with a partner or in a small group. Do you agree with the statements made by Michelle Obama? What do you think needs to happen next? Is there an easy solution to the problem?

# Written work (HL)

In the previous text, Michelle Obama quoted Nelson Mandela, who said:

'Education is probably the most powerful weapon for change.'

Give a personal response to the stimulus and justify it. Choose an appropriate text type which you have studied in class. Write between 150 and 250 words.

# Written work (SL)

Imagine that you were a member of the audience at Michelle Obama's speech. Write an email to a friend sharing your impressions of what you heard. Write between 150 and 200 words.

# 06 Women's achievements in the 21st century

## Objectives

- To consider the current role of women in different societies
- To discuss the role of women in jobs in your country
- To research successful women and their achievements
- To discuss the differences in learning and achievement between boys and girls at school
- To practise the present perfect continuous tense

**Opposite** Female Chair of the Board.

# 6.1 Famous female achievers

## Text 6.1.1 Famous female achievers

In 2013 the Bank of England announced that the novelist Jane Austen would appear on the ten-pound bank note from around 2017. Jane Austen will replace Charles Darwin, thus giving a woman a place on bank notes again after Elizabeth Fry was removed from the five-pound note and replaced by Winston Churchill. The removal of Elizabeth Fry provoked a group of 46 female Members of Parliament to write to the Prime Minister and the Bank of England asking them not to remove women from bank notes. Their appeal was successful. The situation triggered much public debate about the small number of women represented on bank notes, and suggestions were made for other worthy candidates.

The Bank of England's choice of Jane Austen to illustrate a bank note is an acknowledgement of her achievements as an author. She lived between 1775 and 1817 in England and is well known for her romantic novels; many people would say that *Pride and Prejudice* (1813) is one of her most famous works. However, the choice of Jane Austen must have been a difficult one, as there are many other female achievers who could have been chosen to grace a bank note: from Boudicca (AD 60/61), the mighty warrior, to Margaret Thatcher (1925–2013), the first woman to become Prime Minister of Great Britain.

In the context of women in society, it is worth considering other countries and the wide range of talents and abilities that women display. Female achievers are worthy of mentioning because they have often had to compete in a male-dominated world that has not always welcomed competition from women. As a consequence, they had to be strong and self-confident and fight for their place in areas that many considered to be a male-only domain. For example, the British novelist Mary Anne Evans (1819–80) felt that she would only be taken seriously as a writer in Victorian England if she were male. She therefore wrote under the pseudonym George Eliot. Overleaf is a list of some female achievers from around the world.

# 06 Women's achievements in the 21st century

### Louisa May Alcott (1832–88)
American author of the still popular novel *Little Women*, she was the first female author to produce literature in the 19th century that was read by a mass audience – largely teenagers.

### Marie Curie (1867–1934)
Marie was born in Warsaw, Poland, but later moved to France to study maths and physics at the University of Sorbonne in Paris. She was largely responsible for the discovery of radioactivity and received the Nobel Prize in Chemistry in 1897.

### Pearl Buck (1892–1973)
An American who was born in China where her parents worked as missionaries, she developed an insight into Chinese culture and later wrote novels about American and Asian culture. In 1938 she was the first woman to win the Nobel Prize in Literature.

### Mother Teresa (1910–97)
Born in Albania, she became a missionary at the age of 18 years and went on to become a nun in 1931. While working as a nun, Mother Teresa went to Calcutta, India, where she founded a religious group called 'Missionaries of Charity'. She devoted all her life to helping the poorest of the poor in India.

### Frida Kahlo (1907–54)
Frida Kahlo was a Mexican artist who suffered a bus accident at the age of 18; this resulted in a life of pain and suffering that is reflected in many of her works. She is remembered as one of the most important surrealist artists of the 20th century.

## General comprehension

1. Which event caused a large group of female politicians to complain to the Prime Minister of the UK?
2. Which phrase in the text tells you that there was a lot of public interest caused by the complaint?
3. Why is it more difficult for women to be recognised for their successes?
4. According to the text, why did one British writer choose to publish her novels under another name?
5. Look at the examples of the five female achievers above. Write a paragraph answering the following questions: Which ones have you heard something about? Which of the five women was successful in an area that was considered a typically male-dominated domain? Which one would be considered to be doing 'typical women's work'? Give reasons for your decision.

## Text handling

Find words in the text which are similar in meaning to the following.

1. therefore
2. taken away
3. set off
4. deserving
5. recognition
6. decorate
7. area
8. fictitious name

### Individual oral activity

Research some other famous women achievers from around the world. Select two or three and prepare your presentation. It should be three or four minutes long, and you should be prepared to answer questions from the class after you have spoken. When you are preparing your presentation, ask yourself the following questions:

- Have I started by clearly stating the women's names and countries of origin and the period when they lived?
- Have I explained why I chose these women? What made them stand out?
- What achievements are they famous for?
- Have I made my presentation interesting and used words to make the information flow well?

(**Examples:** *first of all, I want to start by, one of the most interesting points is, another fact is, in conclusion*)

Finally, make sure that you practise your presentation to see if you can talk for the given amount of time.

### Written work

Using the information you gathered for your oral activity, create a flyer about four female achievers of your choice. Give clear information about what they have achieved and where and when they lived, and include examples. Use illustrations and bullet points as well as text.

## 6.2 Girls in school

### Text 6.2.1 Building confidence

## Today, girls, it's double maths – in Mandarin

by Sian Griffiths – Education Editor

Girls' school leaders are so concerned about their pupils' reluctance to take risks in the classroom that they are encouraging staff to teach some subjects in a foreign language to encourage pupils to believe that making mistakes is acceptable.

South Hampstead High School in north London is planning to teach 12-year-olds some humanities subjects in Spanish from September. At Oxford High School tutor groups are conducted in French and Mandarin. At Central Newcastle High School geography lessons are taught in foreign languages.

The hope is that the move will free girls up to take risks, be more confident and think more 'outside the box' to solve problems.

The experts say that even though girls are outstripping boys in school and university, they are being overtaken in the workplace because of their fear of failure.

They also hope the initiative will help girls to be bolder in admission interviews under tough questioning from dons.

# 06 Women's achievements in the 21st century

Kevin Stannard, director of innovation and learning at the Girls' Day School Trust (GDST), said: "The curse of the good girl is something we are thinking about a lot. There are a lot of girls who strive for perfection, who have a real fear of looking daft when answering questions and they are in danger of underselling themselves through fear of failure. We are trying to undermine that in girls' schools to get girls to take intellectual risks."

Stannard said he was "really hopeful" that the language initiative "will be a way of helping build girls' confidence." He added: "They see the teacher, who is unfamiliar with the language, taking risks and so they are more prepared to take risks themselves". Along with increasing language confidence comes increasing confidence to take risks and solve problems. "We want them not necessarily to aim for perfection but to aim for effectiveness."

The initiatives follow others designed to boost girls' confidence such as improvised comedy workshops at Putney High School and lessons in boasting at Wimbledon High School. The trust, which represents 24 schools and two academies, has also commissioned research by Cambridge University to identify the styles of teaching that girls thrive on. Helen Fraser, chief executive of the GDST, said that the results would be published in the autumn but girls' schools were already aware of many styles of teaching that did not work. She cited the experience of a head teacher who had taught both boys and girls. "When he was teaching in the boys' school he would lean down close, be very loud and very clear. If you did that to the girls their eyes would fill with tears," she said.

*http://www.thesundaytimes.co.uk/news, July 28 2013*

## General comprehension

1. According to the text, which schools are offering subjects taught in a foreign language?
2. What other courses are being offered to help improve self-confidence?
3. According to Kevin Stannard, what is the aim of the Girls' Day School Trust?
4. What has Cambridge University been asked to research?

## Text handling

Below are some words taken from the text. Choose the word or phrase that could best replace the word given and keep the meaning.

1. reluctance (line 2)
    a) fear
    b) eagerness
    c) unwillingness
    d) desire

2. tutor groups (line 10)
    a) higher level students
    b) teachers' classes
    c) small groups of students
    d) after school activities

3. 'outside the box' (line 16)
    a) creatively
    b) at home
    c) in the hallways
    d) intensively

4. outstripping (line 18)
    a) following
    b) surpassing
    c) copying
    d) lagging behind

5. dons (line 23)
    a) managers
    b) university lecturers
    c) male teachers
    d) interviewers

6. boost (line 44)
    a) lessen
    b) initiate
    c) show
    d) encourage

7. improvised (line 45)
    a) important
    b) organised
    c) difficult
    d) unplanned

8. cited (line 55)
    a) condemned
    b) praised
    c) quoted
    d) remembered

## Individual oral activity

Look at the photograph below and describe what you see. Relate the picture to boys and girls at school and talk about your own experiences and the similarities and differences in achievement and working styles that you have observed. You should plan to speak for three minutes.

## Written work

As a Language B student, you have a vast amount of experience of learning a language and of self-confidence that you have gained from that. Or perhaps you have a different opinion? Reflect on the connection between language learning and self-confidence and present your ideas in the form of a speech that you could deliver to the class. Give examples from your own school experience. Write between 250 and 300 words.

**Tips for writing**

- You need an introduction: it is a good idea to say something general at the beginning of a speech.
- Think who your audience is. Are they students or parents? This may influence your choice of anecdotes, for example.
- Maybe give some general information about the numbers of speakers of English around the world and try to incorporate an anecdote from your own experience.
- Remember also that in a speech you can have rhetorical questions directed at your audience.
- You should use linking phrases such as *first, second, moreover, I would like to add, finally*.
- At the end say 'Thank you for listening'. This is the signal that the speech is over.

# 06 Women's achievements in the 21st century

## 6.3 Meet the women doing 'men's work'

### Text 6.3.1 Katie Gillard

**Katie Gillard, 21, truck driver**

There are 300,000 truck drivers in the UK, of whom 1,600 (0.5%) are women. Katie completed her category C HGV exams in 2010 and started her career at her dad's haulage firm, JL Gillard & Sons in Somerset. She now works for Tarmac at a quarry in Wiltshire.

I left college with a full qualification to work with young children, but decided it wasn't for me. My dad told me that the age limit to get an HGV licence had changed from 21 to 19 and suggested I do the exams. I passed the test first time in 2010 and last year I passed the class 1 articulated lorry test. Walking into the classroom to do the first of my HGV practical exams was really intimidating. I was the only girl.

The first time I sat behind the wheel was terrifying, but I picked it up pretty quickly. I work with my father, Andrew, who owns a quarry. I'm used to people doing a double-take when I'm driving. I get it every day, particularly when I'm sitting in traffic. It doesn't bother me too much. I really enjoy driving.

On some sites, blokes look at you with an expression that says, "Oh, you're only a young girl and you're driving a big lorry." The other day, I had to manoeuvre out of a tight spot and a builder insisted on telling me how to move my lorry, but it was totally the wrong way. People can often be like that, but I just ignore it.

A lot of teasing goes on where I work, but everyone gets the same treatment. Male or female, if you're shy or timid, a quarry would be the wrong place to work.

Some people say more girls are sitting their HGV test. But from what I see, women are always going to be a minority in this industry. It's always going to be seen as a man's world.

http://www.theguardian.com/lifeandstyle/2013/apr/26/meet-women-doing-mens-work

'HGV' stand for 'Heavy Goods Vehicle', commonly referred to as a truck or a lorry.

## General comprehension

1. What are Katie Gillard's qualifications?
2. How successful was her first experience of driving a truck?
3. What are the reactions of her male colleagues in her job?
4. What are Katie Gillard's reactions to male comments about her ability to drive a truck well?

## Text handling

1. Match the words on the left with the definitions on the right. There are more definitions than you need.

   | | | | |
   |---|---|---|---|
   | I | haulage firm | A | lacking in self-confidence |
   | II | a quarry | B | business that transports goods |
   | III | articulated lorry | C | bullying |
   | IV | intimidating | D | building site |
   | V | timid | E | makes you feel scared |
   | VI | to tease | F | truck in two parts: the cab and a trailer |
   | | | G | place where rock is cut out of the ground |
   | | | H | to make jokes about a person and their abilities |

2. Look at these words in context and work out what you think they mean.
   a) wheel
   b) pretty
   c) blokes
   d) teasing
   e) to pick something up

> The RNLI is the Royal National Lifeboat Institution. The network of lifeboat stations around the coast of the UK is a charity funded by donations from the public.

## Text 6.3.2 Fran Wilkins

### Fran Wilkins, 30, coxswain

Of around 5,000 station crew in the RNLI, 8% are female. Fran is the first female coxswain at the Filey lifeboat station in North Yorkshire, and one of only three in the UK. A coxswain is in command of a rescue at sea. Most lifeboat crew are volunteers.

*I joined the RNLI when I was 17, after I left school. It seemed a natural thing to do. My dad is a fisherman, I have a brother in the merchant navy, another in the army as a diver and a younger brother on the same lifeboat crew. So it's in the family. I studied sports at university, but was more interested in this. I became a coxswain last October.*

*The reality is that you are surrounded by men. At first, I felt I had to prove myself. Once I felt I had, it was fine. But the most important thing is that you are doing the job properly. Being in a crew, you get pulled into a very strong team who fully trust each other. I wouldn't have been able to get this far without help from the other members.*

*Male or female, it's not for everyone. And it's definitely not glamorous: you should see me after a rescue in really bad weather.*

*I also work as a watch officer for HM Coastguard. That involves coordinating a response team. Whenever I'm not working in the office, I'm on call. My pager is always on. There are 28 of us on the lifeboat crew and we don't have a rota, so when I'm paged, I go to the station.*

*Operations vary from rescuing people cut off by the tide to looking for missing people. We towed my dad in last year. If my dad or my brother needed to be rescued, I would want a good crew to help them. That's the way I think about it when I go to assist someone: this is someone's father or someone's brother.*

http://www.theguardian.com/lifeandstyle/2013/apr/26/meet-women-doing-mens-work

## 06 Women's achievements in the 21st century

### General comprehension

1. Describe the work of a coxswain.
2. 'So it's in the family.' Explain what Fran Wilkins means when she says this.
3. What is the importance of teamwork in her job?
4. Why do you think there are also men who would not like to be a coxswain?

### Text handling

1. Match the words on the left with the definitions on the right. There are more definitions than you need.

   I   glamorous
   II  pager
   III rota
   IV  to tow

   A  electronic equipment that sends a signal
   B  to pull one vehicle behind another
   C  to rescue
   D  duty list with times
   E  well paid
   F  attractive

2. Look at these words in context and work out what you think they mean.

   a) a watch officer
   b) I'm on call
   c) operations
   d) the tide

### Text 6.3.3 Rachel Martin Peer

## Rachel Martin Peer, 51, London black cab driver

There are 23,000 black cab licences in London and about 10,000 cabs out at any one time. Five per cent of these drivers are women. The first hackney carriage licences were granted in 1654.

*I did the knowledge in three and a half years, which isn't bad. To get through the knowledge you need determination and discipline. If you haven't got them you won't get it, no matter who you are.*

*Yes, I felt like I was entering a very male-dominated world but it was no problem for me – bring it on! It's an equal playing field. They know I have learnt exactly what they have learnt, I am doing the same job and I am being paid exactly the same money. In fact my tips are probably better, but that's another story.*

*The guys treated me like one of the blokes and I don't want to be treated any differently. I felt completely accepted, and of course we are the better drivers!*

*It's a great job and I love it. I've never done a job I don't love. If I don't love it I won't do it anymore, I'll do something else. The knowledge is the hardest thing I have ever done in my life – what a personal journey! I learnt so much about myself it was unbelievable. After doing this I can achieve anything*

as far as I'm concerned. I've been doing it for three years now and I think I will be a 75-year-old driver; I haven't got a pension, for one thing!

Eve Katie Sprange

'The knowledge' is a test that London black cab drivers must pass in order to get their licence – drivers have to memorise 320 routes, 25,000 streets and 20,000 landmarks or places of interest! This takes an average of two to four years.

## General comprehension

1 Of the 23,000 cabs licensed, how many are in use at any one time on average?
2 According to the text, did Rachel feel she had an advantage over the men when she started the job?
3 Why does Rachel feel a sense of equality in her job?
4 What does Rachel feel is the greatest thing she has achieved so far?
5 Why does Rachel say she will still be driving cabs at the age of 75?

## Text handling

1 Match the words on the left with the definitions on the right. There are more definitions than you need.

| | | | |
|---|---|---|---|
| I | granted | A | small amount of money paid in addition to the bill |
| II | determination | B | issued |
| III | tip | C | amount of money paid monthly by the government after retirement |
| IV | pension | D | pieces of useful information |
| | | E | intense feeling that drives you not to give up |
| | | F | small hotel |

2 Look at the words in context and work out what they mean.
   a) male-dominated
   b) blokes
   c) achieve

## Text 6.3.4 Caroline Lake

### Caroline Lake, 41, mechanic

There are around 200 female mechanics compared to 500,000 male mechanics working in the UK (0.04%). Caroline is a mechanic and the founder of Caroline's Cars, a female- and male-friendly garage in Norfolk.

*I have always had a fascination with cars. As a teenager, when my friends had their heads stuck in Smash Hits, I would be reading motor magazines. At 14, I could tell you what time every car model in the UK could do 0–60 in. When I was 16, my father bought me an old Triumph Dolomite to fix up.*

*When I finished school, I studied social studies and marketing – being a mechanic wasn't an option in those days. At 27, I set up a franchise*

101

# 06 Women's achievements in the 21st century

with a Japanese car company. I asked the mechanic to take me on as an unpaid apprentice one day a week. I was the tea girl and the butt of most of the jokes, but I loved the smells, the cars. I started to do more hours, and after a few years the boss asked if I wanted to take the MOT NVQ exams.

Working in other garages over the years, I did feel like an outsider. Some of the guys would make horrible, sexist comments, but I noticed many of the women drivers would want to talk to me. Because the industry isn't regulated, some mechanics will take advantage of people's lack of knowledge. It can be intimidating. That got the cogs going about starting up my own business. Caroline's Cars has been running since 2006. I have taught hundreds of women – and men – basic mechanics.

I think there are so few women because it's a stereotypical male environment, but I plan to change that. There is no reason women can't do it. It's not about brute strength. There is a tool for everything. In fact, women have certain characteristics that make them perfect for the trade. Women are dextrous, patient – they have less of a tendency to throw a spanner across the room. I often speak at schools to promote it to young girls; to tell them that this is actually quite a cool job. I hope to have garages across the country where women can train. The more women that do it, the more other women will see it as an option. I have plenty of customers who say to me, "I wish I could have done this when I was younger", but, like me, they didn't see it as an option.

http://www.theguardian.com/lifeandstyle/2013/apr/26/meet-women-doing-mens-work

---

All vehicles in the UK must be tested annually by the MOT – the Ministry of Transport – for their roadworthiness and safety. An NVQ is a National Vocational Qualification, a competence-based qualification.

## General comprehension

1. What was Caroline's favourite free time activity when she was a teenager?
2. Can you explain what she was able to do at the age of 14?
3. Caroline says that when she left school, being a mechanic 'wasn't an option'. What do you think was the reason for this?
4. What is Caroline's long-term plan?

## Text handling

1. Match the words on the left with the definitions on the right. There are more definitions than you need.

   | | | | |
   |---|---|---|---|
   | I | franchise | A | skilled with tools |
   | II | apprentice | B | tool used in car repairs |
   | III | dextrous | C | person who learns skills on the job |
   | IV | spanner | D | form of business organisation with a chain of companies |
   | | | E | skilled with your hands |
   | | | F | foreign company |

2. Look at these words in context and explain what you think they mean.
   a) to get the cogs going
   b) stereotypical male environment
   c) brute strength

## Text 6.3.5 Charlotte Harbottle

### Charlotte Harbottle, 24, butcher

**Charlotte has just moved from specialist butcher Lidgate's in London's Holland Park to owning her own shop, Charlotte's Butchery, in Newcastle. Of 7,000 butchers in the retail meat industry, Charlotte is thought to be one of only three women (0.04%).**

*There have been a few occasions when I was serving and the customer asked to speak to a butcher. I would say nothing and get another butcher to help them. But my colleagues would usually tell them I'm the best person to talk to anyway.*

*Sometimes, when people hear I'm a butcher, they say, "Do you really cut stuff up?" I don't mind that side of things at all. You don't see it as a living thing. The job is mechanical and very specialist to do right. I am not a feminist. I just think there should be good butchers who know what they are doing with a carcass whether they are male or female. I think the more people realised what a butcher does, the more popular this career would be.*

*I studied theology at York University, and worked in a butcher's shop part-time. When I graduated, I got a job as a proofreader, but I hated working in an office. I realised I would prefer to be a butcher and have the freedom that owning your own business brings. It's strange – relatives in my family are sheep farmers, and my mother grew up on a farm, so I have always known about this industry in some way, but last year my grandmother sent me a picture of my great-great grandfather standing outside his own butcher shop. So it's definitely in the blood.*

http://www.theguardian.com/lifeandstyle/2013/apr/26/meet-women-doing-mens-work

# 06 Women's achievements in the 21st century

## General comprehension

1. What does Charlotte think is the connection between her job and the work of her family and relatives?
2. After Charlotte graduated from university, did she work in the same field of study?
3. Does Charlotte think you have to be strong to be a butcher?
4. Does Charlotte work as a retail or wholesale butcher?

## Text handling

1. Match the words on the left with the definitions on the right. There are more definitions than you need.

   I   carcass
   II  feminist
   III proofreader

   A  university examiner
   B  someone who believes men should do certain jobs
   C  not the full number of hours
   D  someone who believes strongly in women's rights
   E  body of a dead animal
   F  someone who reads texts and checks for errors

2. Look at these words in context and explain what you think they mean.
   a) a few occasions
   b) to graduate
   c) great-great-grandfather

## Zoom in on grammar

**The present perfect continuous**

In the text about Rachel Martin Peer, the London black cab driver, she says:

  'I *have been doing* this *for* three years now.'

This verb tense is called the present perfect continuous, and it is often used with the word 'for' to emphasise the duration of the activity. It gives us two pieces of information:

- Rachel's job started three years ago.
- She is still doing this job.

The present perfect continuous tense can also be used with the word 'since' to emphasise the beginning point of the activity; Rachel could also say:

  'I *have been doing* this *since* 2010.'

## Grammar in context

**The present perfect continuous**

1. Look at the following pairs of sentences and make one sentence using the present perfect continuous of the verb in brackets and the word 'for'.
   a) I started at this school two years ago. I still study here now. (study)
   b) My brother went to China five years ago. He is working for an American company. (work)
   c) My older sister lives in London. She went there some months ago. (live)
   d) Katie Gillard is a truck driver. She started driving trucks six years ago. (drive)

2. Look at the following pairs of sentences and make one sentence using the present perfect continuous of the verb in brackets and 'since'.
   a) I first went skiing on holiday in winter 2013. I love skiing now and I go every year. (ski)
   b) The maths teacher plays in a jazz combo. He started when he was invited to join after he told them he played the trombone. (play)
   c) My sister is looking for a new flat. She started looking after she came back from living in Paris. (look)
   d) I lost my keys on the way to school. I am worried. (worry)

### Interactive oral activity

In groups of three, make lists of what you each consider to be traditionally men's or women's jobs. Compare your lists and see if you have agreed on any jobs. Discuss whether you think men or women are more suited to these jobs and why. Also discuss why you think that in a number of societies the roles of men and women are changing. Do you think the movement is in both directions – i.e. more men are doing women's jobs – or is it just the women who are changing their roles?

Time your activity and talk for no more than ten minutes, making sure that each person gets a chance to talk and give their opinions. Be prepared to share your ideas with the other groups.

## Exam practice

# What is International Women's Day?

International Women's Day (8 March) is a global day **(1)** _____ the economic, political and social achievements of women past, present and future. In some places like China, Russia, Vietnam and Bulgaria, International Women's Day is a **(2)** _____ holiday.

Suffragettes campaigned for women's right to vote. The word 'Suffragette' is derived from the word "suffrage" meaning the right to vote. International Women's Day honours the work of the Suffragettes, celebrates women's success, and reminds of inequities still to be redressed.

International Women's Day has been observed since in the early 1900's, a time of great expansion and **(3)** _____ in the industrialized world that saw booming population growth and the rise of radical ideologies.

The new millennium has witnessed a significant change and attitudinal shift in both women's and society's thoughts about women's equality and emancipation. Many from a younger generation feel that 'all the battles have been won for women' while many **(4)** _____ from the 1970's know only too well the longevity and ingrained complexity of patriarchy. With more women in the boardroom, greater equality in legislative rights, and an increased critical mass of women's visibility as impressive role models in every aspect of life, one could think that women have gained true equality. The unfortunate fact is that women are still not paid equally to that of their male **(5)** _____ , women still are not present in equal numbers in business or politics, and globally women's education, health and the violence against them is worse than that of men.

However, great improvements have been made. We do have female astronauts and prime ministers, school girls are welcomed into university, women can work and have a family, women have real choices. And so the tone and nature of IWD has, for the past few years, moved from being a reminder about the **(6)** _____ to a celebration of the positives.

Annually on 8 March, thousands of events are held **(7)** _____ the world to inspire women and celebrate achievements. A global web of rich and diverse local activity connects women from all around the world ranging from political rallies, business conferences, government activities and networking events through to local women's craft markets, theatre performances, fashion **(8)** _____ and more.

So make a difference, think globally and act locally.

*http://www.internationalwomensday.com*

# 06 Women's achievements in the 21st century

### Exercises

Answer the following questions.

1 Some of the words have been removed from the text. From the list below, choose the words which best fit the gaps and write the appropriate letters in the box below.

| | | | | | |
|---|---|---|---|---|---|
| I  | ☐ | A particular   | I parades    |
| II | ☐ | B throughout   | J ideologies |
| III| ☐ | C celebrating  | K feminists  |
| IV | ☐ | D negatives    | L counterparts |
| V  | ☐ | E turbulence   | M organizing |
| VI | ☐ | F achievements | |
| VII| ☐ | G national     | |
| VIII|☐ | H significant  | |

2 Based on the information in the text, match the first part of the sentence with the appropriate ending. An example has been provided. There are more options than you need.

**Example:** International Women's Day... ☐ C

I   Celebrations of women's achievements... ☐

II  Women have not gained true equality with men... ☐

III Women's pay... ☐

A although great improvements have been made.

B are accompanied by reminders of areas where success is lacking.

C is celebrated in countries all around the world.

D is equal to men's.

E because they have less education.

F is often lower than men's.

G are impressive.

# Further exercises

## Written work (SL)

Based on what you have read about International Women's Day, write a proposal to your school principal suggesting that your school designates a day to celebrate the achievements of women. Your proposal should include some information about the worldwide recognition of International Women's Day and its background. You could propose inviting some speakers to the school: women from the local community who have achieved recognition for the work they do. Explain what kind of activities the women are involved in; they could be from businesses, hospitals, charity concerns, the police or fire services, or any other area of local life. Write between 300 and 400 words.

> Your proposal should be presented as a formal letter addressed to your school principal or head teacher. You must begin with their name or title: 'Dear Mr/Mrs/Dr...' (not 'Dear Sir/Madam'). Write an introduction explaining your reasons for writing the letter. End with a conclusion, politely requesting that your proposal is positively received. Use formal phrases such as, for example, 'I would like to...' and 'Could you consider...'.

### Intercultural activity

The text above mentions suffragettes and the right to vote. Research three or four countries around the world to find out if women have the right to vote, and if they have, when it was granted to them. Make bullet points and then with a partner compare your findings and discuss the information that you found. Was there anything that surprised you? Anything that made you want to know more? Anything that made you want to ask questions/find answers?

Women and men have not always had the right to vote for the same length of time in history. What do you think were the reasons for this?

## Written work (HL)

One of the Higher Level writing tasks in the English B examination is a personal response to a statement. You will have already learnt that there is no right or wrong answer because you will be assessed on your ability to present a clear, logical and reasoned argument, stating your opinions and justifying them.

In the text on page 105 the final sentence is:

'So make a difference, think globally and act locally.'

Think about the statement – what do you think it means? Give examples. To what extent do you agree with this statement? Do you think this statement has been used throughout history – or is it relatively new? Write your response in around 350 words.

# 07 The family

## Objectives

- To practise using colloquial expressions and complex sentences
- To revise the first conditional
- To practise the use of 'tell' and 'say' in reported speech
- To practise writing instructions or guidelines
- To explore the changing roles of parents

**Opposite** What does the family mean today?

# 7.1 The changing face of fatherhood

## Text 7.1.1 Three generations of fathers

# The changing face of fatherhood

by Joanna Moorhead, Sunday June 17 2012

**From hands-off to hands-on, through the traumas of divorce and coming out, three generations of dads talk to Joanna Moorhead about their very different experiences as a man's role in family life evolves**

### John Broughton, 78

**Lives in Newbury, Berkshire. He and his wife, Sylvia, have three children aged 52, 49 and 41**

"Sylvia and I were both 24 when our eldest son, Paul, was born: I was in the RAF [Royal Air Force] at the time, but the pay didn't stretch to funding a family. I suppose, these days, what a couple would do in that situation is both work: but in those days we prided ourselves, us men, on being the breadwinners, and on our wives being able to stay at home. So I left the RAF and set up my own business.

"I worked very long hours when the children were young – I didn't see them as much as I might have done, and I do regret that now. I'd get home too late at night to see them, and leave too early in the morning to see them then: but we made a lot of the weekends. We'd drive down to the coast and we'd all sit there enjoying a picnic whatever the weather.

"Holidays were very important times, too: and as my business became successful, we could afford to go abroad. We took the children to Spain and Mallorca and the south of France: it was all about where we could all have a good time together, and those are very precious memories.

"When I see my grandson, Joel, with his twin babies, I can see that being a father has changed a lot – he takes on as many childcare duties as his wife does. And I know that Paul, when his children were younger, spent more time with them than I did with mine. But I think the important way things haven't changed is that we'd all do anything for our children – being a father is the most important thing to any of us, even though it's perhaps expressed in different ways in different generations."

### Paul Broughton, 52

**Has a son, Joel, 29, by his first marriage, and two children – Jasmine, 18, and 15-year-old Reece – by his second marriage, to Kim**

"I married my first girlfriend, which was quite common in those days, but we split up when Joel was still very young and I moved back home. It meant I wasn't around to see as much of Joel as I'd have liked, especially when I moved to Leicester to work and he was still with his mum in Berkshire. I saw him every other weekend – I tried to do ordinary things with him, trips to the park and feeding

109

the ducks, because I was very aware of the danger of giving him too many treats because his mum and I were divorced.

"When I married Kim and Jasmine and Reece came along, the lovely thing was being able to be with them all the time – it made me realise what I'd missed out on with Joel. I'd come in from work and they'd both come running to meet me, and then we'd read stories and be together all evening.

"These days, Jasmine is at university and only Reece is at home full-time, but older children have different expectations about their parents as providers these days. I remember getting my first pay packet and my mum sitting down and saying, 'well done – now let's talk about how much you're going to contribute to the running of the house'. I can't even imagine Jasmine's face if I said something similar to her! A father like me these days has to accept that he'll go on being a financial provider for some time to come."

### Joel Cronogue, 29

**He and his wife, Charlotte, live near Catterick in Yorkshire. They are the parents of twins Samuel and Sophia, nine months**

"The first thing I remember my dad doing when he came home from work when I was a child was to pick up the toys and pitch in with what was involved with the children – so he was my role model and that's very much how I am, too. For me, having twin babies is a shared job for Charlotte and I – if anything, the fact that I work means I've got the lighter load, because it's easier to get out of the house and have a change of scene at work than it is for Charlotte to be at home with the babies all day.

"When I get home I check out what I can do – give them a bath, sort out the laundry, make up the bottles for the next day. I feel Charlotte will need a break, so rather than coming home and expecting time to myself, I come home expecting to get stuck in.

"When the children are older, though, our plan is for Charlotte to pick up her career again, so we'll both be earners and we'll both be looking after the children. To me, being a dad who's simply an economic provider isn't enough – I want to play an active role as my children grow up. I want to sit down on the couch with them when they're older and remember times we shared.

"I'm in the Army, and now the babies are here I've decided to change my shift pattern and my job so that I can be around more as the children are growing up.

"I'm also opting out of going to places like Iraq and Afghanistan, because I don't think it would be fair on Charlotte to leave her on her own with the babies.

"The Army is a very masculine environment, but the people I work with understand where I'm coming from. One of my bosses said he'd only been around for one of his daughter's 17 birthdays, and if he could turn back the clock he'd do things very differently. He said I shouldn't let anything stand in the way of organising my life so I can spend more time with my children – and that's very much my attitude, too."

http://www.independent.co.uk/life-style/health-and-families/features/fathers-day-the-changing-face-of-fatherhood-7856666.html

## General comprehension

1. Re-read the text about John.
   a) Why did he leave the RAF?
   b) Why was he not able to spend as much time as he wanted with his children?
   c) Describe his happy memories of when the children were younger in your own words.

2. Re-read the text about Paul.
   a) Is Paul still married to his first girlfriend?
   b) How often did he see Joel when he was young?
   c) What did he enjoy especially when Jasmine and Reece were small?

3. Re-read the text about Joel.
   a) What does Joel do for a living?
   b) How does Joel describe his role as a father?
   c) Why does Joel not want to go to places like Iraq or Afghanistan?

4. What do you think are the main differences in the role of the fathers in these texts? Copy and fill in the graphic organiser showing the three men and how their roles are similar and different. Then explain your work in a short paragraph using examples from the text.

5. Although the role of the mother is not explicitly described in the texts, what differences can you identify between the roles of John's wife, Sylvia, and Joel's wife, Charlotte?

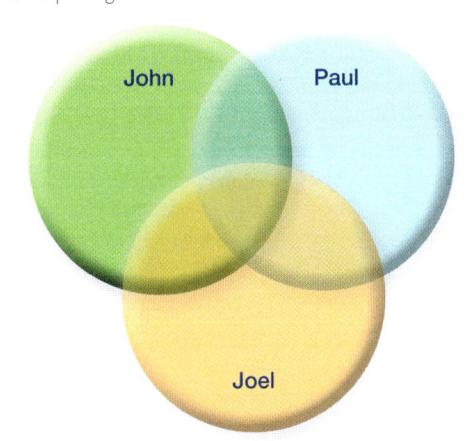

## Text handling

1. True or false? Justify your answer with a relevant brief quotation from the text.
   a) When he was in the RAF, John could not afford to support a family.
   b) John's generation did not allow their wives to go out to work.
   c) Kim is Joel's mother.
   d) After Paul and his first wife separated, he went to live with his parents.
   e) Paul expects to support his children financially longer than his parents supported him.
   f) He expects Jasmine to pay her share of expenses at home.
   g) When Joel comes home, he expects to relax.
   h) Charlotte will always stay at home.
   i) People in the Army understand Joel's attitude towards being a father.

2. Joel's story: Read the text below and replace the missing prepositions. Then go back to the text to check your answers.

   **on / of / back / out / with / around / from / to**

   'I'm in the Army, and now the babies are here I've decided a) _____ change my shift pattern and my job so that I can be b) _____ more as the children are growing up. I'm also opting c) _____ of going to places like Iraq and Afghanistan, because I don't think it would be fair d) _____ Charlotte to leave her on her own e) _____ the babies. The Army is a very masculine environment, but the people I work with understand where I'm coming f) _____. One of my bosses said he'd only been around for one of his daughter's 17 birthdays, and if he could turn g) _____ the clock he'd do things very differently. He said I shouldn't let anything stand in the way h) _____ organising my life so I can spend more time with my children – and that's very much my attitude, too.'

111

# 07 The family

**3** There are several colloquial expressions used in the text. Match them to the correct meaning by using clues in the text to help you.

- **I** We prided ourselves, us men, on being the bread winners
- **II** We made a lot of the weekend
- **III** What I'd missed out on with Joel
- **IV** To pick up the toys and pitch in
- **V** The lighter load
- **VI** Have a change of scene
- **VII** If he could turn back the clock

- **A** do something in a different place
- **B** used it as well as we could
- **C** easier job
- **D** have the time again
- **E** being the only ones to earn money in the family
- **F** join in
- **G** the experiences I didn't have

## Zoom in on grammar

**Reported speech using 'tell' and 'say'**

When we report something another person has said, we often use a tense shift: in this case from the simple present to the simple past. We can also use 'that' in the sentence, as shown below.

'I am cold,' she said.

*What did she say?* 'She said she was cold.' *or* 'She said that she was cold.'

*What did she tell you?* 'She told me she was cold.' *or* 'She told me that she was cold.'

Note: After 'say' there is no indirect object, but after 'tell' there usually is.

## Grammar in context

**Reported speech using 'tell' and 'say'**

Change these sentences from the text to reported speech, using *tell* and *say* for each example to practise the difference.

1. 'I saw him every other weekend.'
2. 'Jasmine is at university and only Reece is at home full-time.'
3. 'A father like me these days has to accept that he'll go on being the financial provider for some time to come.'
4. 'When I get home I check out what I can do.'
5. 'The Army is a very masculine environment, but the people I work with understand where I'm coming from.'

## Written work

How has the role of a father changed in the 21st century? Describe a father's role as you see it. You could ask a father (your own, or maybe a teacher or someone you trust) some questions first about the role he played when his children were small. Write between 250 and 400 words.

---

The culture of childcare and protection has changed dramatically in the Western world over the years. Ask your parents or older relatives how their lives differed from yours today in this respect.

# 7.2 Helicopter parents

## Text 7.2.1 'Helicopter parents' creating a generation incapable of accepting failure

by Hayley Dixon, August 30 2013

*"Helicopter parents" who micromanage their children's lives are creating a generation incapable of dealing with failure, a schools guide has warned.*

Parents who "hover" over their offspring, filling every moment with extra lessons and after-school clubs, are creating too much pressure and should take a step back when they reach adolescence, the *Good Schools Guide* claimed.

If children do not learn to deal with failure they may be unable to cope with defeats in later life, according to the newsletter.

"If we drive our children to define themselves only by success, how will they deal with the inevitable setbacks that come with adulthood?" the guide asks. "Are we creating a generation who won't have a go at something new for fear of failing?"

Some of the country's top girls' schools have already begun introducing measures to encourage their high achieving students to accept defeat.

Oxford High School for Girls is planning a maths test where it is impossible to get 100% to prevent students becoming obsessed with being "Little Miss Perfect", while Wimbledon High School runs a "failure week" to teach pupils to build resilience.

The guide warns that around year nine, when children start to assert their independence, "attentive parenting can mutate into undue pressure". They "strongly advise" parents to take a back seat and allow children to control their own future, the *Evening Standard* reported.

Furthermore, pupils who are pushed toward top A-levels will often struggle to deal with studying independently at University, the letter to parents added.

Earlier this month head teachers warned that "helicopter parents" who intervene in the higher education admissions process by telephoning Universities are actually damaging their prospects by sending the wrong message about their maturity.

The *Good Schools Guide* today reiterated that warning, advising adults to leave it the process to the teenagers.

Helen Fraser, the chief executive of the Girls' Day School Trust, of which both Wimbledon and Oxford High School are a part, has previously explained that they try to teach failure so that the pupils understand that "being perfect is the enemy of learning".

"We need to ensure that their education helps them to become resilient, to encourage them to not be afraid to take risks and to be confident," she said.

Referring to the impossible test she added: "What is important in this context isn't whether the girls get 100% but that they learn that failure is not fatal – what counts is what you learn from the experience and how you bounce back from it."

http://www.telegraph.co.uk/education/10277505/Helicopter-parents-creating-a-generation-incapable-of-accepting-failure.html

# 07 The family

To what extent are helicopter parents a reflection of society in the 21st century?

**TOK**

## General comprehension

1. How would you explain the term 'helicopter parents' in your own words to someone who has never heard of it before?
2. What do parents do when they hover over their children?
3. When does the author suggest that parents should stop hovering over their children?
4. What does the word 'pushy' mean? If the word is new to you, read the text carefully and find clues which help you understand it.
5. What do the children of pushy parents fail to learn?
6. What is the result of this, according to the text?
7. Describe the measures which some top schools have introduced to overcome the problem.
8. After reading the text, which of the IB Learner Profile traits can you connect to ideas in the text and how?

## Text handling

Find words in the text which could be meaningfully replaced by the following; the words are listed in the order they appear in the text.

1. son or daughter
2. teenage years
3. unavoidable
4. change
5. strength
6. to step back
7. to interfere
8. stage of development
9. restated
10. make sure

## Grammar in context

**Reference pronouns**

In the following sentences from the text, identify which words are referred to by the underlined pronouns.

1. Parents who "hover" over their offspring, filling every moment with extra lessons and after-school clubs, are creating too much pressure and should take a step back when <u>they</u> reach adolescence, the *Good Schools Guide* claimed.
2. If children do not learn to deal with failure <u>they</u> may be unable to cope with defeats in later life, according to the newsletter.
3. The guide warns that around year nine, when children start to assert their independence, "attentive parenting can mutate into undue pressure". <u>They</u> "strongly advise" parents to take a back seat and allow children to control their own future, the *Evening Standard* reported.
4. Earlier this month head teachers warned that "helicopter parents" <u>who</u> intervene in the higher education admissions process by telephoning Universities are actually damaging <u>their</u> prospects by sending the wrong message about <u>their</u> maturity.
5. What is important in this context isn't whether the girls get 100% but that <u>they</u> learn that failure is not fatal – what counts is what you learn from the experience and how you bounce back from <u>it</u>.

## Zoom in on grammar

**First conditional**

The first conditional is used for situations where something may or may not happen, but it is possible. It is formed using

> If … + *present*, … + future

For example:

> If it rains, we will get wet.

The sentence can also be turned round:

> We will get wet if it rains.

## Grammar in context

**First conditional sentences**

1. Find two first conditional sentences in the text.
2. Now complete these sentences using the first conditional.
   a) If students always study hard…
   b) If the teachers praise students more…
   c) If parents leave their children to make their own decisions…
   d) If parents and teachers fail to support the students….

# Text 7.2.2 Three mistakes 'helicopter parents' make that prevent their children from growing up

http://www.huffingtonpost.com/michael-s-broder-phd/three-mistakes-helicopter-that-prevent-their-children_b_3741412.html

**Michael S. Broder, Ph.D., posted: 08/14/2013**

The term "helicopter parent" is a relatively new one in our culture, but the practice is quite prevalent. When a child leaves home (for college, for instance, or even overnight camp) the helicopter parent does exactly what the term implies – hovers. Helicopter parents usually have the best intentions – to protect their children from life's hardships and prepare them for adulthood – but as with many other aspects of parenting, the results don't always match the intentions. If this sounds familiar and you find yourself "hovering," here are a few common mistakes to be aware of and what you might want to consider instead:

## Mistake 1

Children get their own cell phones at younger ages every year. While cell phones are great for safety purposes, they make it possible for parents to be in continual contact with their child. Psychologist Dr. Steven Sussman has even referred to the cell phone as "the world's longest umbilical cord." When your young adult child goes off to college, it's easier than ever for you to stay in touch – all the time. But is this a good thing? And it may certainly take on a life of its own when your child calls you to discuss what to eat at the next meal or even uses you as a surrogate alarm clock, with a daily wake-up call. Instead, limit routine communication to a specific time of day. Maybe you and your son or daughter can schedule a time to speak on the phone each evening or a few specified evenings each week. This way, he or she can have the opportunity to try to solve problems on his or her own instead of immediately reaching out to you for the answers.

## Mistake 2

It's quite common for parents to continue to pay for things into adulthood that they began paying for when their child was much younger. For example, many young adults are still on their family cell phone plans and car insurance, and usually let their parents foot the bill for meals out and family vacations. However, while remaining a safety net, you also may

# 07 The family

want to allow them to have some "skin in the game," in order to learn financial responsibility. This means setting firm limits and establishing a clear policy concerning credit cards and other financial matters. As an invaluable preparation for adulthood, gradually hand over small financial obligations, in order to transition him or her to become a financially responsible adult.

## Mistake 3

Intuitively, it makes sense that adolescents need different parenting than infants or toddlers and young adults require different parenting than adolescents, but this change doesn't always happen automatically. For example, it's no longer necessary to punish and reward your children in the same way you did when they were younger. The best parenting is about giving guidance that's age-appropriate and that speaks to your child's unique needs and stage of development. I offer several examples of what this might look like in my new book *Stage Climbing: The Shortest Path to Your Highest Potential*. As your child becomes an adult your role as a parent will shift. For example, you can now become much less of a micromanager and disciplinarian, and more of a role model. Your child will now receive consequences from his or her own environment when poor choices are made, rather than you. This is a good thing. So relish your new role!

**The bottom line is that as a parent your greatest responsibility to your young adult children is to help them develop the skills to make it on their own. By avoiding these mistakes, you've taken a giant step in the right direction toward enjoying the stage of life where you can savour your child functioning successfully as an independent adult!**

http://www.huffingtonpost.com/michael-s-broder-phd/three-mistakes-helicopter-that-prevent-their-children_b_3741412.html

### General comprehension

1. Insert these titles of the three mistakes above the appropriate paragraphs.
   *Parenting in a way that's not age-appropriate*
   *Being in constant communication*
   *Maintaining full financial control*
2. The author believes that helicopter parents have the best intentions. So what is the problem?
3. Identify the advantage and disadvantage of mobile (cell) phones which the author describes.
4. Which unusual phrase does the author use to describe the mobile phone? Explain why the phrase is appropriate.
5. What is his recommendation concerning communication to the parents whose children are at college?
6. What justifications does he give for this recommendation?
7. How does he suggest that financial matters should be organised by parents with young adult children?
8. For the young adult, what is the result of the parent becoming more of a role model than a micromanager or disciplinarian?
9. What is the author's basic idea with regard to the parents' greatest responsibility?

## Text handling

True or false? Justify your answer with a relevant brief quote from the text.

1. The practice of helicopter parenting is rare.
2. Helicopter parents mean well.
3. With a mobile phone, parents can always be in contact with their child.
4. The author suggests that parents should maintain full financial control over their adult children.
5. As the child becomes an adult, the role of the parent does not change.

## Zoom in on grammar

**Sentence structure**

Good writing uses a variety of sentence structures: in particular, complex sentences enrich writing. So far in this book we have introduced a number of complex sentences. Look back over the 'helicopter parents' text and see how many complex sentences you can identify.

Remember, a complex sentence is made up of an independent clause, which can stand alone, and a dependent clause, which cannot stand alone. For example:

> 'While cell phones are great for safety purposes, they make it possible for parents to be in continual contact with their child'.

'While cell phones are great for safety purposes' is not an independent clause and it cannot stand alone as a sentence.

However, 'They make it possible for parents to be in continual contact with their child' is an independent clause and so can stand alone as a sentence.

## Grammar in context

**Complex sentences**

Match the beginnings of these complex sentences to the endings. Check your answers with the text.

1. If this sounds familiar and you find yourself 'hovering',...
2. While cell phones are great for safety purposes...
3. However, while remaining a safety net...
4. As your child becomes an adult...
5. By avoiding these mistakes, you've taken a giant step in the right direction toward enjoying the stage of life...

A. ... you also may want to allow them to have some 'skin in the game,' in order to learn financial responsibility.
B. ... where you can savour your child functioning successfully as an independent adult!
C. ... they make it possible for parents to be in continual contact with their child.
D. ... your role as a parent will shift.
E. ... here are a few common mistakes to be aware of and what you might want to consider instead.

## Interactive oral activity

Discuss the text and the three tips the author suggests with your group. Can you find more tips for the parents? Make a list together and be prepared to defend your choices when you present them to the class.

## Written work

Write an article for your school magazine, explaining the term 'helicopter parents' and pointing out the negative effects such behaviour may have.
Write between 250 and 300 words.

# 07 | The family

## 7.3 Home schooling

### Text 7.3.1 Home schooling in Australia

*Welcome to the world of home education – learning without school! We officially began educating our three children in 1985, when our eldest was five years. In truth, we had helped them learn what they need to learn as they grew and explored and discovered this amazing world since the moment they were each born! I am a passionate advocate of allowing children to learn unhindered by unnecessary stress and competition, meeting developmental needs in ways that suit their individual learning styles and preferences. We are a homeschooling, unschooling and natural learning family! There are hundreds of articles on this site to help you build confidence as a home educating family. I hope that your home educating adventure is as satisfying as ours was!*

**Beverley Paine**

### Teach your children at home!

You won't be alone. Many Australian families choose to educate their children at home. Homeschooling is both rewarding and enjoyable.

You don't need any special educational qualifications to teach your children at home. People from all backgrounds successfully teach their children – people with university degrees, trade certificates, small business owners, factory workers, people working from home, mums, dads – everyone has the ability to teach their children at home!

The only qualification you need is LOVE for your children. Do you qualify? Yes!

Schools can't, and don't, love your children. They can care for them, look after them and teach them, but the essential successful ingredient in home education is love.

### Love brings success to every learning situation.

From the love you offer your children will come the responsibility, commitment and drive to continuously strive for the best education available for your children. Your life-long dedication to your children's health and happiness will drive you to seek out best and most appropriate resources and to facilitate excellent quality learning opportunities and activities for your children. You, too, will become a life-long, passionate learner!

Home education is grounded in love and commitment. A parent's love for a child. A child's love for his or her parent. This is a solid foundation to grow educational success upon.

### Do you want to know more?

Are you interested in building strong, enduring and respectful family relationships? Are you interested in becoming involved in healthy, active and interested communities, dedicated to promoting the educational opportunities and well being of not only children, but adults too?

This web site is packed with information about how you and your family can explore the world of homeschooling. You'll find lots of great ideas and tips to help you navigate your way easily into a happy home learning environment.

### Homeschooling is empowering!

Become personally involved in your children's education. Be there to mark those special learning moments. To share in the delight of discovery. To guide your child through the trials and tribulations of childhood. The excitement, the awe, the anticipation, the wonder.

### Teach your children at home today!

"Little children love the world. That is why they are so good at learning about it. For it is love, not tricks and techniques of thought, that lies at the heart of all true learning. Can we bring ourselves to let children learn and grow through that love?"

**John Holt,** *How Children Learn*

http://www.homeschoolaustralia.com, August 4 2013, 'The Educating Parent'

## General comprehension

1. What does the author believe is the only qualification needed for parents to teach their children?
2. What do the children gain as a result of this, according to the author?
3. Which qualifications are unnecessary?
4. Do you agree with the author's description of home schooling? What disadvantages can you imagine?

## Text handling

Match these words and expressions from the text on the left to their meanings on the right.

| | | | |
|---|---|---|---|
| 1 | passionate advocate | A | difficulties |
| 2 | unhindered | B | necessary |
| 3 | ingredient | C | make possible |
| 4 | dedication | D | looking forward to something |
| 5 | facilitate | E | enthusiastic supporter |
| 6 | enduring | F | not prevented |
| 7 | trials and tribulations | G | part of something |
| 8 | awe | H | devotion |
| 9 | anticipation | I | lasting |
| 10 | essential | J | amazement |

> Home schooling is illegal in many countries of the world and only allowed in special circumstances in others.

# 07 The family

### Interactive oral activity

Discuss the following questions with your group and be prepared to share your ideas with the class.
- How would you describe the tone of the article? How does it make you feel?
- How does it differ from the previous article?
- Which do you find more convincing?

In your group make a list of the advantages and disadvantages of each system. Then decide: if you had to choose, which you would prefer?

### Written work

Write a persuasive speech to deliver to your peers, either in favour of or against home schooling. Plan your work carefully and think about what you are writing (remember the features of a speech), who you are writing for (which will determine the register) and why you are writing. Remember to use separate paragraphs for each main point. Write between 250 and 400 words.

## 7.4 Grandparents

### Text 7.4.1 The changing face of grandparenting

http://www.ageconcern.org.nz/happiness/family/changing-face-grandparenting

# Age Concern New Zealand

http://www.ageconcern.org.nz/happiness/family/changing-face-grandparenting

**Families and patterns of ageing are changing - and grandparents continue to have a vital role in today's families.**

### a) ............................................................................................................................

The relationship between a grandparent and grandchild can be really beneficial and rewarding for both the older person and the child. It's important to remember though, that grandparenting is not necessarily confined to the natural grandparents: a family friend or a neighbour might also step into this role.

*"My grandchildren have enriched my life, given me a sense of purpose and a desire to remain healthy for as long as I can." – Graham, aged 73*

The relationship between grandparent and grandchild is a special one; based on mutual love and affection, but a grandparent can also play several important roles within a family: advisor, spiritual mentor, teacher, safe haven, caregiver, story-teller, friend or family historian. Grandparenting can offer an older person a second chance to participate in parenting and enjoying children. There are usually fewer pressures and demands on grandparents which often means they are able to be more relaxed and tolerant with the grandchild and can help to support the parents.

**Suggestions for grandparents**

- Value your own wisdom and experience as parents
- Respect and support your children's parenting views
- Offer to look after your grandchildren to give their parents a break
- Discuss your availability for childminding and discuss your wishes about frequency of holiday visits
- Most important of all – have fun with your grandchildren!

### b) ............................................................................................................................

*"The nice thing about Nana and Grandad is that they say that we have two homes – one with our parents and one with them." – Thomas and James, aged 8*

Strong friendship bonds often develop between grandparents and grandchildren, helping to overcome generational barriers – the three generations grandparents/parents/grandchildren have much to learn from each other. Effective communication is essential to this learning. Listening to each other and respecting personal differences are particularly important.

**Some ideas on communicating with your grandchild**

- Listen to what the child is saying to you
- Avoid giving unasked-for advice
- Never yell at or hit a child
- Encourage the child to talk about their problems/feelings

# 07  The family

`http://www.ageconcern.org.nz/happiness/family/changing-face-grandparenting`

### c) ........................................................................................................

*"I find it difficult to say to my mother that I think she is sometimes too hard on the children, and it worries me that the children are often reluctant to visit her."* – Carol, aged 37

Parents can play an important role in influencing how well relationships work between the generations. Parents are often pivotal to the success of the grandparent/grandchild relationship but can sometimes feel trapped by the demands of both.

**Suggestions for parents**

- Keep the lines of communication open between the grandparent(s) and yourself
- Encourage the relationship between your children and their grandparents by letting them spend time together without you
- Never assume grandparents are ready-made childminders
- Make any important parenting rules clear, but give grandparents some leeway too
- Remember that children are very versatile and can adapt easily to different codes of behaviour

### d) ........................................................................................................

*"My koro is old on the outside and young on the inside."* – Arawhetu, aged 5

Many families today are made up of people from different ethnic backgrounds and religious beliefs. Discussing and respecting different customs, views and beliefs is important as it can help overcome problems, promote understanding and lead to positive and enriching life experiences for all family members.

**Useful suggestions**

- Ensure grandparents have an opportunity to share aspects of their culture and life experiences
- Ensure all family members talk about the features of differing cultures
- Encourage your grandchildren to learn the language and customs of their cultural backgrounds
- Learn the language and customs of your grandchildren's cultural backgrounds

### e) ........................................................................................................

*"To be a grandparent is an ever changing privilege."* – Mary, aged 72

Many families have grandchildren living throughout the world. A grandchild and a grandparent who have not met for some years may find it difficult relating to one another.

**Suggestions for maintaining a close relationship**

- Keep in contact frequently by phone, mail or by text – or, if you have Internet access, by Skype
- Exchange photographs regularly – via email, Facebook or mail
- Use whatever skills you have to make something special for your grandchild, e.g. sewing, painting, woodwork, cooking

http://www.ageconcern.org.nz/happiness/family/changing-face-grandparenting

**f)** ..................................................................................................................

*"If you would like a warm relationship with your grandchildren don't leave it to chance - praise, encourage and hug them at every opportunity."* – Ta'ase, aged 64

Marriage, the breakdown of a relationship or a remarriage can extend the family network, which can create new challenges and opportunities for families.

Role confusion can arise when several sets of grandparents become part of the same family. Grandparents may feel unsure of the boundaries of their role.

Open communication between all family members is the key to ensuring that relationships are nurtured and strengthened. Having the chance to share in the experience and wisdom of a new grandparent can be very positive for all the members of a family.

**g)** ..................................................................................................................

*"A grandparent is a parent who has a second chance."* – Rowan, aged 59

For some grandparents, raising grandchildren becomes a full time role when mum or dad can't care for the child, or have been found by the court not to be suitable as primary caregiver. This may occur for many reasons, the most common being substance abuse, violence and mental illness.

Raising grandchildren in these circumstances can be very challenging – emotionally, physically and financially. Support and information is available for grandparents in this situation – contact Grandparents Raising Grandchildren Trust on 0800 427 637.

There is no automatic right of access or custody by grandparents to their grandchildren. However, under the Care of Children Act 2004 a grandparent may seek an order from the Court concerning contact with, or care of, the child.

If you are experiencing access or custody difficulties, consult a lawyer or your community law office, who will advise you of the legal situation.

**h)** ..................................................................................................................

*"The notion that I have contributed to two generations gives me an inner sense of acknowledgement and reward."* – Dorothy, aged 81

As people are living longer and are healthier in their older years there should be many years to share with grandchildren – and great-grandchildren!

© 2013 Age Concern New Zealand Inc
http://www.ageconcern.org.nz/happiness/family/changing-face-grandparenting

# 07 The family

> Respect for elders, such as grandparents, varies in cultures around the world. For example, older people are greatly respected in the cultures of Korea, Japan, China, India, the Mediterranean countries, and many others.

## General comprehension

1. Insert the paragraph titles in the appropriate places in the text.

   | | |
   |---|---|
   | Changing families | Cultural differences |
   | Grandparents raising grandchildren | Grandparenting from a distance |
   | A final thought | Parents' role |
   | Inter-generational bonds | What is a grandparent? |

2. What is the basis of a good relationship between grandparents and grandchildren?
3. What are the advantages of grandparenting compared to parenting?
4. What do grandchildren gain from their grandparents?
5. Which two key factors are important in effective communication between the three generations?
6. What problems can occur for parents in the grandchild–grandparent relationship?
7. How can problems be dealt with successfully if family members have different ethnic backgrounds or religious beliefs?
8. In your opinion, or from your experience, which of the three suggestions for maintaining a close relationship is the most useful?
9. When is it likely that grandparents will take on the role of raising grandchildren?

## Text handling

1. Match the words from the text on the left to their meanings on the right.

   | | | | | | | | |
   |---|---|---|---|---|---|---|---|
   | I | confined to | IV | nurtured | A | central | D | limited to |
   | II | yell | V | circumstances | B | situations | E | shout loudly |
   | III | pivotal | | | C | taken good care of | | |

2. True or false? Justify your answer with a relevant brief quotation from the text.
   a) A family friend or a neighbour can also act as a grandparent.
   b) A grandparent can play many roles in a family.
   c) The different generations – grandchild, parent and grandparent – are so different that they cannot learn from each other.
   d) Parents play no part in the relationship between grandparent and grandchild.
   e) Parents should give grandparents strict rules with no exceptions allowed.

## Zoom in on grammar

**The imperative**

Note that the tips listed in the article above always start with a verb in the imperative, the command form, with no subject:

   Value...                Offer...                Respect...

This is also the way instructions are often given, for example, to put a newly bought gadget together, or to make a cake. The instructions are not given as a flowing text, but as a series of bullet points, each beginning with the verb.

## Grammar in context

**The imperative**

There are no specific tips offered to the grandchildren regarding their role and relationships with their parents and grandparents. Write a set of tips, in the same form, for grandchildren. Remember to begin each tip with a verb in the imperative.

## Interactive oral activity

Discuss the role of grandparents you know and include any ideas on how relationships could be improved after reading this text. For example, think about different ways for the generations to communicate and share information. Can the grandchildren help the grandparents with technology in other ways? How can the grandparents support the grandchildren?

# Exam practice

## Changing face of childhood as nurseries take over 'family time'

by John Bingham, Social Affairs Editor, February 16 2013

YOUNG children are spending almost 40 per cent more time with strangers than in the mid-1990s as "formal" childcare increasingly takes the place of family time, official figures show.

According to the Office for National Statistics [ONS], children under five now spend an average of 668 hours a year in paid childcare – up from just 490 hours in 1995.

It follows a drive to enable more women to work and increased Government support for childcare.

But experts said that the reduction in direct contact between parents and children, particularly in the vital early years of their lives, could be storing up problems for the future.

They said it reflected a move to "formalise" and "institutionalise" childhood. The use of formal childcare has increased for all age groups since the mid 1990s – rising by an average of 8.3 per cent. But among the under-fives the average number of hours is up by 36.4 per cent in that period.

It equates to an average of just over two and a half hours of formal childcare per day per child, excluding weekends. But that figure includes many children who are still cared for full-time by a parent, meaning that for others the average is much higher.

Despite a growing reliance on grandparents as working parents try to juggle commitments, the total amount of informal – meaning unpaid – childcare has declined slightly over the period. Nevertheless, according to the ONS, it would be worth an estimated £343 billion a year – almost a quarter of GDP. Its value has almost trebled since the mid 1990s, largely reflecting the soaring cost of childcare.

Experts said the shift towards greater reliance on nurseries and childminders reflects increasing demand in the face of a "long hours" culture. But it also coincides with the growth of a more formal style of supervision with pre-arranged "playdates" replacing opportunities for spontaneous play.

Dr Agnes Nairn, the author of a landmark Unicef report which compared childhood in Britain with that other European countries, said: "Everything is being formalised ... we are all 'hardworking families' so maybe this is about 'hardworking children'."

Sue Palmer, author of the book *Toxic Childhood*, said that while it is important for children over the age of two-and-a-half to spend some time with other children, the decline in "family time" could be storing up social problems for the future.

"Family time is very, very important for children, it is just building a relationship between parent and child which underpins effective discipline and children's communication skills.

"These are very basic social and developmental things, we took it for granted in the past that they will happen because there always has been these opportunities for interaction.

"We don't know what we are losing – these are the building blocks of many human skills, the basic skills of building a relationship, the soft skills which underpin people's well-being."

She added that research in the US had found evidence that "empathy" had declined among college students over a generation.

"Sometimes I wonder whether the problems that we have at the moment in the health service and the culture of care, how much of that is related to the fact that we have really undervalued the family for such a long time," she said.

*http://www.telegraph.co.uk/health/children_shealth/9873008/Changing-face-of-childhood-as-nurseries-takes-over-family-time.html*

# 07 The family

### Exercises

Answer the following questions.

1. Which two factors have led to the increase in the amount of time children under five spend in paid childcare?

   ................................................................................................................................

2. What do experts believe will be the result of less parent–children contact time?

   ................................................................................................................................

3. Which age group is most affected by the developments since the mid-1990s?

   ................................................................................................................................

4. Why do experts believe there has been a shift towards greater reliance on nurseries and childminders?

   ................................................................................................................................

5. What other effect has the growth of formal supervision, rather than informal supervision in the family, had?

   ................................................................................................................................

6. What does Sue Palmer believe is being lost?

   ................................................................................................................................

7. Why does she believe empathy has declined among college students?

   ................................................................................................................................

8. How does she explain the problems in the health service and the culture of care?

   ................................................................................................................................

9. Find words in the text which can be meaningfully replaced with the following.

   A   make possible            ..........................

   B   very important           ..........................

   C   become less              ..........................

   D   increased threefold      ..........................

   E   rapidly rising           ..........................

   F   slight movement          ..........................

**10** True or false? Justify your answer with a brief relevant quotation from the text.

**A** The reduction in direct contact between parents and children will have no negative effects.

...................................................................................

**B** Among the under-fives the average number of hours in formal childcare has increased by about a third since the mid-1990s.

...................................................................................

**C** People are working longer hours now so have become more dependent on nurseries and childminders.

...................................................................................

**D** Children in formal supervision have fewer opportunities for spontaneous play.

...................................................................................

## Further exercises

### Interactive oral activity

Interview your partner about how much they can remember of their early childhood, and ask them to describe any lasting memories. As they are remembering and explaining, be sure to ask any questions necessary for clarification or more information.

## Written work

Write a diary entry as a result of the reading and group discussion, reflecting on your early childhood. Remember, a diary entry is an informal piece of writing that normally would only be read by you, so it may be personal and reflective. Write between 200 and 300 words.

# 08 The English language

## Objectives

- To consider the English language and its role in global communication
- To discuss the factors influencing the choice of a second language
- To revise uses of the –*ing* form
- To practise writing in varying text types: an email in informal English, a formal article and a semi-formal blog
- To practise using 'some' and 'any' in positive and negative sentences
- To practise interviewing others about their experiences and views

**Opposite** What is your mother tongue?

# 8.1 English as a global language

## Text 8.1.1 English as a global language

### Original influences from overseas

The English language can be traced back to the mixture of Anglo-Saxon dialects that came to these shores 1500 years ago. Since then it has been played with, altered and transported around the world in many different forms. The language we now recognise as English first became the dominant language in Great Britain during the Middle Ages and in Ireland during the eighteenth and nineteenth centuries. From there it has been exported in the mouths of colonists and settlers to all four corners of the globe. 'International English', 'World English' or 'Global English' are terms used to describe a type of 'general English' that has, over the course of the twentieth century, become a worldwide means of communication.

### American English

The first permanent English-speaking colony was established in North America in the early 1600s. The Americans soon developed a form of English that differed in a number of ways from the language spoken back in the British Isles. In some cases older forms were retained – the way most Americans pronounce the 'r' sound after a vowel in words like start, north, nurse and letter is probably very similar to the pronunciation in 17th century England. Similarly, the distinction between past tense got and past participle gotten still exists in American English but has been lost in most dialects of the UK.

After the USA received independence from Great Britain in 1776 any sense of who 'owned' and set the 'correct rules' for the English Language became increasingly blurred. The publications of Webster's dictionary in 1786 and 1828 were enormously successful and established differences in spelling such as color and center and were therefore major steps towards scholarly acceptance that British and American English were becoming separate entities.

### English around the world

Like American English, English in Australia, New Zealand and South Africa has evolved such that they are distinct from British English. However,

# 08 The English language

cultural and political ties have meant that until relatively recently British English has acted as the benchmark for representing 'standardised' English – spelling tends to adhere to British English conventions, for instance. As with most of the Commonwealth, British English is the model on which, for example, Indian English or Nigerian English is based. In the Caribbean and especially in Canada, however, historical links with the UK compete with geographical, cultural and economic ties with the USA, so that some aspects of the local varieties of English follow British norms and others reflect US usage.

## An international language

English is also hugely important as an international language and plays an important part even in countries where the UK has historically had little influence. It is learnt as the principal foreign language in most schools in Western Europe. It is also an essential part of the curriculum in far-flung places like Japan and South Korea, and is increasingly seen as desirable by millions of speakers in China. Prior to WWII, most teaching of English as a foreign language used British English as its model, and textbooks and other educational resources were produced here in the UK for use overseas. This reflected the UK's cultural dominance and its perceived 'ownership' of the English Language.

Since 1945, however, the increasing economic power of the USA and its unrivalled influence in popular culture has meant that American English has become the reference point for learners of English in places like Japan and even to a certain extent in some European countries. British English remains the model in most Commonwealth countries where English is learnt as a second language.

However, as the history of English has shown, this situation may not last indefinitely. The increasing commercial and economic power of countries like India, for instance, might mean that Indian English will one day begin to have an impact beyond its own borders.

http://www.bl.uk/learning/langlit/sounds/case-studies/minority-ethnic
© The British Library Board

## General comprehension

1. According to the text, how old is the English language?
2. Has English always functioned as a global language?
3. What historical event influenced the change of the dominant form of British English to American English for many learners around the world?
4. Give some examples of what the phrase 'the USA and its unrivalled influence in popular culture' refers to.
5. What event in the 18th century first established American English as a different form of English?
6. What factors could influence the increase in the significance of Indian English as a language used in international communication?

## Text handling

1. Look at the following idiomatic phrases from the text and explain in your own words what you think they mean.
   a) 'exported in the mouths of colonists'
   b) 'four corners of the globe'
   c) 'scholarly acceptance'
   d) 'British English… as the benchmark for representing "standardised" English'
   e) 'far-flung places'

2. Match the words from the text on the left with the correct definitions on the right.

   | | | | |
   |---|---|---|---|
   | I | overseas | A | coastline |
   | II | shores | B | difference |
   | III | retained | C | influence |
   | IV | distinction | D | abroad |
   | V | blurred | E | first in importance |
   | VI | benchmark | F | kept |
   | VII | adhere | G | indistinct |
   | VIII | principal | H | follow |
   | IX | unrivalled | I | without competition |
   | X | impact | J | reference point |

3. True or false? Justify your answer with a relevant brief quotation from the text.

   **Example:** The English language is derived from Anglo Saxon. TRUE. Justification: It 'can be traced back to the mixture of Anglo-Saxon dialects'.
   a) The English that we speak today has changed considerably since its origin.
   b) English is only an important language in the UK's former colonies.
   c) English as a foreign language is learnt in Japanese and Korean schools.
   d) After the USA received independence from Great Britain in 1776, the rules of American English were fixed.
   e) Indian English may one day have a global influence.

4. What do these underlined pronouns refer to in the text?
   a) Paragraph 1: 'From there it has been exported'
   b) Paragraph 4: 'they are distinct from British English'
   c) Paragraph 5: 'used British English as its model'
   d) Paragraph 5: 'its perceived "ownership" of the English language'

## Interactive oral activity

The text suggests that economic power is the biggest influence on a language being spoken as a second language by people in many countries. In small groups, discuss this idea – say how far you accept this suggestion and what other factors influence the choice of a second language. Give examples from your experiences in your own countries.

Remember to include all group members in the discussion. If someone is hesitant or silent, you may say, 'What do you think?' or 'Would you like to say what you think about this?'. When other people speak, don't forget to react by saying, for example, 'I agree with that', 'That's an interesting point, I hadn't thought about that' or 'I understand what you mean, but I'm afraid I can't agree with you'. You must always remain polite and respectful. However, if someone is dominating the conversation, you can say, 'Just a minute, I think I'll have to interrupt you'.

# 08 The English language

## Zoom in on grammar

**Positive and negative sentences**

In general, we use *some* (and combinations such as somebody/someone/something) in positive sentences and *any* (anybody/anyone/anything) in negative sentences.

**Positive sentences**

We bought *some* CDs.
I'm busy, I have *some* work to finish.
I can see *somebody* in the garden.
I'm bored, I want *something* to read.

**Negative sentences**

We didn't buy *any* CDs.
I'm happy. I haven't got *any* work to do.
I can't see *anybody* in the garden.
I don't have *anything* to read.

**We also use 'any' when we make questions.**

Have you got *any* coins for the parking meter?
Has *anybody* seen my pencil case?
Have you got *anything* to drink?

But we use *some* in a question when we expect the answer to be *yes*. We also use *some* when we offer something – or ask for something.

[I see my friend holding his ankle.] What's up? Have you got *something* wrong with your foot?
Do you want *some* tea?
Do you want *some* of my sandwich?

## Grammar in context

**Positive and negative sentences**

Complete these sentences with 'some' or 'any', or the combinations 'anyone', 'someone', etc., as explained above.

1  I didn't have _____ paper to write on, so I borrowed _____ .
2  Can I have _____ more paper? I need to rewrite my text.
3  Last night I was too tired to do _____ homework.
4  If there is _____ vocabulary in the text you don't understand, check with your teacher.
5  Next week we are going to the museum to study _____ 18th-century documents.
6  Do you have _____ friends in school who speak your mother tongue?
7  Kelly is not in school today; do _____ of her friends know why?
8  It's hot in here; does _____ mind if I open the window?
9  Why are you rummaging in your bag, are you looking for _____ ?
10 I've just made a cake; would you like _____ ?

# 8.2 The history of English

Text 8.2.1 The history of the English language in 100 places

## A project tells the story of the English language through 100 locations, starting in Suffolk and ending in Vienna – with stops in Hastings and Beijing and on the moon along the way

From a piece of farmland in Suffolk, to Vienna, via Hastings, Beijing and even the moon – it may sound like an unusual journey. But these are the places, identified in a new study, which have helped to create, shape and spread the English language around the globe – and beyond. They have all been included in a new project which aims to tell the story of the language through 100 locations. It has been conducted by the English Project, a charity devoted to study of the subject. The scheme was launched in 2010, with a request for the public to help, by providing suggested locations. That phase has now been completed and the first 100 locations are described in a new book, *A History Of The English Language In 100 Places*.

It starts in Undley Common at Lakenheath, Suffolk, in 475 where arguably the first use of English was found on a bracteate – a thin piece of metal worn as jewellery – unearthed by a farmer, and ends in the Austrian capital, in 2012, where the University of Vienna is assembling a database of recordings of more than one million words of English, spoken by people for whom it is not their first language, in order to analyse trends. Between the two, the book tells how English developed on these shores, before spreading around the world in countries like America, India, and Australia, and was then taken up in other parts of the globe where it is not a first language.

Some time in the last decade, the number of people speaking English as a second language is thought to have overtaken those who speak it as a first language. Stops along the way include Hastings, in 1066, when the Norman Conquest led to French influence on the language, and Helsinki, in 1993, where text messaging was developed. Other locations have been chosen to signify a range of historical figures, such as William Shakespeare and William Caxton, movements of people and emerging technology which have helped to shape the language.

For more information on the English Project, go to www.pearsonhotlinks.com, enter the title or ISBN of this book and click on Chapter 8.

Bill Lucas, a professor at the University of Winchester, said: "The language has developed and continuously evolved since its beginnings, some time in the early fifth century. And we are very keen to explore just how significant a role geography has had in these changes, "What began as the language of the Angles, Saxons and Jutes on a small island has become a global property. It is owned and shaped by almost two billion English speakers across the Earth. Through an extraordinary combination of accidents, conquests and technological advances, English is now the language of the world."

# 08 The English language

### York, 866
Norse-speaking Danes occupy the city and establish settlements across the east of the country, bringing with them words which enter the language. There are at least nine hundred words of Norse origin in standard modern English, among them 'egg', 'husband', and 'leg'. Only the French have had such a profound influence on English as the Danes.

### Chancery Street, London, c1419
A letter from King Henry V, on campaign in France, is sent back to his government in England updating them on the latest intelligence he had received about fears of an attack from Scotland. It is thought to have been read out to nobles in the Lord Chancellor's office, increasingly known as the Chancery. Unlike correspondence from previous kings, written in Latin or French, this one was written in English.

### Bruges, 1474
The site of the printing of the first book in English, The Recuyell of the Historyes of Troye. William Caxton, who had translated it himself from French, later returned to England where he set up a printing press in Westminster.

### Northolt, 1551
John Hart wrote The Opening of the Unreasonable Writing of our Inglish Toung. Never published in his life time, it was about English spelling, and it is thought to be the first systematic study of the subject. He suggested spelling should be phonologically based. Thirty-five years later, in Chichester, a schoolmaster published a pamphlet by William Bullokar: Or rather too be saied hiz abbreuiation of hiz grammar for English, extracted out-of hiz grammar at-larg. More generally known as Pamphlet for Grammar, it was the first guide of its kind.

### Nîmes, 1695
Hard-wearing cotton fabrics produced in the French town, "serge de Nîmes", entered the English language in around 1695 as "denim".

The town has been included in the list to show how place names have been used to create new words. Other toponyms, as they are known, include: bungalow, a corruption of 'Bengal', describing the kind of cottages built by European settlers in that part of India; hamburger – minced beef from the German city of Hamburg in the nineteenth century; and magenta, the distinctive crimson colour discovered at the time of the battle of Magenta in Italy, in 1859.

### Salford, 1850
The Royal Museum and Public Library opened in Salford, with 10,000 books. Considered the first public library, it had more than 1,200 visitors a day in its first year. The same year, the Public Libraries Act was passed in England, enabling boroughs to levy a tax to provide free public libraries. The institutions are credited with massively increasing access to reading.

### New York, 1913
The first crossword appears in the New York World. The first in Britain followed in 1922, in Pearson's Magazine. It is included to show the popularity of written word puzzles, which date back to Roman times.

### The Empire State Building, 1941
The first television advertisements – for Bulova watches – are broadcast by WX2XBS – later NBC – from its transmitter on the building, during a baseball game between the Brooklyn Dodgers and the Philadelphia Phillies. Several trade names have themselves become words, including Hoover, Sellotape, Thermos and, more recently, Google.

http://www.telegraph.co.uk/education/educationnews/10405963/The-history-of-the-English-language-in-100-places.html

## General comprehension

1. How was the information for the book collected?
2. At what point in history did English become a language spoken by more people in the world as a second language than as a first language?
3. According to the text, what is a 'toponym'?
4. In the text about Northolt in 1551, what do you notice about the quotation from the mentioned text?

## Text handling

Match the words taken from the text on the left with the words or phrases with similar meanings on the right. There are more options than you need.

**Example:** aims (paragraph 1)   **B**

1. devoted (paragraph 1)
2. unearthed (paragraph 2)
3. signify (paragraph 3)
4. emerging (paragraph 3)

A developing
B intends
C religious
D committed
E buried
F dug up
G represent
H exciting

## Zoom in on grammar

### Using –*ing* clauses

A clause is a part of a sentence. Some sentences have two clauses:

> Feeling hungry, I bought a hamburger.

In this sentence, 'I bought a hamburger' is the main clause. 'Feeling hungry' is the –*ing* clause. In the above text you can find this example:

> A project tells the story of the English language through 100 locations, *starting* in Suffolk and *ending* in Vienna.

When two things happen at the same time, you can use the –*ing* form for one of the verbs. The main clause often comes first:

> She was sitting in the common room *working* on her computer. (= she was sitting and she was working)
>
> She ran out of the room *crying*. (= she was crying when she ran out of the room)

In the above text you can find this example:

> Norse-speaking Danes occupy the city and establish settlements across the east of the country, *bringing* with them words which enter the language.

# Written work (HL)

Imagine you are in an English-speaking country where you are spending some time. Write an email explaining some of the positive and negative experiences you have had speaking English. Who are the people who help you most?

Your email will be informal but you must show that you have a wide range of vocabulary and can use complex sentences. This is what you need to show in the final examination.

Write between 350 and 400 words.

# 08 The English language

## 8.3 The mother tongue

Text 8.3.1 Why your mother tongue is important

**blog**

# The mother tongue

The first language through which I perceived the world was Hindi – the language of Northern India. As I entered kindergarten, I distinctly remember a classroom atmosphere of condescension towards my language. I'm sure that many other schools were different, but that was the tone in my school. As I spent more time in that environment, I slowly began to lose fluency in my own ancestral language. Hindi eventually became a memory stored in the back of my mind. Like so many other children of immigrants in America, English became the only language I could speak fluently.

Language loss among immigrant cultures in the United States is a symptom of many forces operating together. Mass media, the education system, and employment requirements are all parts of the reason. However, I believe the root cause lies with the ugly legacy of centuries of colonialism. Many non-white peoples have been made to feel that their language and culture is somehow lesser.

Eliminating the language of a culture was a primary strategy used by colonialists to assimilate, fragment, and ultimately control peoples. In the United States, Native Americans were taken from their tribes and placed in English schools where they were not allowed to speak their own language. The modern day language loss of so many immigrant children like myself shows that some element of that assimilationist attitude still exists in American schools – even if it's not as overt as before.

Language is like a programming for the mind – it shapes our perception of ourselves and our world. Each culture's language is the embodiment of its unique outlook on life. When I lost Hindi, I lost the key to identifying with my own people – like losing the ability to tune into a certain frequency.

Without our ancestral languages, we may look like one another, but we've lost one of our deepest common bonds. We become isolated from our communities – unable to relate to each other all that differently than we would with a white person, or someone from another culture. A unique and special bond forms when two Armenian-Americans meet and can converse in Armenian, or when Korean-Americans converse in Korean.

Our language unites us. Speaking our language among our people keeps our culture alive, gives us pride in ourselves, and strengthens our bonds. This is why preserving our ancestral languages is key to uplifting our condition in America: language unites us and united we are strong. Divided we are weak.

Although personal sentiments toward immigrant cultures have improved since the time of legislation like the Chinese Exclusion Act, we all know that we're still far from having a fair and equitable system. Non-white communities in America still face systemic prejudice in almost every aspect of their interaction with the establishment. In addition to this, we have less wealth, less social and political power, less access to fresh food, and we tend to live in more polluted inland and urban areas with dirtier water. Our condition needs to be improved. Language loss is fragmenting us. Preserving our languages will help us to maintain more cohesive and strong communities. And strong communities can advocate for themselves.

Children of immigrants like me were socialized as minorities within a majority white culture. Growing up, I feel that they made it seem like European-American culture, historically and currently, has everything right and is always on the path towards progress. On the other hand, cultures like my own had gotten it wrong. It felt like they were saying that we had fallen behind and our cultures were backward.

When I started college at Berkeley, I took it upon myself to relearn Hindi. I took Hindi classes at Berkeley, and arranged to study for a semester abroad in India, during which time I studied more Hindi. After graduating, I went back to the same language school that I went to during my semester abroad, and spent nearly half a year single-mindedly focused on learning Hindi. I regained my verbal fluency completely, and now I can also read and write Hindi with proficiency.

I think that when you know your ancestral language, you can fully understand your culture. You can see that in many spheres, your culture possesses profound wisdom and insight. For example, in the Hindi language, the words for tomorrow and yesterday are the same word: "kal." This reflects the Indian culture's cyclical view of time, in contrast to the Western conception of time as linear. Indians believe in rebirth – not only of people but of the universe itself. During my time in India when I was fully immersed in Hindi, even dreaming in Hindi, I felt how the rhythm of the language made the rhythm of my life different. Life was slower and more musical. It was and is uplifting for me to tune into this different frequency through language.

Connecting with the ancient and historical truths of my culture – which are embedded in the language – has been empowering for me. And I think it would be empowering for any immigrant American to maintain this bond with their culture and community.

*http://www.huffingtonpost.com/rohit-kumar/an-indianamerican-relearn_b_3111708.html*

### General comprehension

1. What did the author feel was the reaction of his school to his native language?
2. According to the text, what three factors influence language loss among immigrants?
3. Why did colonial powers force the people in the countries they colonised to stop speaking their own language?
4. What are the consequences when a speaker's ancestral language is lost?
5. When the author relearnt his ancestral language, Hindi, what insights did he gain into his culture?

# 08 The English language

### Text handling

1. With a partner, find these words in the text and together examine the context to work out the meaning. Afterwards you may check in a dictionary to see how well you worked it out.

   a) condescension
   b) legacy
   c) to assimilate
   d) to fragment
   e) to converse
   f) prejudice
   g) spheres
   h) cyclical
   i) linear
   j) uplifting

2. In the text, notice how verbs and related nouns are used. For example: 'to perceive' and 'perception' can be found. What are the nouns that belong to the following verbs?

   a) assimilate
   b) condescend
   c) converse
   d) lose
   e) believe
   f) isolate
   g) connect
   h) remember
   i) decide
   j) speak

3. True or false? Justify your answer with a relevant brief quotation from the text.

   a) The author felt that school caused him to lose mastery of his own mother tongue.
   b) According to Rohit Kumar, the reason for language loss among immigrants in America is predominantly the school environment.
   c) Native Americans lost their mastery of their language because they wanted to learn English.
   d) Speaking the mother tongue is a way for immigrants in America to improve their self-confidence.
   e) Immigrants of the author's generation were made to feel that their culture was less worthy than the European-American culture.
   f) The author feels that by learning Hindi he gained an inner strength.

## Written work

As a Language B student, your first language is not English. Write a reply to Rohit Kumar in blog form, telling him about your experiences of keeping up or losing your ancestral language. Keep the register semi-formal, but write carefully and communicate your feelings clearly by giving examples and details of your experience.

Write between 350 and 400 words.

### Interactive oral activity

Plan to interview some students and teachers at your school who do not have English as their first language. Decide what questions you will ask them – based on some of the points from the text and new ideas you may have. You may include details of their mother tongue and how much they speak it, the influence of English on their ancestral language, or how they feel when they speak their mother tongue compared to when they speak English. Draw up a list of questions, then find time to carry out your interview as a homework activity. In the next class, be prepared to report your findings to the other students.

# 8.4 Lost in translation

## Text 8.4.1 Getting the English right

The English language is spoken by over 700 million individuals around the world. In the book *Lost in Translation*, the author, Charlie Croker, takes an affectionate look at some of the unintentionally humorous results of people struggling to get right the complexities of a language they are on the way to mastering.

Here is the introduction to Charlie Croker's funny book *Lost in Translation*.

## Introduction

You're in a far-flung corner of the globe, it's the early hours of the morning and you've just checked into your hotel after an exhausting flight. The prospect of a seven-thirty business breakfast is filling you with dread, and you've a nagging feeling you forgot to pack your toothbrush. But then you notice a sign in the corner of the bathroom: 'Please to bathe inside the tub'. Despite your tiredness you can't help but smile. Yes, you're Lost in Translation.

All over the world, from Beijing to Buenos Aires, in hotels and restaurants and taxis and zoos (yes, zoos), these priceless nuggets of verbal dottiness lie in wait, ready to brighten the lives of the jaded voyagers who chance upon them. They are the reward points on your Travel loyalty card. They are the treats we earn for enduring mislaid luggage, deep-vein thrombosis and stony-faced stewardesses. Never failing to amuse, they put a spring in our step with nothing more complicated than an off-balance vocabulary and some iffy syntax. It's English Jim, but not as we know it.

Sometimes you can tell what is meant: 'Our wine list leaves nothing to hope for.' Sometimes you can't: 'Nobody is allowed to sit on both sides of the boat.' Occasionally you're left in doubt as to whether the language is wrong or not. A notice in one Shanghai hotel reads: 'It is forbidden to play the recorder in guest rooms.' Do they really mean 'recorder'? If so, why? Has there been an epidemic of people playing that instrument? Do the Chinese take particular offence at it, even more than we do? Is that possible?

A final word of caution. Amused as we are by other nation's fumblings with our language, we should never forget that their English is infinitely better than our Thai/Polish/Vietnamese. Indeed, sometimes it's better than our English – you'll find several examples in these pages from

English-speaking nations, whether from the land of Shakespeare or the Land of the Free.

So enjoy. Go forth, take the plunge… and get thoroughly Lost in Translation.'

## Can you work out what these signs mean?

### Travelling by plane:
- Instructions on a Korean flight:
  *Upon arrival at Kimpo and Kimahie Airport, please wear your clothes.*
- At Heathrow Airport, London, UK:
  *No electric people carrying vehicles past this point.*

### In the hotel:
- Qatar:
  *Please do not use the lift when it is not working.*
- In a hotel cloakroom, Berlin, Germany:
  *Please hang yourself here.*
- Italy:
  *This hotel is renowned for its peace and solitude. In fact, crowds from all over the world flock here to enjoy its solitude.*
- Taipei, Taiwan:
  *If there is anything we can do to assist and help you, please do not contact us.*
- France:
  *Wondering what to wear? A sports jacket may be worn to dinner, but no trousers.*

### In the restaurant:
- China:
  *Cold shredded children in spicy sauce*
- Cairo, Egypt:
  *French fried ships*

公共旅游卫生间
Public Toilet Tourism →

## Text handling

Check the meaning of these words and phrases from the introduction to *Lost in Translation*: choose the word which best fits the meaning in the text.

1. a far-flung corner of the globe
   a) a disorganised place
   b) a war zone
   c) a distant place

2. dread
   a) hunger
   b) tiredness
   c) dismay

3. priceless
   a) amusing
   b) expensive
   c) strange

4. nuggets
   a) small pieces
   b) little nuts
   c) examples

5. jaded voyagers
   a) old planes
   b) tired travellers
   c) Asian travellers

6. iffy syntax
   a) wrong spelling
   b) foreign phrase
   c) strange word order

7. infinitely
   a) much
   b) completely
   c) endlessly

8. the Land of the Free
   a) Europe
   b) Australia
   c) the United States of America

## Interactive oral activity

Examine the examples from *Lost in Translation* with a partner. Can you identify the errors of language that make the signs humorous? Make a list of the errors and then your suggestions for corrections.

## Written work

There are a number of websites where you can find examples of mis-translated English. A couple of them can be accessed through www.pearsonhotlinks.com. Use these websites, as well as similar ones, to find some examples of mis-translated English, and try to guess what the instructions or phrases are actually supposed to mean. Present your findings in a table.

To access the websites mentioned in the text, go to www.pearsonhotlinks.com, enter the title or ISBN of this book and click on Chapter 8.

## Exam practice

# Esperanto – an alternative to English

Even as a young man, Lazar Zamenhof, from Białystok in Poland, decided at the end of the 19th century that the ethnic divisions in his country would be lessened if the people spoke a language that was not identified with one particular political group, and he thought a completely new language would be the answer. He therefore set about creating a language and Esperanto was born. Zamenhof was convinced that his idea of a politically neutral language would bring cultures together because no single mother tongue would be dominant; he believed that dominant languages had a divisive affect on groups of people speaking a number of languages. In designing this new language, Zamenhof based it on numerous European languages: incorporating words that are already common to most of them, for instance, photograph, theatre, telephone, or tea. The grammar structures were simplified to make it easier to learn and certain difficulties were

## 08 The English language

therefore eliminated. For example, there is no indefinite article (a/an) – only the definite article (the) and verbs do not change for person or number.

Despite a general perception that there are few speakers of Esperanto around the world today, there are in fact a relatively large number of speakers – the Esperanto Society speaks of two million speakers worldwide. Some famous supporters and speakers of the language include the Russian author Leo Tolstoy, former British Prime Minister Harold Wilson, American actor (Star Trek) William Shatner and British actor Peter Ustinov. It is difficult to offer Esperanto in a school curriculum because there is no culture to interact with and there is no fund of literary texts for students to read and study. However, there are schools that offer Esperanto; in fact in over 28 countries around the world an estimated 600 schools offer pupils the opportunity to learn this language.

Enthusiasts who have endeavoured to have Esperanto recognised as a language of international relations have met with resistance from countries with an already acknowledged international status. In the 1920s numerous countries, among them France, objected when a proposal was made at the League of Nations (today called the United Nations) to adopt Esperanto for international communications. Their argument was that a language with an established and recognised position in the world was better than a new language with no cultural heritage.

The Esperanto Society claims that Esperanto has established itself in the top hundred of spoken languages (the worldwide number of languages is generally estimated to be 6,800).

### Exercises

Answer the following questions.

1. In 1887 why did Lazar Zamenhof feel his country needed a new language?

   ..................................................................

2. What did Zamenhof mean when he talked about the need for 'a politically neutral language'?

   ..................................................................

3. What aspects of languages were eliminated from Esperanto and for what reason?

   ..................................................................

4. According to the text, what is the main reason why Esperanto is infrequently put on school curriculums?

   ..................................................................

5   Why did Esperanto supporters lose their appeal to have the language recognised as a language of international communication?

    ............................................................................................

6   Which word in lines 10–15 means 'causing disagreement'?

    ............................................................................................

7   Which word in lines 35–40 means 'a list of courses to be studied'?

    ............................................................................................

8   Which word in lines 45–50 means 'tried to do something'?

    ............................................................................................

## Further exercises

### Interactive oral activity

Find out some further information about Esperanto. Take a look at the website of the Esperanto Society. Consider some points that support using Esperanto and also arguments against it. Make notes, but in your discussion you may only use up to ten bullet points. Discuss the advantages of Esperanto, its origins and the reasoning behind its development, and its chances of survival. You should also think about the advantages and disadvantages of using English and the reasons for its status as a global language.

Your aim should be to come to general agreement in your group. You therefore have to listen to the opinions of each member of the group, and either agree with them or convince them that your ideas are more relevant.

For more information on Esperanto, go to www.pearsonhotlinks.com, enter the title or ISBN of this book and click on Chapter 8.

## Written work

You have been asked to write an article on languages for your school magazine. You decide to conduct an interview and write up the questions and answers.

Base your interview on some of the points you have explored in this unit. There will first be an introductory paragraph about the theme of the interview and the person being interviewed – maybe a student.

Write between 250 and 300 words.

Below are some ideas you could explore.

- Alternatives to learning English in the future as a global language and the feasibility of this alternative.
- The interviewee's own experiences of language learning and their mother tongue.
- What languages are used at home and for work?
- Does it seem that some languages are considered to be more prestigious?
- If the interviewee speaks more than two languages, which language do they use when they are dreaming? Or counting or writing shopping lists?

# 09 Advertising

**Opposite** What kind of world do we live in?

## Objectives
- To discuss the impact of advertising
- To revise modal verbs
- To review the zero conditional
- To revise phrasal verbs
- To discuss connections between advertising and TOK

## 9.1 Advertising in the 21st century

### Text 9.1.1 Message to advertisers: It's the year of newspapers… going mobile

http://www.inma.org/blogs/integrated-advertising-sales/post.cfm/message-to-advertisers-it-s-the-year-of-newspapers-on-mobile

### Industry leaders say a market leader has not yet stepped forward to lead the charge in developing a mobile marketplace. Newspapers should strike while the iron is still hot. by Suzanne Raitt, June 20 2013

What they meant to say is: Newspapers on mobile are hot. More than half of the digital population visits newspaper Web sites, according to the World Association of Newspapers. And those consumers use one or more mobile devices to do so.

In Canada (I imagine similar numbers will be found elsewhere), we have found two out of every six newspaper media visits each day are via mobile (tablet or phone).

If you look at tablet newspaper readers specifically, they visit newspaper sites/apps four times in a day. And mobile phone newspaper readers (looking at our sites or getting updates via e-mail) read us [newspapers on mobile phones] four times in a day.

Furthermore, according to the Pew Research Centre the top two activities each day on a tablet are e-mail (44%) and getting the news (37%). When we move to weekly data, the two activities are essentially tied at 65% and 64%, respectively.

The same research shows the following smartphone activities are key: e-mail (61%), social networking sites (46%), and news (36%). When we move to the weekly data, news pops up and is as dominant as social media (62%), behind e-mail at 80%.

E-mail and news are the top activities on mobile. Interestingly, this is not the case for TV. In January 2013, the Council for Research Excellence undertook research that found only 2% of total TV viewership occurred on a tablet or smartphone.

Randy Cohen, president and CEO of Advertiser Perceptions Inc., commented that — unlike with earlier digital media like search (where Google drove ad innovation) or social (where Facebook and Twitter are driving innovation) — ad executives don't yet perceive any media entity as a market "leader" in developing the mobile marketplace.

Right now, according to Cohen, the mobile advertising marketplace is still looking for leaders who can drive innovation and help organise it from a marketing perspective.

Newspapers are leading in mobile. Advertisers, take note!

*http://www.inma.org/blogs/integrated-advertising-sales/post.cfm/message-to-advertisers-it-s-the-year-of-newspapers-on-mobile*

# 09 Advertising

With a partner or in a small group, consider a collection of ads with TOK eyes. How do your ads connect to the Ways of Knowing? Which Ways of Knowing are most strongly emphasised and does that depend on what is being promoted? Which Ways of Knowing do you think are most important in ads and why? What about ethical issues? How ethical and honest are the ads?

### General comprehension

1. Explain the main arguments of the article in a few, concise sentences.
2. What support does the writer give for these arguments?
3. What audience does the writer want to reach in this article?

### Text handling

1. Explain the following expressions in your own words. If the expressions are unfamiliar, try to find the meaning from the context.
   a) to strike while the iron is hot
   b) newspapers on mobile are hot
   c) digital population
   d) to pop up
   e) to drive innovation
   f) mobile marketplace

2. True or false? Justify your answer with a relevant brief quotation from the text.
   a) Consumers use a variety of mobile devices to read newspapers.
   b) Both mobile phone users and tablet users read their newspapers online four times a day.
   c) The most popular activity on a tablet is emailing.
   d) Watching TV on a tablet or smartphone is as popular as reading newspapers on them.
   e) At present, there is no market leader in the developing mobile advertising market place.

## Written work

Now that you have read about advertising and discussed it at length, do you think this would be a field in which you would like to work? Which of the IB Learner Profile traits do you think a person in advertising needs? Write a paragraph explaining and justifying your ideas about this.

### Zoom in on grammar

**Zero conditional**

The zero conditional is used when a result generally follows an action without exception. It is formed by:

If ... + *present*, ... + *present*

If we heat water, it boils. / Water boils if we heat it.

### Grammar in context

**Zero conditional**

Create zero conditional sentences with the following starters:

1. If you multiply 7 by 9...
2. If the fire alarm goes off...
3. If you lose your wallet...

# 9.2 The effects of advertising

## Text 9.2.1 What does advertising do?

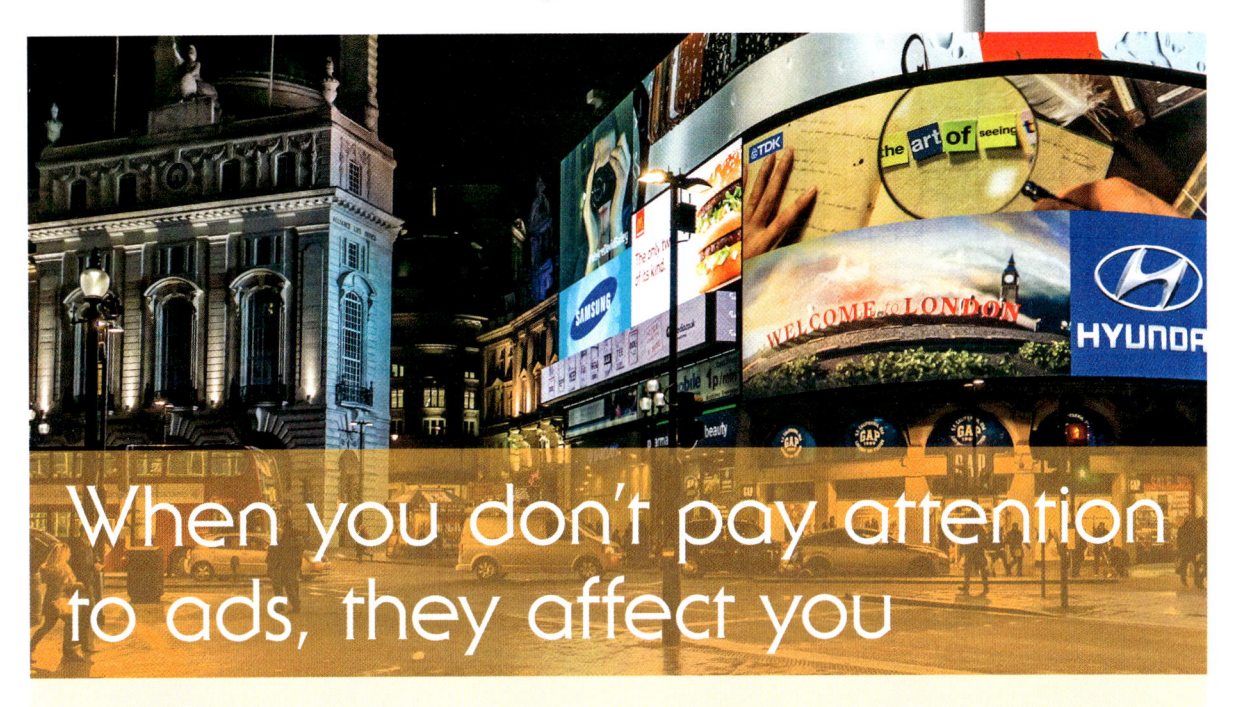

# When you don't pay attention to ads, they affect you

Published on August 31, 2010 by Art Markman, Ph.D. in *Ulterior Motives*

We live in a world of advertising. It is a world of our making, of course. We don't like to pay the full price of things, so we allow other people to pay part of that price in exchange for letting them pass a message to us. So, we open up the pages of our favourite magazine, and there are glossy ads for clothes, shoes, cars, or beer. We turn on the television, and smiling faces on television try to sell us soup, toothpaste, candy, and politicians.

The reason that we accept all this advertising is that we assume that we can tune most of it out. If we don't pay attention to the ads, then they won't have that much of an effect on our behaviour. Sure, the makers of commercials can try to jack up the volume, but at least we have the right to look away. Right?

A paper due to appear in the December, 2010 issue of the *Journal of Consumer Research* by Melanie Dempsey and Andrew Mitchell suggests that the picture might not be so rosy. These researchers did two clever studies that ought to make us think twice about how much advertising we allow ourselves to be exposed to.

We usually assume that advertising functions mostly to tell us about the properties of a product. A particular detergent might advertise that it gets stains out better than competitors, that it smells good, and that it leaves clothes feeling fresh. We believe that these properties are ones that will help us to choose the detergent we want to buy.

However, ads also do other things. One thing they do is to take a product and to put it next to lots of other things that we already feel positively about. For example, an ad for detergent may have fresh flowers, cute babies, and sunshine in it. All of these things are ones that we probably feel pretty good about already. And repeatedly showing the detergent along with other things that we feel good about can make us feel good about the detergent, too. This transfer of our feelings from one set of items to another is called affective conditioning (the word affect means feelings).

# 09 Advertising

In these studies, Dempsey and Mitchell told people about two brands of pens. One brand had better properties than the other. So, objectively, that better brand is the one people should have picked. Before making a choice about the pens, though, some people did what they thought was an unrelated experiment in which they watched pictures on a screen that flashed quickly. Some of these pictures paired the brand name of the pen that had the worse set of properties with a lot of positive items. This procedure is known to create affective conditioning.

So, this experiment put two sources of information in opposition. People had a set of properties about the pens that suggested one brand was better than the other. And the group that did not go through the affective conditioning procedure picked this brand most of the time when asked to choose a pen.

The people who went through the affective conditioning procedure picked the pen that was paired with positive items 70–80% of the time. They chose this pen, even though they had information that the other pen was better. Over the two studies in this paper, the authors found that people chose the pen that was paired with positive objects even when people were given as much time as they wanted to make a choice, and even when the instructions specifically encouraged them to pick the best choice and to say why they were choosing a particular pen.

These results suggest that the most powerful effect of advertising is just to create a good feeling about a product by surrounding it with other things that you like. It is also important to point out that affective conditioning is most effective when you don't realize that it is happening. That is, trying to pay less attention to the ads you see on TV and in magazines may actually make this type of advertising more effective.

So, why do we choose things just because we feel good about them? The world is a busy place. It is hard for us to feel confident that we have all of the objective facts about anything, whether it is products, people, or choices of things to do. The feelings we have are often a good marker of what is safe to do and what is likely to turn out well. If we have to make a choice, and one of the options just feels good to us, then we are likely to go with the one that feels good.

Most of the time, of course, that is a good idea. Often, we feel good about something because we have had positive experiences with it in the past. The problem is that we allow advertisers to have access to our mental world. They have paid for the opportunity to slip information to us about what feels good. That information ultimately affects the way we make choices, whether we know it or not.

http://www.psychologytoday.com/blog/ulterior-motives/201008/what-does-advertising-do

## General comprehension

1. Why do we accept so much advertising?
2. What do advertisers do besides telling us about the properties of a product?
3. What is affective conditioning?
4. How did the researchers create affective conditioning?
5. How effective was this?
6. According to the author, what is the most powerful effect of advertising?
7. In your opinion, how can we defend ourselves against this?

Is advertising moral? Why or why not? **TOK**

## Text handling

True or false? Justify your answer with a relevant brief quotation from the text.

1. People believe advertising has no effect on them if they ignore the ads.
2. Ads just tell us about the properties of a product.
3. Feeling good about other images in an ad does not affect our feelings about the product.
4. Affective conditioning led people to choose the less effective pen.
5. Affective conditioning works best if people are unaware of it.

## Written work

Now that you are aware of one of the strategies used by advertisers, choose an advertisement of the type which this article describes and, using it as an example, write an article for the school magazine to inform your peers about the use of affective conditioning in advertising. Write between 250 and 300 words.

### Zoom in on grammar

**Modal verbs**

Examples of modal verbs include *can, could, must, should, ought, may, might, will, would, shall.*

Modal verbs are used to express that something must or may happen or be done. They are also used to instruct people in how to do something. A modal verb does not have an *-s* or *-ing* ending.

### Grammar in context

**Modal verbs**

Complete the following sentences with a modal verb. When you have finished, check your sentences with the text to see if you chose the correct modal verb or if you altered the meaning of the sentence slightly by choosing an alternative modal verb.

1 The reason that we accept all this advertising is that we assume that we _____ tune most of it out.
2 Sure, the makers of commercials _____ try to jack up the volume, but at least we have the right to look away.
3 These researchers did two clever studies that _____ to make us think twice about how much advertising we allow ourselves to be exposed to.
4 A particular detergent manufacturer _____ advertise that it gets stains out better than competitors, that it smells good, and that it leaves clothes feeling fresh.
5 For example, an ad for detergent _____ have fresh flowers, cute babies, and sunshine in it.
6 That is, trying to pay less attention to the ads you see on TV and in magazines _____ actually make this type of advertising more effective.

## 9.3 The power of language

### Text 9.3.1 Sold on language

http://www.psychologytoday.com/blog/sold-language/201107/think-you-cant-be-persuaded-ads-you-ignore-think-again

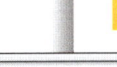

### When mindless persuasion trumps thoughtful deliberation
Published on July 8, 2011, by Julie Sedivy, Ph.D. in *Sold on Language*

We live in the age of Over-Information. Every day, we're doused with thousands of commercial messages alone, let alone all the tweets, pips and squeaks clamoring for our attention from our Twitter, Facebook and email accounts. Why don't our heads explode?

The answer is one that most junior high teachers have known all along: people ignore most of the information that surrounds them.

No one has illustrated our stunning capacity to ignore information more vividly than Daniel Simons and Chris Chabris. If you haven't already

http://www.psychologytoday.com/blog/sold-language/201107/think-you-cant-be-persuaded-ads-you-ignore-think-again

seen the video of their famous study, you might want to watch it before hitting the spoiler alert in the next paragraph. Go on—it'll be worth it.

In this well-known "invisible gorilla" study, you watch a video in which two teams—one in black T-shirts and one in white—pass basketballs to fellow team members. Your job is to count the passes among white team members. It takes some attention, but many people manage to answer accurately. What they often completely fail to see, though, is the gorilla that strolls into the middle of the game, faces the camera and beats its chest before sauntering off to the sidelines. When asked afterwards if they saw the gorilla, many people are gob-smacked.

This hilarious study provides a deep insight that turns out to apply very broadly, namely that we dole out our attention very unevenly, allotting generous dollops of attention to some aspects of our environment, while being enormously stingy with others, to the point of missing information that should have been un-missable.

It'll come as no surprise to advertisers that people rarely devote their full brainpower to the ads that are lobbed at them. But this doesn't necessarily mean that the ads have no impact on consumers. Sometimes, it can mean the opposite.

In the scientific work on persuasion there's a well-known result that, while not quite as funny as the Simons and Chabris study, is very similar to the invisible gorilla effect: it's the finding that people are often apt to ignore the difference between strong and weak arguments in forming attitudes or choosing how to behave.

A pivotal study by Ellen Langer and colleagues provides one of the earliest demonstrations. In this experiment, students in a university library were approached by an under-cover experimenter who asked to jump ahead of them in the photocopying line and make a few copies. Sometimes, the experimenter would justify the request by saying "May I use the Xerox machine, because I'm in a rush?" But other times, no explanation was offered. Not surprisingly, students were more reluctant to grant the favour when the experimenter didn't bother to justify the request. But the justification didn't actually have to provide a good reason—it just needed to sound like one. So, students complied just as readily when the experimenter gave a "placebo" explanation that was utterly without content: "May I use the Xerox machine because I need to make some copies?" Apparently, just decorating the sentence with the word because was enough to sway the students.

Since the Langer study, an enormous amount of research has looked at when and why people are persuaded by weak arguments just as easily as by strong ones, much of this work being led by John Cacioppo and Richard Petty. It turns out that the circumstances under which people are the least sensitive to the quality of an argument are the same situations in which they are most likely to be swayed by very superficial cues such as the attractiveness of a speaker, his or her reputation, or even how many arguments are made—regardless of their content. It seems, then, that where inattentiveness closes one door to persuasion, it opens another.

What determines whether you're likely to engage in thoughtful evaluation as opposed to mindless reaction? Some of the factors that tilt you in one direction or another are not entirely surprising. Anything that reduces your motivation or ability to devote mental power to the issue at hand leads to more mindless persuasion—for example, being distracted, having to process the message very quickly, or not having that much at stake. (In Langer's study, when the experimenter asked to copy a large number of copies, people suddenly sat up and took notice, and rejected the request with the "placebo" justification.)

Some situations are clearly set up to favour the mindless variety of persuasion, and these tend to be the ones that place a lot of emphasis on packaging, or on certain phrases that act as triggers much as the word because did in the photocopying study. You're not likely to be doing much thoughtful deliberation while zipping through the grocery store with a screaming toddler who's stuck a penny up his nose, or while fending off a telemarketer as you put the finishing touches on dinner.

http://www.psychologytoday.com/blog/sold-language/201107/think-you-cant-be-persuaded-ads-you-ignore-think-again

But the research has also yielded some more startling findings. For example, people who are in a good mood can be more susceptible to mindless persuasion than those who are in a bad mood. It seems that feeling crummy makes you think about arguments more carefully. (Note to teenagers: buttering up your mom might be especially important if your best argument amounts to "But everyone's doing it!") And bolstering a feeling of power in someone before they've heard an argument is liable to make them think less deeply about it, which suggests that in order to make the best decisions, presidents and CEOs ought to cultivate a healthy sense of humility.

Much of the time, we're perfectly happy to make decisions based on gut reactions that don't involve our full attention. It is, after all, how we keep our minds from exploding. But when it matters—say, when we're buying a house, or an insurance policy, or choosing a president—it's worth really paying attention. Otherwise, we may miss the gorilla.

http://www.psychologytoday.com/blog/sold-language/201107/think-you-cant-be-persuaded-ads-you-ignore-think-again
© 2011 Julie Sedivy, All rights reserved

## General comprehension

1. Why does the author wonder why our heads do not explode?
2. Which picture does the word 'douse' create in our minds? Do you think the use of the word is effective?
3. Why has she chosen to use the word 'clamor'?
4. What does her decision to mention junior high teachers in paragraph 2 reveal?
5. Have you watched the gorilla video yet? What information does the video give us about our attentiveness?
6. Which word seemed to convince people in the photocopying queue (line) to let experimenters jump ahead?
7. Which three factors reduce our concentration on an issue?
8. Which situations in particular discourage thoughtful consideration?
9. What effect does mood have on our consideration of arguments?

For more information on the work of Daniel Simons and Chris Chabris, go to www.pearsonhotlinks.com, enter the title or ISBN of this book and click on Chapter 9.

## Text handling

1. True or false? Justify your answer with a relevant brief quotation from the text.
   a) People are always focused on events around them.
   b) Everyone notices the gorilla in the video.
   c) Our attention is spread evenly.
   d) People give their full attention to advertisements.
   e) People can be persuaded by both strong and weak arguments.
   f) If you are distracted, you can be more easily persuaded.
   g) Flattering a person and then presenting an argument may make them think less deeply about it.

2. Match the following words from the text on the left to the correct meanings on the right.

   | | | | | |
   |---|---|---|---|---|
   | I | gobsmacked | | A | likely to |
   | II | hilarious | | B | less resistant |
   | III | stingy | | C | humbleness |
   | IV | rarely | | D | supporting |
   | V | apt to | | E | given |
   | VI | yielded | | F | very funny |
   | VII | susceptible | | G | try to avoid |
   | VIII | bolstering | | H | amazed |
   | IX | humility | | I | hardly ever |
   | X | fend off | | J | mean |

# 09 Advertising

### Written work

We all buy things because we have been influenced by advertisements, either consciously or unconsciously. Think about when this happened to you (or if you cannot remember an example, make it up!), and write a diary entry reflecting on what happened and why, and your feelings as a result of the event.

Remember, a diary entry is you writing just for yourself, so it is written in informal language and is very reflective; however, it should still have a clear structure. Write between 200 and 250 words.

## 9.4 Advertising and children

### Text 9.4.1 Seven highly disturbing trends in junk food advertising to children

http://www.alternet.org/food/7-highly-disturbing-trends-junk-food-advertising-children

## ALTERNET  By Laura Gottesdiener

**From bribing children with toys to convincing them to eat a "fourth meal," the industry is glutted with perverse, profit-chasing schemes.**

Ever wonder why one-third of all children in the United States are overweight, if not dangerously obese? According to a slew of recent reports, the cornucopia of junk food advertising to children plays a substantial role in creating this public health crisis. From bribing children with toys and sweepstakes to convincing them to eat a "fourth meal," the industry is glutted with examples of perverse, profit-chasing schemes to capitalize on children's appetites at the expense of their long-term health. Here are 7 most perverse trends in junk food advertising to children.

### 1 ..........................................................................................................................

Junk food marketing to children and adolescents has become billion-dollar industry. According to 2006 data, the most recent numbers available, kids experience at least $1.6 billion worth of food advertising a year – the vast majority of the ads geared toward pushing high-calorie and low-nutrition snacks down kids' throat.

According to data compiled by the non-profit health organization Food & Water Watch, children see nearly 5,000 TV food ads every year, and teenagers get bombarded by almost 6,000 annually.

The vast majority of these ads are specifically geared towards children, using tricks like cartoon characters and sweepstakes prizes to make the sugary cereals and fatty hamburgers all the more attractive. As children's online activity has risen, massive corporations like McDonald's have also designed child-focused websites, complete with video games that teach children brand recognition, that are getting hundreds of thousands of young visitors a month. In the month of February 2011, for example, 350,000 children under the age of 12 visited McDonald's two main websites, HappyMeal.com and McWorld.com.

http://www.alternet.org/food/7-highly-disturbing-trends-junk-food-advertising-children

Most disturbingly, the amount of this advertising is steadily increasing. According to a report from Yale University's Rudd Center for Food Policy & Obesity, the advertising increased dramatically in only two years, between 2007 and 2009. Children between the ages of 6 and 11 saw a staggering 56 percent more ads for Subway, and 26 percent more ads for McDonald's. African American children were disproportionately targeted by this advertising, seeing 50 percent more advertisements for fast food than white children of the same age.

**2** ..................................................................................................................................

While many have complained that sedentary television culture is causing the childhood obesity crisis, new studies suggest that the real culprit may be the constant ads for junk food that children are viewing during commercial break – not the television programs themselves.

A 2006 Institute of Medicine government report stated. "It can be concluded that television advertising influences children to prefer and request high-calorie and low-nutrient foods and beverages."

Even clearer evidence comes from a long-term study in Quebec, where fast food advertising geared specifically toward children has been banned both online and in-print for the last 32 years. There, researchers discovered that the province has the least childhood obesity of anywhere in Canada, and that the ban decreased children's consumption by an estimated two to four billion calories.

In Britain, the president of the Royal College of Pediatrics and Child Heath, has also advocated for the state to ban junk food advertisements on television until after 9 pm, when the majority of children are already asleep.

**3** ..................................................................................................................................

How fat are these television advertisements making kids? According to one recent study, their effects are surprisingly heavy. The experiment compared children's food consumption while watching television programs with food commercials, versus programs that ran straight through without any ads. It concluded that kids consumed almost 50 percent more calories while watching the 30-minute program with commercials – a total of almost 100 calories in only a half an hour. Over the course of a year, that would lead to a 10-pound weight gain.

**4** ..................................................................................................................................

One of the biggest problems with child-specific advertising is that young kids aren't even able to recognize the commercials for what they are: short segments intended to sell them things. As the Food and Water Watch explains, children under the age of four can't even recognize the difference between a television show and the commercials – the line between content and advertising is completely invisible to them. Children between four and eight may understand that advertisements are different from the T.V. program, but they still don't recognize that ads are paid commercials intended to convince them to buy something.

## 09 Advertising

`http://www.alternet.org/food/7-highly-disturbing-trends-junk-food-advertising-children`

However, just because children can't recognize the ads for what they are doesn't mean that these commercials don't affect them. Studies show toddlers are able to accurately identify brand logos and that young children prefer food wrapped in McDonald's packaging.

**5** ................................................................................................................................

A study of one child-geared advertising campaign, launched by Taco Bell, demonstrates how perverse this marketing really is. In 2006, Taco Bell launched a campaign to convince children to eat a "Fourth Meal," which is after dinner and before breakfast. (Essentially, the fourth meal is at the time of night when children should be sleeping or doing their homework.)

The campaign kicked off with a website showing children in their pajamas wandering around outside and eating nachos, tacos and other late-night snacks offered by Taco Bell. The foods being marketed often had more than 400 calories, placing them squarely in the meal category. But the goal isn't just to sell more tacos; it's actually to carve out an entire new post-dinner market where the consumer base is young children.

**6** ................................................................................................................................

Increasingly, these types of ads aren't only on television and online; they are also in schools where the child-marking focus is even more obvious. As budget cuts and austerity measures have swept the nation, schools are increasingly relying on money from vending machine contracts and corporate partnerships. These revenue streams rely on how much food the students buy, meaning that the school earns more money if it stocks these machines with junk food.

**7** ................................................................................................................................

Due to increasing criticism from the public health community and the federal government, the fast food industry undertook the ambitious task of self-regulation in 2006, launching the Children's Food and Beverage Advertising Initiative. Under this initiative, companies pledged to market "better-for-you" foods to children.

Here are selections from the menu they came up with:
- Burger King Kids Meals with "Fresh Apple Slices" and fat-free milk or apple juice
  Assuming the meal is a plain hamburger, the offering has nearly 400 calories.
- McDonald's Happy Meals with fries, apple slices and fat-free chocolate milk
  Assuming the meal is a plain hamburger, the offering has more than 550 calories
- Kid Cuisine Meals Primo Pepperoni Double Stuffed Pizza 480 calories, with 15 grams of fat
- Chef Boyardee Pepperoni Pizza Ravioli 290 calories

Sometimes the industry's definition of regulation, is the best argument for government intervention.

http://www.alternet.org/food/7-highly-disturbing-trends-junk-food-advertising-children, November 29, 2012. This article was published in partnership with GlobalPossibilities.org.

## General comprehension

1. Insert the paragraph headings appropriately (in 1–7) in the text above.

   Children clueless while industry cashes in
   Industry's idea of self-regulation: happy meals with apple slices
   The ads, not the TV, are what's making kids fat
   Ten extra pounds – a year
   Bombarded!
   Holding schools hostage
   A fourth meal?

2. Which of these seven disturbing trends do you find the most serious?
3. Explain the biggest problem with advertising aimed specifically at children in your own words.
4. What is the 'fourth meal'?
5. Why is it possible for fast food to 'hold schools hostage'?
6. What is your opinion of the companies' promise to market healthier food?
7. Did you notice that parents are not mentioned in this article? What do you think their role should be?

## Text handling

Identify the words in the text which can be meaningfully replaced with the following words or phrases. The words are in the order they occur in the text, in the following sections.

**In the introduction**
1. overweight
2. abundance
3. unreasonable

**Section 1**
4. huge
5. worryingly
6. amazing

**Section 2**
7. inactive
8. recommended

**Section 3**
9. advertisements

**Section 4**
10. sections
11. very young children

**Section 5**
12. shows
13. started

**Section 6**
14. income

**Section 7**
15. promised

Fast food has become a way of life in America and Great Britain; people eat on the streets, or public transport, and in front of the TV. Rather than eating three meals a day and little inbetween, people now tend to 'graze'. What is the situation in your country?

## Zoom in on grammar

### Phrasal verbs

Many verbs are formed of two parts – a verb followed by a preposition or an adverb – and these are called 'phrasal verbs'. For example: *look at, think of, believe in, belong to*.

Some verbs can take a number of different prepositions or adverbs, with different meanings. For example: *look in, look out, look after, look for, look round*.

## Grammar in context

### Phrasal verbs

Complete the following sentences with the correct preposition or adverb. Check your answers with the text.

1. Even clearer evidence comes from a long-term study in Quebec, where fast food advertising geared specifically _____ children has been banned both online and in print for the last 32 years.
2. African American children were disproportionately targeted _____ this advertising, seeing 50 percent more advertisements for fast food than white children of the same age.
3. According to data compiled by the non-profit health organization Food & Water Watch, children see nearly 5,000 TV food ads every year, and teenagers get bombarded _____ almost 6,000 annually.
4. The campaign kicked _____ with a website showing children in their pajamas wandering around outside and eating nachos, tacos and other late-night snacks offered by Taco Bell.
5. Here are selections from the menu they came _____.

155

# 09 Advertising

To what extent do fast food restaurants and advertising companies have a moral responsibility to society? Discuss.

**TOK**

### Interactive oral activity

Discuss the article with a partner.

Think about these points, but add other ideas of your own.

- What shocks you the most?
- Who is to blame for this situation?
- What can be done?
- What do you think of the industry's idea of self-regulation?
- Are you affected by this kind of advertising?

### Exam hints

**Preparing for an interactive oral**

- First, decide on the topic of your presentation and do your research. Remember, the presentation should be short, so keep to a limit of two or three minutes, which will give more time for the group discussion.
- Organise your ideas so that the points you make are clear. Do not just give a list of facts, but make it interesting as well as informative.
- Prepare a visual aid to help you present your ideas to the group, but do not use notes.
- Be ready to listen to the other group members and have good questions to ask about their ideas.

### Written work

Write a proposal for your local government suggesting ways for each of the seven highly disturbing trends to be effectively opposed. Make notes first, then organise your work in paragraphs. As it is a proposal for the government, be sure to use a formal register. Write between 250 and 350 words.

## Exam practice

## How has advertising changed?

**by Amy Johnson**

The advertising that we see today is a far cry from the pale, insipid images of the hard-working housewife and her husband in scenes of domestic bliss that were prolific during the 1900s. These advertisements were commonplace in magazines and newspapers as well as on television and billboards. Today, all you need to do is switch on your television to realise that societal values have changed and – consequently – so has the advertiser's message. Naturally, advertising messages now reflect the mindset of a more liberal, international and socially-aware consumer. We know the message has changed; this much is glaringly obvious, but the waves of change are surging even more dramatically in terms of the advertising medium.

## 1

While there are certain core advertising principles that have remained since the industry's inception, the way target audiences consume media and the actual medium itself are almost unrecognisable. Younger generations are changing consumption habits. They're digital babies, nurtured by the internet to actively engage with content. Their consumption habits are influencing households, to the point where televisions are becoming a secondary fixation in relation to online and mobile multimedia channels.

## 2

"Social" is still the word on advertiser's lips as we move into the latter part of 2013. A few years ago, traditionalists dubbed it a fad that would surely pass. However, as Anders Sjostedt of Hyper Island so eloquently puts it:

"A year ago, it was still okay for advertising people — especially if you were over 40 — to simply state 'I don't like Facebook and I hate Twitter' as a reason not to get involved with and understand social media. I think we've reached the tipping point where that is now just considered unprofessional."

The tipping point has definitely arrived, and advertisers have been forced to see their consumers in a different light – as active participants rather than the passive recipients that they once were. Advertising campaigns have to factor in engagement and social outreach to achieve any level of success. Integration is key.

## 3

Who are you talking to? Is your message having the desired response? These are questions that advertisers used to approach somewhat blindly a few decades ago. While market research methods have improved with time, what we're seeing now is quite unprecedented. Massive amounts of online data are available to marketers concerning consumer behaviour and response. The era of responsive marketing and advertising campaigns has arrived.

On the topic of knowing your consumer Gillian Rightford, owner of Adtherapy and Course Instructor on the UCT Foundations of Advertising course, says:

"There's too much playing to the masses and too much losing sight of the one person that actually counts – the person who may do something, buy something, think something, as a result of your ad. [Ads should] speak to the truth of the product and brand benefit, and how people feel about it; and create an ongoing dialogue, online, offline, in people's hearts and minds, about what the ad actually spoke to us about."

## 4

The modern advertiser needs:

- An understanding of digital mediums;
- A good grasp of traditional and digital integration;
- Insight into current consumer behaviour;
- Creativity tempered with a good dose of consumer insight, and
- An eye for competitive advantage.

Fortunately, these are skills that can be acquired. As the saying goes, "change is the only constant", and in the field of Advertising, this is certainly true. Advertisers must adapt to their new and transforming environment or they will drown in the strong tides of change.

Adapted from http://www.getsmarter.co.za/blog-marketing/16653-how-has-advertising-changed.com; this article is published under the Creative Commons Attribution licence.

## 09 Advertising

### Exercises

Answer the following questions.

**1** Insert the four paragraph headings appropriately (in 1–4 above).

Social media: A powerful tool in the advertiser's arsenal
The data candle: Shedding light on unknown variables
Generations X, Y and Z: The modern advertiser's frame of reference
What does the modern Advertiser look like?

**2** Answer the following questions.

**A** Look again at the picture at the beginning of the text. Write a short comparison between it and a modern advertisement you have seen using insights from the text to support your ideas.

..................................................................................................................

**B** Why has advertising changed so much?

..................................................................................................................

**C** How do advertisers see their consumers now?

..................................................................................................................

**D** The author uses the metaphor of the sea to describe the changes in advertising. Find the two examples of this in the text. Why do you think he chose this metaphor?

..................................................................................................................

**3** Match the words from the text with the synonyms on the right. There are more meanings than you need.

| | | | | | |
|---|---|---|---|---|---|
| I | insipid | ☐ | A | numerous |
| II | prolific | ☐ | B | weak |
| | | | C | period of time |
| III | subservient | ☐ | D | belonging to the working class |
| IV | inception | ☐ | E | obedient |
| | | | F | the start of something |
| V | era | ☐ | G | dull and boring |

158

**4** True or false? Justify your answer with a relevant brief quotation from the text.

**A** Advertising today is not dramatically different from advertising in the past.

.......................................................................................................

**B** The core advertising principles have changed.

.......................................................................................................

**C** We are in the period of responsive marketing and advertising campaigns.

.......................................................................................................

**D** A modern advertiser needs to be creative and understand consumers.

.......................................................................................................

**E** These skills cannot be learnt.

.......................................................................................................

## Further exercises

## Written work (HL)

One of the writing tasks in the English B examination is a personal response to a stimulus. There is no right or wrong answer, because students are assessed on their ability to present a clear, logical, reasoned argument stating and justifying their opinion.

Write between 150 and 250 words.

Think about the statement – 'As the saying goes, "change is the only constant".'

Do you agree or disagree? Why? Think carefully about your reasons.

Choose any genre which you have studied and write a response to the stimulus.

### Interactive oral activity

Consider different ways you could present the topic to your fellow students. For example, you could examine how advertising has changed in time as a reflection of society, or through technological development, or because of its changing role in our lives – or maybe you have other ideas. Find some examples of advertising from the present and past to support your arguments.

When everyone is ready, each person in the group should present their findings individually. Then the group can ask questions and discuss the ideas raised.

# 10 Technology in education

**Opposite** Too young to type?

## Objectives
- To practise direct and indirect speech
- To revise the use of 'since' and 'for'
- To review abstract nouns
- To discuss the use of technology in education

## 10.1 Laptops in the classroom

### Text 10.1.1 Interview with an international school technology teacher (Adriaan van der Bergh)

> Good morning Mr van der Bergh, thank you for taking time to answer a few questions about laptops in the classroom.
>
> Do you think laptops are/will be essential for learning in the 21st century?

> Yes, not so much a laptop per se, but a device which is connected to the internet and empowers students by giving them unrestricted access to any knowledge they wish to learn will be essential for learning.

> What are the main advantages of laptops in the classroom?

> The main advantages are that laptops empower students with unrestricted access to knowledge.
>
> They also enable students to create artefacts like movies, animations, cartoons, podcasts and blogs, and instantly share them with a global audience.
>
> They engage students through game-based learning, and collaboration with peers all over the world.

> What about the disadvantages?

**Above** Mr van der Bergh, technology teacher.

# 10 Technology in education

> Well, sometimes technical problems can get in the way of learning and of course if they are not managed properly, laptops could prove to be a great distraction. In addition students may become overly reliant on technology tools.

**Is there a 'best age' to introduce children to laptops in the classroom?**

> In my opinion, 10–11 is the right age to make the transition from tablets (like the iPad) to a more powerful device like a MacBook or other full-fledged laptop.

**Who has the most difficulties with laptops in the classroom? Is it the teachers?**

> This is difficult to say... though it may seem that using a laptop comes more naturally to kids that to adults, I don't think this is the case. It seems that kids learn quicker, but I think this is because they are less afraid of 'breaking something' and feel more comfortable learning through trial and error. Adults are afraid of breaking something, so learning by trial and error is less likely...

**How do parents react to the idea of laptops in the classroom?**

> Most parents are very supportive of this. Most parents who work in a modern workplace see the way their kids will probably work once they leave school is in a place full of technology where being fluent with technology and being able to teach yourself how to use new technology is an essential skill.

**Thank you very much Mr van der Bergh.**

## General comprehension

1. The teacher has listed a number of advantages of laptops in the classroom. Do you agree with them? Can you add any more advantages?
2. Do you agree that the best age to introduce laptops in the classroom is between 10 and 11 years? Explain why you agree or disagree.
3. What do you think about using laptops in the classroom?
4. What do your parents think about this?

## Text handling

Find words in the text which could be meaningfully replaced by the following. The words are in order according to the text.

1. absolutely necessary
2. tool
3. unlimited
4. objects
5. working together
6. dependent
7. move

## Zoom in on grammar

### Direct and indirect speech (reported speech)

Sometimes, when changing direct into indirect speech, you need to change the tense: present tense → past tense, or past tense → past perfect. However, if the information given in the direct speech is still true, a tense change is not used.

There are a number of verbs which can be used for reporting speech; 'say' and 'tell' were discussed in Chapter 7. The following ten verbs are some of those which can be used to report speech with a 'that' link. For example: 'He said that laptops will be essential for learning in the future.'

*Verb + 'that':* admit, agree, believe, consider, feel, know, point out, think, say, tell

Note: When reporting what has been said in indirect speech, it is usual to express the meaning, rather than repeat the exact words.

## Grammar in context

### Direct and indirect speech (reported speech)

Form sentences using the information in the interview and the ten reporting verbs listed above.

*Mr Van der Bergh admits...*

*He agrees...*

*He believes...*

*and so on.*

# 10 Technology in education

Text 10.1.2 Article for a school magazine read by parents and students

## Our School Policy on Laptops
### By Mr J. Smith, Deputy Headmaster

Over the past few months a number of parents have expressed concerns about their children using laptops in the classroom. This has clearly become a topic worthy of discussion, so please allow me to address these concerns as an educator.

Children in the 21st century need to become expert users of technology in their everyday lives. Their future careers will almost certainly depend on technology, and so it is in everyone's interest for them to become proficient users as they grow up. Technology will advance and change in years to come, and it is essential that the children are involved in the changes and developments as they occur.

Technology has become a ubiquitous part of society and can be observed everywhere. Watch people of all ages on the streets, in cafés, at the bus stop, or in an airport and they are inevitably engaged in communicating online in their spare moments. It is a trend that cannot be ignored, but should be harnessed in education. In this way, students are learning for life.

The possibilities for using laptops in the classroom are endless, and the benefits are many. The teachers at our school have investigated the best use of laptops and agree on the following points.

### Taking Notes
Students are often required _____ take notes. These may be related to information that the teacher has presented orally or _____ the board, or from information they have read, or from ideas resulting from experimental work and group discussions. Often, these notes must be made quickly _____ the discussion continues and the ideas are fresh, consequently penmanship may suffer. Notes typed on a laptop are easier to read, edit and organise _____ handwritten notes. Using laptops, the notes can also be shared quickly with other students or the teacher.

### Research
Being able to find relevant information quickly on any topic is an important skill in learning and this can be better accomplished with the laptop. Students learn to determine _____ useful, relevant, or reliable information may be in follow-up discussions with their classmates or teachers. They also learn how important it is not to just copy the work of others, but to analyse, understand and then put the ideas into their own words. In this way they learn that plagiarism will not be tolerated.

### Additional information, tasks, and support
Teachers can also give students more information by sending them links to investigate, or additional exercises from a CD-ROM or the Internet. Research by Educause.edu has shown that students who learn with computers integrated into their studies score better on tests than those who only learn _____ traditional methods.

### Classroom logistics
Using laptops also allows students to stay _____ touch with their teachers during lessons because their vision is not blocked by monitors. The teacher can also see each student easily. As laptops are mobile, seating arrangements in the classroom can also be changed quickly and easily.

### A final word
In addition, the students can carry their laptops from class to class, and from home to school, meaning that they do not have as many books to carry, or even lose. The advantages of laptops in the classroom are very clear to both teachers and students, but we look forward _____ hearing your thoughts as parents.

## General comprehension

1 Why has the deputy headmaster written this article?
2 Why does he think skills in technology are important?
3 Where do you see laptops in daily use?
4 What does he consider the advantages of taking notes on a laptop?
5 Do you agree with the skills he lists which are acquired for research?
6 Can you think of any other advantages of laptops in the classroom?

## Text Handling

**A** Fill the gaps in the text using the words below. There are more words than you need. When you have completed the task, check your answers with the text.

**up, to, while, how, on, over, than, in, by, to, if**

**B** Match the words with their closest meaning, according to the text.

1 proficient
2 ubiquitous
3 plagiarism
4 integrated

I   adaptable   considerate   competent   unskilled
II  unnecessary   found everywhere   unusual   sophisticated
III study of illness   copying someone else's work and taking it as your own   infection   a curse
IV  related to maths   upside-down   combined   impossible

## Interactive oral activity

*Imagine this situation:*
A parent is very worried that their child is spending too much time on the computer and missing out on many other things. The parent has come to talk to the child's teacher in school as the class have now begun to use laptops in the classroom as well.

In pairs, decide who will play the role of the teacher and who will be the anxious parent. Decide yourselves how old the child should be and begin to plan your conversation. To prepare, the parent should make a list of the disadvantages he/she sees, and the teacher should make a list of the advantages. Practise your conversation and be ready to perform the dialogue in front of the class.

## Written work

Your school has a partner school in Africa where the teachers would very much like to introduce laptops for the children. However, the school does not have enough money to buy a computer for every child. Write a proposal for your own school community, suggesting ways that students, parents and teachers could get involved in raising the necessary money to make the laptops possible. Remember to focus on who you are writing to, why you are writing and what (genre) you are writing. Write between 250 and 350 words.

# 10 Technology in education

## Text 10.1.3 A letter from a parent in reply to the magazine article

Dear Mr Smith,

I read your article in last month's school magazine with interest, as I am one of a number of parents who are very concerned about the use of laptops in the classroom.

My daughter is in year seven, and in my opinion she spends far too much time on her laptop and other gadgets. Her homework often takes far longer than I would expect, and this seems to be because she is distracted by other links and related sites. She is very curious by nature – this means that instead of concentrating on the topic she is studying, she often wastes time investigating other things. There is just too much available information that gets in the way because she cannot yet sort the necessary from the unnecessary. If she does a keyword search as part of a homework assignment, she takes a lot of time and ends up looking at topics that are completely unrelated to the information she needs. If she had a dictionary or reference book it would be much quicker and easier.

She thinks a laptop is a toy and has a lot of fun playing with it. There are websites about everything imaginable, and some of them use cartoon characters in order to make the whole thing a lot of fun for her. If she had books to use this would not be a problem.

As well as wasting time with the laptop, she is losing the ability to write by hand. All of her schoolwork and homework seem to be typed up, and she hardly ever uses a pen or a pencil. Is this normal? She is also reluctant to sit and read a book because she thinks playing with her laptop is more fun. I am very worried about this too.

The laptop is just a distraction and often a dangerous distraction. There are so many sites on the Internet that have images and texts which children should not see. There are also people out there who can hurt vulnerable children who are too easily lured into dangerous situations. Children are just not aware of the dangers of the Internet and don't believe that people they chat to online may wish to harm them. The Internet is full of hidden dangers and using laptops in school is like opening a gate and welcoming all of these dangers.

I regularly try to check what she is looking at when she does her homework, but this often causes arguments between us and I am worried about what is happening in school. How do the teachers know what children are doing in lessons when they should be working? How can one teacher check a whole class when they are all looking at their laptops individually? If they were using textbooks, as we did in school, this would not be a problem.

Altogether, I think using laptops in school is a terrible mistake. Children like my daughter are losing their basic skills of reading and writing. They are given too much information that they cannot deal with, and, worst of all, the Internet puts them in real danger. For the sake of our children, please stop using laptops and give the children back their books and pencils, which will not put them in danger.

I hope you will consider my arguments carefully and I look forward to hearing from you.

Yours sincerely,

Mrs Annie Andrews (mother of Annabel)

## General comprehension

1 Make a list of the concrete points the writer makes in the letter which support her claim that laptops are a distraction.
2 What dangers does the writer see in the use of laptops for children?
3 Which basic skills does she think are being lost? Do you agree with her?
4 Why does she say her daughter thinks the laptop is a toy?
5 What does the mother think the school should do? Do you think this is good advice? Why or why not?
6 The writer compares giving children laptops in school to 'opening a gate and welcoming danger'. Do you think this is a good comparison? Why or why not?

## Text handling

**A** Match the words with their closest meaning, according to the text.

1 gadget
2 distraction
3 vulnerable
4 lured into

I    tool to open a lock    a joke    small mechanical or technical device writing implement
II    noticeable difference    average    something which distracts attention a form of subtraction
III    a musical sound    likely to be harmed    unexplained    harmful
IV    tempted into    thrown into    exposed to    midunderstood

**B** To what or to whom do the words underlined refer?

There are also people out there who can hurt vulnerable children <u>who</u> (a) are too easily lured into dangerous situations. Children are just not aware of the dangers of the Internet and don't believe that people <u>they</u> (b) chat to online may wish to harm <u>them</u> (c).

I regularly try to check what <u>she</u> (d) is looking at when she does her homework, but this often causes arguments between <u>us</u> (e) and I am worried about what is happening in school. How do the teachers know what the children are doing in class when <u>they</u> (f) should be working? How can one teacher check a whole class when <u>they</u> (g) are all looking at their laptops individually? If they were using textbooks, as <u>we</u> (h) did in school, this would not be a problem.

a)
b)
c)
d)
e)
f)
g)
h)

## Written work

Use the information in the texts you have read about laptops in the classroom and make a table to compare the advantages and disadvantages. A T-chart would be useful for this.

Add any other points which you can think of yourself. Then, using the table, write a paragraph to answer the following questions.

- Do your findings demonstrate convincingly that laptops are an advantage or a disadvantage?
- Do you agree?

| Advantages | Disadvantages |
|---|---|
|  |  |

# 10 Technology in education

### Interactive oral activity

*Motion: 'This house believes that laptops are a distraction in classrooms and should not be allowed.'*

Plan your arguments carefully; be ready to refute the arguments of the opposition.

Use phrases such as 'I am sorry, I cannot agree', 'I have to disagree', 'on the contrary', 'according to my information', 'if I may add one point'.

## 10.2 Technology in education around the world

### Text 10.2.1 Computers in school in Africa

The following text is an article that may surprise you about the number of computers being used in schools in Africa.

A project to enable students in Rwandan schools to have access to laptop computers was launched in 2008 by President Paul Kagame. Entitled One Laptop per Child (OLPC), the Rwandan Ministry of Education also supported this project, which has the goal of distributing 200,000 computers to primary school children across the country.

Mr. Nkubito Bakuramutsa, the project coordinator, said, 'A consignment of 100,000 laptops worth US$20million, will be arriving this month, and our target is to have distributed 200,000 laptops by the end of December.'

He also added that primary schools had already been given as many as 105,000 XO laptops. This very ambitious project has benefitted more than 145 schools. 'The One Laptop per Child programme is a major driver towards a knowledge-based economy,' he observed.

Rwanda is divided into 416 sectors, and a major problem has been how to distribute the laptops. Due to the high level of interest shown by parents wanting their children to learn the IT skills necessary for life in the 21st century, at least one school in each sector will benefit from the project.

An additional problem is the patchy Rwandan electricity supply – something that is obviously needed to power the laptops. Mr Bakuramutsa stated that schools in each district close to the national grid are collaborating with the Energy, Water and Sanitation Authority (EWSA) to receive a reliable provision of power.

Each school's computers will be connected to a server loaded with software for mathematics, science and English, and teachers are being trained to use the software effectively. So far, the OLPC Project has trained more than 1,500 teachers, with many more waiting to be trained.

In addition, the OLPC project will train two more teachers who are to be responsible for supporting schools and general trouble-shooting. The computers are free for state-supported schools, while private schools can buy them for $200 (approximately RWF120,000) each.

Finally, Mr Bakuramutsa notes, 'I call upon parents and teachers to support the OLPC project. I am optimistic that the beneficiaries will compete favourably on the labour market after completing their studies.'

## General comprehension

1. What is the main aim of the One Laptop per Child project?
2. What difficulties may some schools encounter with the laptop project?
3. Give two ways teachers will be supported in the programme.
4. Can you think of any disadvantages to this programme?

## Text handling

Find words in the text with a similar meaning to the words and phrases below. The words are in the same order as they appear in the text.

1. was started
2. to share out
3. working together
4. solving problems
5. hopeful
6. students who receive the computers

## Zoom in on grammar

**Direct and indirect speech**

Often, in a text, both direct and indirect speech are used to report the content of a discussion. 'According to...' is also used to report what someone has said. To make a text more interesting, a variety of reporting verbs are used – not only 'he said/she said'. Other verbs which may be used include *admit, add, agree, announce, argue, ask, believe, consider, enquire, explain, feel, hear, insist, know, point out, suggest, suppose, understand, wonder*.

## Grammar in context

**Direct and indirect speech**

Re-read the text and make a list of the reporting verbs used. Note how they are used. Write sentences of your own using these reporting verbs.

## Individual oral activity

Research the geography or history of the present situation in Rwanda. Use the information you find to give a three- or four-minute presentation to your class or group. Be ready to answer any questions the other students may have.

# 10 Technology in education

> ### Exam hints
> **Remember**
> - Use just bullet points when you present.
> - Do not learn the presentation off by heart.
> - Look at your audience and talk to them.
> - Make your presentation lively and interesting by using a good range of vocabulary and sentence structures.
> - Look closely at the rubric, which is used to grade oral presentations, and aim to meet the criteria.

In British English, 'hole in the wall' is a slang name for a cash machine.

## Text 10.2.2 The Hole-in-the-Wall project

`http://www.hole-in-the-wall.com/Beginnings.html`

## Beginnings

Dr. Sugata Mitra, Chief Scientist at NIIT, is credited with the creation of Hole-in-the-Wall. As early as 1982, he had been toying with the idea of unsupervised learning and computers. Finally, in 1999, he decided to test his ideas in the field. On 26th January, Dr. Mitra's team carved a "hole in the wall" that separated the NIIT premises from the adjoining slum in Kalkaji, New Delhi. Through this hole, a freely accessible computer was put up for use. This computer proved to be an instant hit among the slum dwellers, especially the children. With no prior experience, the children learnt to use the computer on their own. This prompted Dr. Mitra to propose the following hypothesis:

> The acquisition of basic computing skills by any set of children can be achieved through incidental learning provided the learners are given access to a suitable computing facility, with entertaining and motivating content and some minimal (human) guidance.

Encouraged by the success of the Kalkaji experiment, freely accessible computers were set up in Shivpuri (a town in Madhya Pradesh) and in Madantusi (a village in Uttar Pradesh). These experiments came to be known as Hole-in-the-Wall experiments. The findings from Shivpuri and Madantusi confirmed the results of Kalkaji experiments. It appeared that the children in these two places picked up computer skills on their own. Dr. Mitra defined this as a new way of learning – Minimally Invasive Education.

At this point in time, International Finance Corporation joined hands with NIIT to set up Hole-in-the-Wall Education Limited (HiWEL). The idea was to broaden the scope of the experiments and conduct research to prove and streamline Hole-in-the-Wall. As part of this, more than 30 such clusters of computers or, as they have come to be known, Learning Stations have been set up in India and outside India. The results, which have been uniformly encouraging, show that children learn to operate as well as play with the computer with minimum intervention. They picked up skills and tasks by constructing their own learning environment.

http://www.hole-in-the-wall.com/Beginnings.html

## About the man

Dr. Sugata Mitra is a long-term educationist and a scientist of international repute. He has over 25 inventions and first-time applications in the areas of Cognitive Science, Information Science and Education Technology, to his credit. Dr. Mitra has been the Chief Scientist at NIIT and is currently Professor of Educational Technology at Newcastle University, UK.

Dr. Mitra is a winner of "Man of Peace Award" from Together for Peace Foundation, USA, and "Social Innovation Award" from Institute of Social Inventions, UK. He was also conferred the "Dewang Mehta Award" by the Government of India in recognition for his work related to Hole-in-the-Wall.

## About NIIT

NIIT, the global IT Learning Solutions Corporation, is known for its pioneering work in the field of IT education and training. Its strong research orientation has helped it to continuously innovate in the areas of instructional design methodologies, and curricula development that is cutting-edge.

NIIT's vast education delivery network spread across 33 countries in the Americas, Europe, Asia, Middle East, Africa and Australia/Oceania, blends classroom and on-line learning. The company provides a comprehensive education environment to individuals and enterprises; offering training that is customized to the varied needs of audiences with diverse backgrounds.

http://www.hole-in-the-wall.com/Beginnings.html

To learn more about NIIT, go to www.pearsonhotlinks.com, enter the title or ISBN of this book and click on Chapter 10.

### General comprehension

1. What was Dr Mitra's basic idea behind the Hole-in-the-Wall computer experiment?
2. How did the slum dwellers react to the Hole-in-the-Wall computer?
3. What did the Kalkaji experiment show?
4. How was this later confirmed?
5. What was the aim of the company Hole-in-the-Wall Education Limited?
6. What results has the experiment now had?
7. Can you understand how this was possible?
8. How would you describe Dr Mitra?

### Text handling

1. In the text there are a number of interesting phrases. If the phrases are new to you, try to understand them from the context. Explain these phrases in your own words.

    a) toying with an idea
    b) slum dwellers
    c) freely accessible computers
    d) prior experience
    e) incidental learning
    f) minimal human guidance
    g) Minimally Invasive Education
    h) joined hands
    i) clusters of computers
    j) long-term educationist

2. True or false? Justify your answer with a relevant brief quotation from the text.

    a) Dr Mitra has been thinking about unsupervised learning and computers since 1982.
    b) The first computer was installed far away from the NIIT premises, in a slum.
    c) The children already had experience of computers.
    d) Dr Mitra believes children just need access to computers to learn basic computing skills.
    e) Hole-in-the-Wall Education Limited (HiWEL) was formed by two companies.
    f) All of the results have been encouraging.
    g) Dr Mitra has been recognised across the world for his work, but not in India.
    h) Unfortunately, NIIT is not able to offer training to people with a variety of needs.

# 10 Technology in education

### Zoom in on grammar

#### 'Since' and 'for'

*Since* and *for* are often used in expressions of time with the present perfect.

- *Since* is used with a point in time – since + point in time.
  since my birthday, since Christmas, since you arrived
- *For* is used with a period of time – for + period of time.
  for six weeks, for two years, for as long as I can remember

### Grammar in context

#### 'Since' and 'for'

Complete the following sentences with *since* or *for*.

1 Dr Mitra has been thinking about unsupervised learning _____ 1982.
2 The Hole-in-the-Wall computers have been in use _____ over 15 years now.
3 Slum dwellers have been using computers _____ Dr Mitra had them installed.
4 The Hole-in-the-Wall Project has been known worldwide _____ a long time.
5 The Hole-in-the-Wall computers have been in use _____ 26th January 1999.

### Interactive oral activity

Make some notes about your impressions of Dr Mitra's work and be ready to discuss them with your group. Think of at least four questions which you could ask others in the group to keep the discussion flowing.

## Text 10.2.3 The Flat Classroom project: Introduction

Global collaborative learning experiences are an essential trait of the 21st century school. It is time to move forward in every school and experience the advantages of these projects in classrooms around the world. Global collaboration has evolved since the beginning of the information era and allows classrooms to merge into common experiences and projects. Integrating it into the curriculum is vital to those schools that want to remain relevant, engaged with learners, and known for achievement. Global literacy and global competency are now being discussed as an important part of the curriculum of each school. You can't develop global literacy from a book; it can only come through experience.

### Group work with a difference!

The Flat Classroom project is an exciting learning experience where students from different countries and cultures work together online with their peer-group to research and present their ideas jointly although they never meet face to face and possibly never will!

The Flat Classroom Project allows upper middle and high school levels to study and explore emerging trends and "flatteners" in our world as discussed in Thomas Friedman's book *"The World is Flat"*. Students learn about technology trends in a project designed to let them experience those trends firsthand.

There are two main components: a collaborative group wiki and a personal video. Grouped in cross-school teams, students conduct authentic research and collaboratively edit a wiki on their topic. They can more closely connect with partners on the project's social network through forums, blogs, a live chat, and message walls. Educators, business leaders or pre-service teachers serve as expert advisors on the wiki.

The personal video is a response to the research from a specific creative perspective. Using one of the six senses of the conceptual age from Dan Pink's *A Whole New Mind* a student may tell her or his story using the first-person voice, or another one of the "six senses". Students outsource a section of their video to another student in another classroom. This makes them not just participants studying the forces that make the world flat, but rather those who have lived it. Educators serve as judges to determine the top videos in an awards program at the end of the project. At the conclusion of the project, students report their reflections on post-project blog posts and student summits in the online presentation room.

> For more information about the Flat Classroom Project, go to www.pearsonhotlinks.com, enter the title or ISBN of the book and click on Chapter 10.

Flattening Classrooms, Engaging Minds: Move to Global Collaboration One Step at a Time
*(Pearson Resources for 21st Century Learning)*

## General comprehension

1. What does the expression 'Flat Classroom' mean to you after reading the text?
2. Why does the author think global collaboration is important? Give three reasons.
3. How can global literacy be developed?
4. Who do the students work with on their Flat Classroom projects?
5. What must they produce?
6. How do students connect with their partners?
7. What happens in the awards programme?
8. What makes them not just participants studying the forces that make the world flat, but rather those who have lived it? And why?

## Text handling

Explain the following expressions in the text.

1. collaborative learning
2. essential trait
3. global collaboration
4. peer-group
5. emerging trends
6. authentic

173

# 10 Technology in education

## Text 10.2.4 The Flat Classroom project: Learning is social

Learning is a social experience that can be enhanced with social networking tools and Web 2.0 technologies. Findings from the *Digital Youth Project: Living and Learning with New Media* [a research project which looked at how young people are living and learning with new media] tell us that youths currently engage in peer-based, self-directed learning online.

Although adults can be influential in setting learning goals and in functioning as role models, the use of new media by youth allows them to learn from their peers. Recent research by the Cisco Learning network also supports the power of peer-to-peer learning. Cisco found that in the case of IT professionals, peer-to-peer learning is necessary and just as important as knowledge coming from the instructor.

According to Steve Hargadon, an expert in social media in education and the founder of Classroom 2.0 (an educational network of over 50,000 educators), the impact of Web 2.0 has changed people's relationships to information and extended personal learning opportunities. Educational networking can minimize isolation in learning and create powerful learning conduits between students.

In the Flat Classroom Projects, which typically study technology topics, we see forum posts on topics about novels, history, and other subjects considered to be 'core' and not traditionally considered targets for technology integration. Students want to learn from their peers and make learning social. This inclination towards social learning occurs anytime we connect students for academic purposes.

The traditional classroom that exists as a distinct entity with one teacher and a group of students can no longer close the door on the world. In fact, a new learning landscape has evolved where responsibility for the curriculum, content and learning is equally shared among all learners (teachers and students).

Flattening Classrooms, Engaging Minds: Move to Global Collaboration One Step at a Time
*(Pearson Resources for 21st Century Learning)*

### General comprehension

Decide which of the following statements are true according to the text.
1. Many young people learn through peers, or independently, online.
2. Independent learning is as important as being taught by a teacher.
3. Studying and learning online is lonely.
4. Many of the posts on the Flat Classroom projects have nothing to do with school work.
5. The old idea of one teacher in a classroom with the door closed will never change.

### Text handling

Match the words from the text on the left to the closest meanings on the right. There are more meanings than you need.

1. influential
2. isolation
3. inclination
4. distinct
5. responsibility

A. ignorance
B. arrogance
C. powerful
D. accountability
E. tendency

F. being alone
G. clear
H. necessity

### Interactive oral activity

Can you see a common idea in both the Hole-in-the-Wall project of Dr Mitra and the Flat Classroom project of Julie Lindsay and Vicki Davis? What do you think they have in common and what are the key differences?

After you have discussed the questions in some depth in your group, make a chart or another kind of visual to show the commonalities and differences between the two projects.

## Zoom in on grammar

### Abstract nouns

In the text above there are a number of abstract nouns. These refer to an idea or a quality which is not concrete, meaning that it cannot be seen or touched. For example: *independence*, *integration*, *inclination*, *responsibility*, *isolation*. Abstract nouns often make a text seem more difficult to understand, but if we look closely at the word we can usually identify the meaning by the more familiar verb or adjective form (though not all of these words will exist in all three forms). For example:

| Abstract noun | Verb | Adjective |
| --- | --- | --- |
| isolation | isolate | isolated |
| arrogance | – | arrogant |
| ignorance | ignore | ignorant |
| necessity | necessitate | necessary |
| importance | – | important |

Do you see a pattern emerging with some of these endings?

## Grammar in context

### Abstract nouns

Look at the text again and find at least five abstract nouns. Make a table like the one above. Note: It is possible that not all of the words have each form.

## Exam practice

# Exercises

### Written assignment 1: Essay title (HL)

Re-read three of the texts about technology in the classroom and choose a common theme or area of focus which you could explore in a written assignment. When you have chosen your theme and your main arguments, decide on an appropriate genre. Plan your work carefully; write an outline first and then a rationale. Think about it before you begin the final copy to make sure your arguments are strong and well expressed.

### Written assignment 2: Personal response (HL)

'We need to educate the "net generation" differently not so much because they are different but because the world is different.'

*Dr Eric Brunsell, College of Education and Human Services, University of Wisconsin, Oshkosh, 03/05/2009.*

Based on the stimulus, give a personal response and justify it. Write between 150 and 250 words.

### Written assignment 3: Essay (SL)

You have been asked to explain the Flat Classroom project to a group of middle-school students. Choose whether you would like to do this in a speech, a flyer, or an article for the school magazine. Write between 250 and 350 words.

# 11 Mobile phones

## Objectives

- To revise the imperative form
- To review the passive and active voices
- To review 'used to' and 'get used to'
- To practise using the gerund as a subject
- To practise writing guidelines
- To review prepositional verbs
- To discuss how mobile phones have changed the way we communicate

**Opposite** A life-changing invention?

# 11.1 Mobile phones and manners

## Text 11.1.1 Mobile obsession

> **In little more than a generation mobile phones have become a fixture in our lives. We do not leave home without them. And in a country with a population of about 63 million there are an astonishing 81.6 million mobile subscriptions**

**by Geraint Jones; Sunday, July 7 2013**

Britain's mobile obsession makes staggering reading: in 2011 calls on mobiles exceeded those on landlines for the first time, we sent more than 150 billion text messages and with the spread of smartphones 32.6 million subscribers used mobiles to access the internet (almost 10 million more than in 2010).

But the huge transformation they have made to our lives comes at a price. Chatting, texting and surfing all plunge us into a little world of our own making us lose our awareness of others even when we are in packed public places such as railway stations, shops and high streets.

And it means that far too often we fail to consider those around us and we lose our sense of good manners. Now Debrett's, Britain's definitive guide to etiquette, has produced a list of what is and is not acceptable mobile behaviour.

It tells users: "Don't carry on mobile phone calls while transacting other business – in banks, shops, on buses and so on. It is insulting not to give people who are serving you your full attention.

"People in the flesh deserve more attention than a gadget, so wherever possible turn off your phone in social situations.

"Ensure that your mobile phone conversation is not disturbing other people. Intimate conversations are never appropriate in front of others, try to respect your own and other people's privacy.

"Your mobile phone is not a megaphone, so don't shout.

"Don't use foul language, have full-blooded rows, or talk about money, sex or bodily functions in front of witnesses.

"Monitor the volume of your ringtone; if it blares out and heads turn it's too loud."

The guide adds: "The ways in which this indispensable little gadget can cause offence are legion. Remember, above all, that you are not joined at the hip to this useful device. It is important to be aware at all times of good mobile phone etiquette."

Although Sainsbury's [a well-known supermarket] last week backed a customer after a checkout girl refused to serve her while she was on her mobile, yesterday it promised not to discipline her. It added that it hoped

# 11 Mobile phones

"the discussion this has created leads us all to think twice before reaching for our mobiles and to recognise the great job sales assistants across retail do".

Deputy Prime Minister Nick Clegg also came out in favour of the shop assistant, saying that he had a "sneaking sympathy" for the employee's stance.

Speaking on LBC Radio, he said: "I have sat in numerous meetings where people don't look each other in the eye, they drop in and out the conversation. It drives me round the bend. I have an old-fashioned view that people are supposed to talk to each other."

It is not just our sense of good manners that is suffering because of mobile technology; we are also running increasing risks of physical injury. Using a mobile while driving is illegal and makes us four times more likely to cause an accident, but they can also kill us when we are on our feet. Researchers at Tampere Institute of Technology in Finland found that one in six pedestrians have either had an accident or a near miss while using a mobile and many more were likely to have come close to an accident without even realising it.

Scientists have also shown that those who cross the road while a)_____ on a phone raise their b)_____ of being hit by a car by 15 per cent.

Phone obsession: What are the dos and don'ts when using a mobile? Many people are almost c)_____. Children are especially at risk. In 2011 33 10-year-olds and 93 children aged 11 were killed or seriously d)_____ on their way to or from school. The higher figure for the older group is e)_____ explained by the fact that 11-year-olds are six times more f)_____ to own a mobile phone.

Stephen Glaister, of the RAC Foundation, said mobiles "g)_____ pedestrian reaction times and lead to h)_____ judgements about when and where it is safe to cross roads". While the sight of mobile-using pedestrians walking into lampposts, tripping down stairs or i)_____ with other people might make for amusing footage on YouTube, it can be much more serious for the victims, and efforts are now being made to reduce injuries from what is now classed as "inattention blindness".

Brick Lane in London's East End, which is a seething mass of humanity most weekends, has become the country's first "safe text" street with lampposts padded to protect distracted mobile users. Other experts are advocating the introduction of "texting lanes" which are designated obstacle-free corridors marked with bright lines.

In the US, authorities are considering tackling the problem from a different direction, fining people up to £150 for texting while walking. Nevada state assemblyman Harvey Munford said: "So many people are almost oblivious. They are texting and texting, totally unaware as they cross even six-lane highways. Kids are so addicted to those things, it's almost become a plague."

*Daily Express, 07/07/2013, http://www.express./news/uk/413005/Mobile-phones-and-the-death-of-good-manners-why-we-need-new-etiquette-guides*

## General comprehension

1. Which type of phones do the British use more: mobiles or landlines?
2. What does the author think is the price we pay for this transformation?
3. What is Debrett's?
4. What is the first tip Debrett's gives to mobile phone users?
5. Describe what happened in Sainsbury's in your own words.
6. What was Nick Clegg's opinion of this?
7. Is it permissible to use a mobile phone while driving in Britain?
8. What is the effect mobile phones have on pedestrians called?
9. What has been done to the lampposts in Brick Lane and why?
10. How are the authorities in the USA thinking of dealing with the problem?

## Text handling

1. Replace the missing words in the text with the words below.

   **oblivious / chance / injured / flawed / chatting / possibly / impair / colliding / likely**

2. Find words in the text which could be meaningfully replaced with the words below. The words are all in the first seven paragraphs of the text.

   a) amazing
   b) was more than
   c) change
   d) good social behaviour
   e) private
   f) loudhailer

3. Explain the following expressions from the text in your own words.

   a) sneaking sympathy
   b) drop in and out of the conversation
   c) drives me round the bend
   d) impair reaction times
   e) seething mass of humanity

## Interactive oral activity

How dependent are you on your mobile phone? How long could you exist without it?

In your group, discuss the role of the mobile phone in your life – how often, why and when do you use your mobile phone?

## Zoom in on grammar

**The imperative**
When writing instructions or a definitive guide, like Debrett's, the imperative (or 'command form') is used. For this, the root form of the verb is taken. Negatives are indicated with 'don't' or 'do not'. Extra emphasis can be added to positive instructions by using 'do'.

## Grammar in context

**The imperative**
Look again at the imperative verbs used in the excerpts from the Debrett's guide in the text. You will find that the sentences begin with the root form of the verb and there are no personal pronouns used. For example: 'Ensure… '.

Find other examples in the text.

Now discuss with a partner what other suggestions could be made to improve mobile phone etiquette, and list these ideas in the command form.

# 11  Mobile phones

### Written work (HL)

As a responsible senior student, you have been asked to write a set of guidelines for your school concerning the appropriate use of mobile phones during the school day. These may be used as the basis for school policy, so think carefully. Write between 250 and 400 words.

### Written work (SL)

Which ideas were most surprising or interesting for you in this text? Write a reflection in the form of a diary entry. Write between 250 and 400 words.

## 11.2  The history of mobile phones

### Text 11.2.1 Forty years of the mobile phone

http://www.express./news/science-technology/388974/40-years-of-the-mobile-phone-Top-20-facts.

# 20 TOP FACTS
by Adrian Lee; Wednesday April 3 2013

1. The first mobile telephone call was made on April 3, 1973 by Martin Cooper, a former Motorola inventor, who is known as "the father of the cellphone".

2. From Sixth Avenue in New York he rang the boss of a rival manufacturer who was less than thrilled to discover that he had lost the race to develop a portable, hand-held device. Cooper later recalled: "There was silence at the other end of the line. I suspect he was grinding his teeth."

3. The weight of the phone used to make that call was about the same as a bag of sugar (2lb). The brick-like battery required, which allowed a talk time of just 30 minutes and took 10 hours to charge, made carting it around even more of a chore.

4. A decade later in 1983 the first mobile phones went on sale in the US costing about £2,500 each. By 1990 there were a million users.

5. The first mobile phone call made in the UK was in 1985 when comedian Ernie Wise called from London to Vodafone's offices in Newbury, Berkshire. Mobile phones went on sale here two years later costing £1,200 each and became the must-have gadget of the yuppie. They entered popular culture when Del Boy was seen brandishing one in the hit TV series *Only Fools And Horses*. Nine out of 10 adults in the UK now have a mobile phone.

http://www.express./news/science-technology/388974/40-years-of-the-mobile-phone-Top-20-facts

**6** Voicemail was first added to mobile phones in 1986, followed 10 years later by the first laborious internet access from handsets.

**7** Long before the iPhone there was IBM Simon. Released in 1993 this bulky gadget was the first smartphone and had calendar, fax, touch screen and a host of other features – all for about £500.

**8** The bestselling single model is the Nokia 1100, made in Finland. More than 250 million devices were snapped up, also making the phone the top-selling electrical gadget in history, ahead of the PlayStation 2. The phones are still highly sought after on the second-hand market and sales boomed after a false rumour that a software glitch allowed fraudulent bank transactions to be carried out using the device.

**9** Mobile phone texting was first introduced 21 years ago. Neil Papworth, a 22-year-old software programmer from Reading, sent the first message when he wished his friend Richard Jarvis of Vodafone: "Merry Christmas." At the time mobile phones didn't have keyboards so it was sent via personal computer.

**10** The first photo to be shared using a mobile phone was taken in 1997 by Philippe Kahn. He sent snaps from the maternity ward where his daughter Sophie was born. Kahn, an inventor from France, is credited with developing the world's first camera phone.

**11** Celina Aarons, from Florida, is thought to hold the dubious honour of having racked up the highest ever mobile phone bill. She neglected to change her calling plan to an international one when the phone was used for two weeks in Canada. The result was a £142,000 bill, which was later reduced to £1,800 by the phone company.

**12** In the UK a mobile phone is stolen every three minutes. The Metropolitan Police claim that such thefts account for one third of all street robberies in London. Inventors are working on the idea of keeping your sim card safe by inserting it into your forearm.

**13** The Sonim XP3300 Force is recognised by the Guinness World Records as the toughest phone. It survived after an 84ft drop on to a layer of concrete without suffering any operational damage.

**14** Drivers' reactions are a third slower when talking on a handheld mobile than when under the influence of alcohol.

# 11 Mobile phones

`http://www.express./news/science-technology/388974/40-years-of-the-mobile-phone-Top-20-facts`

**15** Fake trees and cacti, which are used to conceal mobile phone masts, have become an art form and featured in photographic exhibitions. Following complaints about the appearance of the 40,000 masts in the UK, companies have developed ingenious disguises. Next time you're out take a closer look at that chimney, clock, drainpipe or weather vane.

**16** The first cell phone to be used by James Bond was an Ericsson JB988 in *Tomorrow Never Dies* in 1997. The handset contained various fictional extras such as a fingerprint scanner, lock pick, stun gun and remote control for 007's BMW car.

**17** The world's most expensive mobile phone carries a £6.7 million price tag. The height of luxury or vulgarity, depending on your point of view, it's a version of the iPhone. The device is made from solid gold, encrusted with 500 diamonds and comes in a platinum box.

**18** Phantom calls to the police are a big problem. Even if a phone is locked emergency calls can still be made accidentally. At one time UK police forces were receiving 11,000 phantom calls a day. In the US two men were caught breaking into a car after one accidentally dialled 911 and officers overheard everything.

**19** The most common use for a mobile is neither calling nor texting but checking the time. This has prompted concerns texting will bring about the death of the wristwatch.

**20** More than 180 million iPhones have been sold to date. If you turn them sideways and line them up, they measure more than 12,700 miles. Someone has bothered to work out that's long enough to build a bridge from Rio de Janeiro to Shanghai, go halfway around the world or circle Pluto almost three times. Modern devices can weigh less than 3oz and around the world there are now 5 billion mobile telephones. In the UK the volume of calls from mobile phones first exceeded the volume of calls from fixed phones in 2011. The mobile phone industry is the fastest-growing in the world.

*http://www.express./news/science-technology/388974/40-years-of-the-mobile-phone-Top-20-facts*

## General comprehension

1. Create a timeline using information from the text. Starting from 1973, add the information for the dates mentioned up to 2011.
2. Which of the 20 facts surprised you the most?
3. Do you believe all of them? Which ones don't you believe? Why? Why not?
4. How does the weight of your phone compare with that of the earliest phones?
5. Why do you think the mobile phone industry is the fastest-growing industry in the world?
6. What differences do you think there will be between mobile phones now and in ten years from now?

## Text handling

1. Find words in the text that could be meaningfully replaced with the words below. The words are in order according to the text.

   a) competitor
   b) can be carried
   c) task
   d) ten years
   e) young, modern person
   f) funny man
   g) waving
   h) difficult

2. True or false? Justify your answer with a relevant brief quotation from the text.

   a) More Playstation 2 gadgets are sold than mobile phones.
   b) A mistake in the software allowed criminals to make bank transfers on other people's mobile phones.
   c) The highest ever mobile phone bill occurred because the owner used her phone in another country without changing her calling plan.
   d) One third of all items stolen on the streets of London are mobile phones.
   e) Mobile phone masts are often disguised.
   f) Emergency phone calls cannot be made if the phone is locked.
   g) Mobile phones are used most often to text.

**TOK:** To what extent have mobile phones affected communication – for the better or the worse?

## Interactive oral activity

Interview someone you know quite well who is at least 20 years older than you about how life has changed due to the mobile phone. Make a list of questions first, but then try to develop the conversation from their comments. Ask about how they kept in contact with friends in the past, how often they had contact with them, and how this has changed. Ask them about their opinion of the advantages and disadvantages of mobile phones. Share the results with your group.

## Zoom in on grammar

### The passive voice

The passive is formed with *to be* plus a passive participle. For example:

|  | **Active** | **Passive** |
| --- | --- | --- |
| **present simple** | Mother *cooks* dinner. | Dinner *is cooked* by mother. |
| **present continuous** | The class *is reading* Twilight. | Twilight *is being read* by the class. |
| **past simple** | Robbie Williams *sang* the song. | The song *was sung* by Robbie Williams. |

Mobile phones have revolutionized lives in recent years. Talk to your parents or an older relative about how life was different before mobile phones.

## Grammar in context

### The passive voice

Look again at the first sentence of the text.

> The first mobile telephone call *was made* on April 3, 1973 by Martin Cooper, a former Motorola inventor, who is known as "the father of the cellphone".

The sentence is in the past-simple passive, and it tells us who carried out the action. It could be re-written in the active voice.

> Martin Cooper *made* the first mobile telephone call on April 3, 1973.

Re-read the text and find the following.

- One passive sentence in the past simple tense.
- Two passive sentences in the present simple tense.

Then re-write the three sentences in the active voice.

183

# 11 Mobile phones

## 11.3 Mobile phones in the future

Text 11.3.1 Talk to the hand: HOT Watch turns your palm into a mobile phone

http://www.gizmag.com/hot-watch-mobile-phone/28592/

**HOT Watch is a new smartwatch with a directional speaker and microphone embedded in the wrist, allowing the wearer to answer phone calls by cupping their hand to their ear** by Jonathan Fincher; August 6 2013

**1 _____**

The smartwatch market is barely in its infancy, but it's already feeling a bit crowded. With crowd funding success stories like the Pebble and the Agent rubbing shoulders with juggernauts like Apple, Google and Microsoft, a new smartwatch has to bring something truly innovative to the table in order to stand out. PH Technical Labs (PHTL) seems prepared to do just that with the HOT Watch, which has a directional speaker and microphone embedded in the wrist, allowing the wearer to answer phone calls just by cupping their hand to their ear.

**2 _____**

The developers at PHTL designed the watch primarily around their patented Hands On Talk technology, which is where the HOT Watch gets its name. When synced to a smartphone via Bluetooth, users can take calls privately just by using their palms to reflect and amplify the audio directly into their ears instead of relying on a separate headset. Strange as it seems, the designers claim this method delivers incredibly clear sound for both the caller and the wearer.

It's not uncommon these days to see someone with a Bluetooth headset seemingly talking to themselves, but watching a person appear to answer a pretend phone might take more time to get used to. Unlike a regular cell phone though, there's a lot less risk that you'll drop it or accidentally forget it somewhere.

**3 _____**

Aside from this unusual method for answering phone calls, the watch comes packed with almost as many features as a full smartphone. From the HOT Watch, users will be able to access their contacts for caller ID and text messaging, read their email, and even listen to music through their phone's native player. It will also come equipped with some basic apps for checking the weather, stocks, calendar, news, Facebook, and Twitter, amongst many others. PHTL is also planning to provide an SDK so programmers can create their own third-party apps.

**4 _____**

Of course it's still a watch, so wearers will have a choice between different watch faces, along with alarm, timer, and stopwatch functions. You'll still need to take out your regular smartphone however for more advanced functions, like GPS, internet browsing, or the camera. The Bluetooth connection between a phone and the watch usually ranges from 20 to 30 ft (6.1 to 9.1 m). As an added precaution, if they get too far away from each other a proximity alert will sound to let you know if your phone is being left behind or stolen.

**5** _____

A basic HOT Watch measures just 34 x 42 x 8 mm (1.3 x 1.7 x 0.3 in), with a Sharp 1.26-inch E-paper display on the front. The capacitive screen uses multi-touch controls and is made of a smudge-proof, anti-reflective glass that's easy to read even in bright sunlight. Four shortcut buttons are located along the top of the screen, which can be customized to open specific programs. An energy efficient Cortex M3 processor handles most of the watch's basic functions, along with a separate DSP processor just for Bluetooth, call controls, and any audio enhancements. The final design is water resistant up to 50m as well.

**6** _____

The watch is also equipped with a vibration motor as well as a six-axis accelerometer and gyroscope, which opens the door for some unique controls and functions. With the optional HOT Gestures activated, the smartwatch will respond to specific hand motions and touch commands. Moving your hand toward your ear while receiving an incoming call will automatically answer it, while shaking your hand will send it to voice mail, for example. You can also draw letters on the screen to unlock it to specific programs, like "C" for the clock or "D" for the dialpad. There's even an optional program that will detect if the wearer has fallen down suddenly and then automatically text a pre-set emergency number, unless it's canceled within 30 seconds.

**7** _____

The developers launched a Kickstarter campaign to mass produce the HOT Watch and exceeded their US$150,000 goals within the first 30 hours. Anyone who backed the Kickstarter for $119 or more will receive a smartwatch of their own when they ship (from March). The watch is available in Basic, Edge, Classic, and Curve styles with either a gold or silver finish. For the most part, the various models only differ in aesthetics, though the Curve is a bit more expensive and includes a built-in 2,200 mcd flashlight. HOT Watch are taking preorders from their website now: www.hotsmartwatch.com.

### About the author

Jonathan grew up in Norway, China, and Trinidad before graduating film school and becoming an online writer covering green technology, history and design, as well as contributing to video game news sites like Filefront and 1Up. He currently resides in Texas, where his passions include video games, comics, and boring people who don't want to talk about either of those things.

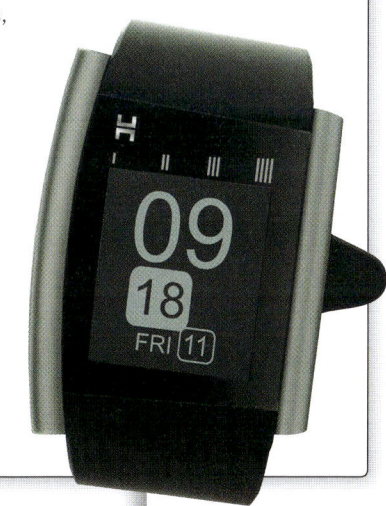

Adapted from http://www.gizmag.com/hot-watch-mobile-phone/28592/

**Above** HOT Watch.

### General comprehension

1. Where does the name HOT Watch come from?
2. Why is there little risk of dropping or losing the smartwatch?
3. What special features does the HOT Watch have?
4. How can you listen to music on the HOT Watch?
5. Is it possible to browse the internet on a HOT Watch?
6. How will you know if your HOT Watch is not with you?
7. What is special about the glass face?
8. How do you send an incoming call to voice mail?

# 11 Mobile phones

### Text handling

1. Put the following paragraph headings in the appropriate places in the text.

   Talk to the hand
   Specifications and other details
   It's your choice
   What's new about the HOT Watch
   Final plans
   The market today
   Other exciting rfeatures

2. True or false? Justify your answer with a relevant brief quotation from the text.
   a) It is unusual to see someone with a Bluetooth headset talking to themselves.
   b) The HOT Watch does not have GPS.
   c) You can answer the HOT Watch just by a hand movement.
   d) If you fall down while wearing a HOT Watch, the emergency services will be called.

3. Explain the following expressions and words used in the text.
   a) cupping their hand
   b) innovative
   c) bring something to the table
   d) embedded in the wrist
   e) enhancements
   f) opens the door for...

### Interactive oral activity

Re-read the text with your partner and make a list of the advantages and disadvantages of the HOT Watch mentioned in the text. Discuss and add any others that may occur to you as you read.

### Zoom in on grammar

**'Used to' and 'get used to'**

1. Jane *used to* live in Australia, but now she is living in Singapore.
2. Jane *used to* smoke, but now she has given it up for her health.

*Used to* expresses the idea that something happened over a long period in the past, as in sentence 1, or happened regularly in the past, as in sentence 2.

To *get used to* something expresses the idea of becoming accustomed to something. We use *get used to* + *-ing*, or *get used to* + noun.

Jane has *got used to* living in Singapore.

Jane had *got used to* feeling fitter.

Bill will *get used to* his new camera.

### Grammar in context

**'Used to' and 'get used to'**

Look at this sentence from the text:

It's not uncommon these days to see someone with a Bluetooth headset seemingly talking to themselves, but watching a person appear to answer a pretend phone might take more time to get used to.

Now write three sentences about yourself using 'used to' and three sentences using 'get used to'.

### Written work

Make a leaflet to advertise the HOT Watch. Try to use your own words and phrases as much as possible, but highlight the many innovative features of the HOT Watch. Write between 250 and 400 words.

## 11.4 Mobile phones and stress

Text 11.4.1 Balancing act: Wellington technology consultant Tilmann Steinmetz has found the perfect way to maintain a good work/life balance – turn your phone off

# Better business

**Stress and overload from cellphones and email are causing workers to be unproductive for an average of four hours each week, new research suggests**

The encroachment of work into after hours and digital distractions in the office have also caused an "invisible pandemic" of poor productivity in the workplace, according to results from the *Workplace Productivity Report*. Authored by behavioural neuroscientist Dr Lucia Keleher and employment specialist Kate Boorer, the report surveyed 435 Australian workers about distraction and overload in the workplace. It found that 85 per cent of respondents could be more productive at work – more than half admitted they were frequently distracted. Describing distraction as the "nemesis" of productivity, the report found each employee was unproductive for an average of four hours per week because of stress and overload. With the digital world meaning people were connected constantly, 80 per cent of workers said they responded to email at home and 72 per cent took work home. This could lead to burnout and poor productivity.

"The results from this study clearly indicate that distraction due to the deluge of 'stuff' we are all incessantly bombarded with has created a 'silent or invisible' pandemic of poor productivity."

The study found workers fell into two broad categories, with 20 per cent coined "early adapters" and the remainder "constrained defeatists". Defeatists believed their feeble productivity was caused by poor culture or outdated practices at their workplaces, while adapters coped well with a 24-hour work cycle and were often employed

# 11 Mobile phones

by progressive businesses. Wellington cloud computing company Xero's general manager of human resources, Natasha Hubbard, said with the company experiencing explosive growth, it was "all hands to the pump". This meant many staff were working long hours, answering emails from home and even taking phone calls while on holiday. To ensure employees did not burn out, it was important the company listened to its workers.

"We promote a culture where it's OK to say: 'I'm tired, I need to come in late tomorrow, I need to take some time in lieu because I worked all weekend'."

Business NZ chief executive Phil O'Reilly agreed the most productive employees were those who felt in control of their situation, and more companies were embracing policies such as flexible working hours to achieve that. It was essential employers and employees agreed on some ground rules about technology.

"It needs to be made OK to turn their phone off and not respond. What's unhealthy is when employers hand out these devices and expect they will get answered at all times of the day and night.

"Treating an employee, and the boss for that matter, simply as a human being is important… I think technology can be empowering rather than some sort of slavery."

Wellington employment lawyer Susan Hornsby-Geluk said while she was not aware of any cases that had focused solely on being available outside work hours, it was becoming more prevalent in general workplace stress cases. Employers had to ensure the health and safety of workers, but employees needed to ensure they were not putting themselves in overwhelming situations. "If an employee said to their employer: 'I'm not prepared to check emails outside of work', an employer could not compel them to do so."

Deputy State Services Commissioner Sandi Beatie said many public servants were required to work outside the office or be on call and mobile technology was a useful tool that allowed them to have more flexible work arrangements.

Tilmann Steinmetz works as a consultant for Eagle Technology and has a clear policy in managing work emails at home, although he admits he does not get as many as some of his colleagues. When the 42-year-old does check his account periodically in the evenings, it is rare for him to respond unless the matter is urgent. "I don't believe anyone [at Eagle] actually expects me to answer right away, depending on the issue. When I'm on leave I actually switch off the [email] synchronisation." Eagle had a flexible work policy and it was lucky to be in an industry where working from home was simple. After taking a day off sick, Steinmetz said it was no problem for him to remain at home the next day and work remotely. But generally he preferred to go into work, then switch off after knocking off for the day. His friend worked from home and set his own hours, which was fine, but not the ideal situation for everyone, he said.

## TIME MANAGEMENT TIPS

Make your calendar, not email, the first thing you open during the day. Email is often given precedence because of its immediacy, but time management coach Chris Macintosh says focusing on the calendar helps workers prioritise their most important work first.

Set out specific periods for checking your emails and stick to them. While not suiting every job, having set times to sort out emails boosts productivity for many people. Make a decision on every email as you read it – either delete it, delegate it, do it now or de-activate it by turning it into a task or appointment on your calendar.

Learn to say no. Just because you are invited to a meeting does not mean you must go. Mr Macintosh recommends busy workers block out time in their calendar with jobs, so they do not feel forced into tasks they have no time to fit in.

Set out what you will do tomorrow before leaving work today. This will help with the next day's efficiency, and it means you will worry less about work and sleep better at night, leaving you refreshed and ready for the day.

http://www.stuff.co.nz/the-press/news/8928152/Digital-stress-overwhelming-workers-study, © Fairfax NZ News

## General comprehension

True or false? Justify your answer with a relevant brief quotation from the text.

1. If workers had less stress and overload, they would not be more productive.
2. The amount of information we are confronted with leads to poor productivity.
3. Workers who successfully manage being constantly connected hardly ever work for progressive businesses.
4. Employers and employees should agree how technology should be used.
5. It must be acceptable for employees to switch off their phones and not reply after working hours.
6. An employer can force an employee to check emails out of work.
7. Although Tilmann Steinmetz may check his emails in the evening at home, he does not always reply.

## Text handling

Look closely at how these words and phrases are used in the text, and try to explain them in your own words.

1. encroachment
2. nemesis
3. deluge
4. pandemic
5. all hands to the pump
6. to work remotely

## Zoom in on grammar

### Prepositional verbs

A prepositional verb is a verb + preposition followed by an object. For example: *ask for (a pay rise)*, *believe in (yourself)*, *complain to (the manager)*, *wait for (a bus)*.

Some prepositional verbs can take more than one preposition and so change the meaning. For example:

- *complain to someone* – means to share your concerns or complaints with someone
- *complain about* someone/something – means you have concerns or complaints about someone or something.

## Grammar in context

### Prepositional verbs

Below are sentences from the text. Without looking back, try to put in the correct preposition for the verb. Check your answers when you have finished.

1. With the digital world meaning people were connected constantly, 80 per cent of workers said they responded _____ email at home and 72 per cent took work home.
2. The results from this study clearly indicate that distraction due to the deluge of 'stuff' we are all incessantly bombarded _____ has created a 'silent or invisible' pandemic of poor productivity.
3. Defeatists believed their feeble productivity was caused _____ poor culture or outdated practices at their workplaces
4. To ensure employees did not burn out, it was important the company listened _____ its workers.
5. It was essential employers and employees agreed _____ some ground rules about technology.
6. Just because you are invited _____ a meeting does not mean you must go.

# 11 Mobile phones

> **Interactive oral activity**
>
> Look again at the time management tips at the end of the text and discuss them with your group. Are they helpful or realistic? Which would be the most useful for you to follow? Do you have any other tips to add to the list?

## Written work

A friend of yours has successfully applied for a job with a prestigious company. You know that the employees there are under a lot of pressure and often suffer from stress. Write an email to your friend congratulating her/him on the appointment, but warning of the dangers of overwork and giving some careful advice on ways to avoid burnout. Be creative and imaginative! Write between 250 and 400 words.

## Exam practice

# The future of mobile phones: A remote control for your life

*In the near future, your mobile phone will be so powerful it'll guide you through your whole life, says William Webb*

It is 2025. Your mobile is now much more than just a communication device – more like a remote control for your life. You still call it a "mobile" from habit, but it is an organiser, entertainment device, payment device and security centre, all developed and manufactured by engineers.

On a typical day it will start work even before you wake. Because it knows your travel schedule it can check for problems on the roads or with the trains and adjust the time it wakes you up accordingly, giving you the best route into work. It can control your home, re-programming the central heating if you need to get up earlier and providing remote alerts if the home security system is triggered. It is your payment system – just by placing the phone near a sensor on a barrier, like the Oyster card readers in use on London transport, you can pay for tickets for journeys or buy items in shops. With an understanding of location, the mobile can also provide directions, or even alert the user to friends or family in the vicinity.

It is your entertainment centre when away from home. As well as holding all your music files, as some phones today are able to do, it will work with your home entertainment system while you sleep to find programmes that will interest you and download them as a podcast to watch on the train or in other spare moments. It will intelligently work out what to do with incoming phone calls and messages. Because it knows your diary it will also know, for example, to direct voice calls to voicemail when you are in a meeting, perhaps providing a discrete text summary of the caller and the nature of their call.

> ❗ The Oyster card is an electronic smartcard used in London; travellers can scan their Oyster card to pay for bus, tube and rail services, and more.

With its understanding of almost all aspects of your life, many new services become possible. For example, a "Good Food" meal planning service could send daily suggestions for your evening meal based on learned preferences, previous selections made and the likely contents of your refrigerator. The latter might work by uploading the bill from the weekly grocery shop and then removing those items it deduces have been used for meals earlier in the week.

Leaving home without your mobile, bad enough already, will become rather like leaving home without your wallet, keys, music player and mobile all at once – quite unthinkable. And in the nicest, most helpful ways, your mobile will guide you through life.

So what will this apparently massive change in our relationships with our mobiles require in the way of new technology or extra expenditure? Actually, surprisingly little. Now that we have widespread cellular coverage, with high-speed data networks in many homes, offices and points of congregation such as coffee shops, we have all we need to get signal to the mobile.

What we do need is better mobiles and more intelligence. Mobiles will continue to get steadily better, with higher resolution touch-screens, speech recognition that really works and much greater memory and storage capabilities. Increasingly intelligent software will be running on these mobiles, and also on home and wide-area networks, able to learn behaviour, predict needs and integrate with a growing number of databases, such as transport updates from major providers. So, instead of the train company just sending you a text to tell you of delays, your mobile will analyse it in conjunction with your travel plans and modify those plans if needs be.

This evolution will be a slow but steady one as every few years mobiles get slightly better, intelligent software evolves and the various providers of all the necessary input data – such as transport organisations and shops – gradually make the data available in formats that become increasingly useful.

Ten years ago the mobile was purely a device for making voice calls. Now it is a camera, MP3 player, organiser and texting device. This is only the start of an evolution that will turn it into our trusted and indispensable companion in life.

http://www.independent.co.uk/student/magazines/the-future-of-mobile-phones-a-remote-control-for-your-life-448816.html

# 11 Mobile phones

### Exercises

Answer the following questions.

1. How will your mobile phone help you with travel plans?

2. Which new features will the mobile phone have for entertainment?

3. How can it help in the kitchen?

4. Will all these features make the mobile very expensive?

5. What is 'intelligent software'?

6. Can you predict any disadvantages that this technology will bring?

7. True or false? Justify your answer with a relevant brief quotation from the text.

A. Your phone will no longer be called a 'mobile' in 2025.

B. Your phone will inform you if there is a security problem at home.

C. You will not be able to pay for goods with your phone.

D. Your phone will be able to tell you if your relatives are nearby.

E. It will find programmes you like and download them for you to watch later.

F. Your phone calls will still come through even if you are busy.

G. It will be able to plan your dinner because it knows what will be in your refrigerator.

H. Leaving home without your mobile phone will be dreadful.

I. This will all demand a lot of new technology.

J. Ten years ago, a mobile phone only made phone calls.

**8** Match the words from the text with the synonyms on the right. Write the appropriate letter in the box below.

| | | | | |
|---|---|---|---|---|
| I | remote control | ☐ | A | in the area |
| II | habit | ☐ | B | together with |
| III | it is triggered | ☐ | C | money spent |
| IV | in the vicinity | ☐ | D | controlled from a distance |
| V | discreet | ☐ | E | huge |
| VI | it deduces | ☐ | F | it is started |
| VII | massive | ☐ | G | cannot do without |
| VIII | expenditure | ☐ | H | something you do regularly |
| IX | in conjunction with | ☐ | I | not noticeable |
| X | indispensable | ☐ | J | it works out |

## Further exercises

### Zoom in on grammar

#### The gerund

As we saw in Chapter 3, the gerund can be used as the subject of a sentence. Often it has several accompanying words, in which case it forms a 'gerund clause'. A gerund is also used after the following sentence beginnings:

*There is no...*

*It is no good...*

*It is useless...*

*It is no use...*

With both 'it is useless' and 'it is no use', the infinitive can also be used: 'It is useless to talk to him' or 'It is no use to try to call him'.

### Grammar in context

#### The gerund

'Leaving home without your mobile, bad enough already, will become rather like leaving home without your wallet, keys, music player and mobile all at once – quite unthinkable.'

Make sentences using the beginnings below which reflect the meaning of the sentence quoted from the text:

**1** It is no good... **2** It is useless... **3** It is no use...

## Written work

Do you think your life will be controlled by your mobile in 2025? Write a reflection on the information in the text and give your own description of life in 2025. Write between 150 and 250 words.

# 12

Mass media and social media

**Opposite** Too much information?

## Objectives
- To revise countable and uncountable nouns
- To practise the use of 'since' for giving reasons
- To revise the use of 'many', 'much', 'a lot of' and 'lots of'
- To revise the differences between 'affect' and 'effect'
- To practise using the possessive form 's
- To consider how mass media and social media influence our lives

# 12.1 Mass media and social media

## Text 12.1.1 Mass media in the 21st century

### How did it all begin?

It may be difficult for many people to imagine that just a generation ago, mass media as we know it today was unthinkable.

It all began following the Industrial Revolution when there was a real need for information to be shared. Postal communication already existed, but that was slow. The first more rapid system of communication was the telegraph.

Before that, Claude Chappe invented a system using flags in 1792. It depended, of course, on people being able to see each other and was called 'semaphore'. In fact, the word 'telegraph' was first coined by Claude Chappe. In 1809, Samuel Soemmering invented the first telegraph system. He transmitted electric signals using up to 35 wires with gold electrodes in water. The message was sent 200 feet, approximately 70 metres, and was created by electrolysis producing bubbles of gas. In 1828, the first telegraph system in the USA was invented by Harrison Dyar who sent electrical sparks through chemically treated paper tape to burn dots and dashes. A number of other systems were then developed to send messages electrically, including the Morse code, which was developed by Samuel Morse in America in 1838.

**Above** A device used to send Morse code.

Two inventors, Elisha Gray and Alexander Graham Bell, invented telephones which could transmit speech in the 1870s, but Bell patented his invention first. The invention of the radio, by Guglielmo Marconi, an Italian inventor, followed quickly in the 1890s and from then the systems were developed and improved upon continuously. Scientists worked on the ways to transmit images; the development of television soon followed.

In 1900 at the World Fair in Paris, a Russian, Constantin Perskyi first used the word 'television' during the first International Congress of Electricity.

# 12 Mass media and social media

Did you know that Charles Dickens' (1812–70) novels appeared first as weekly and monthly instalments in magazines?

In the past, families sat down to watch TV together, but now with modern devices family members often watch different programmes in different rooms.

The first television advertisement was broadcast in 1930 and the British Broadcasting Corporation started regular television broadcasts for three hours a day in 1936. At that time there were about 200 television sets in use worldwide. In 1951 the first colour television was presented in the United States of America.

The first newspapers appeared before any of the electric inventions, but after the printing presses were developed they became one of the most important ways of communicating information. Newspapers were quickly followed by magazines.

And now, in the twenty first century, the Internet and new media supply us with continual news and information as well as entertainment and education. Can you imagine life without it?

## General comprehension

1. What is semaphore?
2. What was a big disadvantage of the postal system?
3. Who patented the telephone?
4. When and where was the word 'television' first used?
5. How do you know what is happening in the world? Which system do you use?

## Text handling

Match the following words on the left to the correct meanings on the right.

| | | | |
|---|---|---|---|
| 1 | generation | A | system of sending messages by electricity/radio signals |
| 2 | telegraph | B | to be the first person to think of/create something |
| 3 | to invent | | |
| 4 | to coin a word | C | fast |
| 5 | rapid | D | to send by an electronic system |
| 6 | to transmit | E | to use for the first time |
| | | F | people of a similar age |

## Written work (HL)

Give a personal response to the following stimulus and justify it, using between 150 and 250 words. Choose any text type you have studied.

> 'The technique is wonderful. I didn't even dream it would be so good. But I would never let my children come close to the thing.'

*Vladimir Zworykin, television developer, interviewed on his 92nd birthday*

### Exam hints

Some tips before you start:
- Who said this and what was he referring to?
- Why do you think he wrote it?
- Do you agree or do you have some reservations?

There is no right or wrong answer for the personal response task. The main point is that you give an organised and logical personal response to the quote.

So, think first about what you want to write and which genre is most appropriate. Then begin to collect the main points you want to make. Organise your ideas and support your arguments.

### Written work (SL)

Imagine you had to exist without any access to mass media for a week. How do you think you would cope? Would it be a relief or a strain?

Write an email to a friend describing how you managed for a full week with no access to mass media. Explain the situation and your reactions to it. Write between 150 and 250 words.

## 12.2 Mass media today

### Text 12.2.1 The influence of mass media

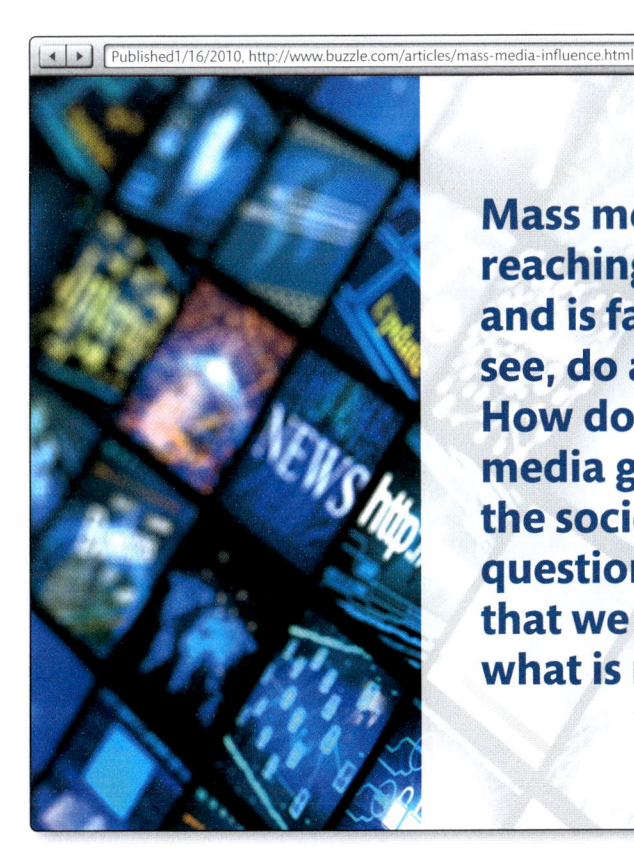

Published 1/16/2010, http://www.buzzle.com/articles/mass-media-influence.html

**Mass media is one of the farthest reaching forms of communication and is fast changing the way we see, do and understand things. How does the modern mass media generate an influence on the society? Before answering this question, perhaps it is pertinent that we address the question: what is mass media?** by Arjun Kulkarni

# 12 Mass media and social media

Published 1/16/2010, http://www.buzzle.com/articles/mass-media-influence.html

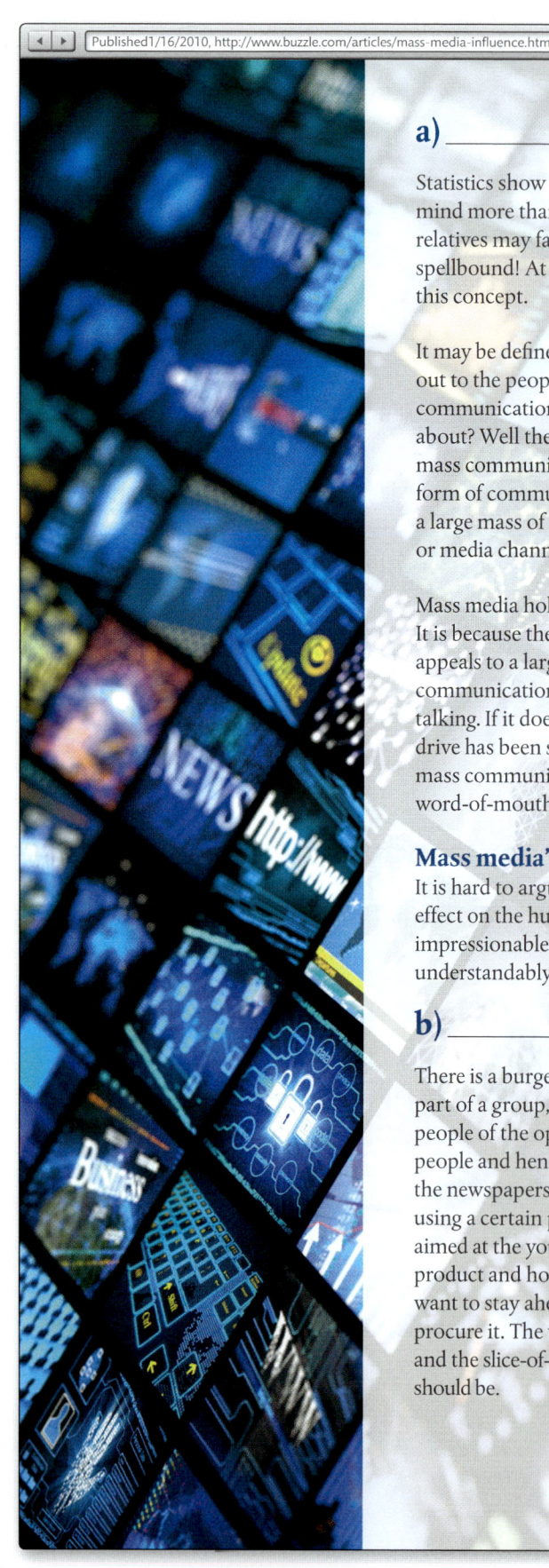

### a) _____

Statistics show that there are few things which impact the human mind more than mass media. The advice of teachers, parents and relatives may fall on deaf ears, but the mass media holds us all spellbound! At this point, it becomes necessary to define this concept.

It may be defined as any form of communication which is meted out to the people at large, through the various forms of communication. What modes of communication are we talking about? Well there can be no static definition for the channels of mass communication as they are increasing all the time. But any form of communication which is seen and understood by a large mass of people can be taken to mean mass communication or media channels.

Mass media holds a kind of mystique in the minds of the people. It is because the communication is designed in such a way that it appeals to a larger demographic segment. The test of a good mass communication marketing drive is to see if it gets the people talking. If it does, then not only does it mean that the advertising drive has been successful, but the organization in charge of the mass communication is also getting publicity by the word-of-mouth channel!

### Mass media's hold

It is hard to argue with the fact that mass media has a compelling effect on the human mind. Especially on minds which are more impressionable. For example, the influence on our children is understandably higher than it is in adults.

### b) _____

There is a burgeoning need amongst the youth to be accepted as a part of a group, to be popular, to have friends and relationships with people of the opposite sex etc. Experts understand this need of the people and hence they come out with advertisements on TV, or in the newspapers, or on websites on how people can be more popular using a certain product. Most advertisements you see which are aimed at the youth generally talk about the 'cool quotient' of the product and how it is going to be the next 'in-thing'. And if you want to stay ahead of the game, it is absolutely vital that you procure it. The visual effect, seeing the things happen in front of you and the slice-of-life effect makes them look a lot believable than they should be.

Published 1/16/2010, http://www.buzzle.com/articles/mass-media-influence.html

Mass media, effective as it is, can be used on the youth to drive home pressing concerns in the country; child obesity, the dangers of alcohol and preteen sexual relations, importance of exercise and fitness etc. If these things can be done, the media will be able to influence the youth for the better and send better messages for the development of the youth than it is sending today.

**c) _____**

Like children and youth, it influences adults too, although perhaps not on the same scale. Most adults with a platonic view of things will resist the temptation of being buoyed up by what entertainment has to offer. While men usually find it difficult to hold themselves back in the face of the allure of sexuality. Other subjects which also appeal to men are financial security and a luxurious hassle-free lifestyle. Women on the other hand are more tempted towards products which guarantee immunity from aging altogether and not just what the previous generation called 'aging gracefully'.

Mass media can yet be used constructively to teach the adults about the importance of insurance, financial education and how to maintain a healthy lifestyle.

As you can see, the mass media hold a large share of importance in society, but if used constructively, it can be more of a boon than the bane which people consign it to be these days. After all, there are two sides to a coin and it is up to us to pick the correct one and take it forward.

Published 16/1/2010, http://www.buzzle.com/articles/mass-media-influence.html

### General comprehension

1. How is mass media defined in the text?
2. How do we know if a good mass communication marketing drive is successful?
3. Give two examples which show how mass media can have a positive effect.
4. True or false? Justify your answer with a relevant brief quotation from the text.
   a) The term mass media is static.
   b) Mass media has little effect on the human mind.
   c) Mass media works if it gets people talking.
   d) Mass media influences adults most.
   e) Mass media influences young people by showing advertisements for products which will make them more popular.
   f) Mass media could have a very positive effect on society.

# 12 Mass media and social media

## Text handling

1  Insert the following paragraph titles appropriately:

The influence on adults
Understanding mass media
The influence on youth

2  What do you think these expressions mean? Work with a partner and see if you can uncover the meaning using context clues.

   a) may fall on deaf ears
   b) hold us spellbound
   c) a kind of mystique
   d) a demographic segment
   e) word of mouth
   f) a compelling effect
   g) more of a boon than a bane

3  The pronoun 'it' is used many times in this text. Re-read the text and try to identify what 'it' stands for in each example below.

   a) It may be defined as... (paragraph 3)
   b) ... designed in such a way that it appeals to... (paragraph 4)
   c) ... to see if it gets the people talking (paragraph 4)
   d) ... is understandably higher than it is in adults (paragraph 5)
   e) ... of the product and how it is going to be the next... (paragraph 6)

## Zoom in on grammar

**Countable and uncountable nouns**

Some nouns can be countable or uncountable, depending on their use; uncountable nouns are often less specific, but a countable noun denotes a particular example.

   We are all members of *society*.

   There are many different *societies* at universities.

## Grammar in context

**Countable and uncountable nouns**

The following abstract nouns from the text are uncountable:

- entertainment
- importance
- influence
- advice
- immunity

Make a sentence for each of the words. For example:

   At 7p.m. the *entertainment* will begin.

## Interactive oral activity

In the text, the writer states:

   'Mass media has a compelling effect on the human mind.'

Working in small groups, divide into two teams.

One team will collect arguments which support this statement (not only those expressed in the article); the other team will find arguments which present the opposite point of view. Take time to prepare your discussion, and make sure everyone in your team has some contributions to make. Do not let anyone dominate the discussion – remember to use expressions like:

- I disagree/I agree
- On the contrary...
- Just a moment, have you considered...
- Well that's all very well, but...

## 12.3 The effects of social media

Text 12.3.1 How does social media affect the way we communicate?

### blog

# Can social media impact day-to-day communication?

If so, does it improve it or stall it? The answer is very simple. Studies have shown that we polish our communication skills when we chat online using various social media sites. The online environment can be shaped by the advanced settings found in our social media sites. We decide who gets to talk to us and who doesn't. We are in control of every piece of information that we wish to share and we can create the image that we want when we try to impress somebody or meet somebody for the very first time.

# 12 Mass media and social media

We can simulate a face-to-face conversation quite easily, since we can use a webcam and a microphone. If we have a shy personality we can easily overcome that by practicing our conversational skills until we reach a point where we feel a bit more confident about ourselves, feeling more capable of engaging in all sorts of conversations.

Social media websites not only enrich the dialogues that we have with people; we can also get in touch with our long distance friends. We can also get other people informed about noble causes or involve in online projects that will help many people benefit from them. We can also promote our business with much more success, if we know how to properly promote our products or services on social media, so as to get people to talk about them.

Using social media websites is a good way of expressing yourself or revealing a part of your personality that you might find difficult to share during face to face communication. As long as we do not forget that online communication is not enough and cannot be a real substitute for face to face human contact, social media can indeed improve the way we communicate.

*http://itviz.com/*

## General comprehension

The writer suggests a number of ways that social media can positively affect the way we communicate. Read the text carefully and make a note of the suggestions.

1  Do you agree with all of her ideas? Explain your answers.
2  Explain the writer's final argument in your own words.
3  How would you describe the writer's attitude to this topic?
   a) critical
   b) positive
   c) accepting
   d) _____ (your own suggestion)

## Text handling

Explain the following terms.

1  to stall something
2  to enrich
3  to engage in
4  to benefit
5  to reveal
6  to promote

## Zoom in on grammar

### 'Since'

*Since* can be used when referring to time with the present perfect:

I haven't had a letter from you since last year.
I have been waiting since 5 o'clock.

But *since* can also be used to give a reason:

Since I have no money, I can't go to the cinema.

### Grammar in context

**'Since'**

Read this sentence from the text again:

> 'We can simulate a face-to-face conversation quite easily, since we can use a webcam and a microphone.'

Which word could we use instead of *since* in the sentence?

### Zoom in on grammar

**'Affect' and 'effect'**

*Affect* is a verb. The most usual meaning is to influence, although there are other meanings.

*Effect* is a noun which means result or consequence, but there are also other less common uses of effect, which you may like to check in your dictionary.

Examples:

> Did studying vocabulary all evening affect (influence) your test score?
> What was the effect (consequence) of studying vocabulary all evening?

### Grammar in context

**'Affect' and 'effect'**

This section of the chapter is entitled 'The effects of social media' and the subheadings are

- How does social media affect the way we communicate?
- How social media networks can affect society negatively.

Look at the use of these two words in the titles.

Now put the correct term in each sentence.

1. How does social media _____ society?
2. What _____ does social media have on society?

## Written work

Write an email to the writer of the text either agreeing or disagreeing with the article and justifying your thoughts. Write between 250 and 400 words.

### Exam hints

Before you begin the work, decide why you are writing and which examples or arguments you will use. Organise your ideas, think about the register/tone and remember that the genre is an email.

# 12 Mass media and social media

### Text handling

Make a T-chart to compare the information given in the article on social media. On one side list the positive attributes, and on the other side list the negative attributes as described in the text. Can you add more examples of your own to the list? When you have finished, compare the finished charts in your group.

| Positive attributes | Negative attributes |
|---|---|
|  |  |

### Written work

Your school principal has asked you, as a representative of the Senior Class, to either make a speech or prepare a set of guidelines for younger students about sensible use of social networks.

- Decide which genre you will use.
- Organise your main ideas with supporting statements or examples.
- Remember the three big ideas:
    - genre – what you write
    - audience – who you are writing for
    - purpose – why you are writing.

### Zoom in on grammar

**'Many', 'much', 'a lot of', 'lots of'**

These are all words which express a large amount of something.

*Many* is used before countable nouns, *much* before uncountable nouns.

- *many ideas* – countable
- *much milk* – uncountable

*A lot of* and *lots of* can both be used before countable and uncountable nouns.

The general rule is that *a lot of* or *lots of* are used in positive sentences, and *much* and *many* are used in negative sentences.

## Text 12.3.2 Tips for dealing with cyberbullying

http://www.beatbullying.org/safety/cyberbullying/

**If you're being cyberbullied, don't ignore it or keep it a secret. Tell someone what's going on. If the first person you talk to doesn't help, don't give up. Try talking to someone else. And if you see cyberbullying going on, report it and offer your support – tell them they can get help at BeatBullying**

**Here are some more tips for dealing with cyberbullying:**

- Don't post personal information online – like your address, your email address or mobile number. Keep personal information as general as possible.

- Save and print out any bullying messages, posts, pictures or videos you receive or see.

- Never respond or retaliate, as this can just make things worse.

- Block any users that send you nasty messages.

- Make a note of the dates and times of bullying messages, along with any details you have about the sender's ID and the URL. Keep a diary of everything that's happening.

- Never let anyone have access to your passwords. Check the privacy settings on accounts like Facebook and make sure you know how to keep your personal information private.

- Think very carefully before posting photos of yourself online. Once your picture is online, anyone can download it and share it or even change it.

- Don't pass on cyberbullying videos or messages about other people.

- Don't ignore it. If you see cyberbullying going on, report it and offer your support.

- If you're being bullied repeatedly, think about changing your user ID, nickname or profile to stop the bullies finding you.

- Always report anything abusive you see online to the site concerned. Flag it, report it, or talk to someone about it.

- You may want to consider marking your photos as private, so that only your friends can view the pictures. On BeatBullying and on other sites, you can set your photos to be seen only by either registered users or friends.

- If someone wants to keep their chats with you a secret, or tells you anything that's a "secret", tell an adult what's happening.

- Google yourself every now and again. It will show you what is online about you and what others can see and you can make changes if you don't like what you see.

http://www.beatbullying.org/safety/cyberbullying/

# 12 Mass media and social media

## General comprehension

1. What is the first, most important, message on this website for people who are being bullied?
2. What is the main message for those who see someone being bullied?
3. Why should the person being bullied never respond?
4. List the things you should not post online.
5. What steps can you take to stop being bullied?
6. How should you react to someone who wants to share 'secrets' with you?
7. Do you have any other tips to add to the list?
8. From what age do you think children should be allowed to go online, without supervision?

## Zoom in on grammar

### The imperative

Did you notice that the tips were all written in the imperative?

- Don't...
- Think...

Sometimes there is an adverb placed before the verb:

- Always...
- Never...

And in other cases the zero conditional is used: If ... + *present*, ... + *present*. For example:

If you're being bullied repeatedly, think about changing your user ID.

## Grammar in context

### Sentence structure

Look again carefully at the text and notice in particular the verbs, adverbs and conditional sentences and how they are used. Note the interesting sentence structures and try to imitate these structures in your own writing.

## 12.4 Social media and the family

### Text 12.4 Alone together

Mark Twain mythologised the adolescent's search for identity in the Huck Finn story, the on-the-Mississippi moment, a time of escape from an adult world. Of course, the time on the river is emblematic not of a moment but of an ongoing process through which children separate from their parents. That rite of passage is now transformed by technology. In the traditional variant, the child internalizes the adults in his or her world before crossing the threshold of independence. In the modern, technologically tethered variant, parents can be brought along in an intermediate space, such as that created by the cell phone, where everyone important is on speed dial. In this sense the generations, sail down the river together, and adolescents don't face the same pressure to develop the independence we have associated with moving forward into young adulthood.

When parents give children cell phones – most of the teenagers I spoke to were given a phone between the ages of nine and thirteen – the gift typically comes with a contract: children are expected to answer their parents' calls. This arrangement makes it possible for the child to engage in activities – see friends, attend movies, go shopping, spend time at the beach – that would not be permitted without the phone. Yet, the tethered child does not have the experience of being alone with only him – or herself to count on. For example, there used to be a point for an urban child, an important moment, when there was a first time to navigate the city alone. It was a rite of passage that communicated to children that they were on their own and responsible. If they were frightened they had to experience those feelings. The cell phone buffers this moment.

Parents want children to answer their phones, but adolescents need to separate. With a group of seniors at Fillmore, a boys' preparatory school in New York City, the topic of parents and cell phones elicits strong emotions. The young men consider, "If it is always possible to be in touch, when does one have the right to be alone?"

Some of the boys are defiant. For one "It should be my decision about whether I pick up the phone. People can call me, but I don't have to talk to them." For another "To stay free from parents, I don't take my cell. Then they can't reach me. My mother tells me to take my cell, but I just don't." Some appeal to history to justify ignoring parents' calls. Harlan, a distinguished student and athlete, thinks he has earned the right to greater independence. He talks about siblings who grew up before cell phones and enjoyed greater freedom: "My mother makes me take my phone, but I never answer it when my parents call and they get mad at me. I don't feel I should have to. Cell phones are recent. In the last ten years everyone started getting them. Before, you couldn't just call someone whenever. My sister didn't have to do that." Harlan's mother, unmoved by this argument, checks that he has his phone when he leaves for school in the morning; Harlan doesn't answer her calls. Things are at an unhappy stalemate.

Several boys referred to the "mistake" of having taught their parents how to text and send instant messages (IMs), which they now equate with letting the genie out of the bottle. For one, "I made the mistake of teaching my parents how to text-message recently, so now if I don't call them when they ask me to call, I get an urgent text message." For another "I taught my parents how to IM. They didn't know how. It was the stupidest thing I could do. Now my parents IM me all the time. It is really annoying. My parents are upsetting me. I feel trapped and less independent."

Teenagers argue that they should be allowed time when they are not "on call". Parents say that they too feel trapped. For if you know your child is carrying a cell phone, it is frightening to call or text and get no response. "I didn't ask for this new worry," says the mother of two high school girls. Another, a mother of three teenagers, "tries not to call them if it's not important." But if she calls and gets no response she panics.

Alone together: why we expect more from technology and less from each other by Sherry Turtle (Basic Books, New York, 2011).

# 12 Mass media and social media

## General comprehension

1. Which term does the author use to describe the process whereby children separate from their parents?
2. What does the term 'tethered parents' mean to you?
3. What is the average age range of children getting their first mobile (cell) phone according to the author? How old were you when you got your first mobile phone?
4. What is the arrangement the author describes between parents and children when they are given a mobile phone?
5. Why don't adolescents always want to answer their phone? Do you always answer your phone?
6. What is another way, described in the text, to avoid answering your phone?
7. Why do some adolescents today feel that always being contactable by mobile phone is unfair?
8. How do some boys view the consequences of teaching their parents to send instant messages?
9. Describe how some parents feel about always being in contact with their children.
10. What is the reaction of parents if they call their children and there is no response?

## Text handling

1. Have you read Mark Twain's book *Huckleberry Finn*? If not, do some research about it; perhaps you can find a plot summary which will help you understand the first paragraph of this text better.

2. Explain the meanings of these words used in the text.
    a) mythology – mythologised
    b) an emblem – emblematic
    c) adolescent
    d) rite of passage
    e) elicit
    f) distinguished
    g) to navigate
    h) urban child
    i) defiant
    j) sibling

3. Without looking back at the text, put the missing words back into the passage. Check your answers with the text after you have completed the exercise.

   **elicits / separate / recent / distinguished / defiant / justify / unmoved / siblings / whether / alone**

   Parents want children to answer their phones, but adolescents need to a)_____. With a group of seniors at Fillmore, a boys' preparatory school in New York City, the topic of parents and cell phones b)_____ strong emotions. The young men consider, "If it is always possible to be in touch, when does one have the right to be c)_____?"

   Some of the boys are d)_____. For one "It should be my decision about e)_____ I pick up the phone. People can call me, but I don't have to talk to them." For another "To stay free from parents, I don't take my cell. Then they can't reach me. My mother tells me to take my cell, but I just don't." Some appeal to history to f)_____ ignoring parents' calls. Harlan, a g)_____ student and athlete, thinks he has earned the right to greater independence. He talks about h)_____ who grew up before cell phones and enjoyed greater freedom: "My mother makes me take my phone, but I never answer it when my parents call and they get mad at me. I don't feel I should have to. Cell phones are i)_____. In the last ten years everyone started getting them. Before, you couldn't just call someone whenever. My sister didn't have to do that." Harlan's mother, j)_____ by this argument, checks that he has his phone when he leaves for school in the morning; Harlan doesn't answer her calls. Things are at an unhappy stalemate.

## Zoom in on grammar

### The possessive

We form the possessive by using apostrophes.

In the singular the apostrophe comes before the s – 's:

- my friend's book (one friend, and one book)
- my friend's books (still one friend but lots of books).

But in the plural form, the apostrophe comes after the s – s':

- my friends' books (lots of friends and lots of books).

There are exceptions to this rule:

- If a plural noun does not end in s, the apostrophe then comes before the s – *the children's books*.
- Words which end in ...one, or ...body and the pronouns 'one', 'each other' and 'one another' all have the apostrophe before the s – *someone's pencil, everybody's garden, each other's hands, one another's work*.

## Grammar in context

### The possessive

In the text, there are a number of possessive forms used. Look closely and find two examples of the singular possessive ('s) and two examples of the plural possessive form (s'). Be prepared to explain each one.

## Interactive oral activity

A parent and teenage son or daughter are discussing how much the teenager should be in contact with the parent when they are in the town with friends in the evening.

Decide with a partner which role you will play, and then make a list of the main points you want to make. Hold a spontaneous conversation. Listen carefully to your partner's comments and react appropriately. Remember to share the talking time.

## Interactive oral activity

Often magazines have surveys about how people spend their time. Fill in the following survey.

Which of the following things do you enjoy? Put a tick by those you like doing.

- Listening to music
- Eating out with friends
- Going to the cinema
- Reading books
- Using technology

Do you own, or have access to, any of these devices? Tick those you own.

- Tablet
- Mobile phone
- Smartphone
- Laptop
- E-reader

How often do you do these things – every day, several times a week, once a week, more often? Fill in the answer for each.

- Listen to music
- Eat out with friends
- Go to the cinema
- Read books
- Use technology

When you have finished the survey, discuss the results with a partner.

## Exam practice

# Cyberbullying

by Anna Edwards

Published: 01:02 GMT, October 21 2013 | Updated: 09:49 GMT, October 21 2013

**HALF of all young people say that cyberbullying is part of everyday life as majority of parents admit they are scared for their children online**

**More than half of children polled said cyberbullying had become a part of life**

**40 per cent of parents said they would not know how to respond if their child fell victim to cyberbullies or how to set up filters online**

**Teachers said their school did not currently teach about cyberbullying**

More than half of children and young people in England I)_____ cyberbullying as a part of everyday life, a new survey has found. But parents and teachers say they do not feel they are equipped to deal with the growing problem of internet abuse. Campaigners warned that cyber bullying had become 'an everyday problem for today's children' and demanded better education to tackle the II)_____. Almost a third of young people said that teaching schools, parents and children about internet safety would be the biggest step in tackling cyberbullying. More than half of children polled – 55 per cent – said cyberbullying had become a part of life for children and young people, while 60.5 per cent of parents also said it had.

Keeping their children safe online is a major worry for parents, with 49 per cent III)_____ that the amount of access their child has to the internet leaves them struggling to monitor their IV)_____ online. And 51 per cent say this makes them scared for the safety of their child. However, the poll suggests that many families would struggle to respond if their child did fall victim to internet abuse. Some 40 per cent of parents said they would not know how to respond if their child fell victim to cyberbullies or how to set up filters on computers, V)_____ and mobile phones that could protect their children.

There were growing calls for online safety to be taught in more schools, with 69 per cent of teachers and 40 per cent of young people calling for it to be included in the national curriculum. Nearly half of teachers – 43 per cent – admitted their school did not currently teach anything about cyberbullying and online safety and 44 per cent admitted they did not know how to respond to cyberbullying. Almost a third – 32.1 per cent – of young people said that teaching schools, parents and children about internet safety would be the biggest step that can be taken to tackle cyberbullying, yet just a fifth of children felt they were taught enough about it at school.

The major new survey, commissioned by the Anti-Bullying Alliance, underlines the struggle many families face trying to protect their children on the internet. Luke Roberts, National Co-ordinator of the Anti-Bullying Alliance, said cyberbullying is one of the biggest VI)_____ facing young people today and called for the Government to ensure it is taught in all schools. He said: 'Our research shows that cyberbullying is an everyday problem for today's children, but teachers and parents are not always able to VII)_____ the advice and support young people need. 'The solution is better education, not only in the classroom but better training for teachers and support for parents. We need a collaborative approach to tackling cyberbullying, so children themselves can take responsibility for their own safety online and know where to turn for help when things go wrong.

'If we get this right, and make cyberbullying a thing of the past, our children will be able to enjoy a digital future that is safe, fun and connected.' He warned online bullying posed such a big threat to young people because it can spread quickly and easily and leave a permanent VIII) _____ in cyber space. He said: 'Cyberbullying can move from online to off line and back online, that is why this conversation is so important. 'Verbal abuse may be the thing most young people IX) _____ in terms of bullying, but cyberbullying can be an extension of that abuse. 'The particular problem with cyberbullying is that what would have been private conversation becomes a public display.

This means the victim, as well as dealing with that X)_____ harm that is caused by the hurtful language, also has to cope with the fact that everyone in their online communities has known about that bullying, and that is really hard to deal with.

'Each time a new app or new social network site comes out it creates its own types of risks. My biggest concern is the anonymity attached to some of these sites, because it is far easier to bully people if you are anonymous.'

He warned that cyberbullying cannot be stopped by simply turning mobile phones and computers off, and called on the Government, parents and teachers to teach young people how to stay safe online. He added: 'It is not up to one area to take this on, it is up to the Government, parents and social networking sites. Everyone needs to come together.'

The survey questioned 2,200 parents, children and teachers across England to launch anti-bullying week, which takes place from November 18–22.

*http://www.dailymail.co.uk/news/article-2469795/HALF-young-people-say-cyberbullying-everyday-life.html#ixzz2lq1CwSxD*

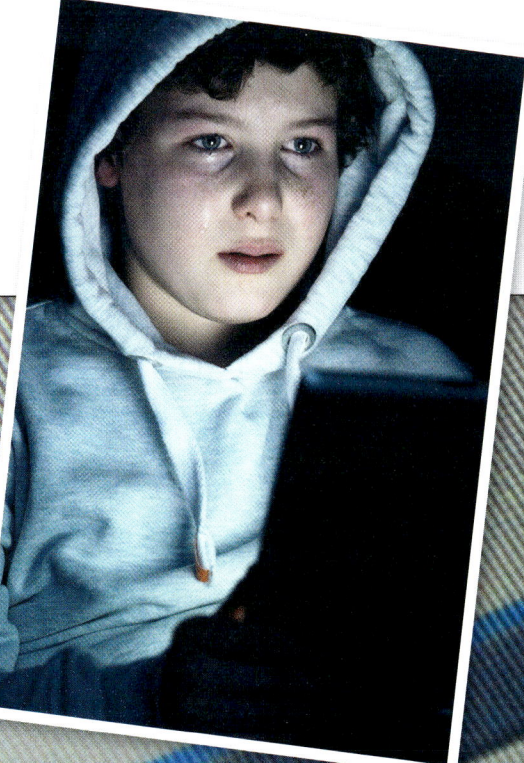

211

# 12 Mass media and social media

### Exercises

Choose the best option from the choices below.

**1** How would you describe the tone of the opening sentences of this article?

    a) excited ☐

    b) enthusiastic ☐

    c) dramatic ☐

    d) threatening ☐

    e) alarming ☐

**2** Answer the following questions.

**A** What do parents and teachers say about the problem?

..................................................................................................

**B** How do the young people quoted think the problem can be approached?

..................................................................................................

**C** What is the major worry of many parents, and why is this a problem for them?

..................................................................................................

**D** Are most parents able to protect their children online?

..................................................................................................

**E** What do many people think is the solution to this situation? Do you agree with this idea?

..................................................................................................

**F** Why is online bullying a major threat to young people?

..................................................................................................

**G** Is cyberbullying worse than verbal abuse? Why?

..................................................................................................

**H** Which factor makes bullying online far easier?

..................................................................................................

**3** Some of the words have been removed from the text. From the list below, choose the word which best fits the gap and write the appropriate letter in the box below.

| I ☐ | IV ☐ | VII ☐ | X ☐ |
| II ☐ | V ☐ | VIII ☐ | |
| III ☐ | VI ☐ | IX ☐ | |

212

| | | | |
|---|---|---|---|
| **A** | tablets | **F** | provide |
| **B** | accept | **G** | encounter |
| **C** | imprint | **H** | initial |
| **D** | issues | **I** | complaining |
| **E** | phenomenon | **J** | behavior |

**4** Of the statements below, only five are true. Identify the true statements. Write the appropriate letters in the box provided, in any order.

**I** ☐       **IV** ☐

**II** ☐      **V** ☐

**III** ☐

**A** Teachers are able to deal with the problem.

**B** The majority of parents know how to set up computer filters.

**C** Cyberbullying is an everyday problem for very few children.

**D** Many parents complain that their children have too much access to computers.

**E** Half of the schools already teach about cyberbullying and online safety.

**F** The solution to the problem is better education.

**G** Cyberbullying is so harmful because it is shared and spread so rapidly.

**H** It is easy to bully people if you can remain anonymous.

**I** Cyberbullying can be prevented if young people turn off their mobile phones and computers.

**J** The research quoted was conducted among a huge group of people.

# 13 Alternative food supplies

## Objectives

- To read about and consider alternative food sources
- To write in formal and informal styles using information from the texts
- To examine uses of colloquial English
- To use the construction 'used to' in sentences
- To examine different uses of the word 'but'

**Opposite** A selection of insects being prepared to eat.

# 13.1 Edible insects

## Text 13.1.1 Why eat bugs?

http://edibug.wordpress.com/why-eat-bugs-2/

# Why eat bugs?

Despite the fact that 80% of the world's cultures eat insects (that's right: the US is in the minority here) most people in our culture consider insects simply to be pests. But when you consider the logic of bugs as food, from an ecological, financial, and global perspective, they start to seem a lot more palatable.

### Insects: The true eco-protein

A United Nations report found that the livestock industry is responsible for generating more greenhouse gas emissions than transport. That means the burgers, chicken, and pork we are eating are technically worse for our environment than our cars. Insects require such fewer resources in terms of food, water, and land space that, as David Gracer of SmallStock Foods puts it, "Cows and pigs are the SUVs of the food world. And bugs—they're the Priuses, maybe even bicycles."

### Top ten reasons to eat insects

**10** Most edible insect species are highly nutritious.

**9** It is up to 20 times more efficient to raise insect protein than beef. That's per pound. This is mainly because bugs don't 'waste' food energy on things like raising their body temperature, or making bones, fur, feathers, and other stuff we can't eat.

**8** Also, it takes less water to raise insects—much, much less: up to 1000 times less.

**7** You are probably already doing it, as the FDA allows a certain amount of insect matter to be present in most commercial foods: an average of 150 or more insect fragments are allowed per 100 grams of wheat flour, for instance—that's a lot of bug!

**6** Most cultures in the world not only eat insects, but in many cases find them to be a delicacy.

# 13 Alternative food supplies

http://edibug.wordpress.com/why-eat-bugs-2/

**5** If insects themselves were deemed a food crop, imagine how much we could cut down on pesticide use, and its associated environmental damage.

**4** Many insects are tasty: some larvae taste like bacon. Who doesn't like bacon?

**3** Many animal rights activists often won't get up in arms over eating bugs, as they are already exterminated on a daily basis (the bugs, not the activists).

**2** Insects may be the food of the future, as scientists are researching their potential as a space food crop.

**1** And the number one reason to eat insects is …

Insects are a great, inexpensive, green source of the protein desperately needed by starving peoples. If we can help create a market and funding for it, there is the potential to help spread nourishment throughout the planet.

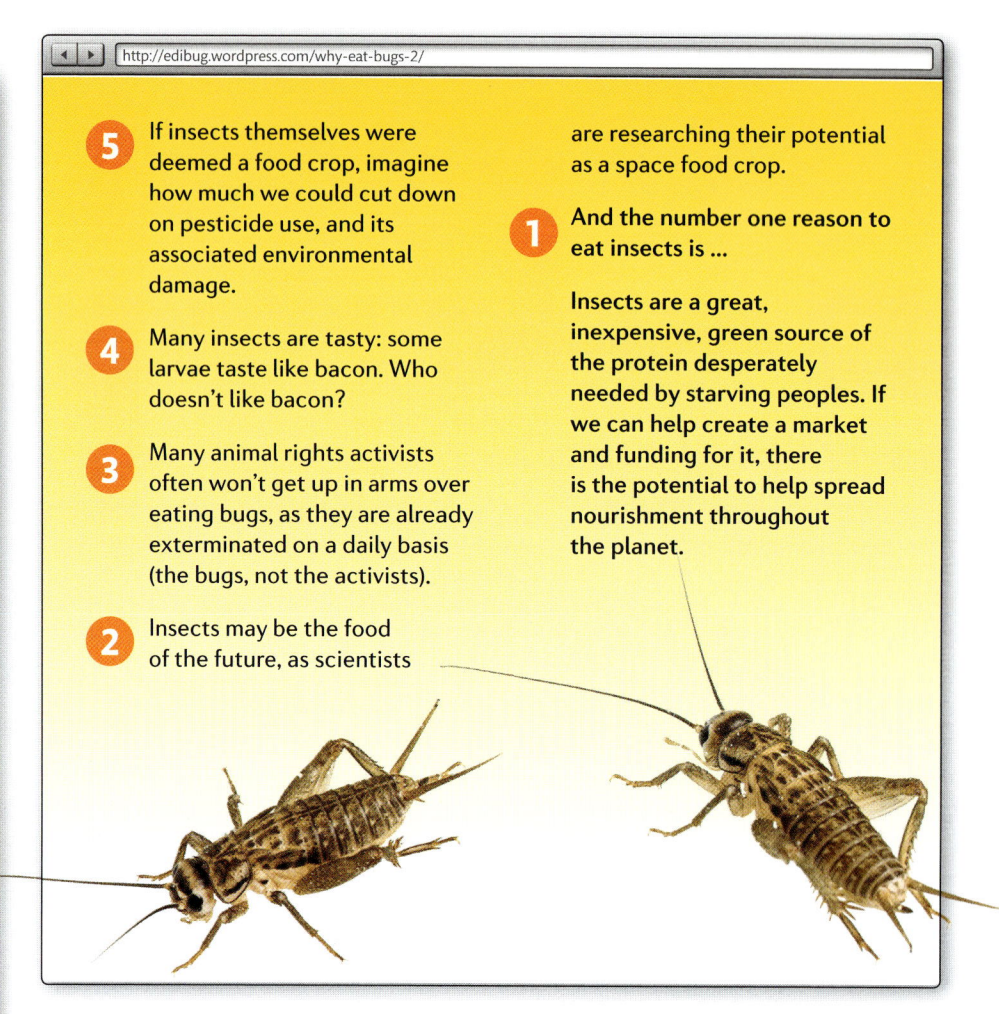

*http://edibug.wordpress.com/why-eat-bugs-2/*

## General comprehension

1 In the first sentence of the text insects are described as 'pests'. What does this mean?
2 Which word in the text is a synonym for 'insects'?
3 The text makes a reference to animals and the environment. What is the comparison?
4 In point 7 of the 'Top ten reasons to eat insects', there is a statement that we already eat insects. In what form is this?
5 In point 4, there is a rhetorical question: 'Who doesn't like bacon?' What does this question imply about bacon?
6 In point 3, you can read a figure of speech: 'many animal rights activists often won't get up in arms about eating bugs'. What does the expression 'to get up in arms' mean?
7 In point 2, where exactly does the author think that insects will be particularly useful as a food source?
8 In point 1, which group of people will especially benefit from eating insects and why?

## Interactive oral activity

Together with a partner, explore some of your opinions about different foods and discuss your likes and dislikes. How specific to your culture are your food preferences? Be prepared to share your ideas with other pairs in the class.

Text 13.1.2 An insect diet may be the solution for a hungry world

http://observers.france24.com/content/20110817-insect-diet-hungry-world-eating

# An insect diet may be the solution for a hungry world

Mexicans eat deep-fried grasshoppers. Japanese love wasp cookies. Leafcutter ants are considered a delicacy in Colombia, as are some caterpillars in South Africa. And in Thailand people cook everything from water beetles to bamboo worms. Even though eating insects has often been dismissed as a cultural eccentricity, it might soon become one of the answers to pressing global problems like hunger and environmental destruction.

Disgusting as the idea of eating insects may be for many, the reality is that eating insects, or entomophagy, is practised in more than half the countries in the world. There are an estimated 1,462 species of edible insects in the world, ranging from beetles, dragonflies and crickets to ant eggs and butterfly larvae, according to research by Wageningen University in the Netherlands. More than 250 species are eaten in Mexico alone.

But more than tasty snacks, insects could become a protein-rich, green and global source of food, according to the Food and Agriculture Organization of the United Nations (FAO). The FAO says the projected growth of the world's population – around 2.3 billion more people by 2050 – will require a significant increase in food production. As a result, demand for livestock is expected to double during the next four decades. However, almost 70% of the land in use for agriculture in the world is for livestock, meaning that the need for more grazing land would bring further deforestation. Agriculture also contributes significantly to greenhouse gas emissions and puts a strain on valuable resources like water. Finding alternative protein sources other than livestock is therefore crucial.

The FAO and scientists around the world are suggesting that insects could be a serious alternative. To begin with, insects have about the same nutritional value as beef, chicken or fish. They are easily raised in a sustainable way, since they require less land and water than cows, pigs or goats. They also reproduce at a quicker pace than mammals. What's more, people in developing countries can harvest them without owning vast properties of land or making huge financial investments.

Currently the FAO is promoting sustainable cricket farms in Laos. Meanwhile, in the United States and Europe, a small but growing number of chefs and foodies are praising the benefits of eating insects and some grocery stores like Sligro in the Netherlands have begun marketing them.

# 13 Alternative food supplies

### General comprehension

1. List the countries mentioned in the first paragraph that already have an established culture of eating insects.
2. Name the European university that has researched entomophagy.
3. What is the main nutritional benefit of insects?
4. Why is 2050 a key date for the subject of food production?
5. Which two factors mentioned in the text are given as reasons why increasing the amount of livestock is not a good option for food production?
6. Which three factors mentioned in the text are given as reasons why eating insects is a serious alternative to eating meat?
7. What is the response to eating insects in the USA and Europe?

### Text handling

1. Here are some words from the text. Which of the definitions given is most appropriate according to the text?
   a) significant: important / considerable / meaningful
   b) strain: demand / damage / species
   c) crucial: possibility / threatening / essential
   d) vast: expensive / huge / rare

2. True or false? Justify your answer with a relevant brief quotation from the text.
   a) Eating insects is frequently considered to be a cultural idiosyncrasy and insects are not regarded as a mainstream food source.
   b) Much research into eating insects has been carried out by a Dutch university.
   c) Insects will only be of food value as a snack because of their small size.
   d) The nutritional value of beef, chicken or fish is much higher than that of insects.
   e) It is not possible to farm insects.
   f) A Dutch grocery chain has started to market insects.

### Interactive oral activity

**TOK** — What is taken for granted about food and eating in your community? How do you decide what you can or cannot eat?

In groups of three discuss the idea of eating insects as an alternative food source. How acceptable do you think it is? Try to persuade the others in your group to accept your arguments.

After your discussion, prepare a brief summary of your discussion points to present to the class.

## Text 13.1.3 Insects are not just an alternative source of food, but they're superior in many ways

http://observers.france24.com/content/20110817-insect-diet-hungry-world-eating-insects-food-colombia-jap

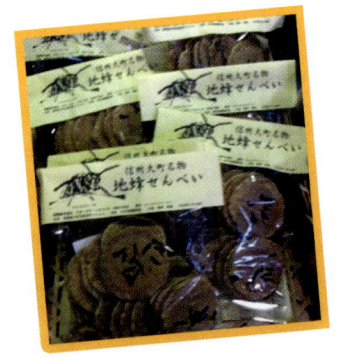

**Danielle Martin is a foodie and insect lover. She posts gourmet insect recipes on her blog 'Girl Meets Bug' and hosts insect cook-offs in museums and schools across the United States**

"I first encountered edible insects in Mexico, when I bought a packet of 'chapulines' [deep-fried grasshoppers]. I remember being suddenly surrounded by a group of children that wanted to eat them right off the table. It really struck me that entomophagy was very much alive.

Since eating insects is so unusual in the U.S., people mainly come to my presentations out of curiosity. There is a sensational aspect to it: they basically want to see the girl eating the bugs. But as they are watching and it smells like regular food to them, there is a moment of realization that bugs can be good.

People go through a whole process when they eat insects for the first time: first they close their eyes tightly, they put the bug in their mouths and their whole body is on guard. As they start chewing, their eyes open and their face sort of blooms. 'That wasn't so bad', they'll say. And then they grab another one… Children are more open-minded: they will go through the same process, but they're more enthusiastic about it.

There are some rules about which insects you can eat. I always say, 'Black, green and brown, swallow it down; red, blue and yellow, leave that fellow'. It's definitely best to avoid insects with flamboyant colours that proclaim to the rest of nature that they're not palatable. I personally prefer to eat insects in their larval stage. My favourites are bee larvae, which taste like bacon and mushrooms, and crickets, whose flavour is a cross between almonds and shrimp. On the other hand, I didn't enjoy eating a walking stick insect because it tasted like leaves. Usually if you eat what they eat, they will probably taste good. For example, waxmoth larvae eat bread and honey, while crickets eat fruits and vegetables.

When people try bugs, they usually describe the taste as either nutty, mushroomy, earthy or shrimpy. Eating insects is an acquired taste, but so are many things that have intense and unusual flavours, like mussels or strong cheeses. In the 1800s lobsters and shellfish were not considered delicacies in America, but fed to livestock or ground and used as fertilizer. This shows us that cultural attitudes change. In Cambodia crickets are so popular that they have even had shortages. So I think it is possible for insects to move from snack to main food source.

Insects are not just an alternative source of food, but superior to traditional protein sources in many ways. Crickets are a great substitute for beef, offering the same amount of proteins but more iron. Waxmoth larvae are high in omega 3, 6 and 9, traditionally found in fish, but have no mercury. And there is no problem in farming them by the thousands. Unlike raising a cow, farming insects is something anybody can do. It requires little expertise, little expense and little space, making eating bugs guilt-free and highly sustainable. I am raising waxmoth larvae in my closet.

In the end, I believe it will be about including something in your diet that is not only good for you, but also tastes great."

Post was written with journalist Andrés Bermúdez Liévano, http://observers.france24.com/content/20110817-insect-diet-hungry-world-eating-insects-food-colombia-jap

## General comprehension

According to the text, two of the following statements are true. Which ones? Cite the relevant parts of the text that support your answer.

1. The audiences at Danielle Martin's presentations are largely there to see someone eating insects.
2. Insects are a snack alternative.
3. In the USA there is a widespread opinion that eating bugs can be good.
4. People usually discover that eating bugs is not as bad as they expect it to be.
5. Farming insects is a specialist activity.
6. Danielle Martin thinks all insects are tasty food alternatives.

# 13 Alternative food supplies

### Zoom in on grammar

**'But'**

In the above text the word *but* is used eight times. Remember that *but* is usually a linking word which brings two ideas together; however, the word *but* can be used in more than one way. Here are two examples from the text:

*'But* as they are watching...' (paragraph 2)

In this example, 'but' is a synonym for 'however'.

In the following example we see the following construction 'not just... but' (paragraph 6):

'Insects are *not just* an alternative source of food, *but* superior in many ways.'

We also see in this example that 'but' is a synonym for 'in addition'.

### Grammar in context

**'But'**

Now find the other examples of sentences with *but* in Text 13.1.3 and examine its function in the sentences.

## Text 13.1.4 Try not to be sick

# Rentokil launches pop-up 'pestaurant' with pigeon, worms and ants on the menu by Heather Saul

**Thursday August 15 2013**

It all got a bit too much for one nine-year old, who had to run off to 1) _____ after devouring "delicacies" such as crickets, ants and pigeon burgers. Pest control service Rentokil has established the world's first "pop-up pestaurant" in the City of London – for 2) _____ day only. The company boasts 85 years of service and will serve up an array of exotic cuisine, including sweet chilli pigeon burgers, salt and vinegar crickets, BBQ mealworms and chocolate-dipped ants. The 'food' is free of charge to everyone feeling 3) _____ enough to try it. The menu may not sound appetising, but it is healthy. Insects have been found to be rich in protein, zinc, calcium and iron while also being low in fat.

Edible insects have recently been identified by a number of different 4) _____ , including the UN's Food & Agriculture Organisation, as a potentially valuable source of food for the world's rapidly growing population. Pigeons are a well-recognised delicacy, and wood pigeon can be found on many Michelin-starred menus across the world.

Nine-year-old Stan Knight showed a bit too much enthusiasm when he scoffed a handful of mealworms and subsequently vomited - but he claims he enjoyed the culinary 5) _____ none-the-less. After putting a handful of the yellow worms in his mouth at once, Stan had to run away from the stall to throw up.

"I don't know. I liked them. They were really nice. I think it was because I had too much of them in one go. They just felt like 6) _____ food," he said.

Tim Guest, 40, from London, tucked into the same mealworms that made Stan vomit, but he was able to keep the "slightly slimy" nibbles down.

"They're not exactly very nice to the touch. It feels wrong on a fundamental level," he said, adding: "It's like a pocket of air with spice on top. It's like a crisp you'd get in the supermarket really.

"I don't really see why anybody wouldn't eat them. I think it's just the concept really, rather than what they actually taste like. I think they taste 7) _____."

Despite believing that they were just like crisps, he said: "I wouldn't go and grab a handful from the wild and shove them in my mouth."

David Cross, head of technical training academy at Rentokil, said: "The Pestaurant is all about celebrating the hard work that goes into keeping the UK's pests under control.

"Common UK pests like wasps, mice, rats, bed bugs, cockroaches, fleas and pigeons, can become a problem for anyone, and can affect both commercial and residential properties.

"Much like the rest of us, they are focused on looking for food and 8) _____ . Once they find a good supply of food and an environment where they feel safe, then they will happily set up home indefinitely. Food will be served until the afternoon.

http://www.independent.co.uk/news/uk/home-news/try-not-to-be-sick-rentokil-launches-popup-pestaurant-with-pigeon-worms-and-ants-on-the-menu-8763550.html

## General comprehension

1. What kind of business is the company Rentokil involved in?
2. Name some of the insect-based dishes on offer in this pop-up restaurant.
3. What do the dishes cost the diners?
4. According to the text, what was the reason for Stan Knight's vomiting?
5. Does Tim Guest feel there is a good reason not to eat worms?
6. What advertising effect does Rentokil hope to gain from this action?
7. Apart from insects, what exotic foods are on offer in the restaurant?

## Text handling

1. In this text certain words have been removed; put the words below back in the text in the correct place.

   **shelter / vomit / fine / one / normal / brave / experience / bodies**

2. True or false? Justify your answer with a relevant brief quotation from the text.
   a) The company Rentokil has existed for over half a decade.
   b) The price of the food in the restaurant is kept low.
   c) Insects are an accepted food alternative for the growing world population.
   d) For British children, insects are not considered a normal food experience.
   e) The idea behind the Rentokil restaurant is to draw attention to the extensive work carried out by the company in the area of pest control.

## Written work

Write an article for your school magazine about the need for alternative food supplies in the next 20 years. Support the argument that world food shortages could be eased by the farming and eating of insects. Write between 250 and 400 words.

# 13 Alternative food supplies

## 13.2 The future is vegetarian!

Text 13.2.1 Why do you need to eat vegetables every day?

### Why do you need to eat vegetables every day?

**You need to eat vegetables every day because you simply cannot find another food group that is as perfectly matched to our everyday human needs as vegetables! Vegetables fit us like a glove. From so many different perspectives, the nature of vegetables and the nature of human health are matched up in a way that simply cannot be duplicated by other food groups, including fruits, legumes, nuts and seeds, grains, seafoods, or poultry and meats.**

**1.**................................................................................

To begin with, vegetables as a group are so low in calories that it is very difficult to gain weight even if you overeat them. (This statement wouldn't apply, of course, to batter-coated and fried vegetables, or to vegetables mixed into a thick cheese casserole.) On average, you are looking at 50 calories (or less) per cup from most of the World's Healthiest vegetables! That amount is astonishingly low, even when you compare it to other food groups within the World's Healthiest Foods. With the World's Healthiest nuts and seeds, for example, you're almost always looking at 750 calories or more per cup. That's 15 times higher than the World's Healthiest vegetables. With legumes, calories per cup fall into the 225–250 range. For fruits, the calories per cup can drop down fairly low for extremely watery fruits (like watermelon, which drops down to about 50 calories per cup), but it can also spike up to more than 400 calories per cup in the case of dried fruits like raisins. The uniquely low-calorie nature of vegetables as a group means that you can be generous with them in a Healthiest Way of Eating and not have to worry about the calories.

**2.**................................................................................

Optimal nourishment is another reason that vegetables are important on a daily basis. You need to eat vegetables every day because you need a supply of vitamins every day. Some vitamins can be stored for future use and others cannot. Some of the vitamins that can be stored in the body are called fat-soluble vitamins such as vitamins A, D and E. For the body to run its best we also need water-soluble vitamins. Found within this group are all of the "B-complex" vitamins, including vitamins $B_1$, $B_2$, $B_3$, $B_5$, $B_6$, $B_{12}$, biotin, choline, folic acid, and vitamin C. We need these water-soluble vitamins every single day because they can't be stored in the body or can only be stored in small amounts. And since the body cannot make these vitamins (or any vitamins), we have to get them from the food we eat. When considered as a group, vegetables are unusually rich sources for a full mixture of water-soluble vitamins. That's why so many health care recommendations (including the U.S. Food Pyramid) encourage 3–5 servings of vegetables per day.

**3** ........................................................................................

When it comes to vegetables, there is also their abundance of phytonutrients to consider. In the science of food, no change has been bigger than the discovery of phytonutrients and their unique place in our health. Phytonutrients include all of the unique substances that give foods their brilliant colors, their delicious flavors, and their unique aromas. They are also the nutrients most closely linked to prevention of certain diseases. Carotenonids and flavonoids are the two of the largest groups of phytonutrients, and there is no food group that provides them in amounts as plentiful as vegetables. The phytonutrients in cruciferous vegetables like broccoli, and in root vegetables like onions and garlic, are unique when it comes to decreased risk of certain cancers, and some of these phytonutrients simply cannot be found in other food groups.

**4** ........................................................................................

Finally are the pleasure of chewing and amazing digestive benefits that come from the high-fiber content of vegetables. Dietary fiber is critical for our health, not only on a daily basis, but on a meal-by-meal and snack-by-snack basis as well. Food cannot move through our digestive tract in a healthy way unless it is fiber-rich. And, vegetables are some of the very richest sources of fiber that exist.

http://whfoods.org/genpage.php?tname=dailytip&dbid=127

## General comprehension

1. The above text presents a number of arguments for eating vegetables. The arguments are presented in four paragraphs. Give each paragraph a title.
2. According to the text, what is the benefit of vegetables in comparison to other healthy foods like nuts and fruit?
3. Is it true that all vitamins can be stored in the body for future use?
4. What is the meaning of the idiom in the first paragraph – 'Vegetables fit us like a glove'?
5. What substances are among phytonutrients?

## Individual oral activity

Write a speech that you will deliver to your grade in an assembly on World Health Day (7th April). You have decided to focus on food in connection with world health: decide which aspects of food you will focus on and write the text of your speech. Write around 400–450 words.

# 13 Alternative food supplies

**13.2.2 Larry Carter, a digital designer in an advertising agency, reflects on the decision he and his wife Amy made to become vegetarian**

*Amy and I both grew up in the country, so for us going veggie was only really down to one thing – we were both mad-keen nature lovers. When I was a kid in Harrogate, I used to go off looking for frogs and sticklebacks after school and Amy, who grew up in Aberdeen, used to spend hours on the beach looking for crabs and jellyfish.*

*When we hooked up we were both studying at Manchester University and had this feeling that there was no such thing as nature any more- 'cos we'd left it. Then, when Amy and I got married, we decided to rediscover nature. Amy'd say 'Come on, let's get our boots on' and we'd spend our weekends walking in the Lake District. Life became a new adventure for us both – bringing back this nature thing.*

*Anyway, when we inherited some money after Amy's grandmother died, we bought a small farm in Ambleside and decided to do it up. Then we started keeping hens and sheep. This was when we started really understanding all the animals. We spent a lot of time tending to them.*

*Then one day when we were having Sunday lunch – we were still eating meat at that time – Amy had cooked roast lamb. It was springtime and outside our lambs were happily running around. I said 'Hey, we're eating one of them'. It just shook us and we said 'Hang on, maybe we don't want to do this'.*

*Well, that was the turning point for us and we made the decision to give up eating meat. It was difficult at first. If we had no meat on the plate, there*

was a gap every time you came to have a meal. Gradually Amy started to fill the hole with pasta or a bit of quiche, or egg dishes made with our hens' eggs. Anyway, meals started to get really good and tasty. We still had the British stuff to fill us up: mashed potatoes and rice pudding!

Well, we really got into this vegetarian thing and started to think about all the millions of animals being shunted into a slaughterhouse. That was hard – in fact it changed our lives. Not just what we ate but the whole spiritual thing.

Our children used to love all the animals we kept and there was no way they were going to eat them or watch Daddy chopping them up. The kids used to be laughed at a bit in school for being vegetarian but they always said they had a clear conscience about the animals.

But times are changing; it's a lot easier to be veggie these days. When Amy and I were kids, vegetarians were weirdos – people in saris and sandals and vegetarian food in restaurants was really rare. But now there's a whole veggie movement. It's great that more people are embracing the idea of eating less meat and more vegetables – even ordinary people. It's perfectly feasible that people want to change their eating habits as society changes. Vegetarianism is becoming mainstream.

### General comprehension

1. What did Amy and Larry have in common when they were growing up?
2. How was Larry brought back to nature?
3. Was Larry a vegetarian when he married Amy?
4. What does this quotation from the text tell you about the family's eating habits? 'It was difficult at first. If we had no meat on the plate, there was a gap every time you came to have a meal.'
5. What does Larry think social change has got to do with becoming vegetarian?

### Text handling

**Using colloquial English**

The above text is a transcript of an interview with Larry Carter when he was asked about why he became a vegetarian. The register of the text is informal. It is the kind of English you hear when a person is speaking. This is quite different from the formal English you use when you are writing an essay.

Look at the words from the text below and decide what the equivalent would be in formal register. Discuss your answers with a partner.

1. a veggie
2. mad-keen
3. we hooked up
4. 'cos
5. Amy'd say
6. do it up
7. kids
8. a bit of quiche
9. the British stuff
10. weirdos

**Opposite** Larry Carter preparing vegetables at home.

# 13 Alternative food supplies

## Zoom in on grammar

**'Used to'**

Using *used to* indicates that something happened regularly in the past but no longer happens:

'When I was a kid, I *used to* go off looking for frogs and sticklebacks.'

The construction 'used to' is placed before the verb.

## Grammar in context

**'Used to'**

Here are some situations based on the text. Change them, using *used to*, so that the meaning indicates that the action was regular in the past but is not true today.

1. Larry lived in Harrogate as a boy.
2. He and Amy ate meat for Sunday lunch.
3. When Larry was a child restaurants didn't serve vegetarian food.
4. Larry and Amy went walking in the Lake District.
5. They weren't vegetarians when they were students.

## Written work

After reading the interview with Larry in a magazine, you decide to write him an email, telling him what you think about his life-style choice. Agree with him and give him some examples from your life to support the arguments for becoming a vegetarian. Write between 250 and 300 words.

## Text 13.2.3 Why do people become vegetarians?

http://teenshealth.org/teen/food_fitness/nutrition/vegetarian.html#

For much of the world, vegetarianism is largely a matter of economics: Meat costs a lot more than, say, beans or rice, so meat becomes a special-occasion dish (if it's eaten at all). Even where meat is more plentiful, it's still used in moderation, often providing a side note to a meal rather than taking center stage.

In countries like the United States where meat is not as expensive, though, people often choose to be vegetarians for reasons other than cost. Parental preferences, religious or other beliefs, and health issues are among the most common reasons for choosing to be a vegetarian. Many people choose a vegetarian diet out of concern over animal rights or the environment. And lots of people have more than one reason for choosing vegetarianism.

### Vegetarian and semi-vegetarian diets

Different people follow different forms of vegetarianism. A true vegetarian eats no meat at all, including chicken and fish. A lacto-ovo vegetarian eats dairy products and eggs, but excludes meat, fish, and poultry. It follows, then, that a lacto vegetarian eats dairy products but not eggs, whereas an ovo vegetarian eats eggs but not dairy products.

A stricter form of vegetarianism is veganism (pronounced: vee-gun-izm). Not only are eggs and dairy products excluded from a vegan diet, so are animal products like honey and gelatin.

Some macrobiotic diets fall into the vegan category. Macrobiotic diets restrict not only animal products but also refined and processed

http://teenshealth.org/teen/food_fitness/nutrition/vegetarian.html#

foods, foods with preservatives, and foods that contain caffeine or other stimulants.

Following a macrobiotic or vegan diet could lead to nutritional deficiencies in some people. Teens need to be sure their diets include enough nutrients to fuel growth, particularly protein and calcium. If you're interested in following a vegan or macrobiotic diet it's a good idea to talk to a registered dietician. He or she can help you design meal plans that include adequate vitamins and minerals.

Some people consider themselves semi-vegetarians and eat fish and maybe a small amount of poultry as part of a diet that's primarily made up of vegetables, fruits, grains, legumes, seeds, and nuts. A pesci-vegetarian eats fish, but not poultry.

### Are these diets OK for teens?

In the past, choosing not to eat meat or animal-based foods was considered unusual in the United States. Times and attitudes have changed dramatically, however. Vegetarians are still a minority in the United States, but a large and growing one. The American Dietetic Association (ADA) has officially endorsed vegetarianism, stating "appropriately planned vegetarian diets, including total vegetarian or vegan diets, are healthful, nutritionally adequate, and may provide health benefits in the prevention and treatment of certain diseases."

### Check the label

Some foods that appear to be vegetarian aren't. Most cheeses are made using an animal-derived product called rennet. Other ingredients that show up in seemingly vegetarian foods include gelatin, which is made from meat byproducts, and enzymes, which may be animal derived.

http://teenshealth.org/teen/food_fitness/nutrition/vegetarian.html#

## General comprehension

Using bullet points, complete the table below to summarize the main points from the text. This will help you to gain an overview of the arguments in the text.

| Reasons to become vegetarian | Different kinds of vegetarianism | Acceptable for young adults? |
|---|---|---|
|  |  |  |

## Interactive oral activity

In groups of three, have a discussion about vegetarianism. You want to discuss why this is an issue for some people.

Here are some things to think about:
- Are you for or against vegetarianism?
- What do you think about the health aspects of eating only vegetables?
- What are the positive aspects and the negative aspects for people in general?
- Is it an idea that is becoming more popular as the world population increases?
- What are some of the problems in the world that make food an issue for future generations?

Prepare some ideas before you begin and be prepared to share your viewpoint with the rest of the group after your discussion.

# 13 Alternative food supplies

## 13.3 Anyone for seaweed?

### Text 13.3.1 Seaweed as a food source

For many ages mankind has known and utilized the ocean grown plants to complement his diet and also provide extra fodder to eager cattle. As human food there are many that are not only edible but also palatable.

Japanese traders are very involved in the harvesting of seaweeds throughout the oceans of the world. Known as a staple part of their food for over 10,000 years, Japan is still the country with largest intake of seaweed in their diet. Because of this factor, goitre is practically unknown and the people share a wonderfully high quality health and youthful appearance with fine hair, teeth and nails.

A range of seaweeds for use in sophisticated eastern cuisine of the Japanese is now commercially available in Australia. But until comparatively recently there has been little knowledge available about seaweeds in the Western world – not enough to give confidence to anyone trying out the various seaweeds found on the beaches. So it is a relief to know that the ones that are well known to the casual experimenter, that the pleasant tasting sea lettuce which is bright green and like a soft endive in character, and the common kelp, are both safe to eat.

Current research and investigation into the nutritional value of the estimated 25,000 different species of edible seaweeds of identified plants is somewhat limited. It is an ever growing sphere of interest to botanists, nutritionists, dieticians, and health conscious people of the world who wish to reduce some of the dangers of land grown produce.

There is an abundance of seawater on our planet and sufficient coastal waters to allow additional cultivation of massive amounts of seaweeds to provide us with alternate foods should this be necessary. At present we should utilize them as food to supplement our soil grown vegetables and herbs and provide us with valuable trace elements and minerals missing from produce grown under modern methods of farming on lands now often contaminated in some way.

Many health conscious people already are familiar with the benefits of kelp and make use of the abundance of this plant on the North American western seaboard. Others in Europe, Britain and Australia are familiar with agar-agar which can be used in additions to commercial products, to make a delicious jelly and employed in the home. Spirulina is already a very popular food supplement worldwide.

So let's extend our interest and try out some new foods.

Try some oriental recipes and tips that will add food value and exciting new tastes to our diet!

*http://www.freelancecommentaries.com/seaweed-as-a-food-source*

### General comprehension

1. What two uses for ocean plants are mentioned in the first paragraph?
2. In the second paragraph the condition 'goitre' is referred to. Research this word and find out what it is.
3. According to the text, which country has the longest experience of using seaweeds in its cooking?
4. After reading the text, what kind of product do you guess 'spirulina' is?

## Text handling

In the table, which word or phrase in the text do the underlined words refer to?

| | |
|---|---|
| 1 For many ages mankind has known and utilized the ocean grown plants to complement <u>his</u> diet. | |
| 2 Known as a staple part of <u>their</u> food for over 10,000 years... | |
| 3 So it is a relief to know that <u>the ones</u> that are well known to the casual experimenter... | |
| 4 <u>Others</u> in Europe, Britain and Australia are familiar with... | |

## Written work

Write a formal letter to the principal of your school suggesting that the school cafeteria should promote alternative foods by having a selection of ocean plants on the menu for a limited time. Support your request with facts you have learned about seaweeds. Write between 250 and 400 words.

## Written work

Write an email to a friend of yours telling him/her about your plan to have a part of the cafeteria's meal plan dedicated to ocean plants. Include some of the arguments from your formal letter but think how the register will be different in an email. Write between 150 and 250 words.

To learn more about seaweed as a food source, go to www.pearsonhotlinks.com, enter the title or ISBN of this book and click on Chapter 13.

# Exam practice

## Exercises

### Written assignment 1: Essay title (HL)

After discussing alternative food sources in your English class, you believe that students at your school should be encouraged to accept changes to the school lunch menu. Write a letter to your school principal explaining your ideas and suggest alternative foods which could be included. Write between 250 and 400 words.

### Written assignment 2: Personal response (HL)

Give a personal response to the following stimulus and justify it. Choose any text type you have studied in class. Write between 150 and 250 words.

'Who controls the food supply controls the people.'

*Henry Kissinger (1923–), American diplomat*

### Written assignment 3: Essay title (SL)

As a member of the school's health committee you have been asked to give a speech to the school about the importance of healthy eating. Write the text of your speech. Write between 250 and 400 words.

# 14 Teenage health

**Opposite** Joy or pain?

## Objectives

- To practise the uses of the gerund
- To review and practise a variety of complex sentence structures
- To review modal verbs in context
- To revise the third conditional
- To discuss the importance of diet and health for teenagers

# 14.1 Teenage health issues

## Text 14.1.1 Text messaging to improve teen health

http://psychcentral.com/news/2013/01/21/text-messaging-to-improve-teen-health/50628.html

# Text messaging to improve teen health

**by Rick Nauert PhD
Senior News Editor**

Reviewed by John M. Grohol, Psy.D. on January 21 2013

Parents understand that teenagers spend a lot of time texting.

However, the magnitude of the text messaging is difficult for middle-agers to comprehend as researchers estimate teenagers receive an average of 3,417 texts a month, or 114 per day.

A new study attempts to turn this innate behaviour of the 'Millennials' or 'Generation Y' subjects into a way in which educational information about nutrition and physical activity is delivered to teens. Investigators studied whether teenagers would be interested in receiving texts about health on their phones and how they would like those messages presented. For a one-year period, researchers studied 177 adolescents, ages 12–18 and discovered that most teens were open to receiving such texts, but the way in which they were worded made a big difference.

"Kids are texting all the time, so it's a communication they're very familiar with and it appeals to them," said Melanie Hingle, University of Arizona assistant research professor of nutritional sciences and lead author of the study. "But we realized very quickly once we got down to the actual development of the messages that we didn't know the first thing about what kind of tone or information kids would be interested in."

Researchers quickly learned—and this may come as no surprise to those with teenagers at home—that the teens didn't like to be told what to do. Therefore, phrases like "you should," "always" and "never" did not go over well, while softer words like "try" and "consider" were much better received. Likewise, texts introduced by the words "did you know" also generally were disliked, with teens saying the phrase made them immediately not want to know whatever came next.

Texts the teens liked best included those that specifically referenced their age group, such as, "American girls aged 12–19 years old drink an average of 650 cans of soda a year!" They also

> Definition: 'Millennials' and 'Generation Y' are terms used to describe people born between the early 1980s and the 2000s.

# 14 Teenage health

liked messages that were interactive, like fun quizzes; messages that were actionable, like simple recipes; and messages that included links to websites where they could learn more about a topic if desired. The teens also appreciated the occasional fun fact not necessarily related to health—some bit of trivia they could share with their friends, like the fact that carrots were originally purple or that ears of corn have an even number of rows. And they didn't want to be inundated with texts—no more than two a day.

Hingle believes text messaging can be a potentially valuable supplement to in-person nutrition education and fitness programs for teens. "A lot of the previous interventions that have been developed in nutrition are very top-down, in that we're the experts and we're telling people what to do," Hingle said. "We didn't want to do that in these text messages, and we didn't think it was very effective, so we had kids at every step of the process working with us to help us to come up with topics and refine the voice and style."

Future research efforts will focus on the development of text message-based programs. "When we started, we didn't even know if this was a good idea because phones are used to contact your friends and for social engagements, not about educational messages," said Mimi Nichter, UA professor of anthropology and co-author of the study. "What we, as anthropologists, wanted to know about the culture of kids was: What does health mean to them, and given that, what do you offer them? What's palatable for them, not just for the mouth, but for their way of thinking?" said Nichter, who has for years studied body image, food intake and dieting among teens.

The texting study was part of a larger USDA-funded study at the UA exploring how mobile technology may be used to promote healthy lifestyles for teens. The interdisciplinary project, dubbed "Stealth Health," has united researchers across the university campus in research and development projects related to mobile health applications. Promoting health and physical activity during the teen years can be critical, with the risk for developing obesity increasing during adolescence, Hingle said. "They're at the age right now that they start making decisions for themselves with regard to food and physical activity," she said. "Up until about middle school, parents are a lot more involved in making those decisions, so from a developmental standpoint, it's a good time to intervene."

The researchers published their work in the *Journal of Nutrition Education and Behavior*.

University of Arizona, http://psychcentral.com/news/2013/01/21/text-messaging-to-improve-teen-health/50628.html

## General comprehension

1. What is your opinion of the estimates given by researchers of the number of texts teenagers receive?
2. Why is this difficult for older people to understand?
3. Which two main ideas did the investigators discover about teenagers' willingness to receive health texts?
4. Which phrases proved to be unpopular with teenagers?
5. Which texts did the teenagers enjoy?
6. Explain in your own words what the anthropologists were hoping to find out.
7. What was the project called and why do you think this name was chosen?
8. Why do researchers believe the teenage years are so important in relation to this issue?

### Text handling

Find words in the text which could meaningfully be replaced by the following: (the words are in the order they appear in the text).

1. size
2. inborn
3. nourishment
4. similarly
5. particularly
6. unimportant information
7. flooded
8. addition
9. agreeable
10. encourage

## Written work HL

Write a personal response to the text explaining your attitude to texting and the role it plays in your life. You could compare these to the facts given in the text or the attitudes of your friends to texting. Write between 250 and 300 words.

### Zoom in on grammar

#### The gerund and the present participle

Both the gerund and the present participle are formed by adding *-ing* to a verb, for example: *playing, reading, sleeping*. If the verb ends in *-e*, the *-e* is generally dropped before adding *-ing*, for example: *make – making, have – having, escape – escaping*.

In some cases the final consonant may be doubled, for example, *stop – stopping, get – getting*.

The form used after the verb 'to be' is called the present participle – i.e. he is *running*; the water was *boiling*; the men had been *working*; the weather will be *freezing*. The gerund, however, is used in many different ways, for example:

- As the subject of a sentence – *Swimming* is a good way to keep fit.
- With a preposition – He was tired after *walking* so far.

### Grammar in context

#### The gerund and the present participle

In the text there are several examples of the use of the gerund.

#### After an adjective and a preposition

Investigators studied whether teenagers would be interested in *receiving* texts about health on their phones.

Make sentences of your own using these constructions followed by a gerund.

1. interested in... *-ing*
2. good at... *-ing*
3. keen on... *-ing*
4. tired of... *-ing*
5. aware of... *-ing*

#### After a verb

'They're at the age right now that they start *making* decisions for themselves with regard to food and physical activity.'

Teens may be recommended to consider *losing* weight for health reasons.

Some verbs can take either the gerund or the *to-infinitive*, for example:

They start *making* decisions. They start *to make* decisions.

Other verbs which can take the gerund or the *to*-infinitive include:

like, love, hate, fear, prefer, dread

For example:

I like *to play* the piano. I like *playing* the piano.

Make sentences of your own using the other five verbs listed above.

---

**TOK**

**Texting and tweeting**

What role do language and emotion play in texting and tweeting for both the sender and the recipient?

# 14 Teenage health

## Text 14.1.2 Healthy eating for teenagers

`http://www.nhs.uk/Livewell/Goodfood/Page/healthy-eating-teens.aspx`

# NHS choices
## www.nhs.uk

A healthy diet can help you look and feel great. Don't follow the latest food fad: find out the truth about eating well. Your body needs energy and nutrients from food to grow and work properly. If you don't eat a healthy, balanced diet, you could be putting your health and growth at risk. A healthy diet also gives you the energy you need and can help you look and feel great. But eating well doesn't have to mean giving up all your favourite foods. A healthy diet means eating a wide range of foods so that you get all the nutrients you need, and eating the right number of calories for how active you are. Beware of fad diets: they're rarely the best way to reach a healthy weight. Instead, use our tips to help you eat more healthily.

### Get started

**1** ..................................................................

Some people skip breakfast because they think it will help them lose weight. But skipping meals doesn't help you lose weight and is not good for you, because you can miss out on essential nutrients. Research shows that eating breakfast can actually help people control their weight. In addition, a healthy breakfast is an important part of a balanced diet and provides some of the vitamins and minerals we need for good health. Whole grain cereal with fruit sliced over the top is a tasty and healthy start to the day.

**2** ..................................................................

They are good sources of many of the vitamins and minerals your body needs. It's not as hard as it might sound: fresh, frozen, tinned, dried and juiced fruit and vegetables all count towards your total. So fruit juice, smoothies and vegetables baked into dishes such as stews all count.

**3** ..................................................................

Foods high in saturated fat include pies, processed meats such as sausages and bacon, biscuits and crisps. Foods high in added sugars include cakes and pastries, sweets, and chocolate. Both saturated fat and sugar are high in calories, so if you eat these foods often you're more likely to become overweight. Too much saturated fat can also cause high cholesterol.

**4** ..................................................................

Aim to drink six to eight glasses of fluids a day: water, unsweetened fruit juices (diluted with water) and milk are all healthy choices.

**5** ..................................................................

you may need more iron in your diet. Teenage girls are at higher risk of being low on iron, because they lose iron when they have their monthly period and they are still growing. Good sources of iron include red meats, breakfast cereals fortified with iron, and baked beans.

**6** ..................................................................

such as wholemeal bread, beans, wholegrain breakfast cereals, fruit and vegetables. Foods that are high in fibre are bulky and help us to feel full for longer, and most of us should be eating more of them.

`http://www.nhs.uk/Livewell/Goodfood/Page/healthy-eating-teens.aspx`

**7** ..................................................., guilty, or upset, or you're often worried about food or your weight, you may have an eating disorder. Help is out there: tell an adult you trust.

**8** ...................................................

Restricting foods (or food groups) or not eating a balanced diet can stop you getting enough of the calories and other important nutrients your body needs. This can lead to weight loss. Being underweight can cause health problems, so if you're underweight it's important to gain weight in a healthy way. Your GP can help with this.

**9** ...................................................

Foods high in fat and sugar are high in calories, and eating too many calories can lead to weight gain. Try to eat fewer foods that are high in fat and sugar, such as swapping to low- or no-sugar fizzy drinks. A healthy balanced diet will provide you with all the nutrients your body needs. Your body mass index (BMI) can tell you whether you are a healthy weight – check yours with our BMI healthy weight calculator.

**10** ...................................................

If you have an overweight BMI, aim to lose weight to bring your BMI into the healthy range. If you want to lose weight, it's important to choose your diet plan carefully. It can be tempting to follow the latest fad diet, but these are often not nutritionally balanced and don't work in the long term: once you stop, the weight is likely to come back. Diets based on only one or two foods may be successful in the short term, but can be dull and hard to stick to and deficient in a range of nutrients. The healthier, long-term way to lose weight is by combining long-term changes towards a healthy, balanced diet with more physical activity. If you're concerned about your weight, your GP can help.

**11** ...................................................

or any eating plans that advise you to cut out whole food groups. This can be unhealthy, because you may miss out on nutrients from that food group. Low-carb diets can be high in saturated fat. Eating too much saturated fat can cause high cholesterol, which can lead to an increased risk of developing heart disease. Other diets may involve cutting out dairy foods such as milk, yoghurt and cheese. These foods are high in calcium, which you need to ensure your bones grow properly. Choose lower fat dairy foods when you can – semi-skimmed, 1% fat or skimmed milk contain all the important nutritional benefits of whole milk, with less fat.

To learn more about healthy eating, go to www.pearsonhotlinks.com, enter the title or ISBN of this book and click on Chapter 14.

*http://www.nhs.uk/Livewell/Goodfood/Pages/healthy-eating-teens.aspx*

235

# 14 Teenage health

### General comprehension

1. The tips below have been taken from the text. Read the text carefully and replace each one at the beginning of the correct paragraph.
   a) If you often feel hungry, try eating more high-fibre foods
   b) Don't follow fad diets.
   c) Don't skip breakfast.
   d) Aim to eat at least five portions of a variety of fruits and vegetables a day.
   e) Make sure you drink enough fluids.
   f) If you're feeling tired and run down,
   g) If you are underweight, you may not be eating enough.
   h) Watch out for 'low-carb' diets,
   i) At snack time, swap foods that are high in saturated fat or sugars for healthier choices.
   j) If eating makes you feel anxious,
   k) If you are overweight, you may be eating too much

2. What can a healthy diet do for you according to the author?
3. If eating a healthy diet is so important, why do you think many people have problems with their diets?
4. How would you explain the term 'fad diet' to someone?
5. How can eating breakfast be beneficial?
6. What are the problems caused by some snack foods?
7. Which foods are most likely to cause people to become overweight?
8. Do you have any other tips for people to improve their diet and their health?
9. How would you describe the tone of this article?

### Text handling

Match the sentence halves to make meaningful, grammatically correct sentences.

1. We should all eat more foods that...
2. Eating too much saturated fat...
3. An increased risk of heart disease...
4. If you are overweight...
5. But eating well doesn't have to...
6. A healthy diet means...
7. It is important to eat...

A ... drinking six to eight glasses of fluids a day may be beneficial.
B ... the right number of calories for how active you are.
C ... eating a wide range of foods.
D ... are high in fibre and help us feel full for longer.
E ... can result in high cholesterol.
F ... may be caused by high cholesterol.
G ... mean giving up all your favourite foods.

### Interactive oral activity

Discuss together which of the IB Learner Profile traits reflect the basic ideas of healthy eating.

### Zoom in on grammar

**Modal verbs**

*Can, could, must, should, ought, may, might, will, would* and *shall* are all modal verbs. Modal verbs are used to express possibility or need. They can be used to tell people what to do, or what they can do, or what is possible or impossible. They never change their form or have endings added. After a modal verb we use an infinitive without *to*. For example:

You *must* study harder.
She *can* take a break now.
We *should* go home now.

### Grammar in context

**Modal verbs**

In the text there are a number of examples of the use of modal verbs. For example:

> A healthy diet *can* help you look and feel great.
> You *may* need more iron in your diet.
> You *may* have an eating disorder.

Re-read the text to find more examples of modal verbs. Think about why they are used and what they express. Try to use modal verbs in your own writing.

### Zoom in on grammar

**Gerund clause**

The gerund clause can be the subject of a sentence.

> *Studying every evening* is hard work.
> *Speaking a new language* can open the door to a new world.

### Grammar in context

**Gerund clause**

In the text there are several examples of the gerund clause as the subject of a sentence.

> *Healthy eating* for teens is important.
> But *eating well* doesn't have to mean giving up all your favourite foods.
> *Being underweight* can cause health problems.
> *Restricting foods* (or food groups) or *not eating a balanced diet* can stop you getting enough of the calories and other important nutrients your body needs.

Now make your own sentences using the following gerund clauses as the subjects of your sentences.

1 Learning a new skill...
2 Meeting new people...
3 Playing an instrument...
4 Cooking for friends...
5 Visiting new places...

## 14.2 Young people and sport

### Text 14.2.1 A third of primary school children 'cannot swim'

> Hundreds of thousands of children are being put at risk by leaving primary school unable to swim properly, according to research published today

by Graeme Paton, Education Editor,
12:01AM BST May 17 2012

237

## 14 Teenage health

Figures show a third of pupils struggle to swim at least 25 metres by the age of 11 – the recommended minimum target set out by the Government.

In some areas, almost three-quarters of children are unable to complete a length of a standard pool, it emerged.

The Amateur Swimming Association blamed a decline of swimming and enhanced life-saving lessons in many schools combined with a lack of encouragement from parents.

It follows criticism over a decision by local council to close large numbers of swimming pools across Britain because of budget cuts – leaving many children without easy access to local facilities.

Critics also fear that school sport has been downgraded in the final year of primary education as children are drilled to pass English and maths exams at the expense of other activities.

Figures suggest that the number of schoolchildren learning to swim is on the decline, with a separate study a decade ago revealing that just a fifth of children nationally failed to hit the 25 metre target.

David Sparkes, chief executive of the ASA, the governing body for swimming in England, said: "Swimming is the only subject on the national curriculum that can save your life so it's essential that government, schools and parents join us in taking action and break the cycle before we create a generation of non-swimmers unable to pass on this life-saving skill to their children in the future."

The study by Kellogg's and the ASA, which was based on Freedom of Information requests made to local councils in England, found that a third of children across the country were unable to swim 25 metres unaided at the end of primary school.

The latest study also showed huge variation nationally, with children in poor areas significantly less likely to swim than those in relatively affluent boroughs.

It emerged that just 26 per cent of children in Middlesbrough could swim the required 25 metres in 2011 compared with 91 per cent in parts of Northamptonshire.

An additional survey of 1,000 parents found that around four-in-10 children who were unable to swim had never been offered lessons by their school. This comes despite swimming forming a compulsory element of the National Curriculum.

Some one-in-six parents admitted never taking their child swimming.

The disclosure led to renewed fears that children were being put at risk close to the sea, lakes and ponds.

Drowning is already the third most common cause of accidental death among children in England, with the number of fatalities increasing by 35 per cent year-on-year.

David Walker, leisure safety manager at the Royal Society for the Prevention of Accidents, said swimming was an "essential skill" that every pupil should master.

"We are concerned to see that so many children are struggling to swim at an acceptable standard," he said.

http://www.telegraph.co.uk/education/educationnews/9269896/Third-of-primary-school-children-cannot-swim.html

## General comprehension

1. What reasons are offered to explain why so many children cannot swim?
2. Who is David Sparkes?
3. Which changes in the primary school curriculum have added to the problem?
4. What makes swimming special in the National Curriculum?
5. Does where a child lives play a role?
6. What part do parents play in this situation?
7. Is it really a problem if a child cannot swim?
8. How have the statistics of swimming ability changed in the last ten years?
9. Which steps must be taken to solve this problem?
10. Can you swim? How did you learn?

## Text handling

1. Match the sentence halves to make meaningful, grammatically correct sentences.

   I  Three-quarters of children are unable…
   II  We are concerned to see…
   III  The disclosure led to renewed fears…
   IV  This comes despite…
   V  Swimming is the only subject on the National Curriculum…
   VI  Figures suggest that…
   VII  Some one-in-six parents admitted…
   VIII  A third of pupils struggle to…

   A  … that children were being put at risk close to the sea, lakes and ponds.
   B  … swimming forming a compulsory element of the National Curriculum.
   C  … to complete a length of a standard pool.
   D  … swim at least 25 metres by the age of 11.
   E  … that so many children are struggling to swim at an acceptable standard.
   F  … never taking their child swimming.
   G  … that can save your life.
   H  … the number of schoolchildren learning to swim is on the decline.

2. Match the meanings to the words as they are used in the text. There are more meanings than you need.

   I  renewed
   II  decline
   III  enhance
   IV  decade
   V  disclosure
   VI  fatality
   VII  affluent
   VIII  compulsory

   A  enclosed space
   B  prosperous
   C  something you have to do
   D  recycled
   E  started again
   F  turn down
   G  improve
   H  decrease
   I  rotting
   J  death
   K  ten years
   L  revelation

## Zoom in on grammar

### 'To be able to' / 'unable to'

*To be able to* has the same meaning as *can* in the present tense.

    She *can* speak Urdu well. She *is able to speak* Urdu well.

To form the negative of *be able to* we can use *be unable to* or *not be able to*.

    However, she *is not able to* write Urdu. However, she *is unable to* write Urdu.

*Be able to* is used to replace *can* in these tenses, where *can* is not possible:

- present perfect – He *hasn't been able to* go to school this week.
- past perfect – He *hadn't been able to* call, as he had no time.
- -ing form – *Being able to* swim is an advantage.
- with 'will' – After the exams, you *will be able to* relax.

# 14 Teenage health

> **Grammar in context**
>
> **'To be able to' / 'unable to'**
>
> In the text there are three sentences using *able to/unable to*. Scan the text and find the examples.
>
> Now write three sentences of your own using *able to/unable to*.

### Text 14.2.2 Too much sport 'may be bad for teens' health'

## Too much sport 'may be bad for teens' health'
Thursday 21 November 2013 – 12am PST

Teenagers have long been told that being active and **a)**_____ in sports is good for their health. But new research suggests that too much sport for teenagers could negatively **b)**_____ their well-being just as much as too little sport. The US Department of Health and Human Services recommends that young people aged between 6 and 17 years carry out at least 60 minutes of physical activity a day, **c)**_____ 7 hours a week. But researchers from Switzerland and Canada say their study, published in the BMJ journal *Archives of Disease in Childhood*, suggests that 14 hours of physical activity a week is best for **d)**_____ good health in teenagers. However, they found that more than 14 hours appears to be detrimental to their health.

To reach their findings, the investigators **e)**_____ more than 1,245 teenagers aged between 16 and 20 from Switzerland. All participants were required to answer questions regarding demographics, height and weight, socioeconomic status, sports practice, sports injuries and well-being. Their well-being was **f)**_____ using the World Health Organization (WHO) Well-Being Index, which provides scores between 0 and 25. A score below 13 is an indicator of poor well-being. Of the participants, 50.4% were male with a mean age of 17.95 years. Almost 9% of these males were overweight or obese. The overall average well-being score for all participants was 17.

The researchers categorized sports participation as low (0–3.5 hours a week), average (3.6–10.5 hours), high (10.6–17.5 hours), and very high (more than 17.5 hours). Low sports activity was found in 35% of subjects, 41.5% had average activity, 18.5% had high, while 5% had very high.

## Very high activity 'just as bad' as low activity

The investigators found that participants in the low and very high activity groups were more than twice as likely to have well-being scores below 13, compared with subjects in the average group. The researchers say this corresponds to an "inverted U shaped" link between weekly duration of sports practice and well-being. They also found that the highest well-being scores were obtained by participants who carried out around 14 hours of physical activity a week, but beyond 14 hours resulted in lower well-being scores.

Commenting on their findings, the researchers say: "Physical activity has been associated with positive emotional well-being, reduced depressive, anxiety and stress disorders, and improved self-esteem and cognitive functioning in children and adolescents. We found that sports practice apparently ceased to be a protective factor and became an independent risk factor for poor well-being when practicing more than twice the 7 recommended hours per week."

The investigators note that their study highlights the importance for physicians caring for adolescents to monitor their level of sports practice and ask them about their well-being.

"Regardless of their decision to pursue their level of practice, these adolescents probably need a supportive and closer follow-up of their health and well-being. Our findings can inform guideline panels who produce recommendations on sports practice for adolescents," they add.

http://www.medicalnewstoday.com/articles/269133.php

**Discussion: truth tests**
Which truth tests would be useful to confirm the validity of the Knowledge Claims in this article?

# 14 Teenage health

## General comprehension

1. According to the text, what is the optimal amount of sport a teenager should undertake for personal well-being?
2. How many hours of sport per week have a negative effect on well-being?
3. Apart from taking part in sport, which activities can you list which are detrimental to a teenager's health?
4. How many hours of sport do you take part in per week? After reading the article, do you think this is a cause for concern?
5. Look up the 'World Health Organization (WHO) Well-Being Index' to see how the scores mentioned in the text were reached. What is your score?

## Text handling

1. Replace the following words and phrases in the appropriate places in the text.

    impact / surveyed / equating to / promoting / assessed / taking part

2. Locate the following vocabulary in the text.
    a) Find an adjective in the text which means 'having a negative effect'.
    b) Find a phrase which means 'average age'.
    c) Find a phrase which means 'mental ability'.
    d) Find a verb which means 'to stop'.
    e) Find an adjective which means 'upside-down'.

## Creativity, action, service

Creativity, action and service (CAS) involves students in a range of activities alongside their academic studies throughout the Diploma Programme. *Creativity* encourages students to engage in the arts and creative thinking. *Action* seeks to develop a healthy lifestyle through physical activity. *Service* in the community offers a vehicle for a different kind of learning with a practical value. The three strands of CAS enhance students' personal and interpersonal development through experiential learning and enable journeys of self-discovery.

*ibo.org*

Do you think it is important that exercise and physical well-being are an element of CAS? What effect do your CAS activities have on your health? How does this compare to the facts given in the article?

## Zoom in on grammar

**Noun clause**

A noun clause can start with *that*, or a question word – *where, why, who,* etc. – or *if* or *whether*.
A noun clause can be the object of a sentence:

New research suggests *that too much sport for teenagers may be detrimental*.

Some verbs which can be used before a noun clause beginning with 'that' include:

agree, assume, believe, consider, feel, know, find, suggest, understand

## Grammar in context

**Noun clause**

Re-read the text and find examples of noun clauses following 'that'.
Write sentences of your own using three of the verbs in the list above.

Text 14.2.3 Why team sports really do improve grades: Link between self-esteem and better performance in the classroom

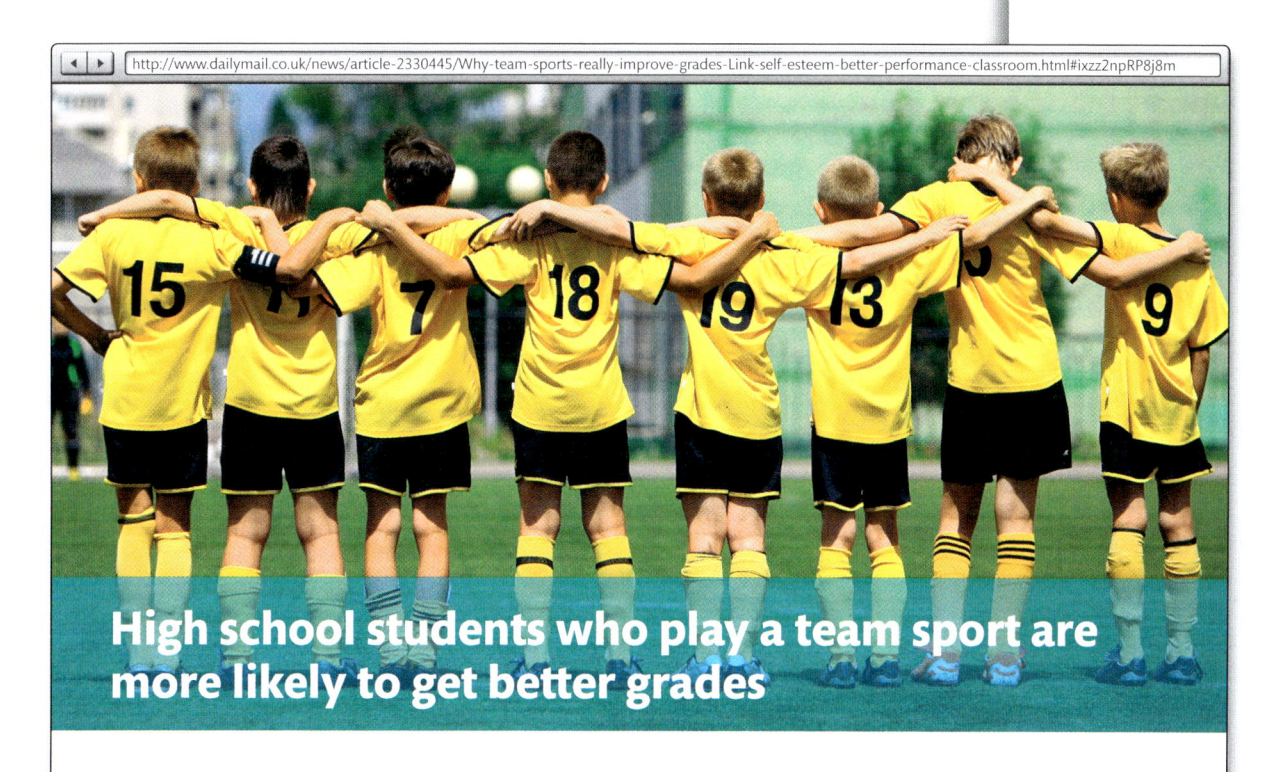

http://www.dailymail.co.uk/news/article-2330445/Why-team-sports-really-improve-grades-Link-self-esteem-better-performance-classroom.html#ixzz2npRP8j8m

## High school students who play a team sport are more likely to get better grades

A survey of 14–18-year-olds shows that competitive sport has a bigger impact on a student's grades than joining the debating or drama club

**by Sarah Harris**

*Published: 18:44 GMT, May 24 2013 |
Updated: 19:23 GMT, May 24 2013*

Team sport is the only extracurricular activity to make a significant difference to students' academic grades, new research has revealed. Teenagers who belong to sports clubs – as opposed to activities such as drama or debating – are also more likely to complete their education and enter higher education. The findings come after a recent survey revealed that physical education in schools has been reduced despite a surge in enthusiasm for sport after the London Olympics.

### Competitive spirit

Experts say teenagers who join sports teams rather than debating or drama clubs have the self-esteem and determination that makes them more likely to succeed academically. Academics from the University of South Carolina and Pennsylvania State University, both in the US, studied data from 9,700 high school students aged 14–18. They attended schools in urban, suburban and rural areas and participated in a variety of extracurricular activities, including academic and vocational clubs, performing arts societies and team sports. The academics looked for correlations between the types of after-school activities undertaken by the teenagers and their school success, including the likelihood of progressing to higher education. They found that students who lived in the countryside were more likely to take part in all kinds of extracurricular activities than their city-dwelling and suburban peers.

But the researchers' most significant findings came when examining the effect of these after-school clubs on students' academic achievements, according to the *Times Educational Supplement*. Team sport was the only

# 14 Teenage health

http://www.dailymail.co.uk/news/article-2330445/Why-team-sports-really-improve-grades-Link-self-esteem-better-performance-classroom.html#ixzz2npRP8j8m

extracurricular activity to have a consistent and significant effect on students' grades across all schools. Matthew Irvin, assistant professor in the Department of Educational Studies at the University of South Carolina, and the paper's lead author, said: "Team sport is significantly related to higher grade-point averages and a higher likelihood of completing high school and enrolling in college." This was true even once students' race, sex, previous academic achievement and socio-economic background were taken into consideration, he added.

Professor Irvin said: "Sport allows you to develop a mentoring relationship with adults and with positive, school-oriented peers. They help socialise you into being more focused on school, and may help develop time-management skills, initiative and an ability to work with others." Other activities had benefits – in urban high schools, for example, students who enrolled in academic clubs were likely to progress to college. And rural students who signed up for vocational or performing arts societies were also likely to go on to enrol on a degree course.

These positive effects remained the same regardless of students' socio-economic backgrounds. But only sport had a consistently positive effect across all schools and all measures of academic success. Professor Irvin added: "Sport is often what brings a community together."

Eileen Marchant, of the UK's Association for Physical Education, said that being "physically able and physically competent often complements academic ability". She said: "It raises self-esteem and self-belief, and there's an absolute correlation between believing in yourself and what happens in other areas of the curriculum. So much of extracurricular sport is focused on games, which are competitive. Additionally, you're competing against yourself in PE, even in something like dance or gymnastics. Success does breed success. There's no doubt about it."

Rod Goldswain, acting head teacher of Northampton School for Boys, which places particular emphasis on extracurricular activities for its 11- to 18-year-old students, said: "Those who do well in life are those who put the maximum effort into their sporting activities. That doesn't mean they have to represent their university. It doesn't mean they have to play on a national level. But when they take part, they're determined. When they train, they want to do their best."

Earlier this month, a report from the Smith Institute, a Left-wing think-tank, revealed that more than a third of teachers reported a reduction in time set aside for PE over the past two years. A lack of funding and, as a consequence, pressure on time were the main reasons given for the decrease. Under Coalition reforms, the £162 million-a-year "school sport partnerships" scheme – which funded sports coaches to work in schools and clubs – was abolished. Ministers also scrapped targets requiring pupils to engage in two hours of sport a week and introduced an Olympic-style "school games" programme to increase access to competitive sport. In March the Government announced £150 million of funding for the next two years with an emphasis on competitive team sports.

http://www.dailymail.co.uk/news/article-2330445/Why-team-sports-really-improve-grades-Link-self-esteem-better-performance-classroom.html#ixzz2npRP8j8m

## General comprehension

True or false? Justify your answers with a relevant brief quotation from the text.

1. Academic grades are not influenced by school sport.
2. After the success of the Olympic Games in London, the amount of sport in schools has increased.
3. Debating and drama clubs have the same effect as sport on academic success.
4. The researchers investigated links between academic success and after-school activities.
5. Students who live in urban areas do fewer after-school activities than students who live in rural areas.
6. The link between academic success and team sports also depends on race, sex and other factors.
7. Time management is one of the areas negatively affected by team sports.
8. There has been a reduction in PE time in schools due to a lack of teachers.

## Text handling

1. Replace these words in the text below.

   **significant / enter / surge / revealed / opposed / complete / extracurricular / recent**

   Team sport is the only _____ activity to make a _____ difference to students' academic grades, new research has _____. Teenagers who belong to sports clubs – as _____ to activities such as drama or debating – are also more likely to _____ their education and _____ higher education. The findings come after a _____ survey revealed that physical education in schools has been reduced despite a _____ in enthusiasm for sport after the London Olympics.

   Now check your answers with the text.

2. Match these words with their meaning below.

   | I | competent | A | notable |
   | II | debate | B | opinion of self |
   | III | correlation | C | regular |
   | IV | scrap | D | discard |
   | V | consistent | E | capable |
   | VI | significant | F | discuss |
   | VII | self-esteem | G | link |

## Interactive oral activity

In small groups, review the text once more and decide whether or not you agree with the author. Does your own personal experience support what is said, or do you have other ideas? Listen to your group carefully and share your ideas.

## Zoom in on grammar

### Prepositions: 'despite' / 'in spite of'

*Despite* and *in spite of* are both used with a noun phrase or an *-ing* form. We can also say *despite the fact that...* or *in spite of the fact that...* .

For example:

> The soccer game went ahead *despite/in spite of* the heavy rain.
> The soccer game went ahead *in spite of the fact that / despite the fact that* it was raining.

Another construction – *despite there being / in spite of there being* – is a rather complicated structure which could easily be replaced with *although* without any change in the meaning.

> The soccer game went ahead *despite there being* a lot of water on the field.
> The soccer game went ahead *in spite of there being* a lot of water on the field.
> The soccer game went ahead *although* there was a lot of water on the field.

## Grammar in context

### Prepositions: 'despite' / 'in spite of'

Read the text again and find examples of the use of *despite*. Can you re-write those sentences using a different form? Work with a partner and then share your answers with the class.

245

# 14 Teenage health

## 14.3 What really matters in life

Text 14.3.1 'I wasted so many years dieting, trying to be sexier and worrying about the size of my thighs'

**Melanie Reid broke her neck and back falling from a horse in April 2010. She writes a weekly column for *The Times Magazine***

**Not so long ago, a media report said one school girl in ten has an eating disorder. Another day, another report, and we're told 25 per cent of girls in some parts of the country are obese. All in all, millions of lovely kids storing up a lifetime of unhappiness with their own bodies**

At times like these, I wheel into my bathroom, the only place where there is a mirror low enough, and gaze quizzically at myself. How can I square what I see – a wrecked body, forcibly removed from the demands of being physically attractive – with the plight of healthy yet desperately dissatisfied young women?

There are some things you don't learn until it is too late. One is that a woman's relationship with her own body image is a totally unnecessary war. I was never a fashion victim or particularly preoccupied with my own appearance, but I look back now on the things about myself that I wanted to change, and the energy I wasted in 30 years of low-key yo-yo dieting and self-criticism.

If I could reclaim even half of it now, how much better I would have spent it – dancing, running, travelling, kissing, talking, laughing, reading, playing sport. Instead of trying to be thinner and sexier, I should have striven to be freer; to be braver; not to give a damn how others thought I looked; to relish every single second I had with a fit, healthy body.

Hindsight is a cruel companion. How, from my present vantage point, do I bridge that chasm of wisdom? How to tell young women, so many of them psychologically crippled by the tyranny of aspiring to a sexy body image, what really matters?

Instead of rejoicing in their health and opportunities, girls are being schooled by their mothers, their peers, the internet and the media to criticise their bodies. It's far worse now than when I was young. More and more poor souls are being screwed up by the pressure to look like stupid celebrities when they should be exploring the freedom to be themselves. We all know off by heart that destructive internal dialogue: my thighs are too fat; I hate my nose; my breasts are too big or too small or too saggy. Sisters take it from me: turn off the negative sound track and get out there and live.

The most sexy thing in the world is being alive, confident, active and interesting. Had I known that I would end up with a spinal injury, I would never have wasted a nanosecond on the width of my thighs, because these things are infinitely shallow and irrelevant. When your body doesn't work anymore, and you are sexually *hors de combat* the concept of body image becomes as blackly funny as it is possible to be. Physical imperfection is real, not some neurotic indulgence.

After my accident, reduced to a bag of bones for the first time in my life, I remember the irony of being told by a nutritionist to choose high-calorie options. I remember the shock of seeing myself naked in the mirror for the first time – great bony shoulders and visible ribs and fleshless hollow armpits. That was the look I once craved, but never like this, slumped helpless in a chair. God, I'd get into a pair of size 10 jeans now, I whispered, except I couldn't, not unless I was suspended from the ceiling and a team of carers tugged them up like they were stuffing sausages.

In my head, I wrote a dark parody of a typical women's magazine "How to lose two stone overnight" feature: easy – break your neck. I remembered how once I contemplated getting Botox (I was scarred between my eyebrows after an encounter with a horse's swinging head); now here I was, face addled with suffering, receiving Botox on the NHS to straighten my paralysed fingers and legs.

I do not speak for others, only for myself. Conventional standards of beauty and elegance are lost when you cannot move, when people look at you with pity, if they look at all. Adult body image involves sexual identity, desirability, power and pride; and when you lose that joy and frisson, you become a changed person. Only the hurt, the gnaw of envy, remains. Oh, you can be as thin as you like, can wear make-up and nice earrings and pretty scarves to make the face brave, but truly, you don't know what you've got till it's gone.

Never mind. There are small compensations for not being sexy. Rhododendrons, for example. My heroic husband pushed me up the slope into the back garden, where I hadn't been for three years, to see the blooms. And I've noticed something significant: the muscles in my chest have recovered enough to let me blow my nose properly again. So, stronger nose blowing too. Honestly, why fret?

The Times Magazine. 01.06.2013

## General comprehension

1. Match the first part of the sentence with the appropriate ending on the right. There are more endings than you need.

   I   Melanie Reid can only see herself...
   II  She feels that women waste time...
   III She wasted years...
   IV  She wishes now...
   V   Girls learn to be critical of their bodies...
   VI  Melanie Reid was slightly injured...

   A ... by a horse turning its head.
   B ... in a low mirror in the bathroom.
   C ... suspended from the ceiling.
   D ... dieting and being self-critical.
   E ... she had spent the time so much better.
   F ... instead of enjoying good health and opportunities.
   G ... from a variety of people and the media.
   H ... riding a horse.
   I ... worrying about their bodies.

2. Explain Melanie Reid's message to young women in your own words.
3. What was the irony of Melanie's situation after the accident?
4. Which two small things give Melanie comfort according to this article?
5. How would you describe the tone of the article?

# 14 Teenage health

## Text handling

Find the words in the right-hand column that could meaningfully replace the words from the text on the left. There are more options than you need.

| | | | |
|---|---|---|---|
| 1 | plight | A | imitation |
| 2 | relish | B | encouraged |
| 3 | chasm | C | lost |
| 4 | irrelevant | D | large gap |
| 5 | craved | E | pain |
| 6 | parody | F | unhappy situation |
| | | G | enjoy |
| | | H | not straight |
| | | I | not important |
| | | J | argument |
| | | K | longed for |

## Interactive oral activity

**The IB Learner Profile**

Discuss the following in small groups.

- Consider the traits of the IB Profile. Which of these do you think Melanie Reid displays and how are they positive for her?
- Think about your situation in comparison to Melanie's. Which traits of the IB Profile do you display? What have you learned from her?

## Zoom in on grammar

**Third conditional**

The third conditional is used to describe a past possibility that did not occur.

> If I *had known* the buses stopped at 11 o'clock, *I would have left* the party earlier.
> If … + *past perfect*, … + *would* + *past perfect*

*Could* can also be used in the *if*-clause:

> If I *could have* known the bus times in advance, I would have caught the last bus.

## Grammar in context

**Third conditional**

Melanie Reid also uses the third conditional to describe what might have been:

> If I could reclaim even half of it now, how much better I would have spent it.
>
> Had I known that I would end up with a spinal injury, I would never have wasted a nanosecond on the width of my thighs…

What about you? What do you wish you had done or not done in the past? Write five sentences using the third conditional.

**TOK**

In the article, Melanie Reid discusses perception: our own perception of our bodies and our lives and the perceptions of others. Discuss the role of perception as described in the article and the role you feel it has in the lives of your peers.

# Exam practice

## Exercises

**Written assignment 1: Essay title (HL)**

Obesity is becoming a serious health issue in the 21st century. Write an essay explaining why this is the case and suggesting ways in which the problem could be solved. Write between 250 and 400 words.

**Written assignment 2: Personal response (HL)**

Give a personal response to the following stimulus and justify it. Choose any text type that you have studied in class. Write between 150 and 250 words.

> '[T]ruly, you don't know what you've got till it's gone.'

*Melanie Reid*

**Written assignment 3: Essay (SL)**

As a member of the school's student sports committee you have been asked by the sports director to give a speech in assembly to the younger students to encourage more participation in the extra-curricular sports programme. Write the speech. Write between 250 and 400 words.

# 15 Multicultural Great Britain

**Opposite** Cultural diversity.

## Objectives

- To practise interactive oral skills
- To develop writing skills in semi-formal English
- To revise the use of the passive
- To examine the use of adjectives in a sentence
- To think about the use of idiomatic language
- To consider the idea of a country being a 'melting pot' of nationalities

## 15.1 The making of a nation

Text 15.1.1 'The British' by Benjamin Zephaniah

### The British

Take some Picts, Celts and Silures
And let them settle,
Then overrun them with Roman conquerors.

Remove the Romans after approximately 400 years
Add lots of Norman French to some
Angles, Saxons, Jutes and Vikings, then stir vigorously.

Mix some hot Chileans, cool Jamaicans, Dominicans,
Trinidadians and Bajans with some Ethiopians, Chinese,
Vietnamese and Sudanese.

Then take a blend of Somalians, Sri Lankans, Nigerians
And Pakistanis,
Combine with some Guyanese
And turn up the heat.

Sprinkle some fresh Indians, Malaysians, Bosnians,
Iraqis and Bangladeshis together with some
Afghans, Spanish, Turkish, Kurdish, Japanese
And Palestinians
Then add to the melting pot.

Leave the ingredients to simmer.

As they mix and blend allow their languages to flourish
Binding them together with English.

Allow time to be cool.

Add some unity, understanding, and respect for the future,
Serve with justice
And enjoy.

*Note:* All the ingredients are equally important. Treating one ingredient better than another will leave a bitter unpleasant taste.

*Warning:* An unequal spread of justice will damage the people and cause pain. Give justice and equality to all.

> The Picts, Celts and Silures were tribes in ancient Britain who fought the Roman invaders in the first century AD. The Germanic tribes – the Angles, Saxons and Jutes – invaded Britain in the fifth and sixth centuries and were followed by the Vikings in the eighth to eleventh centuries. Later, the other people mentioned in the poem migrated peacefully to Britain.

Benjamin Zephaniah, *The Wicked World Anthology*. Published by Puffin Books (Penguin) in January 2000, ISBN: 0141306831

# 15 Multicultural Great Britain

### General comprehension

1. What do you think Benjamin Zephaniah is saying about the British nation in this poem?
2. In the poem you see the verbs *take*, *remove*, *add*, *mix* and *sprinkle*. Do these words make you think of another genre of English writing?
3. What is the 'warning' in the final verse referring to?
4. What is the difference between the two phrases 'allow time to cool' and 'allow time to be cool'? (The second phrase is used in the poem.)

### Zoom in on grammar

**Idiomatic language**

In the poem 'The British', Benjamin Zephaniah talks about a 'melting pot'. He uses the phrase literally – referring to a cooking pot.

The phrase 'melting pot' is often used idiomatically. That means the words are used with a different meaning from their original, literal meaning. We may sometimes refer to a city as being 'a melting pot of cultures': this means that people from different cultures and backgrounds become integrated. In the poem, Benjamin Zephaniah is showing the reader how the British are the result of over hundreds of years of different peoples living together; Britain is a melting pot of nationalities.

When you are reading, always be aware of this aspect of the language and look out for idiomatic phrases.

### Individual oral activity

Before you read the poem aloud you could search on YouTube for 'BBC poetry season – Zephaniah and students perform The British' and listen to the performance.

In groups of three or four, read the poem again but read it aloud. Then talk together and discuss what the poem is saying about the British. Quote lines that you think are particularly meaningful. Consider the idea of a country as 'a melting pot'. Think of your own experience in countries you have lived in, or visited, and discuss whether the idea of a melting pot of nationalities is true of those countries. The USA is often referred to as a melting pot. Do you think this is true?

To see Benjamin Zephaniah and students performing 'The British', go to www.pearsonhotlinks.com, enter the title or ISBN of this book and click on Chapter 15.

## Text 15.1.2 Benjamin Zephaniah: biography

Dr Benjamin Obadiah Iqbal Zephaniah was born in 1958 in Birmingham, England, where he grew up and went to school. He is currently one of the most acclaimed British poets, with a following far beyond the British Isles. Benjamin Zephaniah has been in love with words and poetry his whole life, despite leaving school at the age of 13 unable to read. He says that his school in Birmingham played no role in his love of poetry. In fact, he says he was always most strongly influenced by the music and poetry of Jamaica, the home of his parents.

Always concerned with the lives of ordinary people, Benjamin Zephaniah relates closely to what he calls 'street politics', and was first inspired to write poetry when he was a teenager living in Handsworth, where he performed locally and gained a strong following. He is also engaged with the promotion of equal rights – both for black and white people – and local and international politics. His first book, *Pen Rhythm*, was published in 1980 when he was just 22.

## Growth of fame

The 1980s was a time of high unemployment and social unrest in Britain, and the newly introduced SUS laws triggered numerous demonstrations and protests. Benjamin Zephaniah's poetry could be often heard at these gatherings and he became an iconic figure; photographed, interviewed and admired. His particular form of performance was dub poetry, and he brought this indigenously Jamaican style into the homes of large numbers of the people of Britain for the first time.

Benjamin Zephaniah's fame and popularity spread in the 1990s to countries far beyond Great Britain. Much of the success is due to his own passionate poetry performances, and he feels it is extremely important to keep the oral tradition alive, not only in countries where access to books is limited. His poems are delivered with passion and spirit, and audiences are captivated by his energy.

## Writing for children

Children and young people love the way Benjamin Zephaniah plays with words, the way he is sometimes shockingly provocative and gives voice to thoughts that many people have, but are unable, or do not dare, to formulate. His first anthology of poetry for children, called *Talking Turkeys*, had to be reprinted after only six weeks on the market because it was so popular. And it is not only poetry – in 1999 his first novel *Face* was published, directed especially at boys who might be considered to be 'reluctant readers'. The success of the novel is proof that focusing on themes that are of interest to teenagers and writing in a fast-paced, realistic style can make avid readers of all young people.

## Still going strong

Benjamin Zephaniah continues to be an inspiration to people of all ages. Rappers, aspiring young poets, writers of fiction, all those who do not have a voice in our society and anyone who loves poetry acknowledge his engagement with their cause. *The Times* newspaper has included him in their list of the 50 greatest post-war writers.

---

ⓘ SUS Laws existed in the UK in the 1970s and 1980s – they allowed police to stop and search a person considered to be 'suspicious'. There was a perceived belief that police officers targeted young black men.

ⓘ Dub poetry is a form of performance poetry of West Indian origin, which evolved out of dub music consisting of spoken word over reggae rhythms in Jamaica in the 1970s.

# 15 Multicultural Great Britain

## General comprehension

1. According to the text, what was the extent of the influence of school on Benjamin Zephaniah's life-long love of poetry?
2. Benjamin Zephaniah's first book, *Pen Rhythm*, made his poetry accessible to a wider audience in Great Britain. Where had his popularity been established prior to this?
3. What do you think the phrase means 'to keep the oral tradition alive'?
4. What information in the text tells you that Benjamin Zephaniah is also popular as a writer of children's poetry?
5. Benjamin Zephaniah's 1999 novel, *Face*, was a big success among teenage boys. According to the text, what were the reasons for this success?

## Text handling

1. Which word in paragraph 1 means 'a group of fans or supporters'?
2. Which word in paragraph 5 means 'unwilling'?
3. Which word in paragraph 5 means 'enthusiastic'?
4. Which word in paragraph 6 means 'hoping to achieve something'?
5. 'Still going strong'. Which of the following definitions best explains this phrase?
    a) continuing to be powerful
    b) continuing to be successful
    c) continuing to be loud

## Zoom in on grammar

**Adjectives**

Example: In the first paragraph you read:

His poetry is *strongly influenced* by the music and poetry of Jamaica and what he calls 'street politics'.

When two adjectives are used together consecutively in a sentence to describe something in this way, the first adjective is a modifier (modifying the adjective) and functions like an adverb. In the example the two adjectives are *strong* and *influenced*.

Look at these other examples.

It's terribly cold today. (not 'it's terrible cold')

The painting is incredibly expensive. (not 'incredible expensive')

The examination was amazingly difficult. (not 'amazing difficult')

## Grammar in context

**Adjectives**

Choose two words (one from each box) and use them to help you complete each sentence.

| absolutely | slightly  |
|------------|-----------|
| badly      | extremely |
| reasonably | terribly  |

| cheap   | damaged |
|---------|---------|
| changed | ill     |
| quiet   | sorry   |

1. Although the new restaurant is in the city centre, _____.
2. The maths class is usually noisy but today the students were _____.
3. The student ate the dish of shrimps and the next day he was _____.
4. After the storm the roof of the gym was _____.
5. After the renovation work the house was only _____.
6. I am _____ but I have left my homework on the bus.

## 15.2 Cultural diversity

### Text 15.2.1 What is cultural diversity?

http://www.mylearning.org/jpage.asp?jpageid=2022&journeyid=441

# Cultural diversity

The phrase 'cultural diversity' means a range of different societies or peoples with different origins, religions and traditions all living and interacting together. Britain has benefited from diversity throughout its long history and is currently one of the most culturally diverse countries in the world!

The food we eat, the music we listen to, and the clothes we wear have all been influenced by different cultures coming into Britain. Ethnic food, for example, is part of an average British diet. One of Britain's favourite dishes is Indian Curry. Britons have enjoyed Curry for a surprisingly long time – the first curry on a menu was in 1773!

Even English is based on the languages spoken by Anglo-Saxons, Scandinavian Vikings and Norman French invaders, with words added from the languages of other immigrants over the years!

#### Valuing our cultural diversity

In Britain today there is an estimated 'ethnic minority' population of just over 4 million. We live in a country rich in cultural heritage; but the value in this diversity is sometimes not fully seen.

Valuing our diverse culture in Britain today is all about understanding and respecting other peoples beliefs and ways of life (as we would expect someone to respect ours). It is about supporting individuals in keeping their cultural traditions alive and appreciating the fact that all these different cultural traditions will enrich British life both today and in the future.

#### A diverse history

Cultural diversity in Britain goes as far back as the history books go! In fact it is only when we consider our history that we get a true picture of how diverse Britain today really is.

Each one of these settlers brought with them different foods, fashions, languages, beliefs and lifestyles. People from all over the world have contributed to the Britain we live in today and they continue to do so.

http://www.mylearning.org/jpage.asp?jpageid=2022&journeyid=441

# 15 Multicultural Great Britain

### General comprehension

1. What are the similarities between the text 'What is cultural diversity?' and the poem 'The British' by Benjamin Zephaniah?
2. According to the text, what are the things that settlers in a country bring with them that enrich its culture?
3. According to the text, Britain has 'benefited' from cultural diversity. In your opinion, what examples of this enrichment are not specifically mentioned in the text?
4. What influences do immigrants have on the language of the country they settle in?
5. The ethnic minority population in Great Britain totals some 4 million; is this group generally considered to be a positive contribution to the country?
6. Suggest another word for 'diversity' in the text.

**TOK**: To what extent does your own cultural background and experience influence your understanding of the term 'cultural diversity'?

### Interactive oral activity

With a partner, imagine you are taking part in an interview for the local radio station in the city where you live. The radio station is doing a series of broadcasts on cultural diversity and the interviewer is interested to know about your home country and your experiences of living abroad.

One of you takes the role of interviewer and together you should prepare the questions you think might be asked about your culture. Then do the interview as realistically as possible.

You might record it and then share it with the rest of the class.

## Written work

There are a number of English-speaking countries in the world – for example, Australia, New Zealand, the USA and Canada. All of these have a culturally diverse population. Choose one of these countries, do some research into the extent of cultural diversity there and present the results of your research in a genre of your choice: it may be an essay, a flyer or the text of a speech to be given to fellow students.

Word count: at least 400 words.

**Below** Inner-city housing.

## 15.3 Manchester, UK

### Text 15.3.1 Europe's most exotic city? It's Manchester! 153 languages spoken by a population of 500,000

by Nick Fagge

Its detractors try to portray it as a cold, wet and sometimes insular place.

But Manchester is actually one of the most exotic cities in the world, researchers claim. This is due to its cultural diversity, with at least 153 languages spoken.

Two-thirds of Mancunian school children are bilingual, with the number of languages likely to increase, according to the study by Manchester University.

The city is more diverse than London, and rivalled only by New York and Paris for its ethnic and linguistic mix, claims Professor Yaron Matras, who carried out the research.

"Manchester's language diversity is higher than many countries in the world," Professor Matras said. "It is very likely to be the top of the list in Europe, certainly when compared to other cities of its size."

With a population of 500,000, Manchester is much smaller than London, where more than 300 languages are spoken by eight million inhabitants.

Professor Matras said: "There are certainly a greater number of languages spoken in London but these are by people who are passing through – diplomats, businessmen, etc – but in Manchester, the foreign language speakers are residents.

"Around two-thirds of Mancunian school children are bilingual – a huge figure which indicates just how precious its linguistic culture is. As immigration and the arrival of overseas students to the city continues, it's fair to say that this already large list is set to grow."

Manchester's rapid growth began during the Industrial Revolution, with the city's textile trade attracting workers from across the empire, setting the pattern for diversity.

The policy of recruiting from abroad for public services, such as the NHS, has helped bring in some of the more obscure languages, the professor says.

These include more than a dozen Indian languages, ten from West Africa, three Kurdish dialects, various forms of the Romany language of Eastern European gypsies, Uyghur – which is spoken by the Muslims of north-west China – and even Nahuatl, the tongue of the ancient Aztecs of Mexico.

Professor Matras said the Census data released last week underestimated the number of multi-lingual households in the UK, as respondents were asked to name their main language.

"Most multi-linguals speak a language other than English at home, but use English at work, in their place of study, so they will answer that English is their main language, even though this is not strictly accurate."

http://www.dailymail.co.uk/news/article-2248956/Europes-exotic-city-Its-Manchester-153-languages-spoken

### General comprehension

True or false? Justify your answer with a relevant brief quotation from the text.
1. Only a small number of schoolchildren are bilingual.
2. New York and Paris are less diverse than London.
3. The population of Manchester is half a million.
4. Diplomats and businessmen in London who speak a language other than English are usually residents.
5. The National Health Service (NHS) employs staff only from the UK.

# 15 Multicultural Great Britain

## Zoom in on grammar

**The passive**

Example from the text:

... 300 languages *are spoken* by eight million inhabitants.

Here, *are spoken* is an example of the use of the passive.

A passive verb is a form of *be* + a passive participle. The passive can be formed in all tenses. Look at the table of examples below.

|  | Active | Passive |
|---|---|---|
| *Present simple* | We bake the bread here. | The bread is baked here. |
| *Present continuous* | We are baking the bread. | The bread is being baked. |
| *Present perfect* | We have baked the bread. | The bread has been baked. |
| *Past simple* | We baked the bread yesterday. | The bread was baked yesterday. |
| *Past continuous* | We were baking the bread. | The bread was being baked. |
| *Future* | We will bake the bread. | The bread will be baked. |

Other tenses are constructed in the same way.

**Active and passive**

Active: The boy *broke* the window.
Passive: The window *was broken* (by the boy).

Question: Why do we need the passive?

Answer: It depends on the subject.

'The boy *broke* the window.' The subject of the sentence is 'the boy'.
'The window *was broken*.' The subject of the sentence is 'the window'.

So, it depends on *who* or *what* is the subject of your sentence and what you are focusing on: the choice of the subject depends on the information you want to convey.

Is it important to say who broke the window? Then use the active form of the verb.

Is it important to say that there is a broken window? Then use the passive form of the verb.

## Grammar in context

**The passive**

Using the words in brackets, make passive sentences. There are past and present tenses. The first one is an example.

**Example:** Where's my phone? (it / stole)

*It has been stolen.*

1 A: Last Saturday someone broke into our house.
   B: Oh dear. (anything / take?)

   ..................................................................................................

2 Facebook is a very popular social network. (every day / it / use / millions of people)
   Every day it ..................................................................................................

3 A: There is no PE class today.
   B: Really? (when / it / cancel?)

   ..................................................................................................

4 A tree was lying across the road. (it / blow down / in the storm / yesterday)

   ..................................................................................................

5 Mr Green can't use his office at the moment. (it / redecorate)

   ..................................................................................................

**6**  A: Is the science teacher popular?
    B: Yes. (she / like / everybody in school)

    ..................................................................................................................

**7**  A: Is the meeting at 4 p.m.?
    B: No. (time / change)

    ..................................................................................................................

## Text 15.3.2 Restaurants reflect cultural diversity in Manchester: The Curry Mile

### Rusholme Curry Mile restaurants

The Curry Mile in Manchester is world famous thanks largely to the sheer number of bright neon-lit (mainly Bangladeshi and Pakistani) restaurants and takeaways.

Located along Wilmslow Road in Rusholme, just two miles south of the city centre, the area comes to life late at night with many restaurants staying open until 3 or 4am (even later on busy nights).

With a mixture of award-winning restaurants and fast-food curry houses, The Curry Mile is the ideal place to start or end your evening.

It's claimed there are over 70 Asian takeaways, shisha cafes, sweet houses and restaurants in Rusholme within less than a mile stretch. There's a massive choice of Indian, Pakistani, Bangladeshi and Persian restaurants with the late night openings making them particularly popular with students and party goers.

*http://www.manchesterrestaurants.com/rusholme.htm*

### General comprehension

1  According to the text, why is the Curry Mile in Manchester famous?
2  Where is this street located?
3  What do you think is the meaning of 'award-winning restaurants'?
4  According to the text these restaurants are popular with students and people who go to parties. What do you think is the reason for the restaurants being popular with these groups?
5  In the first sentence 'sheer' is used as an adjective. Which of the following three explanations of the use of the adjective do you think is correct?

   a)  It describes the kinds of building.
   b)  It emphasises the large quantity of eateries.
   c)  It refers to the brightness of the signs.

# 15 Multicultural Great Britain

**Below** A selection of whole and ground spices.

> ### Individual oral activity
> 
> Based on research that you do individually, choose one of the following themes and prepare a three-minute presentation for your class.
> - Manchester – the home of the football club Manchester United
> - Karl Marx and Manchester
> - Studying in Manchester
> - Manchester and the Industrial Revolution
> - Art galleries and museums in Manchester
> - Manchester and its surroundings

## Text 15.3.3 What exactly is a curry?

The word curry was invented by British colonialists in the 18th century. Most likely a corruption of the Indian word *kari* (meaning sauce), it refers to a number of saucy dishes flavored with curry powder or curry paste.

The idea of curry began in India. By the beginning of the 18th century, the Dutch and the British were selling standardized curry powders. At the Universal Paris Exhibition of 1889, a curry decree set the composition of curry as having prescribed amounts of tamarind, onion, coriander, chilli pepper, turmeric, cumin, fenugreek, pepper, and mustard.

Today, curry powder may also include cloves, cardamon, ginger, nutmeg, fennel, caraway, ajowan seeds, dried basil, mustard seeds, mace, poppy seeds, sesame seeds, saffron or cinnamon. The mix depends on the cook, as curry recipes can be found in the cuisines of India, Pakistan, Bangladesh, Sri Lanka, Nepal, Indonesia, Malaysia, Thailand and the Caribbean.

While there is no rigid definition of 'curry,' many restaurants use it as a generic term for sauce-based dishes that can vary in spice content and heat, and can contain meat, poultry, seafood, vegetables, coconut milk, onions, fresh ginger, kaffir lime leaves and other ingredients.

Curry powder's flavors fade quickly, and Indian curry powder is ideally made to order depending on the dish. Madras curry powder is named after the southern Indian region from which it comes. Be careful if you're not used to it, as it tends to pack a lot more heat.

http://www.cookthink.com/reference/955/What_exactly_is_a_curry

### Text handling

Match the definitions on the left with the correct word from the text on the right.

1  style of cooking             A  prescribed
2  to lose freshness            B  contain
3  change resulting from use    C  cuisine
4  laid down as a rule          D  generic
5  referring to a whole group   E  corruption
6  consist of                   F  fade

## Written work

Imagine you have spent a weekend in Manchester with your parents. One of the most impressive moments was going to Rusholme to eat curry; you went there because your mother had read an article about the restaurants there in a Sunday newspaper.

Describe your impressions of the area and the restaurants. Which one did your family choose and why? Write about your enjoyment of the experience. What did the other members of the family think about it? Write between 250 and 300 words.

# 15.4 Colourful London

## Text 15.4.1 Spitalfields, London. Cultural diversity is not a new thing in London's East End

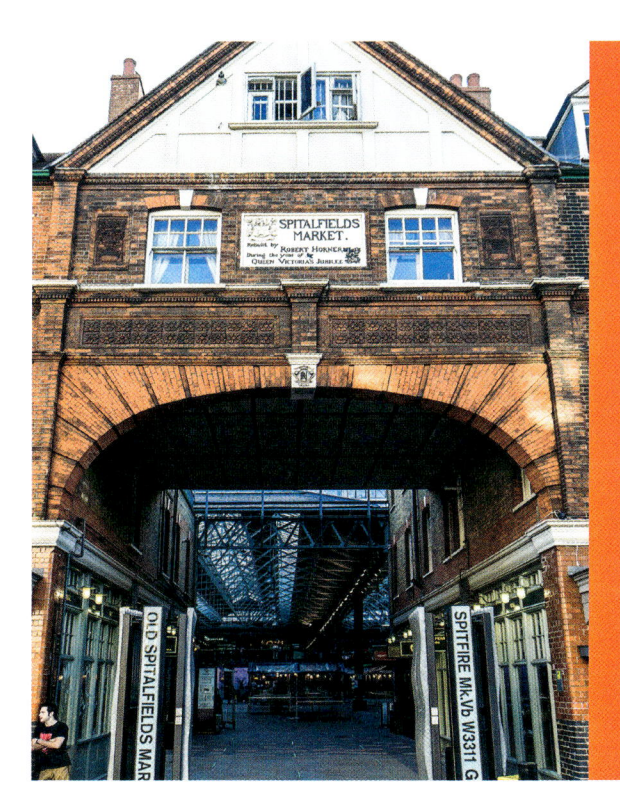

Spitalfields takes its name from the hospital and priory, St. Mary's Spittel that was founded in 1197. Lying in the heart of the East End, it is an area known for its spirit and strong sense of community. It was in a field next to the priory where the now famous market first started in the thirteenth century.

As an international city, London is celebrated for its diversity in population. The East End has always been recognised for the wealth of cultures represented. Spitalfields served as a microcosm of this polyglot society, the 'melting pot' fusion of east and west. Historically, it has played host to a transient community – primarily for new immigrants.

Spitalfields had been relatively rural until the Great Fire of London. By 1666, traders had begun

# 15 Multicultural Great Britain

operating beyond the city gates – on the site where today's market stands. The landmark Truman's Brewery opened in 1669 and in 1682 King Charles II granted John Balch a Royal Charter giving him the right to hold a market on Thursdays and Saturdays in or near Spital Square.

The success of the market encouraged people to settle in the area and following the edict of Nantes in 1685, Huguenots fleeing France brought their silk weaving skills to Spitalfields. Their grand houses can still be seen around what is now the conservation area of Fournier Street. Today these houses are home to many artists including Gilbert and George.

The Huguenots were soon followed by Irish labourers in the mid-1700s escaping famine, many of whom would work on the construction of the nearby London docks. As the area grew in popularity, Spitalfields became a parish in its own right in 1729 when Hawkesmoor's Christ Church was consecrated.

The Irish were followed by East European Jews escaping the Polish pogroms and harsh conditions in Russia; as well as entrepreneurial Jews from the Netherlands. From the 1880s to 1970s Spitalfields was overwhelmingly Jewish and probably one of the largest Jewish communities in Europe with over 40 Synagogues.

By the middle of the 20th century the Jewish community had mostly moved on. Since 1970s a thriving Bangladeshi community has flourished in the area, bringing new cultures, trades and business to the area including the famous Brick Lane restaurant district.

Evidence of the people and communities that have given the area its unique character can still be seen – a Huguenot church, a Methodist chapel, a Jewish synagogue, and Muslim mosque stand among traditional and new shops, restaurants, markets and homes.

Spitalfields is no longer considered just a Sunday destination – it has evolved into one of London's favourite and most vibrant areas.

*http://www.spitalfields.co.uk/about_history.php#.Ut0Qt_sxlkg, © Spitalfields.co.uk*

### General comprehension

1. Who do you think this article was written for? Choose one of the groups listed below and explain briefly why you have chosen it.
    a) students of history
    b) companies thinking of setting up business in Spitalfields
    c) tourists visiting the area
    d) people who have moved to Spitalfields to live
2. Where did the name 'Spitalfields' originate?
3. For how many years has there been a settlement there?
4. For what reasons do you think the following groups settled in the area?
    a) people belonging to the Huguenot religion
    b) Irish labourers
    c) Jewish people
5. What event in the mid-1700s triggered a large wave of emigration from Ireland?
6. In the sixth paragraph, the Jewish immigrants from the Netherlands who settled in London are described as 'entrepreneurial'. Which of the following definitions do you think best fits in the text?
    a) widely travelled
    b) good at starting businesses
    c) religious

### Individual oral activity

Describe the picture below and then relate it to one of your options themes. Talk for three minutes, making connections to ideas that you relate to the subject of the picture.

**Left** For sale: objects representing the country's cultural heritage – or junk?

Text 15.4.2 Visit Brick Lane, London: An app for tourists

## We've made a top 10 list of things you MUST do if you visit Brick Lane

Brick Lane and the surrounding areas have so much to offer – so many things to do and see and experience.

**1** **Sweet and Spicy:** We wouldn't normally recommend one restaurant over another on Brick Lane, but Sweet and Spicy are very different. They've been around for 40+ years. The food served is very unique and unlike any of the other restaurants in the area – or anywhere in the world!

**2** **Whitechapel Art Gallery:** Think modern art, Tate Britain and similar. Very trendy and fashionable and great works of art. 2 minutes' walk from Brick Lane.

# 15   Multicultural Great Britain

**3**   **Sunday market:** A carnival festival where you literally can't walk because of the crowds – this is what happens every week in Brick Lane. Not a carnival, but with a million different places to buy just about anything you can imagine. A must for any tourist.

**4**   **Indoor food market:** Food, food, glorious food – from every corner of the world. The place is *jam* packed with people. The food is typically cooked in front of you and served piping hot. Treat yourself and visit on a Sunday.

**5**   **Vintage clothes:** Clothes recycled and refashioned. Words can't describe the array of vintage fashion ware for sale. There must be more than 10 shops scattered in and around Brick Lane, and then you have the indoor Vintage Market – with 20+ sellers.

**6**   **Graffiti art:** People come from around the world to view and take pictures of the graffiti art dotted around Brick Lane. Famous is the massive pelican – must be more than 50ft high. Look closely and you'll see work from Banksy and many other artists.

**7**   **Beigel Shop:** Open 24 hours a day. The bagels are unique and different to anything made anywhere in the world. In fact, I wouldn't even call it a bagel! It doesn't look like the traditional bagel! Come any day, any time and they'll be open and happy to serve you – open 24 hours 365 days a year.

**8**   **Go for a curry!** OK, this had to be on the list. There exists nowhere else like it in the world. More than 100 curry houses in the area – with nearly 50 on Brick Lane itself. If you want a curry, then visit Brick Lane – food is typically cheap and hard to beat for taste and quality.

**9**   **Buy a cake from Suzzle:** Newly opened and only open on select days of the week, Suzzle gives you a unique partnership of mouth watering delicatessens and art. Melanie cooks the food herself at the back of the shop – you won't get fresher anywhere else. You won't be able to walk past without stopping and staring!

**10**   **Nightlife:** A great one for the night owls and adventure seekers. The crowd changes into fun-loving clubbers – join the party, it starts from 11pm and finishes in the early hours every single night!

And there's more… so much more. Brick Lane is a narrow road, maybe not even a mile long. The area surrounding gives a unique experience in so many different ways – something you won't find anywhere. There many others that we could have put in our top 10, like Spitalfields Market, Boxpark, Petticoat Lane market, Commercial Street and many more – we'll leave that to future write ups and videos we'll create for our app.

http://bricklane.co.uk/app/tourist-guide/index.html

**Above** An example of graffiti art done by famous UK-based artist Banksy.

## Text handling

### Informal English

The register in the above text is informal: it is written in a style that we normally associate with spoken English. Examine these examples taken from the text and suggest alternative, formal ways of expressing the same ideas.

1 they've been around for 40+ years
2 very trendy
3 a must for any tourist
4 jam packed with people
5 OK
6 a great one for the night owls
7 fun-loving clubbers

## Written work

You are helping to organise a trip for eleventh grade students. You have decided to go to London and you will have one whole day to explore Brick Lane. Plan and create a hand-out for the day's activities. Provide information about times and the meeting point. Your hotel is in the Spitalfields area so you can do everything on foot. Make suggestions about things to do and places to see. Use the app to help you plan, but the hand-out should be in semi-formal English.

To learn more about Brick Lane, go to www.pearsonhotlinks.com, enter the title or ISBN of this book and click on Chapter 15.

**Left** Brick Lane, a tourist attraction offering street food, trendy shops and the exciting buzz of a multicultural market.

265

# 15 Multicultural Great Britain

## Text 15.4.3 Carnival in London

Carnival in London? You could be forgiven if you thought that London would not be the place to go to find carnival being celebrated. In fact, most people associate carnival with Brazil or Italy, but not England, not London. However, carnival has been celebrated in London for over fifty years. And where in London? In Notting Hill, where there has long been a large West Indian migrant community.

It is generally agreed that this annual event was first held in 1959, when the celebration took place indoors – in St Pancras Town Hall. It was the fruit of the labours of Claudia Jones, a journalist and politically engaged member of the Trinidad community, who was responding to the political climate of London in the late 1950s – a time of racial tension and unrest that came to a head in the Notting Hill riots. The carnival was intended to be a peaceful way to defuse tensions – it was considered a success and certainly an event to be repeated, although it was not until 1966 that the fun was moved outside and the street carnival took off. The plan was to create cultural unity, to bring people together so that they could enjoy themselves and become aware that there are more things that bring different cultural groups together than keep them apart. It was from 1966 onwards that the steel band (a traditional West Indian band in which the drums can be played while the musicians are moving) became a key part of the music. This kind of music had not been heard on the streets of Britain before, and from these beginnings developed the Notting Hill Carnival that is known today as an event firmly anchored in the fabric of London and the Notting Hill community in particular.

So did it attract many people in the first years? Well, in 1976 there were an estimated 150,000 people lining the streets to watch the extravagantly costumed dancers and listen to the vibrant music in a distinctly Caribbean atmosphere. Since those early days it has grown to become a highlight of the August bank holiday weekend on which it is held, attracting more musicians and bands, more floats decked out with flowers and steel drummers, more groups of dancers in the procession, and a huge increase in the number of spectators lining the streets. Recent years have seen numbers topping 2.5 million, watching 50,000 performers and listening to 38 sound systems playing music ranging from soca to dub, from jazz to reggae and calypso.

Yes, from its modest beginnings, when it was just a party for the local community, the carnival has grown and developed into a massively popular spectacle attracting a diverse multicultural following not only from Notting Hill and the rest of London, but also from other countries. The Notting Hill Carnival is an accepted demonstration of West Indian culture in London that unites a wide range of people from all ethnic backgrounds.

## General comprehension

**1** There are several dates and numbers in the text. Complete the table to explain the reference in each case.

| Date/Number | Reference |
|---|---|
| 1959 | |
| 1966 | |
| 150,000 | |
| 2.5 million | |
| 50,000 | |
| 38 | |

**2** Summarise the main points of the text in no more than 60 words.

**3** There are several kinds of music mentioned in the text. Do some research and then briefly describe the genres of music.

**4** What do you know about the celebration of carnival in other places? Where does the name originate?

> A steel band is the name given to a group made up of people playing steel drums, or pans as they are called. Different types of pans create the different musical registers. This form of percussion comes from early-20th-century Trinidad and Tobago.

## Written work

For your school magazine, you have offered to write a report of your visit to the Notting Hill Carnival in the summer holidays. Say why you enjoyed yourself and describe some of the things you saw. Comment on the different nationalities you encountered in the streets while you were there and what impression this made on you.

Write between 350 and 450 words.

# Exam practice

## Exercises

### Written assignment 1: Essay title (HL)

You are taking part in a class debate on the motion: 'Immigrants enrich a country by introducing aspects of their own culture and celebrating them openly.' Write the text of the debate's opening speech, either agreeing or disagreeing. Write between 250 and 400 words.

### Written assignment 2: Personal response (HL)

Give a personal response to the following stimulus and justify it. Choose any text type you have studied in class. Write between 150 and 250 words.

'To have another language is to possess another soul.'

*Charlemagne (Charles the Great), King of the Franks and Christian Emperor of the West*

### Written assignment 3: Essay title (SL)

Your school has just celebrated a day of internationalism and cultural diversity. Write a blog entry about your impressions of the day. Write between 250 and 400 words.

# 16 The role of culture in our lives

## Objectives
- To actively acquire more vocabulary
- To practise the use of abstract nouns and noun phrases
- To practise writing diary entries
- To review the passive
- To consider cultural diversity from a number of perspectives

**Opposite** How important are flags in the 21st century?

# 16.1 What is culture?

## Text 16.1.1 Cultural differences and how they can be observed

**Observable** may or may not be obvious

behaviours
appearance  dress
language  habits
customs  beliefs  traditions

**Non-observable** usually out of our own and others' awareness

beliefs
norms   expectations   perceptions
time orientation    space    orientation
learning styles              personality styles
rules        roles        values
assumptions
thought processes

The chart above shows many different aspects of cultures. An iceberg is a popular representation of culture. With an iceberg we can only see about 10% and the other 90% is hidden under the water. Similarly with culture we can observe some elements of culture but there is much which we cannot observe. We can see how people a)_____, how they dress, what they look like, and we can hear how they speak. In certain situations we can also observe their customs and traditions. We can see the kind of foods they eat, the typical events at their festivals or on special occasions, and we can begin to appreciate their b)_____ if we observe their places of worship.

However, there are very many other cultural differences which we cannot observe easily and which may surprise us. These are the cultural differences which are hidden 'under water'. For example these include peoples' values, learning styles, beliefs or expectations

### Some research about cultural differences

Professor Geert Hofstede is a Dutch researcher in cross-culture. He carried out a c)_____ research project between 1967 and 1973 of over thirty countries investigating the areas of cultural differences d)_____ in business and in the work place. He developed a framework to compare cultures called the Hofstede Dimension of National Culture. This framework had four main areas: Power Distance, Individualism versus Collectivism, Masculinity versus Femininity and Uncertainty Avoidance.

# 16 The role of culture in our lives

**Simply explained –**

- **Power Distance** describes the degree to which less **e)**_____ people in a society accept that power is unequally shared. If a society has high Power Distance it means that the members accept that everyone has their place in society. With low Power Distance people want to share the power or want **f)**_____ explained and justified.

- **Individualism versus Collectivism** means in some societies each individual takes care of themselves and their close family only, whereas the **g)**_____ collectivism means the society is closely knit and members take care of their families and each other. The difference is also clearer when we see the difference between people's emphasis on "I" or "we".

- **Masculinity versus Femininity.** In a masculine society the emphasis is on high achievement, heroism, assertiveness and reward for success. It describes a competitive society. In contrast a feminine society is cooperative, modest people care for each other and the quality of life. There is harmony and **h)**_____ within the group.

- Hofstede's description of **Uncertainty Avoidance** is a cultural concept which describes how comfortable people feel with uncertainty and **i)**_____. Societies with a high level of Uncertainty Avoidance try to control using **j)**_____ rules and codes of belief and behaviour.

Hofstede's work has been continued and developed so if this is an area which interests you, do try to do some research about the latest findings.

Of course the results of his findings describe generalities, and there are many exceptions with a society as people are very different. Maybe if you think of an American, you would decide their society has a high level of Individualism, but of course this does not apply for every American individual. Not every American has the characteristics of Individualism. Many Americans care very much about the society as a whole. Similarly not every British person feels happy with high levels of uncertainty and ambiguity so that we must be aware that these dimensions are generalisations.

## General comprehension

1. Using your own words, explain the difference between elements of culture above and below the water in the iceberg diagram.
2. What are the main areas of Hofstede's cultural framework?
3. How does he describe high Power Distance?
4. Can you think of a typical situation in your life where high Power Distance is predominant?
5. Does your culture emphasise individualism or collectivism, or a mixture of both? Give some examples to illustrate your answer.

## Text handling

Replace the missing words in the text.

**massive / inequality / especially / powerful / beliefs / consensus / opposite / rigid / ambiguity / behave**

## Zoom in on grammar

### Abstract nouns

Abstract nouns are uncountable and so take a singular verb. Some abstract nouns do not take an article.

*Beauty* is in the eye of the beholder.

*Culture* is an important part of who we are.

*Feminism* is an important issue in the 21st century.

*Ambiguity* is often the cause of misunderstandings.

## Grammar in context

### Abstract nouns

In the text a number of abstract nouns are used which are uncountable, meaning they do not form a plural and do not generally take an article: *avoidance, collectivism, individualism, femininity, masculinity.*

Find other forms of these words, following the example below:

**Example:** *avoidance – to avoid* (V), *avoidable* (ADJ)

1  collectivism –
2  individualism –
3  femininity –
4  masculinity –

## Individual oral activity

Choose two of the pictures below and compare and contrast the cultures they depict:

1  from what you can see in the picture (the tip of the iceberg), and
2  from other cultural attributes which you can imagine may be true.

Explain your choices, and try to take your own cultural bias into consideration.

> **TOK**
>
> To what extent do you think Hofstede's ideas are still valid in the 21st century? Think about your own culture and the cultures of others in your classes. Make your own notes, then discuss the question in small groups.

# 16 The role of culture in our lives

**Below** There are no specific French dishes or ingredients in the Gallic candidacy, which centres instead on the social rituals of the festive meal in a country where food is a key part of social life

## 16.2 Celebrating cultural diversity

### Text 16.2.1 UNESCO declares French cuisine 'World intangible heritage'

http://www.telegraph.co.uk/news/worldnews/europe/france/8138348/UNESCO-declares-French-cuisine-world-intangible-heritage.html

**By Henry Samuel in Paris**
**November 16 2010, 7.00pm GMT**

Experts from the UN cultural organisation, gathered this week in the Kenyan capital, said France's multi-course gastronomic meal, with its rites and its presentation, fulfilled the conditions for featuring on the list.

The 'world intangible heritage' list, which until now numbered 178 cultural practices – including the Royal Ballet of Cambodia and Mexico's Day of the Dead festival, was drawn up under a 2003 convention, now ratified by 132 countries.

It seeks to protect cultural practices in the same way as UNESCO protects sites of cultural value or great natural beauty.

The UNESCO experts singled out French gastronomy as a 'social custom aimed at celebrating the most important moments in the lives of individuals and groups'.

France's ambassador to UNESCO Catherine Colonna hailed the inclusion, saying it 'makes a contribution to cultural diversity'.

'The French love getting together to eat and drink well and enjoy good times in such a manner. It is

http://www.telegraph.co.uk/news/worldnews/europe/france/8138348/UNESCO-declares-French-cuisine-world-intangible-heritage.html

part of our tradition – a quite active tradition,' she added.

How wines are paired with dishes, how the table is dressed, the precise placing of glasses, for water, red and white wine, knife blade pointing in and fork tines down, are all seen as part of the rite.

Francis Chevrier, chief delegate of the French mission in charge of submitting the UNESCO bid, also welcomed the decision. 'It's very important that people realise, in villages in Africa and everywhere, that when you have knowledge of food it is a treasure for your community, and something worth cherishing,' he said.

Songs, dances and traditional know-how from 31 countries were up for consideration at the Nairobi meeting, ranging from Spanish Flamenco, to China's traditional art of Peking opera.

http://www.telegraph.co.uk/news/worldnews/europe/france/8138348/UNESCO-declares-French-cuisine-world-intangible-heritage.html

## General Comprehension

1. What did the UNESCO experts feel was so special about French food?
2. Which other cultural practices are featured on the world intangible heritage list?
3. Explain two of the practices that are seen as belonging to the rite.
4. List the first three foods that you think of under the heading 'French food'.
5. Which French food have you eaten?
6. Describe some practices that are part of the rite of food in your own culture.
7. Why does the French chief delegate think knowledge of food is important? Do you agree?

## Text Handling

Choose the most appropriate meaning for each of the following words

| 1 | intangible | tasteless | invisible | unable to be touched | without roots |
| --- | --- | --- | --- | --- | --- |
| 2 | rite | not wrong | a ceremony | an irritation | a piece of music |
| 3 | ratify | to explain | to defend | to formally agree | to trap vermin |
| 4 | delegate | delicate food | a person sent to represent others | a rare plant | a cook |

## Interactive oral activity

Describe the best meal you have ever eaten to your partner. The listener should think of at least three questions to ask after hearing the presentation.

# Written work

Write the recipe and method to make a favourite dish from your home country.

# 16 The role of culture in our lives

Text 16.2.2 World Day for Cultural Diversity for Dialogue and Development, 21 May

## Ten simple things YOU can do to celebrate the World Day for Cultural Diversity for Dialogue and Development

**1** Visit an art exhibit or a museum dedicated to other cultures.

**2** Invite a family or people in the neighborhood from another culture or religion to share a meal with you and exchange views on life.

**3** Rent a movie or read a book from another country or religion than your own.

**4** Invite people from a different culture to share your customs.

**5** Read about the great thinkers of other cultures than yours (e.g. Confucius, Socrates, Avicenna, Ibn Khaldun, Aristotle, Ganesh, Rumi).

**6** Go next week-end to visit a place of worship different than yours and participate in the celebration.

**7** Play the "stereotypes game." Stick a post-it on your forehead with the name of a country. Ask people to tell you stereotypes associated with people from that country. You win if you find out where you are from.

**8** Learn about traditional celebrations from other cultures; learn more about Hanukkah or Ramadan or about amazing celebrations of New Year's Eve in Spain or Qingming festival in China.

**9** Spread your own culture around the world through our Facebook page and learn about other cultures.

To access the Facebook page, go to www.pearsonhotlinks.com, enter the title or ISBN of this book and click on Chapter 16.

**10** Explore music of a different culture.

There are thousands of things that you can do – are you taking part in it?

http://www.un.org/en/events/culturaldiversityday/tenthings.shtml

### General comprehension

1 Of the ten things to do to celebrate the World Day for Cultural Diversity for Dialogue and Development, which would you find the easiest? Why?
2 Which of these activities would you choose not to do and why?
3 Think about your own situation, both in school and out of school: which other beneficial activities could you add to the list?

### Creativity, action, service

Write a set of guidelines for an activity of your choice to celebrate the World Day for Cultural Diversity for Dialogue and Development. Write between 150 and 250 words.

### Individual oral activity

Prepare a speech of about four minutes to deliver in the school assembly to encourage other students to take part in the World Day for Cultural Diversity for Dialogue and Development. Be prepared to answer questions from your audience.

### Exam hints

**Preparing a speech**

Before you start to outline your speech, make a list of the main points which you want to make, with supporting information. Arrange these points in order. Think which rhetorical devices would make your speech stronger. Can you open the speech with a rhetorical question? Will you use 'we' or 'you' in the speech? How will you keep the audience's interest? Do you have a strong closing remark?

Remember – do not learn your speech off by heart, but:

- use note cards, not a full script
- speak clearly and loudly
- be confident
- try to look at the audience while talking.

**TOK — Discuss the following in small groups:**

- What does the World Day for Cultural Diversity for Dialogue and Development mean to you?
- In your daily life at school, do you interact with students from other cultures?
- How can you be more active in this area to initiate meaningful dialogue and improve development between the cultures you meet on a daily basis?
- To what extent does your own culture influence your perceptions of other cultures?

## 16.3 Personal comments on cultural diversity

### Text 16.3.1 Excerpt from a diary

Do you remember your first day at a new school, when you could not speak the language that everyone else was speaking? Do you remember the emotions you experienced? The excerpts below are translated from the first diary entries written by a Japanese boy whose family moved to Europe. Maybe you shared some of the feelings he expresses.

#### 3pm February 5th 2001

I just got in from school and mum and dad are both home. What a surprise, they are normally still at work when I get home, so what's going on? They said they have something to tell us over dinner. I do hope it isn't anything dramatic. It must be pretty serious or they would have told me straight away. Yuki isn't home yet, as usual she has gone for extra ballet lessons. How can she enjoy that stuff? I guess she just likes wearing pretty dresses and showing off. How boring. Still I had better get on with my homework as there is so much to do and I want to stay top of the class now that I really know I will be going to the absolutely best, most exciting middle school in March. All that work really paid off and if I keep it up I will move into their high school and then, with luck, straight to the university. You can see why it is called an "escalator" school, once you are on it, you just ride to the top. Here I come! I can't believe I made it. I am really ambitious so I can't stop working now – I have to keep it up.

# 16 The role of culture in our lives

### 8pm, the same day

The news from our parents was the worst ever for me. How can they be so pleased and excited when my life has just been ruined? My father has been promoted and we are moving to Europe for at least three years. There was no chance to discuss it, they have made up their minds and so this is what will happen. I am devastated. My life is destroyed. All my plans, all my hopes, all my dreams count for nothing and no one understands me or even cares. I worked so hard to pass those entrance exams, I have done so well. Everyone says so. Why did I bother? What's the point? Now they say we will have to go to an international school and learn in English. How can I do that? I can hardly speak English. In class the teacher talks and we listen. It's only funny because he puts on his glasses when he is being "English" and when he needs to explain something he takes them off and is "Japanese" again. My Japanese is so good because I study and study. I am usually top of our class in the Kanjii tests. What will happen to me in a school where no one speaks Japanese? My English is awful, I will be at the bottom of the class not the top.

Oh, I have just thought – what about my friends? I won't be able to hang out with Masanori and Yuki or go to basketball practice with Yoshihiro and the others. This is so unfair, how can my parents do this to me. How can I tell them I am leaving?

My sister is over the moon. Typical, she always gets excited about the dumbest things. "Ballet is very important in Europe. The best ballet dancers and teachers are all there," she says. How does she know that? She thinks she will go to ballet classes with people from all over the world, but how will she understand? She will soon wake up when she realizes she can't understand anything either.

My father just came in to talk to me. He understands, or he says he understands, how I feel and how disappointed I am but he says I can do this and I will be a good student in the new school too. It's OK for him, he is getting what he wants and the rest of us have to go along with it. But not me!

I know – I will go and live with grandma and grandpa, then I can stay here and go to the school of my dreams and be successful! My life will be saved. Easy! That's what I'll do! Tomorrow morning, over breakfast, I will tell them I am not coming and there is nothing they can do to make me. I have found the perfect solution.

Thanks for listening diary, time for me to sleep now my problems are all solved.

### General comprehension

1 What has recently happened to the writer that makes him feel very pleased?
2 Why is there a difference between the way the writer feels and his sister's feelings?
3 Do you understand the boy's emotions?
4 Describe the English lessons which the boy has experienced, in your own words.
5 Can the boy speak English?
6 How do you think the parents will react to the boy's suggestions?

## Text handling

**1** Explain the following expressions from the text.

a) That work <u>really paid off</u>
b) I can't believe <u>I made it</u>
c) <u>Showing off</u>
d) <u>An escalator school</u>
e) I have to <u>keep it up</u>
f) Those dreams <u>count for nothing</u>
g) <u>To hang out</u> with friends
h) <u>Over the moon</u>
i) She will soon <u>wake up</u>

**2** Match the words with the correct meanings.

to be promoted

a) To be entered in a competition
b) To be encouraged strongly
c) To be given a higher position at work
d) To go to a dance

to be destroyed

a) To be broken into pieces
b) To be part of a ship
c) To be instructed
d) To be left behind

to be devastated

a) To be discouraged from something
b) To be moved up
c) To be seen to do something
d) To be terribly disappointed

**3** Which words from the text are indicated by the underlined pronoun?

a) and if I keep <u>it</u> up
b) once you are on <u>it</u>,
c) no chance to discuss <u>it</u>
d) How can I do <u>that</u>?
e) he takes <u>them</u> off

# Text 16.3.2 Excerpt from a diary

### March 1st 2001

Dear Diary,

Sorry for the long break in communication. Re-reading what I wrote on February 5th, I can hardly believe how naïve I was and how easily I thought the problem would be solved. I didn't reckon with the power of adults and their inflexibility. They are only thinking of themselves and they keep telling me I should be excited and happy like my sister. Then they say what an amazing experience this will be and how jealous my friends will be! How do they know that? They have no idea!

When I told them that I could live with grandma, mum and dad both immediately said "No, you must come with us." They had all sorts of reasons for this, ranging from "Grandma is too frail to take care of you" to "this is the most exciting experience of your life". They have got to be joking. All my hard work to get into a good school and then they take my dream away from me as if it is nothing! Well they can just get used to the fact that I hate it here. I absolutely loathe it and nothing, I mean nothing, will make me change my mind. I didn't want to come and they can't make me like it.

Of course diary, my patient friend, you don't know what has happened, do you? Well, first we had a huge argument and I went off to school crying for the first time in my life. But

# 16  The role of culture in our lives

they were not a bit sorry for me. I don't think they care at all. Within days they were packing up and before anyone knew what was happening we were on the plane to Europe. We stayed in a hotel for a few days and now live in a house with a garden, which is OK except there is no-one to kick a ball around with me and that's no fun on your own.

On Monday we went to the school. It's huge and raucous and everyone, yes everyone, speaks English. The students were laughing and shouting. I guess it was recess as they were all walking around eating snacks and drinking fizzy drinks. No-one was wearing school uniform and some were even wearing jeans and T-shirts, or sports kit. Some of the girls looked like they were going to the beach, with shorts and flip flops on – maybe it was a dress-down day? That looked strange to me. Some kids even had earrings and others had dyed their hair – and they were still allowed to be in school!

We met a woman who showed us round and took us back to her office, and my mother and father sat down while I just stood there. Then she said "Take a seat" to me. What? Take a seat? Where to? Where should I go? Then she laughed and my parents laughed at me too, till I understood that I should just sit down. How humiliating. I knew it would be like this, I hate it here even more now.

She talked to my parents really fast and I didn't understand anything. I don't think they understood much either, and that serves them right! Then the worst part happened! She took us up to a classroom and took me in. I guess she was introducing me to the class, then she turned round and walked out. I wanted to follow her but the teacher caught my arm and pulled me back in and the class laughed. I was so embarrassed I could have died. I had no idea what to do. The teacher sat me down next to a boy who showed me what they were doing. It looked like maths to me and pretty soon I realized it was stuff we did in grade 6, how easy! What kind of school is this? But there was lots of writing around the numbers and I couldn't understand any of that! But do you know what, diary? I am not even going to try! If I am a failure and the absolute worst in the class, my parents will have to send me home. What a plan! Anyway the day went from bad to worse. The woman came to fetch me and then I had to do a test in English and the English teacher came to talk to me. She was trying to be kind but by then I had made up my mind. I will be the worst student ever and no one will be able to help me, then I can go home! Anyway she kept on talking and showing me pictures and trying to get me to speak, but I didn't look at her and kept just staring at my hands. Then she took my hand and moved it away! She touched me! Eugh! And then she called me "dear" and she doesn't even know me. How does she know I am "dear", and anyway she is a teacher and I am NOT her "dear". What an awful day. When I got home my sister was jumping up and down with excitement. Of course she says she understood everything the teacher said. The teacher was so nice and she has already met a girl who does ballet and they will meet again tomorrow to go to ballet classes together after school. It is OK for her, her life has not been ruined.

### General comprehension

1. Why didn't the boy's alternative plan work?
2. What reasons did his parents give?
3. What surprised him in the new school?
4. Explain the misunderstanding he had in the office. Why did this happen?
5. What did the English teacher do to upset him?
6. Can you remember your first day in a new school? Compare your memories with those of the boy.

### Text handling

Explain the following words and expressions from the text in your own words.

a) hardly
b) to be naïve
c) to reckon with something
d) frail
e) raucous
f) loathe
g) a dress-down day
h) humiliating

### Interactive oral activity

How could this student have been helped to feel more comfortable when he visited the school for the first time? Discuss your ideas with a partner and then share them with the class.

### Written work

Write an account of your first day at a new school, either as a diary entry or in a letter to a friend. Write between 150 and 250 words.

## 16.3.3 Excerpt from a diary

### May 3rd 2001

Gosh, reading what I wrote then, I can hardly believe how things have changed. At first it was dreadful. I had no one to help me. I couldn't understand what they said to me, or the timetable or where to go or what to do. I didn't know what the teachers were talking about and just followed the other kids around from class to class. I ate lunch on my own and had never felt so lonely in my life. All I wanted to do was to go home and stay there. I even developed headaches and stomach aches but my mother still made me go to school. I hated everyone and everything. Each day was worse than the one before. My life was a never-ending nightmare!

After about 2 weeks of this unbearable life, a teacher came to me with a Japanese lady I had never seen before. She is the mother of an older Japanese student and I got to talk to her over lunch. She was a stranger really, but she listened to me and I was so glad to have someone, anyone, listen to me and seem to care. Anyway, she told me about her kid and how he found it so hard at first, too, and how it got better slowly as he learned more English. Then she had an idea – maybe I should join a sports club at school or try some other activity that I could enjoy after school. Honestly, diary, I couldn't imagine anything being fun, but I used to do athletics, so she made me promise to try out for that team. We arranged to meet a week later so I could tell her about it.

I found out about the team from her son and he told me what to do. The first training was the next day, so I went along. A lot of the guys looked at me strangely, they were pretty unfriendly, but the coach asked me about my events and I told him I was a sprinter. We did all the warm-ups and drills, and then we had sprint run-offs. Guess what, diary? I beat them all! I was the fastest – can you believe that? The other guys all wanted to know where I learned to run so fast, and I could even understand those questions, although instead of answering I just shrugged my shoulders. The next morning in class, everyone knew about it and somehow they looked at me differently. At break the other track guys asked me to sit with them. They tried to talk to me and I tried, I really tried to answer. From then on slowly everything changed and got better and better.

Hey diary, I have to stop writing now and pack my kit for training! I'll write some more soon!

# 16 The role of culture in our lives

### General comprehension

1. What was the biggest problem the boy had to face?
2. How did he try to avoid going to school?
3. Who was the first person to really listen to him?
4. What did she suggest?
5. Was this a good idea?
6. What changed the whole situation for him?
7. What would you have suggested if he had talked to you about his problems?

### Text handling

Explain the following words and expressions in your own words.
1. hardly
2. a never-ending nightmare
3. unbearable
4. pretty unfriendly
5. shrugged my shoulders

## Written work

Imagine you are the boy who wrote these diary entries. Write the next diary entry for about a month later. Write between 150 and 250 words.

## 16.4 A political view of cultural diversity

### 16.4.1 Robin Cook's Chicken Tikka Massala speech

This evening, I want to set out the reasons for being optimistic about the future of Britain and Britishness. Indeed, I want to go further and argue that in each of the areas where the pessimists identify a threat, we should instead see developments that will strengthen and renew British identity.

**Multicultural Britain**

The first element in the debate about the future of Britishness is the changing ethnic composition of the British people themselves. The British are not a race, but a gathering of countless different races and communities, the vast majority of which were not indigenous to these islands.

In the pre-industrial era, when transport and communications were often easier by sea than by land, Britain was unusually open to external influence; first through foreign invasion, then, after Britain achieved naval supremacy, through commerce and imperial expansion. It is not their purity that makes the British unique, but the sheer pluralism of their ancestry.

London was first established as the capital of a Celtic Britain by Romans from Italy. They were in turn driven out by Saxons and Angles from Germany. The great cathedrals of this land were built mostly by Norman bishops, but the religion practised in them was secured by the succession of a Dutch Prince. Outside our Parliament, Richard the Lionheart proudly sits astride his steed. A symbol of British courage and defiance. Yet he spoke French much of his life and depended on the Jewish community of England to put up the ransom that freed him from prison.

The idea that Britain was a 'pure' Anglo-Saxon society before the arrival of communities from the Caribbean, Asia and Africa is fantasy. But if this view of British identity is false to our past, it is false to our future too. The global era has produced population movements of a breadth and richness without parallel in history.

Today's London is a perfect hub of the globe. It is home to over 30 ethnic communities of at least 10,000 residents each. In this city tonight, over 300 languages will be spoken by families over their evening meal at home.

This pluralism is not a burden we must reluctantly accept. It is an immense asset that contributes to the cultural and economic vitality of our nation.

Legitimate immigration is the necessary and unavoidable result of economic success, which generates a demand for labour faster than can be met by the birth-rate of a modern developed country. Every country needs firm but fair immigration laws. There is no more evil business than trafficking in human beings and nothing corrodes social cohesion worse than a furtive underground of illegal migrants beyond legal protection against exploitation. But we must also create an open and inclusive society that welcomes incomers for their contribution to our growth and prosperity. Our measures to attract specialists in information technology is a good example.

Our cultural diversity is one of the reasons why Britain continues to be the preferred location for multinational companies setting up in Europe. The national airline of a major European country has recently relocated its booking operation to London precisely because of the linguistic variety of the staff whom it can recruit here.

And it isn't just our economy that has been enriched by the arrival of new communities. Our lifestyles and cultural horizons have also been broadened in the process. This point is perhaps more readily understood by young Britons, who are more open to new influences and more likely to have been educated in a multi-ethnic environment. But it reaches into every aspect of our national life.

Chicken Tikka Massala is now a true British national dish, not only because it is the most popular, but because it is a perfect illustration of the way Britain absorbs and adapts external influences. Chicken Tikka is an Indian dish. The Massala sauce was added to satisfy the desire of British people to have their meat served in gravy.

Coming to terms with multiculturalism as a positive force for our economy and society will have significant implications for our understanding of Britishness.

The modern notion of national identity cannot be based on race and ethnicity, but must be based on shared ideals and aspirations. Some of the most successful countries in the modern world, such as the United States and Canada, are immigrant societies. Their experience shows how cultural diversity, allied to a shared concept of equal citizenship, can be a source of enormous strength. We should draw inspiration from their experience.

*http://www.theguardian.com/world/2001/apr/19/race.britishidentity*

## General comprehension

1. What is the tone of this speech – sarcastic, humorous or positive?
2. Why does Robin Cook say the British are not a race?
3. Identify three reasons given in the text for the fact that Britain is culturally diverse.
4. What has been enriched by cultural diversity in Britain according to the author?
5. True or false? Justify your answer with a relevant brief quotation from the text.
    a) The majority of British people are in fact from somewhere else.
    b) Britain was open to external influence because it was an island.
    c) Population movement has increased greatly in the global era.
    d) Multinational companies are reluctant to set up in Britain because of the cultural diversity.
    e) The arrival of new communities influences only the economy.
    f) Young Britons do not understand the benefits of cultural diversity.
    g) Chicken Tikka Massala has remained a truly Indian dish.
    h) National identity is the result of race and ethnicity only.

> Robin Cook was a British politician. He was Foreign Secretary in Tony Blair's Labour government and later became Leader of the House of Commons. He died in a climbing accident in Scotland in 2005.

# 16 The role of culture in our lives

### Text handling

1  Identify to whom or to what the underlined pronouns refer.
   a) London was first established as the capital of a Celtic Britain by Romans from Italy. They were in turn driven out by Saxons and Angles from Germany.
   b) The great cathedrals of this land were built mostly by Norman Bishops, but the religion practised in them was secured by the succession of a Dutch Prince.
   c) Outside our Parliament, Richard the Lionheart proudly sits astride his steed. A symbol of British courage and defiance. Yet he spoke French much of his life and depended on the Jewish community of England to put up the ransom that freed him from prison.

2  Complete the sentences on the left with the endings on the right. Check your answers against the text.

| | | | |
|---|---|---|---|
| I | It is not their purity that makes the British unique, ... | A | ... but a gathering of countless different races and communities. |
| II | Every country needs... | B | ... but the sheer pluralism of their ancestry. |
| III | Legitimate immigration is... | C | ... has been enriched by the arrival of new communities. |
| IV | The British are not a race, ... | D | ... firm but fair immigration laws. |
| V | It isn't just our economy that... | E | ... the necessary and unavoidable result of economic success. |

### Zoom in on grammar

**Noun phrases**

Many of Robin Cook's sentences begin with very long phrases as the subject of the sentence. For example, look closely at this sentence:

> The first element in the debate about the future of Britishness is the changing ethnic composition of the British people themselves.

Can you identify the subject of the sentence?

### Grammar in context

**Noun phrases**

Find three more sentences with noun phrases as their subject.

## 16.5 An example of cultural diversity in action

### 16.5.1 Singapore

Singapore is a very small island, only 42 kilometres wide and 23 kilometres long, but it has a population of over 4 million people from many different cultural backgrounds. Walking through the streets of Singapore you can hear English, Malay, Mandarin and Tamil spoken. In addition, for a real experience of cultural diversity you can walk from the Indian quarter to the Chinese area and then through the Arab quarter. The people live peacefully alongside each other and share their customs and traditions. But how did this come about? What is the history of Singapore?

a) ............................................................
The first inhabitants of Singapore were Malay

fishermen, based on the island. According to legend, Singapore received its name from a prince in the 14th century. While out hunting he saw an animal he had never seen before, but thought it may have been a lion. He thought this was a good omen and so founded the city on the spot where he saw the animal. He named it Singapura from the Sanskrit language 'simha' meaning lion and 'pura' meaning city.

Singapore became firmly established as a trading post by Sir Stamford Raffles, an English colonial administrator who first visited the island in 1819. The city, which he designed to have several distinct ethnic areas, began to grow and flourish rapidly as it became increasingly important for trade between the East and West. There is still evidence of the British rule during the colonial years in the building styles of some of the older houses, the district and street names. In 1819 there were only 150 people living on the island but this increased dramatically to over 80,000 by 1860. The population then was mostly Chinese, Indian and Malay.

Singapore was occupied for three and a half years during the Second World War by the Japanese and was then administered by the British becoming a Crown Colony in 1946. In 1959 the first elections were held for self government. The country was merged with Malaysia in 1963, but became an independent sovereign nation in 1965.

b) ..................................................................

Through the ethnic diversity of its people, Singapore is truly a melting pot. The official language is Malay but English is used for business. Now, however, there is a strong Chinese business community and also a thriving Indian business community. A lot of foreigners working in Singapore tend to be in hi-tech, finance, research and development. Singapore is welcoming to talented immigrants who are also able to settle there permanently.

Society in Singapore is multi-cultural. The different cultural groups live, work and play alongside each other and together with exceptional tolerance and understanding of racial and religious differences. The individual districts of the city, the Arab quarter, Chinatown and the Indian are good neighbours. The cultural differences are also reflected in building styles, shops, places of worship and food of course. The typical cultural celebrations are shared by all as everyone is welcome to join in and the celebrations often spread across the city. Of course with so many diverse cultures in such a small area, the food also reflects the many cultures of the city. The individual areas have their own typical food on sale, but there are also the famous Hawkers markets where a huge variety of foods are available under one roof. These are very popular with the Singapore citizens and the tourists because the food is good and very cheap.

c) ..................................................................

There is an interesting tradition which shows how many people from a variety of cultures in a small place can cooperate together. There are seats available but also crowds of people coming and going. In order to reserve a seat while choosing your meal, the tradition is to put a small packet of paper tissues on the seat you plan to occupy. This way you can be sure your seat will be free when you return with a tray full of steaming hot delicious food.

# 16 The role of culture in our lives

### General comprehension

1. What is remarkable about the linguistic and cultural diversity in Singapore?
2. Explain the origin of the name Singapore, in your own words.
3. Why did Singapore become important as a trading post?
4. What evidence is still to be found of British rule?
5. Which languages are used in Singapore?
6. Why do you think English is mostly used for business? Do you think that may change in the future? Explain your answer.

### Text handling

1. Make a time line of the history of Singapore as described in the text.
2. Re-read the text and make your own suitable headings for the sections a–c.

### Zoom in on grammar

**The passive**

Often when history is told, the passive form is used, describing what happened rather than who did what. The person doing the action is called the agent.

The passive is formed using *be* + passive participle.

Example (the agent = Sir Stamford Raffles):

> **Passive sentence:** The layout of the city of Singapore *was planned* with several distinct ethnic areas.
>
> **Active sentence:** Sir Stamford Raffles *planned* the layout of the city of Singapore with several distinct ethnic areas.

### Grammar in context

**The passive**

Find two more examples of passive sentences in the text where the agent is identified, and change the sentences into the active form.

**Below** Cultural diversity in a visible form.

**Left** What's the hurry?

## Exam practice

# Exercises

**Written assignment 1: Essay title (HL)**

You feel that the diversity of cultures in your school is not celebrated. Write a proposal for a school 'day of culture' which does not only focus on flags, food and festivals.

**Written assignment 2: Personal response (HL)**

Give a personal response to the following stimulus and justify it. Choose any text type that you have studied in class.
Write between 150 and 250 words.

> 'No culture can live if it attempts to be exclusive.'

> *Mahatma Gandhi (1869–1948)*

**Written assignment 3: Essay title (SL)**

Write a diary entry describing your first few days in a new school and the cultural challenges you faced. Write between 250 and 400 words.

# 17 The changing face of leisure

## Objectives

- To discuss adventure sports
- To practise writing in various genres
- To prepare and deliver a persuasive speech
- To revise the use of adverbs of frequency
- To examine some examples of idiomatic language in context

# 17.1 Adventure sports

## Text 17.1.1 The history of adventure sports

**1** ............................................................................................................

The idea of people engaging in sports and exercise is an ancient one; in fact, the prehistoric cave paintings in Lascaux, France, seem to show men engaged in wrestling while spectators stand watching. These paintings are thought to be over 17,000 years old, and are certainly some of the oldest recorded examples of sport. The term 'adventure sports' is a relatively new name for sporting activities which frequently involve a high level of speed, height, physical exertion, special equipment and not only that, in many of these sports there is also a high level of danger. This is a contrast to the traditional view of sports as being a moderate activity, sometimes carried out individually, but more often in teams (usually in schools), with the aim of keeping physically fit. Adventure sport is more to do with pushing yourself to the limits and experiencing excitement and an adrenaline rush while engaging in an activity that is often not a team sport but more of an individual challenge.

**2** ............................................................................................................

The question is, how new is the idea of adventure sport – or extreme sport as it is sometimes called? If you consider the level of physical exertion, one of the most demanding sports is long distance running. The marathon is the most well-known long distance run that covers 42.195 km (26.22 miles) and has become a popular activity involving international competitions held in many countries around the world every year. But the marathon is not a modern invention; it is a commemoration of the first ever run that is recorded in the history books. In the year 490 BC, a Greek soldier and messenger ran to Athens from the city of Marathon to announce the news of the Greek success over the Persians at the Battle of Marathon. However, it wasn't until 1896 that the idea of running 'a marathon' was introduced as a sports event. In that year, the first modern Olympic Games were held in Athens, and the idea of the long-distance run was born.

**3** ............................................................................................................

Students at one of the most famous universities in Great Britain founded the Dangerous Sports Club of Oxford University in the 1970s and organised the first bungee jump from the Clifton Suspension Bridge in Bristol in 1979: an activity considered so dangerous at the time that all the participants were arrested by the police. But it wasn't until 1999 when the Extreme Sports Channel was launched in Amsterdam that the public acceptance for extreme sports started to grow. The channel, available on cable TV and the internet, became popular with thousands of

**Opposite** Bungee jumping.

### Why is the marathon race 42.195 km?

The original distance of the Olympic marathon was 40 km (24.85 miles). However, in 1908, when the Olympics were held in London, it was the British royal family who were responsible for the distance being changed. The route, from the Olympic stadium to Eton, had to be lengthened so that the royal family could watch the end of the race from the east terrace of Windsor Castle. It wasn't until 1921 that the International Athletics Federation finally decided that the internationally accepted distance of the marathon would be 42.195 km.

# 17 The changing face of leisure

**Below** Snowboarding.

people and was watched in over 60 countries. Fans of extreme sports could watch surfing, skateboarding, wakeboarding, bungee jumping and BMX biking – to name but a few. It was probably a result of this channel and the successful marketing strategies that helped make adventure sport so attractive.

**4** ........................................................................................................................................

Many kinds of sporting activities now attract people of all ages who are searching for new challenges. Schools provide opportunities for activities ranging from trekking in mountainous regions to rock climbing and off-road mountain bike experiences. Travel agencies offer white water rafting holidays, courses in hang gliding and a range of 'family' activities like snowboarding or jet skiing. What used to be considered dangerous has now become mainstream – you no longer gasp with horror when someone tells you that they went bungee jumping at the weekend or climbed Sydney Harbour Bridge in their holidays. However, some sports still remain controversial: paintball is often criticised for being too martial and glorifying the idea of fighting in war-like situations, and wingsuit flying seems to have caused a number of accidents and is particularly life-threatening. Nevertheless, the attraction of extreme sports seems to provide many people with the chance to experience a sense of adventure in a world which often seems to be increasingly regulated and safe.

## General comprehension

1. According to the text, what does 'adventure sport' mean?
2. Describe the difference between the modern idea of adventure sports and the traditional idea of sport.
3. What seems to have triggered the popularity of adventure sports?
4. According to the text, what is the connection between an event in Greece over 2,000 years ago and today's Olympic Games?
5. Name at least eight extreme sports that are mentioned in the text.

## Text handling

Choose a suitable heading for each paragraph from the list below.

| | | |
|---|---|---|
| 1 Adventure! | 4 The dangers | 7 Finding adventure today |
| 2 Sport! | 5 How to market adventure | 8 Bungee jumping |
| 3 Sport in prehistoric times | 6 Sport and the Greeks | |

## Zoom in on grammar

### Adverbs of frequency

Adverbs of frequency indicate when or how often something happens.

Their position in a sentence can change.

- Some adverbs go with the verb in the middle of the sentence:

    Surfers *always* practise a lot.     I *frequently* use my laptop in class.

- If the verb is one word, as above (*practise* and *use*), the adverb is before the verb.
- If the verb is two or more words (*can remember*, *don't eat*, *has lived*), we usually put the adverb after the first part of the verb:

    I can *never* remember the date.     Su doesn't *usually* eat breakfast.
    He has *always* lived in that old house.

## Grammar in context

**Adverbs of frequency**

Look at the text above and make a list of the adverbs of frequency in the first two paragraphs. Find three in the first paragraph and two in the second paragraph.

When you have identified the adverbs, compose a paragraph of your own about a theme of your choice – perhaps sports – and use adverbs of frequency in your text.

## Individual oral activity

Describe the picture and then relate it to one of your options themes. Talk for three minutes, making connections to ideas that you relate to the subject of the picture.

**Right** Fox hunting – a tradition that has been part of British culture since the 1700s.

# 17.2 Three athletes talk about what motivates them

## Text 17.2.1 A passion for running

Interviews with three passionate runners, each with a different motivation.

### Running to win – Kota, aged 16

"I guess my love of running started in seventh grade in elementary school when I chose Track & Field for my after-school activity in my home town of Shiga, in Japan. The challenge of getting faster and improving my times, as well as the thrill of crossing the winning line first really drew me into the sport. My distance is 400m and so far my best time is 52.77secs. As every run is timed you get a very clear picture of your progress – to the split second and that is part of what drives me. I just love running, when I'm in a competition it's just me and the track, I don't see or hear anything else. But that doesn't mean I don't care if I win or lose, no I definitely go out there to win. Nothing beats the feeling I have when I'm standing on that top block of the winners podium. Although it does mean hard work; I train for two and a half hours at least three times a week in my club and if I suffer an injury and can't run I get really frustrated and bad-tempered. It also means that I have to sometimes put my training first, and say no to my friends when they are planning weekend activities."

# 17 The changing face of leisure

## Running for fun - Paul, aged 55

"All my life I've been involved with some kind of sports: whether swimming, volleyball or weight-lifting, but I started running when a doctor suggested I needed to pursue a sport that would strengthen my knees rather than weaken them. So I started jogging, alone at first and only fifteen minutes a day but that gradually increased. I didn't really start to enjoy running until I joined a club and started to run in a group. We met twice a week and ran together in the nearby woods and always ran at a pace that made it possible for us to talk and exchange jokes. I guess that is why it was on one of these runs that we had the idea to have a go at a marathon. Training suddenly became more intensive and we ran up to 100km a week. That was vital to build up the necessary stamina needed to run 42km. Anyway, since then I've taken part in a marathon annually and have enjoyed picking out a different country to run in every year! It's difficult to explain the feeling to someone who has never done any serious running but it's great when you know you're running with 35,000 other runners and just as many are cheering you on – as we did in London, which was when I ran my best time of 3hr30mins. That might sound fast but the fastest runners cut that time almost in half! But I never worry about my time – it's the fun of the run that counts and the feeling of elation when you get your finisher medal!"

## Running for charity – Andy, aged 35

"I ran my first marathon in 2002. It started as a fun idea, my sister and I both used to race-walk and knew all about long distance training and decided to run our first marathon together. We literally finished hand-in-hand in a respectable 4hr18min. That was the start; it wasn't the very painful cramps and muscle aches that actually lasted for almost 5 days after the race and kept me from walking normally or even getting up stairs that I remembered, no, it was the feeling of achievement having finished a marathon. It takes me 4-5 hours to run the 42km but I enjoy so many aspects of the run: the excitement in the air minutes before the start, the constant 'taptaptap' of the trainers on the asphalt, the hundreds and thousands of supporters at the side of the course supporting each and every runner, and the bands that brighten the mood along the course. However, it was my work as a vet that brought me to sponsored running. Some of my patients are guide dogs. For a blind person a guide dog is not just 'man's best friend' but also the eyes to the world. The charity Guide Dogs for the Blind is involved in breeding, training, supporting and educating dogs. So it didn't take long for me to decide to combine my running with collecting money for this charity, though sometimes I find it more arduous to reach my target of money to be raised (£2,000) than the training and the run itself. But I see it as a cause worth striving for and spend at least 3 months' training before the event in all weathers. It has always been part of the London Marathon tradition to have people run for charity. And this is the ideal place to find support for my guide dog charity."

## General comprehension

1. According to the runners, what is their motivation for doing this sport?
2. What do each of the runners find most rewarding about their involvement with running?
3. How did Kota, Paul and Andy get involved with running?
4. Andy talks about using the marathon as a way to collect money for guide dogs. How do you think he does this?

## Text handling

1. Look carefully at the interviews and decide what questions the interviewer may have asked the three sportsmen. Write three or four questions for each person.
2. In the interview with Kota, identify one thing he sometimes has to give up.
3. In the interview with Paul, what does he say was the reason for running up to 100 km a week?
4. What does Andy find most stressful about preparing for a sponsored run?
5. Find a word in the 'Running to win' section that has the same meaning as:
   a) excitement
   b) motivates
   c) simply
   d) platform
6. Find a word in the 'Running for fun' section that has the same meaning as:
   a) take up
   b) swap
   c) necessary
   d) euphoria
7. Find a word in the 'Running for charity' section that has the same meaning as:
   a) enliven
   b) animal doctor
   c) teaching
   d) demanding

# 17.3 An unusual place to go climbing

## Text 17.3.1 Sydney Harbour Bridge – Climb it!

**Left** An aerial view of Sydney Harbour showing two of the best-known tourist sights: the Opera House and the Bridge.

291

# 17 The changing face of leisure

**Climb to the top of Sydney's iconic Harbour Bridge at night. Experience a 3.5 hour guided journey to the top of the Sydney Harbour Bridge. It takes you along the outer arch of the Bridge on catwalks and ladders all the way to the highest point of the structure.**

## What's included

In climb groups of up to 14 people, you'll be led by one of BridgeClimb's professional Climb Leaders on an adventure of the world's most recognisable Bridge. The steady incline to the summit leaves you free to focus your attention on your Sydney experience, with opportunities to witness 360 degree views of Sydney.

When you reach the top you will have a sense of achievement that you will remember for ever – you've conquered an Australian icon recognised the world over!

A Night Climb has a character all of its own. There's a quiet, magical quality to the city at night and the Bridge has a mysterious feel as you make your way to the summit guided by the light of the specially provided headlamp for Night Climbers. You're wrapped in a blanket of darkness, with just the Bridge lights illuminating the structure against huge shadows. Then, at the top, Sydney blazes before you in an electric-light show.

## The Bridge Climb is the ultimate Sydney experience.

Professional Climb Leaders will take pictures of you on the Climb and at the end you will receive a commemorative Climber Certificate, Climber Cap and a complimentary group photograph, with all Climbers in the group receiving an identical photo. For safety reasons Climbers cannot take up personal items onto the Bridge (including cameras).

http://www.redballoon.com.au/adventure-sports/bridge-climbing/harbour-bridge-night-climb-child

Sydney Harbour Bridge is the world's largest steel arch bridge and was opened in 1932 after six years of construction. Today the Bridge and Sydney Opera House are the two best-known international symbols of Australia. The Bridge's design was influenced by the Hell Gate Bridge in New York.

### General comprehension

1. According to the text, what makes a Night Climb special?
2. Climbers are not allowed to take cameras. Suggest reasons why you think cameras are not allowed.
3. What is the maximum number of climbers in a group?
4. Why do you think the adjective 'iconic' is used when describing Sydney Harbour Bridge?

### Text handling

1. Find a verb in the text which means 'shines brightly'.
2. Find a noun in the text which means 'a narrow pathway'.
3. Find a noun in the text which means 'the highest point'.
4. Find an adjective in the text which means 'free of charge'.
5. Find an adjective in the text which means 'exactly alike'.

### Written work

Imagine you are on holiday in Australia and have just taken part in the Night Climb of Sydney Harbour Bridge with your family. Write an email to your friend back home telling him/her all about your experience and your feelings during the climb.

Write between 150 and 250 words.

## 17.4 Paintball – more than just a game of tag?

### Text 17.4.1 What is paintball?

`http://socialpaintball.com/2013/09/22/what-is-paintball/`

## This is such a simple question, but not an easy one to answer. Let me, as a parent, explain to you, a parent, about paintball

In its basic form, paintball is a game of tag using balls made with gelatin shells filled with water-soluble dye. The "paintballs" are fired by a gun using compressed gas, but the team sport of paintball is a lot more complex.

That's right; I just used the words team, sport and paintball together.

Surprised?

Let's look at how paintball is played. I will get into the various forms of paintball further into the article, but they all have a few things in common.

There is a set of rules for the field of play, such as: keeping your mask on, the field's boundaries, not over-shooting someone, and when you are tagged by a paintball you are out, along with other similar guidelines.

There are referees on the field to ensure that these rules are followed.

There is an objective to the game. That is right: we are not just running around on a field shooting each other. It could be 'tag all the players on the other team', 'capture the flag', 'touch the other team's bunker', 'rescue a down pilot' or a number of other scenarios. We are about teams.

### Types of paintball

I am going to break down paintball into two game types: speedball and woodsball.

#### Woodsball

Woodsball, also known as Rec Ball, is the original form of paintball and is mainly played outside in a natural or semi-built-up environment. For most new parents to paintball, this is usually the first view you have of a paintball field.

Types of field include indoor fields and fields built up with multi-storey buildings and vehicles. Some fields in Europe are composed of entire villages.

Versions of Rec Ball include Tactical-Milsim paintball, which uses tactical or simulated military (milsim) gear, game play and objectives; and big game scenarios which can take place over a few days on large fields.

#### Speedball

Speedball is played on level fields of grass or artificial turf. These fields look like a small soccer field. The bunkers are air-filled and made out of fabric. Speedball fields are mainly found outdoors, but can also be found indoors.

# 17 The changing face of leisure

`http://socialpaintball.com/2013/09/22/what-is-paintball/`

Speedball games are usually faster and shorter and use significantly more paintballs than a woodsball game.

**About the author: Gordon More**

A graduate of the Outdoor Recreation Management Program at Capilano University, North Vancouver, Canada. He is an outdoor recreation fanatic who operates a kayaking company, has managed a ski resort and lives for paintball, skiing and kayaking. He started playing paintball in 2000, but he didn't really get into the sport until his son was 12.

*http://socialpaintball.com/2013/09/22/what-is-paintball/*

### General comprehension

1. According to the text, what are the differences between the two variations of paintball: woodsball and speedball?
2. According to the text, there are four main rules that players must observe during the game. What are they?
3. The sport is called 'paintball'. How did this name originate?

### Text handling

1. Which definition best describes the verb 'to tag' as used in the text?
   **to label / to touch / to shoot at and hit a player**
2. Which definition best describes the word 'bunker' as used in the text?
   **hole in the ground / object to hide behind / seat**
3. Which definition best describes the word 'turf' as used in the text?
   **grass / asphalt / wood**

## Text 17.4.2 The debate about paintball: A positive or negative influence?

`http://socialpaintball.com/2013/07/09/paintball-and-a-childs-mental-health/`

I'm going to dive into the debate about the positive or negative effects paintball has on a child's mental health with some good hard solid facts. Unfortunately, there has been no peer reviewed scientific research into the direct effects of playing paintball on children.

When talking about paintball some experts will cite a 2004 study completed by two researchers by the names of Carnagy and Anderson from Iowa State University who had participants play one of three versions of the same race-car video game – one where all violence was rewarded, another where violence was punished, and the final version which was nonviolent. The participants were then measured for aggressive affect, aggressive cognition and aggressive behavior.

The results suggested that video games that reward violent actions can increase aggressive behavior by increasing aggressive thinking.

http://socialpaintball.com/2013/07/09/paintball-and-a-childs-mental-health/

But a group from the Texas A and M International University and the University of Wisconsin-Whitewater looked at two studies examining the relationship between exposure to violent video games and aggression or violence in the laboratory and in real life. They concluded "that playing violent video games does not constitute a significant risk for future violent criminal acts." In fact, they argue that "the pathway to violent criminal acts occurs through a combination of innate propensity and exposure to violence in the family."

There are two significant differences between paintball and video games. One of these differences is paintball is a physically demanding sport. The average paintball player will burn 420 calories per hour while playing paintball.

In 2007, Dr. James Blumenthal, a clinical psychologist at Duke University assigned sedentary adults with major depressive disorder to one of four groups: supervised exercise, home-based exercise, antidepressant therapy or a placebo pill. After four months of treatment, Blumenthal found patients in the exercise and antidepressant groups had higher rates of remission than did the patients on the placebo. Exercise, he concluded, was generally comparable to antidepressants for patients with major depressive disorder.

In 1992, a group of researchers from the Psychological Clinic at the University of South Alabama assigned a small group of psychiatrically institutionalized adolescents to a 3 day per week running/aerobic exercise program or a regular physical activity class for 9 weeks. At the end of the trial, the adolescents showed improvements in depression, anxiety, hostility, confused thinking and fatigue.

In December 2011, the American Psychological Association published an article written by Kirsten Weir, citing a huge list of research on the positive benefits and encouraged exercise as a part of client's therapy.

So, it's clear that the physical exercise children received from a paintball game over a video game is a major positive for children.

The other difference between paintball and video games is that paintball is played in a group social environment with face-to-face human interaction, not in a bedroom behind closed doors without any face-to-face interaction like you would find in playing a video game.

I put out a challenge to the Psychology Profession to do a peer review study on the effects of paintball on children. There is so much anecdotal evidence that children burn off their aggression and learn to work through their feelings through activities like paintball.

By Gordon More

http://socialpaintball.com/2013/07/09/paintball-and-a-childs-mental-health/

## General comprehension

1. As there has been no widely recognised research into the positive/negative effects of paintball, which activities are sometimes quoted as having similar effects on young people? Where was this research done?
2. Identify the two differences, given in the text, between paintball and video games.
3. Which two studies, according to the text, proved that physical exercise was a benefit to mental health?
4. In the text, two studies carried out at American universities are referred to which say that violent criminal acts are the result of people's 'innate propensity for violence and exposure to violence in the family'. In your own words, explain what you think this means.

## Individual oral activity

A group of students at your school want to set up a paintball club. There has been a lot of controversy and discussion about this in the school among students, teachers and parents. Prepare a persuasive speech to give at assembly about paintball – either for or against the sport.

Plan to talk for three to four minutes.

# 17 The changing face of leisure

## 17.5 An exhilarating activity for those who don't mind getting wet

### Text 17.5.1 White-water rafting

Growing up in Scotland, I loved sports lessons at school; whether it was tennis, hockey, or rounders, I couldn't get enough. However, when I went to college to study sport, I discovered a far more exciting range of activities. I had never heard of some of them, and a whole new world opened up. There is nothing like the challenge of standing in front of a rock face, all harnessed up, your team behind you, and thinking, 'I can never climb this!' And then you do, and the adrenalin rush, together with the thought, 'I'm a rock climber now!' is the reward.

But the most thrilling activity I discovered, and the one that has kept me fascinated for the past ten years, was white-water rafting. It is a team sport and your 'raft' is not the kind of construction many people might associate with Huckleberry Finn on the Mississippi River – it is a sturdy inflatable boat. Together with your team, you negotiate the fast-flowing water from which the sport gets its name: the waves and plumes of spray created by the water as it rushes round boulders in the river are white.

In the USA, where I now live, white-water rafting is a sport offering something for all ages and levels of experience. Rivers are categorized according to difficulty, and range from Class I to Class VI. The easiest categories are I and II, in which the water is not very 'white', the boulders are relatively small, and the rivers flow at a pace that gives you time to think and manoeuvre. Classes III and IV can be called 'intermediate', and as you might imagine are more difficult and present more technical challenges. It is Classes V and VI that are the real adventure, presenting the greatest challenges on the fastest flowing rivers. The water is not just fast, it

**Below** Shooting the rapids.

is wild and turbulent, and your raft is tossed around like a leaf in a storm. There are crosscurrents, powerful waves, and hidden boulders – but these are the conditions that experts in search of a challenge are looking for!

It is an interesting fact that there is a difference between rivers on the East Coast and rivers on the West Coast of the USA: it is well-known among rafters that the East Coast rivers, with their many boulders, demand high technical ability in order to navigate them safely; West Coast rivers, on the other hand, tend to be steeper in descent and consequently have faster-flowing water.

Some rivers are famous in their own right – for example the Ocoee River in Tennessee, which was the location for the 1996 Olympic Canoe/Kayak White-water Slalom competition, and the Chattooga River in Georgia, where the film 'Deliverance' was shot.

With all the technical aptitude that is needed, it is little surprise that white-water canoe racing is an Olympic sport. It first made an appearance at the Games in 1972, following in the wake of the flat-water canoe events that had been Olympic disciplines since the 1930s. All of these events events test the stamina, strength, and hard-earned level of skill of the athletes.

If you love water and you love excitement, then white-water rafting is for you!

### General comprehension

1. According to the text, how does this water sport get its name?
2. There are six levels of difficulty in the sport of white-water rafting. What influences the increased difficulty levels?
3. What are the differences between East Coast and West Coast rivers in the USA?
4. Explain the Olympic connection to this adventure sport.
5. Which river was the location for a film? Research the content of the film and find the connection to white-water rafting. Present your findings in a brief text.

### Text handling

Match the beginnings of the sentences taken from the text with endings to make new, meaningful sentences.

1. However, when I went to college to study sport,
2. There is nothing like the challenge
3. Together with your team,
4. Some rivers...
5. The Chattooga River...
6. West Coast rivers...

A ... was the location for a successful film.
B ... you'll need to be physically fit before you start.
C ... tend to be more difficult to negotiate.
D ... I was unable to pursue my old hobbies.
E ... cannot be used for rafting.
F ... of trying something that looks impossible.

## Written work

Summarise the sporting activity 'white-water rafting' in approximately 100 words.

# 17  The changing face of leisure

## 17.6  Parkour

### Text 17.6.1 Ryan Doyle: One of the best-known parkour stars in the UK

**parkour (n)**

**Definition:** A sport or athletic activity in which the participant seeks to move quickly and fluidly through an area, often an urban locale, by surmounting obstacles such as walls and railings and leaping across open spaces, as in a stairwell or between buildings.

http://www.thefreedictionary.com/parkour

Hi, my name is Ryan Doyle.

My discipline is parkour and free running. My friends call me Rad. I was born on 22 September 1984 in Liverpool, UK. My special talent is constantly adapting to new experiences and environments. My philosophy of life is don't live in fear of making mistakes, just go for it. My favourite food is crispy chilli beef with egg fried rice.

August 13 2013
WFPF / WFPF Athletes

http://www.redbull.com/en/athletes/1331578990766/ryan-doyle

### General comprehension

Look at Ryan Doyle's profile. There are six sentences and each one is the answer to a question. Write down the six questions.

### Written work

Using the questions you have written for the above activity, write your own answers to create a profile about yourself.

Be prepared to share your profile with others in the class.

# Text 17.6.2 Ryan Doyle: Biography

For the last 12 years, Ryan Doyle has set the boundaries and continues to raise the bar in discovering what the human body is capable of, especially when it is not suppressed by what society says is "socially accepted behaviour". Ryan was influenced by movement from age 1, walking at only 7 months old, he quickly learned about gravity and its consequences when he broke his arm doing a front flip at 3 years old.

While growing into his teen years and discovering Jackie Chan, Ryan joined a Korean martial arts class until he got his 1st degree black-belt in KUK-SOOL-WON. Combining martial art skills with self-taught gymnastics, Ryan discovered "Tricking" and went on to become a National Tricking Champion in 2006, 07, 09 & 2010.

Ryan became the first international Freerunning Champion, winning the Red Bull – Art of Motion in Vienna 2007. Then went on to be the parkour Ambassador for Red Bull and the Art-of-Motion Consultant.

Co-starring in MTV's Ultimate Parkour Challenge, and *Freerunner The Movie*, Ryan continues to be a 'voice' for the discipline of parkour and delivers the messages of this inclusive art around the world.

The WFPF (World Freerunning Parkour Federation) adopted Ryan as a founding athlete in 2007 and together with several athletes from the UK, USA and Europe, took the art to America where it exploded into the youth culture.

Since then, he has become an international champion, Ambassador of Parkour for Red Bull, and the Art of Motion Consultant.

Ryan was born in Liverpool, UK, in 1984 and studied Media at Hope University. He continues to teach at his Freerunning Academy founded in 2004 in Liverpool.

To learn more about Ryan, go to www.pearsonhotlinks.com, enter the title or ISBN of this book and click on Chapter 17.

http://www.wfpf.com/athletes/ryan-doyle/

## General comprehension

Complete the table below to show Ryan's achievements.

| At the age of seven months | Was able to walk |
|---|---|
| While he was a teenager | |
| In 2004 | |
| In 2006, 2007, 2009 and 2010 | |
| In 2007 (two events) | 1 |
| | 2 |

# 17 The changing face of leisure

> **Text handling**
>
> **Examples of idiomatic English**
>
> 1  The first sentence says that Ryan 'continues to raise the bar'. In this example of the use of idiomatic English, what does the reader understand about Ryan's achievements as a parkour runner?
> 2  In the text an idiom is used when talking about parkour being introduced into the USA in 2007: 'it exploded into the youth culture'. What does the choice of this idiomatic use of the word 'exploded' tell the reader?

## Written work

Do some research into parkour and free running. Using the information that you find, write a short essay to introduce this new adventure sport and explain the differences between the traditional ideas of running and jogging and this challenging sport.

Write between 200 and 250 words.

## 17.7 Bungee jumping

### 17.7.1 Pure adrenaline – bungee jumping

**However you spell it – bungi jump, bongee jump, bungy jump or bungee jumping – it is the same thing and the most awesome adrenaline experience Scotland has to offer!**

**It is a personal challenge. A state of mind. An exploration of limits. A few seconds of heart-thumping bliss. An experiment with gravity. Great, exhilarating, safe fun**

## Highland Fling Bungee jumping in Scotland

What is it? Bungee jumping is once-in-a-lifetime free-fall experience of 40 metres towards water from a bridge Bungee jump platform. An airborne flight of a few seconds at over 50 mph before a special bungee jump cord springs you back to normal, upright, life. A safe and unforgettable adrenaline-packed experience using the latest technology and safety equipment, led by experienced, qualified Bungee Jump Masters.

Where is it? The UK's first static bungee jumps take place near to the famous site of the Battle of Killiecrankie. A specially constructed bungee jump platform is suspended below the Garry Bridge over the beautiful River Garry near Pitlochry in Highland Perthshire, Scotland. It is perched above a dramatic gorge surrounded by ancient trees. The site is operated from the visitor centre in Killiecrankie.

Who does it? Free spirits, thrill seekers, outdoor enthusiasts, sports enthusiasts, adrenaline-lovers, taxi drivers, accountants, landscape gardeners, astronauts, plumbers. Get the idea? That's right: anyone from age 14 to 114 with a sense of fun and adventure.

How do you do it? Find a date that's available and book. You can book online, using our Book Online Service. After that, get yourself to the location on the day and put yourself in the hands of the Highland Fling Bungee jump experts and enjoy.

When do you do it? Highland Fling Bungee jumping offers the only bungee experience of its kind in the UK that is open all year round. Check our Booking Page for jump times.

Why do it? Because you are alive. Because it's there. Because you can.

Want to learn a bit more about bungee, its history and why so many have done it and loved it? Check out the Why Bungee Page. See Fact File below for more things you need to know about jumping with Highland Fling Bungee.

## Fact file

**Height:** 40 m or 132 feet

**Jumping over:** Water

**Cost:** £75 per person per jump, 2nd jump by the same person on the same day £30pp

**How long is the experience:** Allow 1 hour

**Recovery:** Winch back up to the bridge

**What to wear:** Sensible clothing and footwear

**Minimum age:** 14 years old

**Maximum age:** 114 years young

**Maximum weight limit:** (for a solo jumper, we do not do tandems, yet!): 120kg or 18.9 stone

**Waist Harnesses:** Fit waist size of 40cm (15.7 inches) to 125cm (49.2 inches).

**T/shirts:** Available onsite – £15

**Photos:** Available onsite – £20

**GoPro video:** Available onsite – £35

**Do I need to pre-book:** Essential

**Car parking:** Available at the Killiecrankie Visitor Centre

**Spectators:** All welcome, come and enjoy this magnificent area!

**See more at:** http://www.bungeejumpscotland.co.uk/page/bungee#sthash.ALp4uaYA.dpuf

http://www.bungeejumpscotland.co.uk/2_bungee.html

# 17 The changing face of leisure

### General comprehension

1. In the introduction there are five sentences which are not, in fact, sentences because they do not contain a verb. The author of the text has chosen to do this for a specific reason. What effect is created by this style of writing?
2. The advertisement is organised for easy understanding. What do you notice about the structure of the text that makes it easy to understand?
3. Participation in this bungee-jumping activity in Scotland is not possible for everyone. What restrictions are there that exclude some people from jumping?

### Interactive oral activity

Work in pairs. One student has never heard of bungee jumping and does not have any idea about it; the other student explains the sport and tries to answer questions from the first student. Before you begin, you should both prepare for the activity by thinking about what you will have to ask or answer.

## Written work

The advertisement says that the centre is 'near to the famous site of the Battle of Killiecrankie'.

Do some research and find out some facts about this battle. Present your answers in a paragraph.

## Text 17.7.2 Bungy jumping Down Under: Two men put New Zealand on the adventure tourism map

A. J. Hackett and Henry van Asch, who met while skiing in Wanaka, New Zealand, set about developing and testing Bungy cords with the help of Auckland University scientists. They were both convinced that others would pay to experience the adrenaline rush associated with Bungy.

After some extensive testing on latex rubber cords a series of extreme jumps were made, first in Tignes, France from a ski area gondola 91 metres above the snow.

Once tried and tested by AJ, Henry and quite a few of their mates. They agreed that they needed a very public confirmation of their complete faith in the newly-created Bungy ropes. To achieve this, a PR coup was set up involving a Bungy Jump from the Paris Eiffel Tower in June 1987. AJ snuck up the Eiffel tower and slept there overnight, then first thing in the morning he Bungy Jumped down off the tower. He was immediately arrested and released five minutes later. The Jump made international headlines and [the] phenomenon had begun.

Shortly after, in November of 1988, despite the fears of sceptics who thought it was a tourism operation which would never catch on, the world's first commercial Bungy operation opened up at the Kawarau Bridge. At that stage they were given license to operate for just 30 days from the Department of Conservation. Many assumed that Bungy Jumping was a tourist fad with limited consumer appeal and commercial viability. During that year, twenty-eight people paid $75 each to leap off the 43-metre bridge with a Bungy cord attached to their ankles.

AJ and Henry knew they had a safe product, but in order to convince the tourism industry and the public, they needed an independent method of safety assurance. So they worked to develop a 'Bungy Code of Practice', which went on to provide the framework for the New Zealand/Australian Bungy Jump Standard. AJ and Henry's company was the first in the world to be awarded the "S" Mark for exceptional safety and quality assurance in Bungy Jumping, with the Standards Association of New Zealand completing an independent audit of all jump sites every six months. The launch of the Kawarau Bridge Bungy site has been hailed as the birth of adventure tourism in New Zealand, and was integral towards putting New Zealand on the world adventure tourism map.

http://www.bungy.co.nz/who-we-are/history

### General comprehension

True or false? Justify your answer with a relevant brief quotation from the text.

1. A.J. Hackett and Henry van Asch are Auckland University scientists.
2. Comprehensive preparations were made before the first jump in France.
3. A.J. Hackett jumped from the Eiffel Tower for a bet.
4. The Eiffel Tower jump was done without permission from the authorities.
5. Many people thought the Kawarau bungee-jumping operation would not be successful.
6. In the first year fewer than three dozen people did the bungee jump.
7. The first jump was from a 43-metre tower.
8. No other bungee-jumping company had previously been awarded a certificate for 'safety and quality'.

## Written work

In this chapter you have read about a variety of adventure sports. Create a one-page flyer to distribute among the student body giving an overview of the different sports and why they are worth trying out. Your flyer should state the positive aspects of the sports.

## Exam practice

# Exercises

**Written assignment 1: Essay title (HL)**

You have taken part in a very exciting sporting activity for the first time while on your holiday in Canada. Write an email to your friend about your experiences. Write between 250 and 400 words.

**Written assignment 2: Personal response (HL)**

Give a personal response to the following stimulus and justify it. Choose any text type you have studied in class. Write between 150 and 250 words.

> 'Man needs difficulties; they are necessary for health.'
>
> *Carl Gustav Jung, psychologist*

**Written assignment 3: Essay title: (SL)**

You have been on a week's course learning how to bungee jump. Write a diary entry at the end of the week. Write between 250 and 400 words.

# 18 How we spend our free time

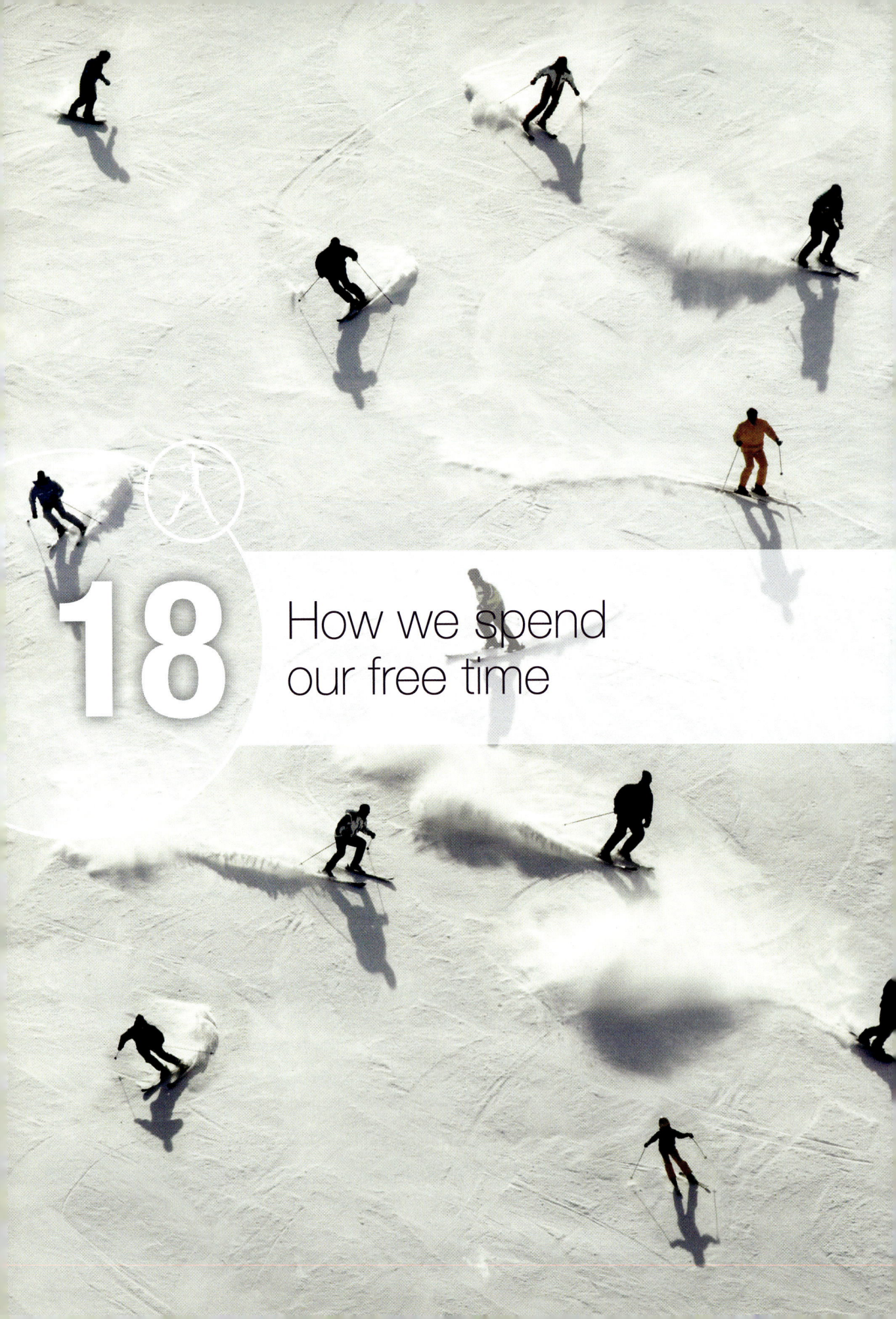

## Objectives

- To revise the possessive form
- To revise comparative and superlative adjectives
- To revise the past perfect
- To practise the zero conditional
- To practise sentences with a noun clause as object
- To reflect on the role of leisure in our lives

**Opposite** Total, perfect freedom?

## 18.1 What role does leisure play in our lives?

### Text 18.1.1 What is leisure?

Leisure is generally agreed to be the time we spend not working, not studying, not doing domestic chores and not sleeping. It is the time when we are involved in satisfying activities which we choose freely. These activities give us time for enjoyment and make us feel good.

These activities may be creative, artistic or athletic. We may be working on puzzles, reading or writing for enjoyment. Some people help others in their leisure time, but the key to any activity is that it gives us pleasure. *We* have chosen the activity, which can be done alone or we may meet other like-minded people and enjoy our leisure time together. These activities can be indoors or outdoors, at home or in a special place. Leisure activities can be very cheap, such as walking or reading, or more expensive, such as owning a motor boat or yacht.

According to the British Government's research from the Department for Culture, Media and Sports for 2010, 23.7% of adults had volunteered in the previous 12 months. The majority of these volunteers had helped raising money for sponsored events, or helping to organise or run an activity. They found that people in rural areas were more likely to volunteer than those in urban areas, young people aged 16–24 were most likely to volunteer, and women tended to volunteer more than men.

With regard to sport, the research showed that 80.9% of adults said they could swim and 85.2% said they could cycle. Of those who could swim, 30.2% reported that they could swim more than 250 metres. From the cyclists, 36.0% were confident riding longer journeys and to work. Over 50% of adults had done sport in the previous 12 months, and the percentage of those doing three or more 30-minute sessions of moderate exercise was 25.4%.

The number of people who were actively involved in culture and had visited a museum, gallery or archive was 47.2%. Libraries were visited by 39%. The results also show a significant number of people participating digitally in culture: for example 41.6% had visited theatre and concert websites, 35.7% had visited sport websites and 24.6% museum or gallery websites.

Statistics from https://www.gov.uk/government/uploads/system/uploads/attachment_data/file/77449/Taking_Part_Y6_Q3_Jan-Dec10.pdf/

# 18 How we spend our free time

### General comprehension

1. According to the definition of leisure in the text, how much leisure time do you have per week?
2. How do you spend your leisure time? Make a chart of how your time is divided now. Compare your finished chart with a classmate. Are the charts very similar?
3. Do your leisure activities fit under the headings Creative, Artistic, Athletic?
4. Do you enjoy your leisure activities with like-minded people or alone?
5. Are your leisure activities generally cheap or expensive?
6. Which information given in the British Government's statistics about volunteering surprises you?
7. What would your replies be if you were asked the research questions about swimming and cycling?
8. It appears that less than 50% of British people take part in cultural activities; how do you think this can be explained?

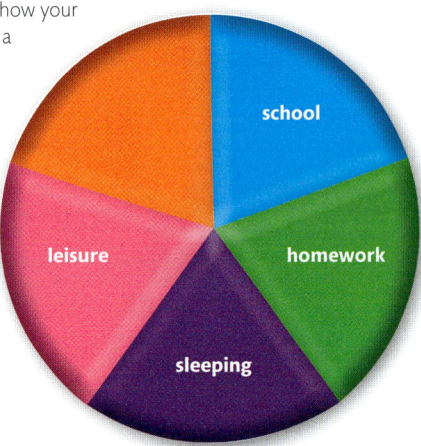

## 18.2 Reflections on leisure

### Text 18.2.1 A poem – Leisure

## Leisure

What is this life if, full of care,
We have no time to stand and stare.

No time to stand beneath the boughs
And stare as long as sheep or cows.

No time to see, when woods we pass,
Where squirrels hide their nuts in grass.

No time to see, in broad daylight,
Streams full of stars, like skies at night.

No time to turn at Beauty's glance,
And watch her feet, how they can dance.

No time to wait till her mouth can
Enrich that smile her eyes began.

A poor life this is if, full of care,
We have no time to stand and stare.

**William Henry Davies
(1871–1940)**

http://www.poemhunter.com/poem/leisure/

## General comprehension

1. How would you describe the mood of the poem?
2. It was written in the first half of the last century; do you think the cares of life at that time can be compared to those of today? Explain your answer.
3. Describe in your own words what the poet thinks we should have time to enjoy.
4. If you were writing a similar poem today, which objects would you want to stand and stare at?

### Text 18.2.2 Men have more leisure time than women, says new report

## Men enjoy half an hour more of leisure time each day than women, a report claims. Women have 30 minutes less to enjoy themselves every day

By Laura Roberts
7:00AM GMT March 9 2010

The international survey found that men spent longer watching television, meeting friends, playing sport or pursuing hobbies than the fairer sex.

The Organisation of Economic Co-operation and Development, made up of the world's richest nations, said that British men ranked close behind France and America in the league table of countries where women work harder than men. The report, released to mark International Women's Day, called for greater equality for women. It said that "governments and firms need to do more to tackle the gender equality gap."

Previous OECD reports have suggested that the difference may be more to do with how each sex chooses to spend its time which was not taken into account in the new report. The OECD concluded that shopping, soaking in the bath, grooming, having a lie-in or taking a long lunch all count as work rather than leisure. If these are taken into account British men have only 10 minutes more spare time a day than women.

The report said: "Men universally report spending more time in activities counted as leisure than women. Gender differences in leisure time are wide across OECD countries." The 32-minute leisure advantage for men in Britain compares with 38 minutes in the US, 33 minutes in France, 50 minutes in Belgium and 22 minutes in Germany. Italian men spend nearly 80 minutes a day more than women on leisure time. Across the OECD countries, 62 per cent of women have jobs, and women earn a fifth less than men, said the *Daily Mail*. Officials said the gap was a result of women taking time off work to concentrate on bringing up their children.

http://www.telegraph.co.uk/news/newstopics/howaboutthat/7400675/Men-have-more-leisure-time-than-women-says-new-report.html

# 18 How we spend our free time

## General comprehension

1. Does your own experience confirm the findings of the report?
2. Why do women have less leisure time, do you think?
3. Do you agree with previous reports that the difference may be due to how people choose to spend their time?
4. Would you count shopping as leisure? Explain your answer.

## Text handling

1. True or false? Justify your answer with a relevant brief quotation from the text.
   a) Men have more free time than women.
   b) In France and the USA, women work harder than men.
   c) Taking a long lunch is definitely considered to be work.
   d) In OECD countries the differences in leisure time between men and women are minimal.
   e) Italian men have considerably more leisure time than Italian women.

2. Explain the following terms in your own words.
   a) the fairer sex
   b) to tackle
   c) the gender equality gap
   d) grooming
   e) having a lie-in

## Zoom in on grammar

**More, most, less, least, fewer, fewest**

These words are used to compare quantities of both countable and uncountable nouns.

**Examples**

- I have more *books* to read than I expected. (*books* = countable)
  I have more *time* to read than I need. (*time* = uncountable)
- She has the most *questions* to answer. (*questions* = countable)
  She has the most *work* to do on this assignment. (*work* = uncountable)

## Grammar in context

**More, most, less, least, fewer, fewest**

Make sentences using *more*, *most*, *less* and *least*, and content from the text.

1. Italian men / time
2. Men / leisure
3. Women / leisure time
4. Women / spare time

## 18.3 The cost of leisure

### 18.3.1 How 'cheap' leisure pursuits can hit your wallet

*Telegraph* consumer expert Jessica Gorst-Williams outlines some spoilers that can turn summer fun into an expensive mistake  By Jessica Gorst-Williams  6:00AM BST June 14 2013

**a)** .................................................................................................................

Do this and you may be fined up to £2,500. Police do raids on fishing lakes to check customers, so beware. You can buy one or 8 day licences or, for regular anglers, full season ones. Concessions for those aged 65 and aged 12 to 16 apply and under 12s do not have to pay. Buy at the Post Office or via its website www.postoffice.co.uk. Or call the rod licence sales line on 0844 800 5386.

**b)** .................................................................................................................

Take a book you have borrowed from a library back late without having renewed it and there could be financial consequences. Typically a standard book loan period from a mainstream library is 21 days.

Check your local library and see the slip or the written note in the book label. Although it may vary from council to council, council lending library fines tend to average around 15p per day to a maximum of £6.

There are concessions for under 18s, children's books and over 60s. Mobile libraries differ. University libraries may charge more particularly for books in high demand.

**c)** .................................................................................................................

If there is no right of way, it is likely that you are trespassing. If that is all you are doing, this isn't usually a criminal issue except where it is on railway and sometimes military training land.

However, an angry landowner could take an offender to a civil court which could result in a nominal fine for the offender and paying the landowner's legal costs.

Other more physical consequences which could happen even when someone is keeping to a public footpath is being attacked by farm animals such as a herd of stampeding cows, a bull or a ram. Such injuries and fatalities are not uncommon. Although it can happen to anyone some farm animals find a dog particularly provocative.

**d)** .................................................................................................................

Boating on certain rivers whether in a powered or unpowered boat requires the payment of a navigation fee. This goes toward upkeep of locks etc. Failure to pay and display valid registration could result in prosecution and a fine. Find out more from www.environment-agency.gov.uk. Or call 03708 506 506.

**e)** .................................................................................................................

There are fines for leaving litter so picnic rubbish should be carefully disposed of. Realistically the odd paper bag dropped while feeding the ducks or a crisp packet is unlikely to lead to a problem although there is no guarantee it will not catch the eye of a nit-picking jobsworth.

**f)** .................................................................................................................

Watching TV at home without a licence is a criminal offence and could incur a fine of up to £1,000 not including legal costs.

# 18 How we spend our free time

**Above** Don't forget your rod licence!

In London there are nine Royal Parks, which in the past were owned by the reigning king or queen. Nowadays these parks are under the control of the government. The names of the nine parks are Bushey Park, Green Park, Kensington Gardens, Greenwich Park, Hampton Court Park, Hyde Park, Regent's Park, Richmond Park and St James's Park.

**g)** ..................................................................................

This won't damage your own budget but could mar your day. As reported in this paper last week having a fitness session in a Royal Park with a personal trainer could turn unpleasant if the trainer doesn't have a licence. The cost of keeping client's figures in trim in Royal Parks runs into a three figure licence fee for trainers and those without them are likely to be waylaid.

http://www.telegraph.co.uk/finance/personalfinance/consumertips/10119037/How-cheap-leisure-pursuits-can-hit-your-wallet.html

## General comprehension

1. Insert the following paragraph headings appropriately.
    a) Walking in a stranger's field
    b) River boating
    c) Fishing without a rod licence
    d) Being a litterbug
    e) Jogging or doing yoga with a personal trainer in a Royal Park
    f) Not renewing library books
    g) Viewing TV without a TV licence
2. What is the most expensive mistake people can make in their leisure activities, according to the text?
3. For which age groups is fishing cheaper?
4. What is the usual library lending period?
5. What should you do before your book is overdue?
6. What action can a farmer take against people who walk on his land?
7. When would trespassing be a criminal act?
8. Why can trespassing sometimes be dangerous?
9. What happens if you fail to pay the navigation fee for a boat?
10. Are people who drop litter always fined?
11. What could be expensive in a Royal Park?

## Text handling

Match the words and expressions on the left to the meanings on the right.

| | | | |
|---|---|---|---|
| 1 | concessions | A | ruin the day |
| 2 | mobile libraries | B | deaths |
| 3 | trespassing | C | special prices |
| 4 | nominal fine | D | just one bag |
| 5 | consequences | E | walking on private land |
| 6 | fatalities | F | libraries in a bus |
| 7 | provocative | G | annoying |
| 8 | a litterbug | H | small fine |
| 9 | the odd paper bag | I | results |
| 10 | mar your day | J | someone who drops litter |

### Zoom in on grammar

**The possessive form – 's and s'**

We use 's to form a singular possessive: the *boy's* books (one boy and his books).

s' forms the plural possessive: the *boys'* books (more than one boy and their books).

Some plural nouns have endings without -s – for example, *children* and *women* – and the possessive form for these nouns is formed with 's: the *children's* books, the *women's* voices.

### Grammar in context

**The possessive form – 's and s'**

Re-read the text, find examples of 's or s' and explain each one.

### Grammar in context

**Zero conditional**

In the text there are some examples of the zero conditional (see the 'Zoom in on grammar' box for Text 9.1.1):

> If there is no right of way, it is likely that you are trespassing.
> If that is all you are doing, this isn't usually a criminal issue.

Build your own examples of the zero conditional with the following openers:

1. If the phone rings, …
2. If you stop talking now, …
3. If you hurry, …

## Text 18.3.2 Free leisure activities – the crossword

# The crossword

A lot of people enjoy leisure pursuits which involve mental challenges. These distract from other daily problems or thoughts and give a sense of satisfaction at the end on completion of a tricky puzzle. One of the most popular of these pursuits is the crossword puzzle.

The first crossword puzzle was diamond shaped with just 31 clues and was printed in the *New York World* newspaper on December 21st, 1913. The creator was Arthur Wynne, an Englishman from Merseyside. His father was a newspaper editor, and in 1905 Arthur moved to New York to work in the newspaper industry. It was not immediately popular, but ten years later a book of crossword puzzles was published by two young men with a new publishing house, Simon and Schuster. The aunt of one of them asked them to publish a book of crossword puzzles. It became a huge success and had to be reprinted, selling over 100,000 copies. More collections of crossword puzzles were produced, and solving crossword puzzles became a very popular leisure activity.

The crossword puzzles today are similar to that first one created by Arthur Wynne, but are

# 18 How we spend our free time

square shaped. As well as books of crossword puzzles, a lot of newspapers and magazines include one or more crossword puzzles in their editions. There are different kinds of puzzles; they may be theme based, they may have straightforward clues, for example:

'Flowing through England's capital city' – *the Thames*

Or they may have cryptic clues, which take a lot more thought. Cryptic means mysterious, with a hidden message. Cryptic clues in crosswords, according to the *Longman Dictionary of Contemporary English*, are 'those with difficult clues with hidden meanings, rather than simple straightforward ones'. Cryptic clues are more difficult to solve and could be anagrams or other kinds of word play, for example:

'Unusually remote celestial body' – *meteor* (the letters of 'remote' rearranged spell 'meteor')

Crossword enthusiasts often work against the clock to solve their crosswords, and many people solve the daily crossword over breakfast or on the train to work.

Longman Dictionary of Contemporary English 6e *ISBN* 9781447954194

## General comprehension

1 When and where was the first crossword puzzle published?
2 Was it immediately a success?
3 Are crossword puzzles today the same as the first puzzles?
4 Which aspects of puzzles have changed?

## Text handling

Complete the crossword using words from the text.

**Across**

3. An activity such as a sport or hobby.
6. Someone who is very interested in a particular activity or subject.
7. Relating to the mind and thought, or happening only in the mind.
8. A word or phrase that is made by changing the order of the letters in another word or phrase.

**Down**

1. Having a meaning that is mysterious or not easily understood.
2. Simple and easy to understand.
4. A shape with four straight but sloping sides of equal length, with one point facing directly up and the other directly down.
5. To take someone's attention away from something by making them look at or listen to something else.

Text 18.3.3 Free leisure activities – Scrabble

# Another popular leisure pursuit is the game of Scrabble

Scrabble is a word game, played with letters of the alphabet written on small tiles. The tiles are worth a variety of points, depending on their frequency. The object is to make words and collect as many points as possible to win. Scrabble is an excellent way to increase vocabulary.

Each player begins the game with seven tiles taken from the bag and places them on a rack in front of him. There can be between two and four players who each take turns to create words on the board, taking new tiles from the bag to replace the ones used. The game is over when all the tiles have been used, or no new words can be created.

In Scrabble there is often a good deal of discussion about whether a word is really valid or not, and lists of acceptable words can be found in handbooks and on the internet.

### General comprehension

1. What is the goal when playing Scrabble?
2. How do the players earn points?
3. When is the game over?
4. What causes debate in the game of Scrabble?

# 18 How we spend our free time

## Text 18.3.4 Free leisure activities – Sudoku

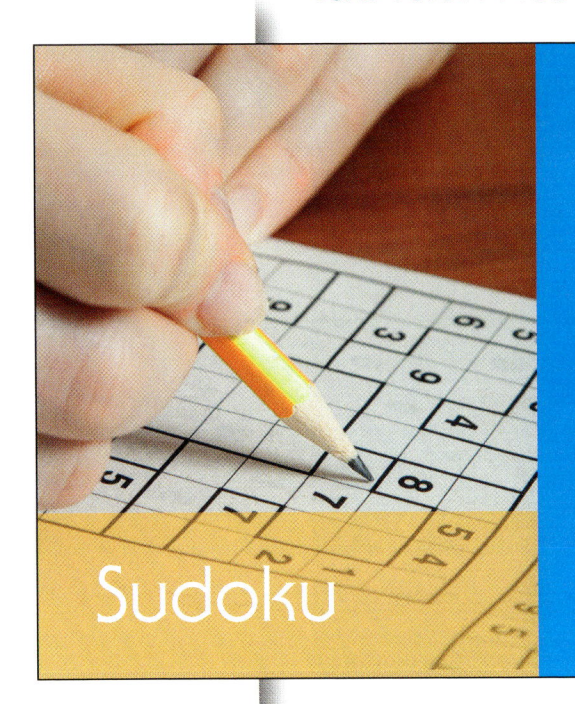

Both crossword puzzles and Scrabble are word games which require good concentration and a wide vocabulary, but another very popular leisure game is Sudoku, which does not require vocabulary knowledge because it is a number game. Here the goal is to fill nine squares with the numbers 1 to 9. Each horizontal and vertical row and each 3x3 box must have all the digits from 1 to 9. So this is a game of logical thinking. It has not been popular for as long as crossword puzzles or Scrabble, and is thought to have been first designed in its present form in 1979 by an American, Howard Garn, who called the game Number Place. It became popular in Japan in 1984 and was then called Sudoku, *su* meaning number and *doku* meaning place. This game has become extremely popular, and a lot of newspapers and magazines include Sudoku puzzles of varying complexity on a regular basis.

### General comprehension

1. Of the puzzles and games presented here, which have you played before and which would you like to try?
2. Which do you think would be most difficult for you and why?
3. Which would be easiest for you and why?
4. Are there typical puzzles or games in your native country?
5. Choose one game and write your own basic instructions on how to play it.

## Text 18.3.5 Great novels can change your life… and your brain

Getting lost in a good book can actually change your brain, with neural paths forming in the same way as if you were actually living the experience, scientists have found

**By Sarah Knapton, Science Correspondent**
**2:15PM GMT January 6 2014**

Atticus Finch claimed you can never understand a person until you climb into his skin and walk around in it. But reading *To Kill a Mockingbird* could make your brain believe that it is actually experiencing events happening to the literary characters between the pages, neuroscientists believe. Researchers found biological changes in the brains of those asked to read books, in an experiment designed to prove that novels can have a significant impact on the mind. They found that a powerful story has the ability to create 'muscle memory' in the brain in the same way as if the events had actually happened to the reader.

Neuroscientist Professor Gregory Berns, of Emory University in Atlanta, Georgia, said: "Stories shape our lives and in some cases help define a person. We wanted to understand how stories get into your brain, and what they do to it. The neural changes that we found associated with physical sensation and movement systems suggest reading a novel can transport you into the body of the protagonist. We already knew that good stories can put you in someone else's shoes in a figurative sense. Now we're seeing that something may also be happening biologically."

Some stories are so powerful they may even permanently alter the way the reader's brain works, the study concluded. The neurological effects could be seen for days after the volunteers had stopped reading the books. Researchers enlisted 21 students to read the novel *Pompeii* by bestselling British author Robert Harris chapter by chapter over 19 consecutive days while monitoring their brains. The students were quizzed at the end on the book – a fictional love story set around the erupting volcano Vesuvius that destroyed the Roman city – to make sure they had read it.

Results of the brain monitor showed that changes in brain functions during the period in which they read the book, stayed with the individuals for at least five further days of tests. The brain areas more affected were those which controlled the left temporal cortex which influences a person's 'receptivity to language'. It also heightened the function of the brain which links thoughts to actions – the bit which, for instance, can make a person want to go running when they think about running. Such heightened brain activities may be expected during the reading of a book, but not once the reading had finished, the researchers said.

Prof Berns added: "It remains an open question how long these neural changes might last. But the fact that we're detecting them over a few days for a randomly assigned novel suggests that favourite novels could certainly have a bigger and longer-lasting effect on the biology of your brain."

The study was published in the journal *Brain Connectivity*.

http://www.telegraph.co.uk/science/science-news/10553579/Great-novels-can-change-your-life...and-your-brain.html

# 18 How we spend our free time

## General comprehension

1 What did Atticus believe? Explain this with an example of your own.
2 What changes did researchers find in the brains of people who read books?
3 What effect can powerful stories have on the brain?
4 How long can these effects last?
5 How did researchers ensure that the students had read the set book?
6 What did the researchers discover?
7 What is still unknown?
8 What effect may favourite novels have?

## Text handling

Explain the following words and expressions.

1 to get lost in a good book
2 literary characters
3 physical sensation
4 protagonist
5 bestselling author
6 to permanently alter something
7 consecutive days
8 receptivity to language
9 an open question
10 randomly assigned

## Grammar in context

### Noun clauses

Re-read the text and identify examples of noun clauses as objects (see the 'Zoom in on grammar' box for Text 14.2.2). You should easily be able to find at least three examples.

Now write sentences of your own using the following starters.

1 I know that…
2 He believes that…
3 We agree that…
4 I realise that…
5 The answers show how much…

## Individual oral activity

Think about a book you have read and prepare a three- to four-minute talk about it. Summarise the plot very briefly, but use most of the talk to explain why you chose this book and what effect it had on you. You could also describe who you would recommend the book to.

## Zoom in on grammar

### The past perfect

The past perfect is formed using *had* + a past participle.

'Had' is used for all persons, i.e. there are no changes: I *had*, you *had*, he *had*, they *had*, etc.

The past perfect is used to describe something which happened before another event being described in the past.

    Mary went to choose a book as she *had* already *finished* the exercises set by the teacher.

The sentence describes events in the past: before she went to choose a book, Mary had already finished the exercises set.

We could also say:

    When Mary had *finished* the exercises, she went to choose a book.

Or:

    After Mary had *finished* the exercises she went to choose a book.

The past perfect is also used in the third conditional:

    I would have called you, if I *had had* my phone with me.

### Grammar in context

**The past perfect**

Sarah Knapton wrote:

> The students were quizzed at the end on the book [...] to make sure they had read it.

She uses the past perfect tense, and we understand that this is used to describe something that happened before the students were quizzed. She could also have said:

> Before they were quizzed, the students had read the book.

Make sentences of your own using the following starters:

1. After we had eaten dinner...
2. She would have read the book if...
3. When he had written the essay, he...

## 18.4 Active leisure

### Text 18.4.1 Exploring your world – the River Thames

In their leisure time, a lot of people like to travel and explore new places. One very popular place for leisure activities in England is along the banks beside and on the River Thames. You can explore the River Thames by boat, by bike or on foot. The river is maybe most familiar to you as it flows through the city of London, but in fact it has already travelled a long way before it reaches London. The Thames is the longest river in England, about 215 miles long from the source in Kemble in the Cotswolds to the North Sea.

The River Thames is often mentioned in English literature. In the famous novel *Three Men in a Boat* by Jerome K. Jerome, the three men travel by rowing boat from Oxford to Kingston on the River Thames. *Alice in Wonderland* was inspired by a boat trip on the Thames taken by an Oxford don named Charles Dodgson and three girls, one of whom was named Alice. As they rowed down the river he told them a story about a girl called Alice and her adventures. The story pleased the girls, so under the pen name Lewis Carroll the story was published in 1865. The famous novel *The Wind in the Willows*, by Kenneth Grahame, is also set beside, on and in the River Thames. The main characters are water-loving creatures, Mole, Ratty and Toad. Sir Arthur Conan Doyle also used the River Thames as part of the setting for some Sherlock Holmes stories. The River Thames in Charles Dickens' novels is a very different place from the delightful scenery in *Alice in Wonderland* or *The Wind in the Willows*. Dickens concentrates on the inner city River Thames in the poorer areas of London, polluted, derelict and he called it 'a deadly sewer'.

As the tourist information says:

> From its source in the Cotswolds, through the heart of some of England's most beautiful and relaxing towns, right into the centre of London, the River Thames has something for everyone. Whether you are hoping to discover more about Britain's history and

317

# 18 How we spend our free time

wildlife, or simply after a great place for boating, walking or cycling, you'll certainly find what you are looking for on the Thames. Pubs by the river, historic university towns, canoeing adventure, epic castles... the only problem is knowing where to start.

The River Thames has been described as 'liquid history' as along its banks you can visit the place where King John signed the Magna Carta at Runnymede. This is a very important early legal document which was written to protect the rights of the barons. At that time a baron was a nobleman who owned land. Further along the river is Windsor Castle, one of the world's oldest inhabited castles. Hampton Court is also on the River Thames. It was King Henry VIII's favourite palace and is very beautiful.

## Five free things to do beside the River Thames

(www.visitthames.co.uk)

**1 Pick some locks**
Each lock along the Thames has its own story to tell and there are 44 in total! Whichever you visit, you can relax and watch the boats go by, and perhaps even chat to the lock keepers about the river's secret history.

**2 Spot wildlife**
The River Thames has an abundance of wildlife all year round. From voles, kingfishers, red kites and swans to the rare otter, there's a world of nature to be discovered. Don't forget to take your camera!

**3 Get active**
If getting active is your way of relaxing, you can explore the entire river by walking the length of the Thames Path National Trail. If you are looking for a faster pace there are some areas of the river that you can cycle, including particularly beautiful stretches of bridleway between Reading and Goring, passing the beautiful area of Mapledurham and Hampton Court to Kingston. Cycling is also a great way to discover the Jubilee River, a man-made flood channel, buzzing with wildlife that runs between Maidenhead and Windsor.

**4 Make a date**
The Thames is there to enjoy any day of the year, but don't forget to look out for special events, too. Sporting spectacles include the Henley Royal Regatta and the Royal Windsor Triathlon, while Reading's Children's Festival and Henley's Food Festival are also worth putting in your diary.

**5 Catch a whopper**
Don't just walk beside the river – get stuck in! With around 30 species of fish, the Thames has some of the best coarse fishing in the country. All you need to do is buy a rod licence (www.envirnment-agency.gov.uk/rodlicence) and find out about day tickets, free fishing sites and special permits for lock and weir fishing.

---

Some of these paragraphs have humorous titles:
- The title of the first paragraph 'Pick some locks' has a double meaning. It could mean 'choose some locks', but the phrase is more familiar to native speakers as meaning 'break open some locks'.
- Paragraph five's 'Catch a whopper' means to catch a very big fish. A whopper is something very big but it can also be a huge lie!

http://www.visitthames.co.uk/dbimgs/Visit%20Thames/Revealing_the_River_Thames.pdf

### General comprehension

1. What range of activities is available on or near the Thames?
2. What can you do when you visit a lock?
3. Why is the Thames called 'liquid history'?

## Zoom in on grammar

**Prepositions with forms of transport**

We use *by* as the preposition in front of a form of transport:
   *by* boat, *by* plane, *by* ferry, *by* car, etc.
BUT we say *on* foot.

## Text 18.4.2 A poem about the River Thames

# 'Tamasá Reaches' *by Jenyth Worsley*

Near the railway bridge on the road to Cirencester
you pass a sign which says, 'Source of the River Thames'.
Its underground spring comes up for breath
through banks that are hardly higher than the water.
Trout are here, otters and water voles.
Take the meandering river's path through Lechlade,
whose stone-built houses keep their hidden views,
until, near Oxford, wider waters offer
residence to house-boats, fishermen and geese.

From Putney to Mortlake
leaning and pulling
oars on the rowlocks
dipping and twisting
past Barn Elms and Hammersmith
sweatshirts sodden
with splashes and straining
megaphones shouting
to dark blue and light blue
victors triumphant
stride through the water
but slumping defeated
the losers stay listless
Where fretful salt meets yellow-brownish sludge

The old Thames sang of rotting wood and skulls,
barbyl, flounders, spearheads, bits of rope.
Its pre-Celt name was Tamasá, dark river.
At this forum of city stone and water
the old trades are gone. Docks and wharves,
where two thousand masts once glittered on the water
with cargoes of tea and sugar, silk and oranges,
and steamers to the Empire bruised the oceans
with holds of steel and missionary trunks –
all are transformed by the new commerce,
the new river gods, Finance and the Media.
Below their elegant glass powerhouses
sailboards catch the wind
and wine and coffee bars displace
oyster and apple stalls.

Jenyth Worsley, © May 2003, www.riverthamessociety.org.uk/poetryc4.htm

## General comprehension

1. How does the poet structure the poem? Think about where she begins and ends the poem for a clue.
2. The first stanza is relatively peaceful but the second stanza is full of movement. What is the poet describing? Who are the people on the river?
3. What was the old name of the River Thames?
4. What changes does the final stanza describe? What has been lost and what is new now?

# 18 How we spend our free time

The boat race described in this poem is an annual rowing competition on the River Thames between Oxford and Cambridge Universities. The first race was in 1829. The course is 4.2 miles (6.8 km). The race is held at the end of March or beginning of April. There are eight rowers in each team plus the cox. Cambridge are the light blues and Oxford the dark blues. Thousands of people watch the race from the banks of the river and millions more watch it live on television.

## Text handling

Match the following words to their nearest meanings according to the text.

1. meander
2. triumphant
3. sodden
4. megaphone
5. slump
6. listless
7. sludge
8. glitter
9. displace
10. wharf/wharves

move slowly and aimlessly / force out / jetty / sparkle / loudhailer / lacking energy / very happy / very wet / fall or sink down / thick mud.

## Zoom in on grammar

**Comparative and superlative adjectives**

|  | Adjective | Comparative | Superlative |
|---|---|---|---|
| Short adjectives | cold | colder | coldest |
| Long adjectives i.e. those with 2 or 3 syllables | exclusive | more exclusive | most exclusive |
| **SPELLING HINTS** | | | |
| Words which end in *e* | fine | finer | finest |
| Words which end in *y* | heavy | heavier | heaviest |
| Some consonants are doubled | big | bigger | biggest |

## Grammar in context

**Comparative and superlative adjectives**

Text 18.4.1 uses superlatives to help describe and promote the River Thames and the attractions around it ('The Thames is the *longest* river...', 'Further along the river is Windsor Castle, one of the *oldest* inhabited castles...').

Write your own sentences, using superlative adjectives, to describe the River Thames. Use the following starters and the superlative form of the adjective that follows. An example is given.

**Example:** The River Thames / longest

The River Thames is the longest river in England.

1. *The Wind in the Willows* / famous
2. scenery along the Thames / varied
3. King John / rich
4. Hampton Court / beautiful
5. otters / rare
6. cycling / fast
7. fishing / fun

## Interactive oral activity

After reading the poem, use the following questions to begin a discussion in small groups.

- What have you learnt about the River Thames from this poem?
- How does the river change along its course?
- What impression does it make on you at each of the three stages?
- Who/what lives and plays along the river?
- What does the poet mean by the expression 'the new river gods'?
- What is your impression of this poem?

## Text 18.4.3 Safety from flooding

### The Thames Barrier

The River Thames flows into the North Sea, but of course there is always a danger of flooding if there is a tidal surge. London is protected by the Thames Barrier.

The Thames Barrier is one of the largest movable 1 _____ barriers in the world. The Environment Agency runs and 2 _____ the Thames Barrier as well as the capital's other flood defences.

The barrier spans 520 metres 3 _____ the River Thames near Woolwich, and it protects 125 square kilometres of central London from flooding caused by tidal surges.

It became operational 4 _____ and has 10 steel gates that can be raised into position across the River Thames. When raised, the main gates stand as high as a five-storey building and as wide as the opening of Tower Bridge. Each main gate 5 _____ 3,300 tonnes.

### Visiting

Visiting the Information Centre is a great way to learn more about the Thames Barrier. Open Thursday to Sunday to the public and groups. Open Monday to Wednesday for private group talks and conferences.

*http://www.environment-agency.gov.uk/homeandleisure/floods/38353.aspx*

### General comprehension

1. What is the aim of the Thames Barrier?
2. In the event of a flood, which area would be the worst affected?
3. Does the Thames Barrier prevent flooding caused by heavy rain?
4. Is the Thames Barrier always raised?
5. When is the Information Centre unavailable to the public?

### Text handling

Choose the correct words to fill the spaces in the text.
1. flood, fire, swamp, riot
2. holds, defends, maintains
3. below, above, across, beneath
4. in 1982, at 1982
5. holds, carries, weighs, remains

# 18.5 Leisure activities around the world

## Text 18.5.1 Surfing in Scotland

Surfing in Scotland is a totally exhilarating experience, and once tried it's hard to fight off the bug to give it a go again and again. Once the first rush of cold is over, it makes little difference whether you're in Hawaii or Machrihanish, as Scotland has some of the best surf conditions in Europe.

# 18 How we spend our free time

For many surfers based in the UK the 5mm neoprene wetsuit has probably been the greatest invention ever created. It's what keeps the cold out when the waves are at their best, normally in mid winter!

**Where to go:**
If you're lucky enough to own your own gear then you have a wide choice of surf spots to choose from. Our Surf Scotland factsheet gives much more detailed information.

Some of the best spots for surfing can be found between East Lothian near Edinburgh and Eyemouth in the Scottish Borders in the east.

In the west there are great breaks off Machrihanish in the Kintyre peninsula, the Island of Tiree and particularly off the west coast of Lewis in the Outer Hebrides.

In the north the waves off Thurso are an expert's dream and this area has also hosted the O'Neill Highland Open for the last two years.

**Want to get started?**
There are a number of excellent surf shops situated near the best surf spots and with tuition starting from £30 for the afternoon (incl. hire) you'd really have to be a couch potato to miss out on those waves!

*http://active.visitscotland.com/activeoffers/water/surfing/*

## General comprehension

1. When you think of surfing, which countries come to mind?
2. Had you heard about surfing in Scotland? Why (not)?
3. What is special about surfing in Scotland?
4. What kind of equipment is needed?
5. When is the best time to go surfing?

## Text handling

Complete the sentence beginnings below by choosing the best ending. Check your answers against the text.

1. Surfing in Scotland is...
2. Our Surf Scotland factsheet gives...
3. It's what keeps the cold out...
4. There are a number of excellent surf shops...
5. You'd really have to be a couch potato...
6. The 5mm neoprene wetsuit has probably been...
7. It's hard to fight off the bug...
8. In the north the waves off Thurso are...

A ... an expert's dream.
B ... the greatest invention ever created.
C ... to miss out on those waves!
D ... situated near the best surf spots.
E ... much more detailed information.
F ... to give it a go again and again.
G ... when the waves are at their best.
H ... a totally exhilarating experience.

## Grammar in context

**Superlative adjectives continued**
Find and list the superlatives used in the text.

### Individual oral activity

Describe the picture below and then relate it to one of your options themes. Talk for three minutes, making connections to ideas that you relate to the subject of the picture.

**Left** A new world view?

## Text 18.5.2 New Zealand: Sports and leisure

### Sports and leisure

New Zealanders have always been good a) _____ making their own fun – pottering b) _____ the garden, reading, walking c) _____ the hills or heading d) _____ the beach. But they're also happy to pay e) _____ pleasures such as dining f) _____, taking a flutter g) _____ Lotto, going to the movies or the theatre, or to professional rugby matches. Whichever way it comes, Kiwis enjoy their time h) _____ play.

**1** _____

For many New Zealanders, home is still where they like to spend their leisure hours – watching television, reading books, or working on their houses. Three in five adult New Zealanders spend time in their gardens. Increasingly, Kiwis are finding fun in the city by eating out, listening to live music, watching movies, or cruising the shops.

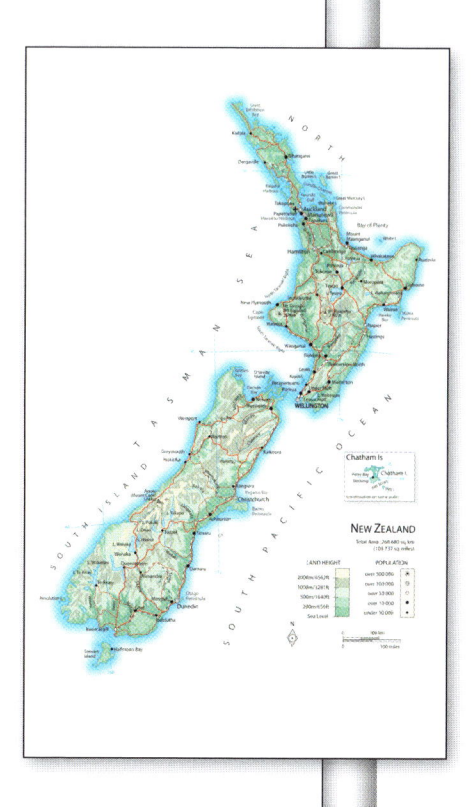

# 18  How we spend our free time

### 2. ............................................................

For much of the 20th century New Zealanders gambled either on horse races or on lotteries, especially the Golden Kiwi. Since 1989 new forms of gambling have emerged: Lotto, gaming machines, casinos and betting on sports results.

### 3. ............................................................

Almost three-quarters of New Zealanders go walking for enjoyment. Some are keen trampers, and in winter, skiing and snowboarding are popular. Others hunt pigs, deer or goats.

The beach is a favourite place for New Zealanders to enjoy themselves. They swim, surf, snorkel, dive, sail and windsurf. A quarter of adult New Zealanders go fishing, whether angling for trout, surfcasting at the beach or netting whitebait.

More people are involved in informal recreation than in organised sport.

### 4. ............................................................

New Zealand has as many passionate followers and fans of sport as other Western countries – and probably a higher percentage of people who actually play sport.

The most popular sport to play is golf. New Zealand has more golf courses per head than any other country.

Rugby (rugby union) is the most popular sport to watch. It has been regarded as the national game since a famous tour to Britain by the All Blacks team in 1905. Rugby is now a professional game, as are rugby league and soccer. Cricket is the major organised summer sport.

Among women the most popular sport to play and watch is netball.

*Jock Phillips. 'Sports and leisure', Te Ara – The Encyclopedia of New Zealand, updated December 20 2012,*

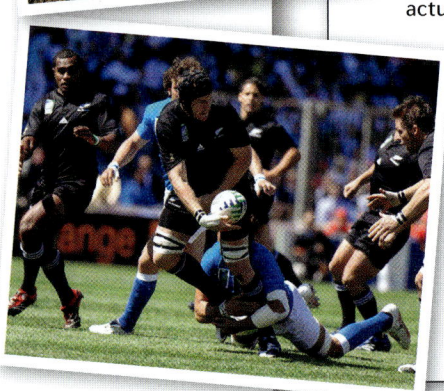

http://www.teara.govt.nz/en/sports-and-leisure

**Above** Outdoor pursuits in New Zealand

## General comprehension

1  Replace the missing paragraph headings.

  a) Organised sports     c) Gambling
  b) Informal sports      d) Home and city

2  True or false? Justify your answer with a relevant brief quotation from the text.

  a) A lot of New Zealanders enjoy pottery.
  b) New Zealanders do not enjoy eating out.
  c) Leisure time spent at home is very popular in New Zealand.
  d) New Zealanders love going on a cruise ship.
  e) Gaming machines and casinos have always been popular in New Zealand.
  f) There are few activities to do at the beach.
  g) The percentage of people in New Zealand who play sport is higher than in other Western countries.
  h) Organised sport is more popular than informal sport.
  i) New Zealand has more golf courses than people.
  j) Rugby is top of the popular spectator sports.

## Text handling

1. Replace these prepositions in the first paragraph:

   at / on / for / in / out / in / for / at

2. Explain the following expressions from the text in your own words.
   a) good at making their own fun
   b) pottering in the garden
   c) taking a flutter
   d) whichever way it comes
   e) cruising the shops
   f) keen trampers
   g) passionate followers

## Individual oral activity

Do more research about New Zealand and prepare a three- to four-minute presentation on your findings.

## Interactive oral activity

Choose one of the photos alongside the text to discuss. Describe what you can see and what connections you can make, and talk about the related lifestyle, with any possible advantages and disadvantages which you may imagine. The talk should be between three and four minutes.

## Exam practice

# Exercises

### Written assignment 1: Essay title (HL)

You recently read a newspaper article which claimed that young people have no interests other than the internet. You disagree strongly with this and have decided to write to the editor explaining why.
Write the letter. Write between 250 and 400 words.

### Written assignment 2: Personal response (HL)

Give a personal response to the following stimulus and justify it.
Choose any text type that you have studied in class.
Write between 150 and 250 words.

> 'Guard well your spare moments. They are like uncut diamonds. Discard them and their value will never be known. Improve them and they will become the brightest gems in a useful life.'
>
> *Ralph Waldo Emerson (1803–1882)*

### Written assignment 3: Essay title (SL)

You have been asked to write an article about a sporting activity for the school magazine. You decide to interview one of your sports coaches, who is an enthusiastic athlete.
Write the transcript of interview in 250–400 words.

325

# 19 Customs and traditions around the English-speaking world

Opposite  Maori mask from Rotorua, New Zealand.

## Objectives
- To practise formal letter writing
- To revise the comparative and superlative uses of adjectives
- To compare the use of two past tenses: the present perfect and the past simple
- To read about customs and traditions
- To discuss customs and traditions from your own country

# 19.1 New Zealand: Maori

## Text 19.1.1 Maori culture and tattoos

Have you noticed that tattoos have emerged as a fashion statement? They have become a form of body art that is loved or hated depending on your age, culture, or both. Some work environments ban tattoos and some cultures deem them to be socially unacceptable, while in others they are considered an integral part of their identity. However they are viewed, the history of tattoos and tattooing is a long and fascinating one.

**Maori are the indigenous people of New Zealand and they represent a fascinating and mysterious culture, with origins thought to be traceable to the islands of Eastern Polynesia. An important part of the Maori culture is the application of tattoos – each tattoo having a traditional design and representing a specific event in the life of the wearer, recognizable as such by all Maori.**

### Ta moko

The tattoo, or *ta moko* as it is named in the Maori language, is the permanent marking of the body and face, and is applied to both men and women at various stages in their life. Although it is often referred to as a Maori 'tattoo', it is different from Western tattoos because the skin is not punctured with needles, but is chiselled with a sharp instrument (*uhi*) before being filled with ink. The result is that if you run your hand over a Maori tattoo there are grooves that you can feel – a tattoo done with a needle is, on the other hand, perfectly flat. The *moko* is an outward and visible demonstration – it shows the commitment and respect that the wearer has for his or her culture, and has designated areas where it may be placed; for men, these include the face, lips, arms, thighs, and buttocks, while women traditionally wear tattoos on their chin and lips.

### A Maori ritual

The adolescent Maori would receive a first tattoo to mark their 'coming of age' in a ritual attended by members of his or her family and tribe. Other tattoos would be symbols of courage or status, and as such were far more than mere decoration. The tattoo process was painful, with tattoos done to the face particularly liable to cause initial swelling and make eating and drinking agonizing. Thus, many of the rituals would be accompanied not only by music and dance, but also by periods of fasting.

327

# 19 Customs and traditions around the English-speaking world

### European influence

The arrival of European settlers in New Zealand had an influence on the Maori and their culture, with the general consensus being that it was a negative one. The new settlers had little appreciation or respect for the traditions and customs of the Maori and imposed their own on the native people. As a result, in the 19th century the tradition of tattooing lost its attraction. It is only since the 1980s that there has been a revival of the Maori culture and a sense of pride restored, bringing with it a renewed interest in the old traditions.

### Cultural renaissance

It can be said that the Maori culture has undergone a renaissance since the 1980s. The popularity of the Maori tattoo has extended far beyond New Zealand to Western Europe and America, where, with the tribal-style tattoo increasingly popular, young people wear *ta moko* designs, sometimes without even realizing their significance. The past two decades have not only brought a revival of the traditional chiselled tattoos – an interest in the Maori language has reawakened and the cultural heritage has flourished, finding expression in a range of courses that have been offered to help the Maori access their own traditions.

---

In his novel *Whale Rider*, Witi Ihimaera, the New Zealand author, writes about the legend of the beginnings of the Maori and connects it to present-day life.

## General comprehension

1. New Zealand is home to the Maori people. According to the text, where did they come from?
2. In the first sentence of the text, which word tells you that Maori are the original inhabitants of New Zealand?
3. 'The Maori culture has undergone a renaissance.' What is the meaning of the word 'renaissance'? What implications does this have for Maori culture?
4. According to the text, Maori tattoos have always been more than merely decoration. What is their significance?
5. What was the effect of the European settlers on the Maori?
6. What part of the ritual of tattooing was determined by a physical necessity?

## Text handling

Match the beginnings of the sentences with the most suitable endings.

| | | | |
|---|---|---|---|
| 1 | The history of the Maori people... | A | ... is a long and fascinating one. |
| 2 | The migration of the Maori people from Polynesia... | B | ... is now popular with non-Maoris. |
| 3 | Maoris must have had... | C | ... were originally made by carving into the skin. |
| 4 | In the past fifty years... | D | ... probably did not occur in one journey. |
| 5 | The traditional Maori tattoos... | E | ... excellent navigation skills. |
| 6 | Important events in life... | F | ... a decline in many Maori traditions. |
| 7 | European settlers in the 19th century caused... | G | ... were commemorated by adding tattoos to different parts of the body. |
| 8 | The typical design of Maori tattoos... | H | ... there has been a re-awakening of interest in Maori culture. |

## Zoom in on grammar

**Present perfect or past simple?**

In the above text there are a number of sentences containing the present perfect tense or the past simple. Let us examine the difference in usage.

The following sentences contain the present perfect form of the verb.

> The Maori culture *has undergone* a renaissance since the 1980s.
> An interest in the Maori language *has reawakened*.
> The past two decades *have* not only *brought* a revival of the tattoo.

The present perfect is used because the writer is talking about an event in an unfinished period: 'Since the 1980s' and 'In the past two decades' are periods that continue up to the present and are not finished. The present perfect always has a connection with the present.

Now look at this example from the text in the past simple.

> In the 19th century the tradition of tattooing lost its attraction.

The past simple is used because the writer is talking about the 19th century – a period which is finished. The past simple tells us only about the past.

## Grammar in context

**Present perfect or past simple?**

Put the verb in the correct form, present perfect (*I have done*) or past simple (*I did*).

**Example:** I *didn't play* (not/play) tennis last year.

1. My grandfather died 15 years ago. I _____ (never/meet) him.
2. Our director _____ (be) at this school since 2014.
3. Susan _____ (live) in France before she came here.
4. We _____ (eat) a lot of cake at the school picnic.
5. Since the 1960s there _____ (not/be) a band as good as The Beatles.
6. The carnival celebrations at school _____ (start) after the first break at ten o'clock.
7. There _____ (be) three accidents in the gym this week.
8. Ian loves London; he _____ (live) there for six years and does not intend to return to his home country.
9. When I _____ (live) in London I went to the theatre as often as possible.
10. I don't know the new PE teacher; I _____ (not/meet) him yet.

## Interactive oral activity

Tattoos have become popular in many cultures among young people in recent years. In groups of two or three discuss the following question:

> To what extent are tattoos an expression of fashion amongst teenagers and should be accepted by parents and schools as a matter of individual choice?

Be prepared to share your opinions with the class.

## Individual oral activity

Describe the picture and then relate it to one of your options themes. Talk for three minutes, making connections to ideas that you relate to the subject of the picture.

**Right** Beauty is taught and learned.

# 19 Customs and traditions around the English-speaking world

## 19.2 The traditions of Christmas

### Text 19.2.1 St Nicholas to Santa: The surprising origins of Mr Claus

`http://news.nationalgeographic.com/news/2013/12/131219-santa-claus-origin-history-christmas-facts-st-nicholas/facts-st-nicholas/`

## Santa's evolution includes a round-the-world ride that rivals the one he does on Christmas Eve *by Brian Handwerk*

Any kid can tell you where Santa Claus is from—the North Pole. But his historical journey is even longer and more fantastic than his annual, one-night circumnavigation of the globe.

The modern American Santa was born in the Mediterranean, evolved across northern Europe, and finally assumed his now-familiar form on the shores of the New World. Who is this Santa, and how did he get here?

Images of St. Nicholas, Santa's original ancestor, vary considerably, but none of them look much like the red-cheeked, white-bearded old man we see everywhere today.

**From St. Nicholas to Santa**

How did this St. Nicholas become a North Pole-dwelling bringer of Christmas gifts? The original saint was a Greek born 280 years after Christ who became bishop of Myra, a small Roman town in modern Turkey. Nicholas was neither fat nor jolly but developed a reputation as a fiery, wiry, and defiant defender of church doctrine during the "Great Persecution," when Bibles were put to the torch and priests made to renounce Christianity or face execution.

Nicholas defied these edicts and spent years in prison before Constantine brought Christianity to prominence in his empire. Nicholas's fame lived long after his death (on December 6 of some unknown year in the mid-fourth century) because he was associated with many miracles, and reverence for him continues to this day independent of his Santa Claus connection.

Nicholas rose to prominence among the saints because he was the patron of so many groups, ranging from sailors to entire nations. By about 1200, explained University of Manitoba historian Gerry Bowler, author of *Santa Claus: A Biography*, he became known as a patron of children and magical gift bringer.

http://news.nationalgeographic.com/news/2013/12/131219-santa-claus-origin-history-christmas-facts-st-nicholas/facts-st-nicholas/

For several hundred years, circa 1200 to 1500, St. Nicholas was the unchallenged bringer of gifts and the toast of celebrations centred around his day, December 6. The strict saint took on some aspects of earlier European deities, like the Roman Saturn or the Norse Odin, who appeared as white-bearded men and had magical powers like flight. He also ensured that kids toed the line by saying their prayers and practicing good behavior.

But after the Protestant Reformation, saints like Nicholas fell out of favor across much of northern Europe. "That was problematic," Bowler said. "You still love your kids, but now who is going to bring them the gifts?"

Bowler said that, in many cases, that job fell to baby Jesus, and the date was moved to Christmas rather than December 6. "But the infant's carrying capacity is very limited, and he's not very scary either," Bowler said. "So the Christ child was often given a scary helper to do the lugging of presents and the threatening of kids that doesn't seem appropriate coming from the baby Jesus."

### St. Nicholas in America

In the Netherlands, kids and families simply refused to give up St. Nicholas as a gift bringer. They brought "Sinterklaas" and his enduring name with them to New World colonies.

But in early America Christmas wasn't much like the modern holiday. The holiday was shunned in New England, and elsewhere it had become a bit like the pagan Saturnalia that once occupied its place on the calendar. "It was celebrated as a kind of outdoor, alcohol-fueled, rowdy community blowout," Bowler said. "That's what it had become in England as well. And there was no particular, magical gift bringer."

In 1821 an anonymous illustrated poem entitled "The Children's Friend" went much further in shaping the modern Santa and associating him with Christmas. "Here we finally have the appearance of a Santa Claus," Bowler said. "They've taken the magical gift-bringing figure of St. Nicholas, stripped him of any religious characteristics, and dressed this Santa in the furs of those shaggy Germanic gift bringers."

In 1822 Clement Clarke Moore wrote "A Visit From St. Nicholas," also known as "The Night Before Christmas," for his six children, with no intention of adding to the fledgling Santa Claus phenomenon. It was published anonymously the next year, and to this day the plump, jolly Santa described therein rides a sleigh driven by eight familiar reindeer.

"It went viral," Bowler said. But familiar as the poem is, it still leaves much to the imagination, and the 19th century saw Santa appear in different-colored clothing, in sizes from miniature to massive, and in a variety of different guises. It wasn't until the late 19th century, he added, that the image of Santa became standardized as a full-size adult, dressed in red with white fur trim, venturing out from the North Pole in a reindeer-driven sleigh and keeping an eye on children's behavior.

*Published*
*December 20 2013*

http://news.nationalgeographic.com/news/2013/12/131219-santa-claus-origin-history-christmas-facts-st-nicholas/

## General comprehension

1. Which saint is the figure of Santa Claus based on?
2. Do some research and find out more about the Bishop of Myra, who became a saint.
3. What is the significance of 6 December in the Santa Claus tradition, and why was this date chosen?
4. According to the text, how did the tradition of Santa Claus become established in the USA?
5. Two poems are mentioned in the text; both had a significant influence on the development of the Santa Claus tradition. What were the titles of the poems and when did they appear?
6. According to the text, what was the status of the Christian religion in the time when the Bishop of Myra lived: 280 years after Christ?
7. At what point in history did the idea of a sleigh pulled by reindeers emerge?

# 19 Customs and traditions around the English-speaking world

### Text handling

The register of the text is semi-formal. Look at the following expressions from the text and suggest more formal ways of writing the sentences they appear in.

1 to put to the torch
2 to toe the line
3 a rowdy community blowout
4 keeping an eye on children's behavior

### Interactive oral activity

Christmas is celebrated around the world by both Christians and non-Christians. In groups of three, share your own experiences of the Christmas celebrations in the countries you have lived or stayed in. In addition – if you have lived in a country where these traditions are not recognised, discuss the reasons for this. Are there other traditions that involve the giving of presents to children and adults?

At the end of your discussion share your thoughts with the other groups.

## 19.3 The traditions of Valentine's Day

Roses are red
Violets are blue
Sugar is sweet
And so are you

When I wake in the morning, I think of you
When I sleep at night, I dream of you
When I see you, I know it's true
I love you

Happy Valentine's Day to the sweetest valentine I could want. You are my sweetheart, and I am glad you're mine.

My Valentine!
So many of my smiles begin with you

Even though we are apart
You are my special Valentine
Your voice warms my heart
I'm so glad that you're mine

Longing to tell you
Of this dream I have
Vision of the future
Ever together…

## Text 19.3.1 Valentine's Day

14th February is (Saint) Valentine's Day, an important date on the calendar in English-speaking countries around the world, and in recent years it has also spread to countries where the first language is not English! Celebrations are held in the name of St Valentine, but who was this mysterious saint? And why do the celebrations involve boys and girls exchanging tokens of love by sending each other gifts and romantic cards containing verses of the sweetest kind?

Valentine's Day is supposed to have originated in the days of ancient Rome but the romantic traditions became known in their present form in Victorian England. It was in the nineteenth century that the tradition of exchanging cards started. Today they frequently contain the colours pink or red, and many include the image of a heart: an international symbol which depicts love. Although these tokens may often express friendship and affection amongst all age groups, for girls and boys the most exciting part of receiving a Valentine's card is the element of mystery, because the card can often be sent anonymously to someone they admire or love.

### The legends of St Valentine

There are numerous accounts of the origins of Valentine's Day, but all are united in the name of the man who gave the day his name. One story is that Valentine lived in third-century Rome and was a priest. The Emperor Claudius II at that time considered soldiers to be more efficient if they did not have wives and families and he banned marriage for his soldiers. Valentine thought the idea was harsh and unfair, and he performed marriages in secret for young lovers. When Valentine's defiant actions were discovered, Claudius ordered his death.

Another story suggests that Valentine helped Christians who suffered imprisonment in the time of the Roman persecution. For these actions he was himself imprisoned and wrote love letters to his girlfriend, which he signed 'from your Valentine', an expression which is frequently used today.

You may choose which story you prefer, and even do some research and find more explanations of who this person was, but the truth behind the stories will probably remain hidden from us. He is nevertheless considered to have been a sympathetic, heroic and romantic figure.

Valentine's Day is celebrated in the United Kingdom, the United States of America, Canada, Mexico, many European countries, Australia and New Zealand. Around 1900 the advances in printing technology made it possible for greetings cards to be sent in large numbers. Today, the Greeting Card Association estimates that 1 billion Valentine's cards are sent each year.

### General comprehension

1. Is Valentine's Day a tradition limited to the USA?
2. In what period of history did our present-day form of celebrating Valentine's Day originate?
3. According to the text, what is the attraction of an anonymous card?
4. Is the story of St Valentine historical fact?
5. Which three adjectives are used to describe the historical figure of Valentine?
6. What technological development accelerated the popularity of sending cards?

# 19 Customs and traditions around the English-speaking world

> ### Grammar in context
>
> **Comparative and superlative adjectives**
>
> Make a list of at least ten adjectives used in the text. Identify how the comparative and superlative forms will be constructed – you can refer to the 'Zoom in on grammar' feature for Text 18.5.1 (page 320) to help you with this.

### Written work

Your class has been working on a project to support the work of a local hospice for terminally ill children. You have decided that it would be a good idea to raise money for this hospice by selling Valentine's Day cards that your class has made. Write a formal letter to the principal of your school explaining your plans and asking for permission to sell the cards in school.

Your letter will contain information about the reasons for your request to sell Valentine's Day cards. It will be persuasive, but at the same time polite and respectful.

Write at least 250 words.

## 19.4 Superstitions

### Text 19.4.1 The surprising origins of common superstitions

Superstition is widespread. It is not limited to any period in history and is not a phenomenon linked only to a certain group of people. Even those who consider themselves to be well-educated and intelligent will sometimes indulge in some acknowledgment of superstition. Maybe they will not want to stay in room 13 in a hotel, or they will make a detour around a ladder leaning against a wall rather than walking under it.

Psychologists tell us that the root of superstition is based on the need to have control. It is a form of self-possession in situations where the outcome of events may be uncertain. Some superstitious forms of behaviour are widespread – such as that associated with the number 13 – whereas others are individual, such as in the case of an athlete who always wears the same socks in a competition. It is the belief that we can somehow influence the outcome of events positively by adhering to certain behaviours.

### "It's bad luck to open an umbrella indoors"

Many people avoid opening an umbrella indoors – but why? In some countries umbrellas offer protection from the sun (in the form of a parasol) rather than the rain. In ancient Egypt it was considered that opening your sunshade indoors was disrespectful to the sun god, and that he would punish you with a curse of bad luck. But the idea of bad things being a consequence of opening an umbrella also has more practical associations. In Victorian times, the awkward, spiky metal frames could easily knock over frangible ornaments in the over-furnished sitting rooms and parlours, thus bad luck was said to follow the opening of the umbrella.

### "It's bad luck to walk under a leaning ladder."

This superstition is also said to have originated 5,000 years ago in Egypt. The Egyptians had deep respect for the power of the triangle, as is demonstrated in the construction of the burial tombs of their leaders. The triangle represented the trinity of the gods, and there was a belief that you should not knowingly pass through a triangle because of its supernatural powers. A ladder leaning against a wall forms such a triangle, hence there would have been a need to avoid walking under it. Christians later usurped this superstition, adopting the ladder as a significant omen because one had rested against the crucifix on which Christ died. It therefore became associated with betrayal and death.

### "When you spill salt, always toss some over your shoulder to avoid bad luck"

In Roman times salt was a much-valued commodity. It was even used as payment for work done – a fact that is reflected in the origin of the word 'salary'. From the same period, the saying 'he is not worth his salt' was a show of disdain for a soldier, as members of the army were given salt allowances. But the idea that salt is powerful enough to ward off evil dates back to three-and-a-half thousand years before the birth of Christ; if an ancient Sumerian spilled some salt, they would throw a pinch over their shoulder because they believed that spilling salt was a warning that an evil spirit – one that could be repelled by salt! – was behind you.

### "Always 'God Bless' a sneeze"

There is a common custom in English-speaking countries to say 'God bless you' when a person sneezes. Originally, people explained the act of sneezing by saying that the body was expelling evil spirits that were trying to establish themselves in it. This link to something unpleasant was consolidated in the Middle Ages, when disease and illness could have a terrible effect on communities as they spread from one person to another. In AD590, Pope Gregory exhorted the phrase 'God bless you' to be used as an appeal for divine intervention because sneezing was a common sign that a person was in the first stages of the deadly bubonic plague, and that death was on its way.

### "A black cat crossing your path is lucky/unlucky"

In some cultures the black cat is a lucky sign, but in some cultures it is quite the opposite. The ancient Egyptians had a cult of cat worship, and human sacrifices would sometimes be made in the temple where the cats resided. When potential victims had been brought there, the person to be sacrificed would be the one in front of whom the cat sat – bad luck! If the cat passed you by, however, that was naturally seen as good luck. This may explain the root of the conflicting good and bad luck beliefs. In addition, during the Middle Ages, black cats in Britain were always considered to be the companions of witches, and it was also believed that witches could change themselves into cats. Furthermore, the colour black is, of course, always associated with the devil and bad luck.

# 19 Customs and traditions around the English-speaking world

**"Hang a horseshoe on your door open-end-up for good luck"**

This superstition is said to have originated in Greece and was later taken up by the Romans, who carried the superstition to other parts of Europe. In ancient Greece, iron was considered to have the ability to ward off evil. Horseshoes were made of iron, and they had an added element of appeal in being shaped like a crescent moon, which was considered by the Greeks to bring fertility and good luck. Thus the horseshoe became a good luck charm. In Britain in the Middle Ages there was widespread fear of witchcraft, and people latched on to whatever they thought could help protect them from the evil powers that they perceived were lurking everywhere. Horseshoes were one of the objects that people would fix to their doors – being careful that the 'open' end was at the top, otherwise the good luck contained in the horseshoe would drain out. People also thought that witches were afraid of horses.

## General comprehension

1. 'It's bad luck to open umbrellas indoors.'
    a) According to the text, what two reasons are given for declaring it to be unlucky to open umbrellas indoors?
    b) The word 'frangible' is seldom used, but by looking at the context, what do you think it means?
    c) Which of the two explanations do you think most contributes to the idea of bad luck?

2. 'It's bad luck to walk under a leaning ladder.'
    a) What mathematical shape had religious symbolism for the ancient Egyptians 5,000 years ago?
    b) Explain the belief that became established 3,000 years later.
    c) Which word in the text means 'took over'?

3. 'When you spill salt, toss some over your left shoulder to avoid bad luck.'
    a) Explain the connection between 'salt' and 'salary'.
    b) Which of the following definitions do you think probably best fits the meaning of 'opprobrium'?
        payment / strong criticism / praise
    c) Why do you think salt was considered to be so valuable in Roman times?

4. 'Always "God bless" a sneeze.'
    a) When did the phrase 'God bless you' become linked to disease?
    b) How do you think this phrase spread to countries other than the one in which Pope Gregory lived?
    c) According to the text, what did sneezing mean before people associated it with deadly disease?

5. 'A black cat crossing your path is lucky/unlucky.'
    a) Why were black cats thought to be unlucky in Britain during the Middle Ages?
    b) This superstition is the only one mentioned that is associated with contradictory beliefs. What are they?
    c) If black is associated with evil, what do you think white is associated with?

6. 'Hang a horseshoe on your door open end up.'
    a) For the ancient Greeks, what was a symbol of fertility?
    b) Describe the shape of a 'crescent' without using your hands.
    c) Which phrasal verb in the text has the same meaning as 'to repel' or 'turn aside'?

### Interactive oral activity

In groups of three, discuss the superstitions that exist in the countries you come from. You may not know the origins but you probably know the beliefs. Listen to each other and ask questions about what you hear to help the conversation flow more smoothly.

## Written work

Follow up the oral work with some research into superstitions in your country and their origins. Think about how you will present the results of your research. Write an introduction to the country you are from before you start explaining the superstitions.

Write between 350 and 400 words.

## Exam practice

# Exercises

### Written assignment 1: Essay title (HL)

Your school magazine is running a series of articles on international-mindedness. You interview a student from your school about one of the traditions in their country. Write an article for the magazine based on the interview. Write between 250 and 400 words.

### Written assignment 2: Personal response (HL)

Give a personal response to the following stimulus and justify it. Choose any text type you have studied in class. Write between 150 and 250 words.

> 'It takes an endless amount of history to make even a little tradition.'
>
> *Henry James, American writer*

### Written assignment 3: Essay title (SL)

You are an ambassador at your school and hear that a new student is starting soon. Write an email welcoming them to the school and tell them about a tradition that is being celebrated in the area at the time when they arrive. Write between 250 and 400 words.

# 20

## Commonwealth customs and traditions

## Objectives
- To review the use of 'too' and 'not... either'
- To review the expression of quantity using 'of' + an uncountable noun
- To practise making comparisons
- To practise sentence structures with 'although/but'
- To discuss and compare customs and traditions in other cultures and our own

**Opposite** An embroidered royal crown – but what does that mean in the 21st century?

# 20.1 An introduction to the Commonwealth

## Text 20.1.1 The Commonwealth

The Commonwealth has existed for 60 years. Countries which were colonies of the British Empire became independent but maintained their ties to Great Britain by becoming member countries of the Commonwealth. Many of these countries have retained customs and traditions from the time when they were British colonies, as well as their own special customs and traditions.

English has remained the language most used in the Commonwealth countries. There are 50+ member countries with over 2 billion people. These member countries are in Africa, Asia, the Americas, Europe and the Pacific and are among the world's largest, smallest, richest and poorest countries. The members agree to The Commonwealth's values and principles and share a commitment to world peace, democracy and human rights. All member countries have an equal say in discussions and debates – no matter how large or small, or how rich or poor they are. As a result, even the smallest member countries are heard and have a full voice in decision-making.

The British monarch, at present Queen Elizabeth II, is the head of the Commonwealth, but this is only a symbolic position. Members of the Royal Family regularly visit Commonwealth countries.

The Commonwealth countries have a shared common interest in sports, culture and education. For example, cricket, rugby, rugby 7s and netball are popular sports in Commonwealth countries. The major sporting event, which attracts a great deal of media attention and reminds everyone that the Commonwealth exists, is the Commonwealth Games, which take place every 4 years. It is the third-largest multi-sports event after the Summer and Winter Olympic Games. The venues for the Commonwealth Games are spread across the member states: New Delhi, India, in 2010; Glasgow, Scotland, in 2014 and the Gold Coast, Australia, in 2018. There are ten core sports which must always be offered at the Commonwealth Games, including track and field, lawn bowls, netball and rugby 7s. Up to seven additional sports, such as cycling or gymnastics, can also be included. This amounts to a maximum of 17 sports over 11 days.

# 20 Commonwealth customs and traditions

## Member countries by region

### Africa
Botswana, Cameroon, Ghana, Kenya, Lesotho, Malawi, Mauritius, Mozambique, Namibia, Nigeria, Rwanda, Seychelles, Sierra Leone, South Africa, Swaziland, Uganda, United Republic of Tanzania, Zambia

### Asia
Bangladesh, Brunei Darussalam, India, Malaysia, Maldives, Pakistan, Singapore, Sri Lanka

### Caribbean and Americas
Antigua and Barbuda, Barbados, Belize, Canada, Dominica, Grenada, Guyana, Jamaica, St Kitts and Nevis, St Lucia, St Vincent and the Grenadines, Trinidad and Tobago

### Europe
Cyprus, Malta, United Kingdom

### Pacific
Australia, Fiji, Kiribati, Nauru, New Zealand, Papua New Guinea, Samoa, Solomon Islands, Tonga, Tuvalu, Vanuatu

## General comprehension

True or false? Justify your answer with a relevant brief quotation from the text.

1. Any country can join the Commonwealth.
2. Many of the Commonwealth countries have dropped the old British customs and traditions.
3. In the Commonwealth, although some countries are very poor, they are still included in decision-making.
4. The head of the Commonwealth is the reigning British monarch.
5. The Commonwealth is an organisation which people often hear about.
6. The Commonwealth Games are larger than the Olympic Games.
7. Some unusual sports are played in the Commonwealth Games.
8. The countries of the Commonwealth are spread across the world.

## Text handling

Match the words to their meanings as used in the text. There are more meanings than you need.

| | | | |
|---|---|---|---|
| 1 | to maintain | A | the school head |
| 2 | to retain | B | to keep |
| 3 | commitment | C | many different sports |
| 4 | symbolic | D | kind of deer |
| 5 | monarch | E | to sustain |
| 6 | venue | F | representative |
| 7 | multi-sports | G | where something takes place |
| 8 | colony | H | royal ruler |
| | | I | to keep clean |
| | | J | loyalty |
| | | K | country controlled by a more powerful country |

## Individual oral activity

Do some more research about the Commonwealth or the Commonwealth Games and prepare a four-minute talk for your class.

## Individual oral activity

Describe the picture and then relate it to one of your options themes. Talk for three minutes, making connections to ideas that you relate to the subject of the picture.

**Right** Power play?

## Exam hints

- Do not learn your speech off by heart: use note cards with short headings.
- Make your talk lively and interesting.
- Have a clear beginning and ending.
- Think about using rhetorical questions to keep the audience's attention.
- Structure your speech carefully to help the listener follow your points.
- Look at the audience when you are speaking.
- Speak clearly and confidently.
- Be ready to answer questions at the end.

## 20.2 Customs and traditions of some Commonwealth countries

### Text 20.2.1 Scotland

Although people sometimes think Scotland and England are the same, or that Scotland is part of England, in fact Scotland has many customs and traditions which the English do not share.

http://www.scotlands-enchanting-kingdom.com/hogmanay-customs.html

# Hogmanay customs

Hogmanay is an important part of the Scottish Calendar, as well as celebrating Burns Supper, so let's explore some traditional Hogmanay Customs. First of all, 'What is Hogmanay?' If this is a word you are unfamiliar with – it means "New Year's Eve". While bringing in the New Year is celebrated around the world, it is probably more important to many Scots than the celebration of Christmas. The origins of the word are not clear. Some say it is the celebration of the winter solstice among the Nords, while others say it is part of the Gaelic New Year's celebration of Samhain. In Europe, the winter solstice celebrations came from the ancient celebration of Saturnalia, which originated from a Roman winter festival. Other folk believe it came from the celebration of the 'Yule' by The Vikings which later contributed to the Twelve Days of Christmas. Other occasions we celebrate include Valentine's Day and of course St Andrew's Day.

# 20 Commonwealth customs and traditions

http://www.scotlands-enchanting-kingdom.com/hogmanay-customs.html

During the Protestant Reformation period, Christmas was banned as it was seen as being Roman Catholic and the celebrations were banned in Scotland for hundreds of years. Indeed it wasn't even a public holiday and many people had to work, and somewhere along the line New Year became the time for having time off work, celebrating with family and it became a much bigger and more important celebration than Christmas. But the excesses of Hogmanay were not liked by the Church either, and many of the celebrations went 'underground'. These days, however, all the Hogmanay customs and celebrations are seen as a huge part of Scottish culture, and now have spread throughout the world.

## The pre-Hogmanay preparations

The 31st December was often a busy day, a day of preparing to see the Old Year out, and to bring in the New Year. Many businesses closed early to allow the workforce time to go home and clean their houses from top to bottom. This cleaning began in the days when everyone had open fires, and fireplaces in particular had to be cleaned. It was considered bad luck by some to go into the New Year with a dirty house. The tradition of cleaning the house for New Year still exists today.

Debt was another thing that was seen as unlucky and most households would endeavour to get rid of all debt before midnight on 31st. It wasn't good to go into the New Year with debt. It's a pity this tradition has stopped as we now live in times when most people enter the New Year with the debt of over-spending at Christmas.

## Midnight

Having family and friends together and partying is one of the main Hogmanay customs. As soon as the clock strikes 12, bells are rung in every town and village throughout the land. Many places have street parties with the villagers for example all meeting in the village square to bring in the New Year together. These days of course fireworks are also set off, so it can be quite a spectacular sight, depending on where you are. So even if you don't want to go outside, you can open your curtains, see the fireworks, hear the bells and the music.

Immediately after midnight it is traditional for everyone to stand in a circle, cross over their arms, hold hands with people on either side and sing Robert Burns' "Auld Lang Syne". People from around the world sing this, although they often only know the chorus:

*"Should auld acquaintance be forgot and never brought to mind?*
*Should auld acquaintance be forgot and auld lang syne?*

*For auld lang syne, my dear, for auld lang syne,*
*We'll take a cup o kindness yet, for auld lang syne."*

But of course the hospitable Scottish welcoming of family, friends and neighbours also extended to strangers, and is still very much a custom today. Everyone is in a happy mood, with or without a "drink" and the belief is very much that a line is drawn under the Old Year and the New one welcomed in on a happy note.

## First footing

This is another one of those Hogmanay customs which is still practised today. It literally means the "first foot" to step into a house after midnight is still common in Scotland. This is still full of tradition and even superstition. In order to ensure good luck for the house, the "first foot" over the door should be male, dark; and of course everyone "first footing" should take symbolic gifts such coal, shortbread, salt, black bun and whisky. (Blonds & redheads, and especially females with this hair colouring, first-footers were considered "bad luck".) These gifts meant the household would be safe and warm and have enough food for the year. These days, however, whisky and perhaps shortbread and the famous black bun are the most common gifts first-footers take. Of course most hosts would have plenty of food and drink in to offer to their guests.

> 'Auld lang syne' is an old Scots phrase which means 'times gone by'.

http://www.scotlands-enchanting-kingdom.com/hogmanay-customs.html

## General comprehension

1. What does the word 'Hogmanay' mean?
2. Can the origins of the word be explained?
3. In Scotland, why was New Year celebrated more than Christmas in the past?
4. Which other Scottish celebrations are mentioned in the text?
5. What happens on 31 December in Scotland?
6. In the past, what was the general opinion about still having debt from the old year in the new year?
7. Why does the author think it is a pity that the tradition of getting rid of debt has died out?
8. Describe three things that happen at midnight.
9. What is necessary for the first footing to bring good luck?
10. What constitutes good luck according to the text?

## Text handling

1. Explain the following sentences from the text more simply in your own words.
   a) But the excesses of Hogmanay were not liked by the Church either, and many of the celebrations went 'underground'.
   b) In order to ensure good luck for the house, the 'first foot' over the door should be male, dark.
   c) But of course the hospitable Scottish welcoming of family, friends and neighbours also extended to strangers, and is still very much a custom today.

2. Match the words to the meanings below. Note: There are more meanings than you need.

   | | | | |
   |---|---|---|---|
   | I | hospitality | A | very old |
   | II | endeavour | B | people with red faces |
   | III | spectacular | C | friendliness |
   | IV | redheads | D | breathtaking |
   | V | ancient | E | try |
   | | | F | people with red hair |
   | | | G | wearing spectacles |
   | | | H | near a hospital |
   | | | I | superstition |
   | | | J | belief in magic |

## Interactive oral activity

Make groups of three; as far as possible each should be the member of a different cultural group. Write some bullet points about the traditions your culture has to celebrate the New Year. If more than one person is from the same cultural group, think about other countries you have visited where you may be able to talk about the New Year traditions practised there. If this is also challenging, think about your own family's traditions for New Year.

Each person should take a role for this discussion: one person is the opener, who begins the discussion; one person is the facilitator, who makes sure everyone contributes; and the third person is the time-keeper, who makes sure no one speaks for too long. Remember to listen carefully to each other and to ask questions too.

## Zoom in on grammar

### 'Too' and 'not... either'

With *too*, if something is true of one part of a sentence, it is also true of the other. The sentence is positive.

The Scots celebrate Valentine's Day, and the English do *too*.
= The Scots and English both celebrate Valentine's day. It is true of both.

With *not... either*, if something is not so for one part of the sentence, it is the same for the other. The sentence is negative.

I can't ski, and my husband *can't either*.
= Neither person can ski.

343

# 20 Commonwealth customs and traditions

> ### Grammar in context
>
> **'Too' and 'not... either'**
>
> Make sentences using *too* or *not... either*.
>
> 1. She loves ice cream... (her sister)
> 2. He can't remember when Valentine's Day is... (his best friend)
> 3. He hasn't got a motorbike... (I)
> 4. She has finished all her homework... (her friend)
> 5. I am tired... (my brother)

## Written work

Imagine that you were staying with a Scottish family at Hogmanay. Write a diary entry which describes your impressions and feelings after being part of this celebration. Write between 250 and 400 words.

## Text 20.2.2 Sri Lanka

Sri Lanka is a tear-shaped island south of India in the Indian Ocean. The capital city, Colombo, is on the west coast. Sri Lanka has a very interesting population demographic, which is a mix of diverse ethnicities: Sinhalese, Sri Lankan Moors, Indian Tamils and Sri Lankan Tamils. With such a range of ethnic groups, a number of religions are practised on the island. Approximately 69% of the inhabitants are Buddhist, 7% Muslim, 7% Hindu, 6% Christian, with a smattering of other smaller religious groups.

Sri Lanka has a history of colonization, with Portuguese settlers first arriving in the 16th century. Next came the Dutch, who took over from the Portuguese in the 17th century, and finally the island was subsumed into the British Empire in the 18th century. The country became independent in 1948, changing its name from Ceylon to Sri Lanka in 1972.

The language spoken by the majority of inhabitants is Sinhala (or Sinhalese or Singalese): sinhala means 'lion's blood'. The name 'Sri Lanka' is also easily interpretable: sri means 'blessed' and lanka means 'island'. The second most widely spoken language is Tamil, while English is often used for business. With such a wide variety of ethnicities in the population, there are obviously many different, but also many shared, customs and traditions; these also vary from region to region.

The main staple food is rice, which is eaten at most meals, often with vegetables, eggs, meat, or fish. Chilli peppers, spices, and coconut milk are also used in Sri Lankan cooking. Sri Lankans tend to drink tea, with or without milk, to accompany their food.

When meeting and greeting people, older Sri Lankans clasp their hands with the palms together and hold them at chin level, as if in prayer. This is called namaste. Younger people also shake hands when greeting each other.

Sri Lankans celebrate the New Year in April, and their calendar follows the movement of the moon. The celebrations begin with a thorough cleaning of the house, followed by the preparation of a meal of special traditional dishes, possibly taking a bath in coconut milk, and then the lighting of an oil lamp. After a family has celebrated together, the festivities continue outside with their neighbours and friends.

Types of traditional clothing vary, of course, according to religious belief. Muslim women usually wear black. Other women who are close to marrying age or are already married often wear a kadyan sari. The name kadyan comes from the last royal capital of Ceylon, Kadyan, which is about 120 kilometres from the present capital Colombo. Men traditionally wear a sarong, which is a piece of cloth tied around the waist like a towel. This can be worn long, or folded in half to be shorter in hot weather.

As a result of the British colonization of Sri Lanka, or Ceylon as it was called at that time, many typically British sports such as football, rugby union, cricket, tennis, badminton, and netball were introduced and are still popular with Sri Lankans today. A traditional Sri Lankan pastime is stilt fishing, a method wherein the fisherman sits on a cross bar called a petta tied to a vertical pole driven into the sand a few meters offshore; from this high position, the fisherman casts his line and waits until a fish comes along to be caught.

Music and dance are also very popular. One of the oldest traditional types of dance is the Kandyan Dance, which has been performed for over 2,500 years. According to legend, it originates from a magic ritual that freed a king who had been bewitched by a spell. It is traditionally danced only by men wearing elaborate headdresses and costumes, and is accompanied only by percussion, with instruments including finger bells, drums, and cymbals. Some Kandyan Dances are named after animals and based on their movements, such as the slow and stolid sway of an elephant, the way a horse trots or gallops, or the gliding and swooping of a hawk.

### General comprehension

1. Describe the shape of Sri Lanka in your own words.
2. What is unusual about the population of Sri Lanka?
3. Which three languages are used in Sri Lanka the most?
4. Describe the food eaten in Sri Lanka.
5. How do traditional older citizens greet each other?
6. When is the New Year celebrated?

### Text handling

Replace the missing words correctly in this passage. Then check your answers against the text.

Sri Lanka is a tear-shaped island a)_____ of India in the Indian Ocean. The b)_____ city Colombo is on the west coast. Sri Lanka has a very interesting c)_____ demographic, which is a d)_____ of diverse ethnicities: Sinhalese, Sri Lankan Moors, Indian Tamils and Sri Lankan Tamils. With such a e)_____ of f)_____ groups, a number of religions are g)_____ on the island. Approximately 69% of the h)_____ are Buddhist, 7% Muslim, 7% Hindu, 6% Christian, with a smattering of other smaller i)_____ groups.

range, practised, religious, inhabitants, ethnic, mix, capital, population, south

## Written work (HL)

'The customs and fashions of men change like leaves on the bough, some of which go and others come.'

*Dante Alighieri, Italian writer*

Write a personal response to the stimulus and justify it. Choose a suitable text type from those you have studied to make your writing most effective.
Write between 150 and 250 words.

# 20 Commonwealth customs and traditions

## Text 20.2.3 The Bahamas

`http://www.bahamas.co.uk/about-the-bahamas/facts/history`

Over the centuries, each new population that has settled in The Bahamas, with their different backgrounds, traditions and beliefs, has shaped Bahamian culture into the unique, colourful patchwork of life and lifestyles that it is today.

The Islands of The Bahamas gained independence from Great Britain on 10 July 1973, which is celebrated as Bahamian Independence Day. As a member of the British Commonwealth, The Bahamas has a symbolic link to Great Britain, with an appointed Governor-General representing the Queen of England, and as an example of the continued British influence on Bahamian government, who continues observance of the historical Changing of the Guards. There is much pomp and ceremony, as the Royal Bahamas Police Force Band performs. The ceremony takes place at Government House (the office and residence of the Governor-General) in Nassau every two weeks.

- The name "Bahamas" comes from the Spanish *baja mar* meaning shallow sea, and is an archipelago of over 700 islands stretching over 258,998 square km in the western Atlantic Ocean.

- The Lucayan Indians were the original inhabitants: they lived throughout The Bahamas between 900 and 1500 A.D.

- Christopher Columbus (the first European visitor) made his first landfall in the New World on San Salvador (called Guanahani by the Lucayan Indians) in 1492.

- The first English settlers on Eleuthera shipped braselitto wood to Boston to thank the people of Massachusetts for the support they had given. The proceeds from the sale of this precious wood were used to purchase the land for Harvard College, which eventually became Harvard University.

- Charles Town on New Providence Island was burnt to the ground by the Spanish in 1684, but later rebuilt and renamed Nassau in 1695 in honor of King William III (formerly prince of Orange-Nassau).

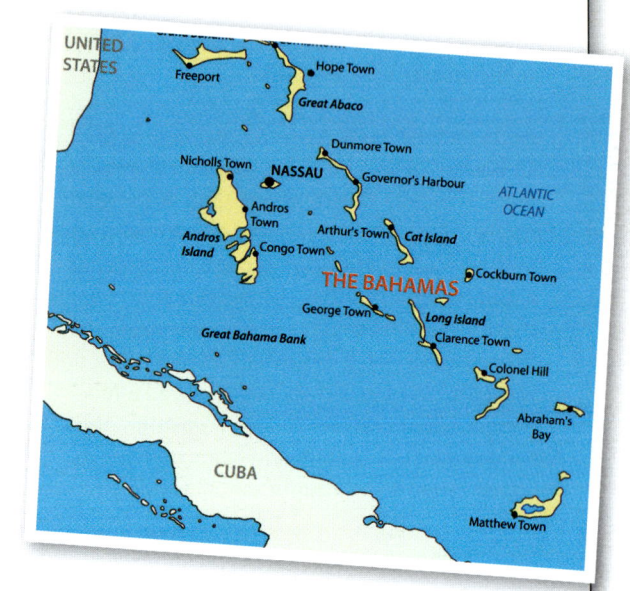

- The Bahamas House of Assembly first officially convened in 1729.

- In 1788 The Bahamas exported 450 tons of cotton to Britain.

- Nassau was officially promoted as a fashionable winter season resort in 1898 with the Hotel and Steam Ship Service Act.

- The Bahama Islands became the free and sovereign Commonwealth of The Bahamas on 10 July 1973, ending 325 years of British rule (but remains part of the Commonwealth).

- The Bahamas, with over 270 years of democratic rule, is one of the most politically stable countries in the world.

- The Bahamas does not have an army.

## The festival of Junkanoo

Although the roots of the Junkanoo parade remain subject to long and passionate debates, what is agreed is that, after centuries of practice, today's cultural extravaganzas have become the most entertaining street carnivals of not only The Bahamas, but also the world at large.

With the costumes, dance and music inspired by a different theme each time, preparations for the Boxing Day, New Year's Day and summer time Junkanoo literally take months and bring together men and women from all different walks of life.

### The history of The Bahamas Junkanoo

Legend has it that you haven't needed an excuse to party in The Bahamas for well over 500 years. But ask folks here at the top of the Caribbean how The Bahamas Junkanoo Tradition got started and they'll all tell you a different story; with many believing it was established by John Canoe, a legendary West African Prince, who outwitted the English and became a local hero; and others suspecting it comes from the French 'gens inconnus,' which translates as 'unknown' or 'masked people'.

The most popular belief, however, is that it developed from the days of slavery. The influx of Loyalists in the late 18th Century brought many enslaved people who were given three days off at Christmas, which they celebrated by singing and dancing in colourful masks, travelling from house to house, often on stilts. Junkanoo nearly vanished after slavery was abolished but the revival of the festival in The Bahamas now provides entertainment for many thousands.

Long before the spectacular 'rush-out', the exuberant Junkanoo dance troupes – groups of up to 1,000 – will have been busy rehearsing their dazzling routines. The musicians will have perfected the hypnotic rhythms they'll perform day and night on a cacophony of goatskin drums, cowbells, whistles and horns, and the imaginative costume designers will have worked non-stop to weave their own special magic with beautifully coloured crepe paper and cardboard.

As the Junkanoo parade moves through the streets of downtown Nassau in the early hours of the morning (generally from 2am to 10am), the energy of the dancers and the beat of the music motivates the vast crowds of supporters and spectators to start moving in their seats, or on their feet, or in the trees, or on balconies - wherever they have found a spot from which to watch this soul-stirring festival! At the end of the famous Junkanoo procession, judges award cash prizes for the best music, best costume and best overall group presentation.

http://www.bahamas.co.uk/about-the-bahamas/facts/history

| General comprehension |
|---|

1   When did The Bahamas become independent?
2   How long was the British rule in The Bahamas?
3   Which typically British ceremony still takes place regularly in The Bahamas?
4   Who was the first European in The Bahamas?
5   Where did the money come from to buy the land for Harvard College?
6   Is the origin of the Junkanoo festival clear? Which theories do people have?
7   How did the slaves use to celebrate their free days?
8   Which musical instruments are used to accompany the dancing?
9   When do the Junkanoo festivals take place?
10  What effect does the music have on the audience?

# 20 Commonwealth customs and traditions

## Text handling

Find words in the text which have the closest meanings to the words below. The words are in the order they appear in the text.

1. first people who lived there
2. first piece of land seen after a long sea voyage
3. holiday place
4. outsmart
5. not free
6. discontinued / done away with
7. full of energy
8. loud noise of various different sounds together
9. union / joining together
10. mostly

## Written work

Imagine you are on holiday in The Bahamas. Write an email to a friend describing where you are, what kind of activities you are enjoying and so on. Write between 250 and 400 words.

### Exam hints

- Remember, an email to a friend is an informal piece of writing, so choose your register and tone appropriately.
- Remember to structure your work carefully and use paragraphing effectively.
- Use descriptive language with a good range of vocabulary to make your writing interesting.

### Zoom in on grammar

**Sentence structure**

Read the following sentence from the text again:

> *Although* the roots of the Junkanoo parade remain subject to long and passionate debates, what is agreed is that, after centuries of practice, today's cultural extravaganzas have become the *most entertaining street carnivals of not only The Bahamas, but also the world at large.*

*Although* has a very similar meaning to *but*, so that the sentence could be re-arranged in this way:

> It is agreed that, after centuries of practice, today's cultural extravaganzas have become the most entertaining street carnivals of not only The Bahamas, but also the world at large, *but* the roots of the Junkanoo parade remain subject to long and passionate debates.

### Grammar in context

**Sentence structure**

Change these sentences from 'although' to 'but'.

1. Although Mary studied very hard, she didn't pass the exam.
2. Although the weather is really bad, we will still go for a run.
3. Although we had never met before, we understood each other immediately.

Now change these sentences from 'but' to 'although'.

4. She had a terrible headache, but she still went to the concert and enjoyed it.
5. Sarah speaks Chinese well, but she cannot write it at all.
6. I would love to come to visit you, but I really do not have the time.

### Zoom in on grammar

**Comparison**

We can compare two things by using a comparative adjective followed by *than*:

I think English is *easier than* Arabic.

Or we can use *less... than*:

A holiday near home is *less expensive than* a holiday in The Bahamas.

Alternatively, we can use *the least*:

Camping is *the least expensive* holiday

To express equality, we can use *as... as*:

A holiday in the Bahamas is *as expensive as* a holiday in Sri Lanka.

### Grammar in context

**Comparison**

Now write your own sentences using all four forms in the above examples at least once, comparing Sri Lanka with The Bahamas.

## 20.3 England

In countries throughout the Commonwealth some British customs and traditions continue to be followed. One of these is the tradition of drinking copious amounts of tea, which you may have heard about. But how did this begin? Here are some quotes about tea from famous people.

### Text 20.3.1 Afternoon tea

"If you are cold, tea will warm you;
if you are too heated, it will cool you;
If you are depressed, it will cheer you;
If you are excited, it will calm you."

— *William Ewart Gladstone*

"Take some more tea," the March Hare said to Alice, very earnestly.

"I've had nothing yet," Alice replied in an offended tone, "so I can't take more."

"You mean you can't take less," said the Hatter: "it's very easy to take more than nothing."

"Nobody asked your opinion," said Alice.

— *Lewis Carroll,* Alice in Wonderland

"You can never get a cup of tea large enough or a book long enough to suit me."

— *C.S. Lewis*

http://www.goodreads.com/quotes/tag/tea

# 20 Commonwealth customs and traditions

## Text 20.3.2 The origins of tea

## What is tea?

Tea is a drink that is produced from the combination of cured leaves of the Camellia Sinensis (tea) plant with hot water. Tea is the second most popular beverage in the world, after water. The Camellia Sinensis plant thrives growing in tropical and sub-tropical climates, hence its origins on the continents of Asia and Africa.

The first recorded consumption in the history of tea was in China, as early as the 10th century BC. Soon, it spread to Korea and Japan. During the 16th century Portuguese exploration of the Far East, tea was traded with the West and as a result, the tea plant spread to the rest of the world. It has been said that Catherine of Braganza, the Portuguese queen consort to King Charles II, introduced the drinking of tea in the UK.

It wasn't until the 19th century until tea drinking became a common pastime for all the social classes. Now, tea drinking occurs as a daily occurrence not just as a component of afternoon tea or a tea party. In the UK, it has become a 'national drink' of sorts and an integral part of British culture.

### Types of tea

There are (at least) four different types of tea: white tea, green tea, oolong tea and black tea. The type of tea depends on the type of tea processing it undergoes. Tea leaves are liable to wilt and therefore oxidise, if they are not dried quickly. As the chlorophyll breaks down, the tea leaves darken and release tannins; this process is called fermentation in the tea industry.

Tea as we know it in the UK is more often sold as teabags. Most popular brands of teabags are usually made by blending a variety of different teas together. Tea is renowned for

**Below** Different types of tea leaves.

containing numerous antioxidants and less caffeine than coffee. There are also certain teas used in diets and tea for weight loss.

## Afternoon tea

Afternoon tea is a tea-related ritual, introduced in Britain in the early 1840s. It evolved as a mini meal to stem the hunger and anticipation of an evening meal at 8pm.

Afternoon tea is a meal composed of sandwiches (usually cut delicately into 'fingers'), scones with clotted cream and jam, sweet pastries and cakes. Interestingly, scones were not a common feature of early afternoon tea and were only introduced in the twentieth century.

Afternoon tea was initially developed as a private social event for ladies who climbed the echelons of society. It was only when Queen Victoria engaged in the afternoon tea ritual that it became a formal occasion on a larger scale, known as 'tea receptions'.

These receptions could have as many as two hundred guests with an open 'at home' invitation to visit between 4pm and 7pm, during which they could come and go as they pleased; this was the genesis of the afternoon tea as we know it.

In Britain today afternoon tea is usually enjoyed as an occasional indulgence or to celebrate a special event such as a birthday, or a pre-wedding or baby shower party with a group of friends.

http://www.afternoontea.co.uk/information/the-afternoon-tea-menu

**Above** A typically British afternoon tea.

### General comprehension

1. What kind of climate does the tea plant need to grow and thrive?
2. Where did tea drinking begin and when?
3. Who is said to have introduced tea drinking to the UK?
4. When did tea drinking become normal for everyone in the UK?
5. What determines the kind of tea that is produced?
6. Why must tea leaves be dried quickly?
7. Is tea healthy? Why?
8. Why did the custom of taking afternoon tea develop?
9. What are the main ingredients of afternoon tea?
10. Is afternoon tea taken on a regular basis nowadays?

# 20 Commonwealth customs and traditions

## Text handling

**1** Add the relevant verb or noun to complete the table below.

| Noun | Verb |
|---|---|
| combination | |
| consumption | |
| occurrence | |
| | to produce |
| | to grow |
| exploration | |
| | to introduce |
| | to oxidise |
| fermentation | |
| | to indulge |
| | to develop |
| anticipation | |
| | to celebrate |

**2** Look again at the text and find the terms below. Try to understand them using context clues and then explain them in your own words.

a) liable to wilt
b) to stem the hunger
c) ladies who climb the echelons of society
d) the genesis of
e) an occasional indulgence
f) a baby shower party

**3** Replace the missing words and expressions from the list below. Then check your answers with the text.

occasion / invitation / genesis / renowned / initially / engaged / blending

Tea as we know it in the UK is more often sold as teabags. Most popular brands of teabags are usually made by a)_____ a variety of different teas together. Tea is b)_____ for containing numerous antioxidants and less caffeine than coffee. There are also certain teas used in diets and tea for weight loss.

Afternoon tea was c)_____ developed as a private social event for ladies who climbed the echelons of society. It was only when Queen Victoria d)_____ in the afternoon tea ritual that it became a formal e)_____ on a larger scale, known as 'tea receptions'.

These receptions could have as many as two hundred guests with an open 'at home' f)_____ to visit between 4pm and 7pm, during which they could come and go as they pleased; this was the g)_____ of the afternoon tea as we know it.

## Zoom in on grammar

**Expression of quantity using 'of' + an uncountable noun**

We say: a cup *of tea*, a pot *of tea*, a glass *of milk*, a litre *of milk*, a bucket *of water*, two litres *of water*.

Before uncountable nouns (tea, milk, water, etc.) we can express the quantity:
- as a container – a cup, a pot, a bottle, a bucket, etc.
- or as a measurement – a litre, two litres, a pint, etc.

Before *of* + an uncountable noun, we can also use other words, for example, *a piece* of cake, *a slice* of bread, *a loaf* of bread, *a bar* of chocolate.

## Grammar in context

**Expression of quantity using 'of' + an uncountable noun**

Complete the following sentences using an *of*-construction.

**Example:** She ate a _____ chocolate. *She ate a piece of chocolate.*

1 She cut a _____ bread.
2 He drank a _____ beer.
3 He bought a _____ land.
4 She made a _____ tea.
5 The bucket holds a _____ water.

## Individual oral activity

Describe the picture below and then relate it to one of your options themes. Talk for three minutes, making connections to ideas that you relate to the subject of the picture.

**Left** Traditions prevail across time and place.

## Written work

Write an article for your school magazine about the importance of preserving cultural identity (see the *Exam hints* feature for Text 1.3.1 for some helpful tips). Write between 250 and 400 words.

# Exam practice

## Exercises

**Written assignment 1: Essay title (HL)**

Recently you visited a country with some very interesting customs and traditions. Write an email to a friend describing what you experienced. Write between 250 and 400 words.

**Written assignment 2: Personal response (HL)**

Based on the following stimulus, give a personal response and justify it. Choose any text type that you have studied in class. Write between 150 and 250 words.

'If you reject the food, ignore the customs, fear the religion and avoid the people, you might better stay at home.'

*James A. Michener, American author*

**Written assignment 3: Essay title (SL)**

Write a blog about some of the differences between the customs and traditions of your own country and those of another country which you have studied or visited.

# 21 Repairing the body

## Objectives

- To discuss the ethical implications of some methods
- To practise writing a diary entry
- To use the construction 'to look forward to something'
- To examine the use of 'may' and 'might'
- To read about scientific solutions to the need to repair the body

**Opposite** X-ray showing a human skull.

## 21.1 Transplanting a limb

**Below** Plastic surgeon Simon Kay with Mark Cahill, the first person to receive a hand transplant in the UK.

### Text 21.1.1 UK's first hand transplant patient describes progress

**The first person in the UK to have a hand transplant has spoken about his progress nearly two months after the operation**

2:45AM GMT Feb 19 2013

Mark Cahill, 51, told the *Radio Times* how he is learning to live with his new limb after the pioneering operation at Leeds General Infirmary on December 27.

The former pub landlord, from Greetland, near Halifax, West Yorkshire, is looking forward to the future after being unable to move his right hand for five years.

Mr Cahill told the *Radio Times* he has had no problems accepting the new hand, despite it being smaller, paler and more freckled than the other.

"I've always seen it as my hand, since the moment I woke up after the operation," he told the magazine.

He said he also feels that the fingernails have become his own.

"They grow at the same rate on both hands and they've already been cut three times. So whatever it is that makes your nails grow must come from me," he said.

Mr Cahill said he would not have been able to accept a hand that looked out of place – such as one from a female donor – but he felt anything was better than his existing hand, which he lost the use of due to severe gout.

He said: "I can see why people with two hands don't understand. But going from a hand that can't do anything, it doesn't seem unusual. Having a hand that is warm, that feels, that is part of you, is much better than a prosthetic limb."

The new limb is already able to feel pins and needles if Mr Cahill taps a nerve in his arm and the next stage of his recovery should see the feeling returning.

Within the next few months, he should be able to use his hand to pick things up and tie his shoelaces.

Mr Cahill has no regrets about the surgery, despite having to take immunosuppressant drugs for the

# 21 Repairing the body

rest of his life and suffering a rejection scare three days after the operation.

"The future's changed. Now I've got something to look forward to," he said.

Leeds Teaching Hospitals announced in late 2011 that it was starting to look for candidates for hand or arm transplants. Potential patients went through a series of health checks and psychological assessment to ensure they had carefully considered the implications of the procedure.

Mr Cahill, who is married to Sylvia and has one daughter, was one of two potential candidates when the donated limb became available on Boxing Day. The hospital said he was selected because he was the best tissue match.

The operation, by a team led by consultant plastic surgeon Professor Simon Kay, used a new technique which involved Mr Cahill having his non-functioning right hand removed during the same operation as the donor hand was transplanted.

This procedure allowed very accurate restoration of nerve structures and it is believed to be the first time this approach has been used, surgeons said.

http://www.telegraph.co.uk/health/healthnews/9879513/UKs-first-hand-transplant-patient-describes-progress

## General comprehension

1. What was the reason Mark Cahill needed a hand transplant?
2. According to the text, what are two indications that the transplanted hand has been accepted by Mark Cahill's body?
3. The operation was the first of its kind. Which word in the text makes this clear?
4. What is Mark Cahill looking forward to doing within the next few months?

## Text handling

Match the words on the left with the meanings that are closest to their usage in the text. There are more choices than you need.

| | | | | | |
|---|---|---|---|---|---|
| 1 | limb | A | quantity | F | hand or arm |
| 2 | freckled | B | artificial | G | weak |
| 3 | rate | C | false | H | possible |
| 4 | prosthetic | D | having small brown spots | I | speed |
| 5 | potential | E | donated | | |

## Zoom in on grammar

**'To look forward to something'**

*To look forward to something* means to hope for something in the future and to be happy about it. Examine these examples.

> He is *looking forward to* the future.
> He is *looking forward to* using his hand to tie his shoelaces.

When *to look forward to* is followed by a verb – *looking forward to using* – the verb after the preposition is in the *-ing* form.

**Letter writing:** Formal letters frequently end with the phrase, 'I look forward to hearing from you.'

**Note:** 'I am looking forward to' (using the present continuous) is semi-formal and 'I look forward to' (using the present simple) is formal.

## Written work

You have read about Mark Cahill's operation. Write a letter to him telling him about your reactions to this operation after you read about it. Give a reason for being interested in the information in the newspaper article. Wish him success for the future.

Remember to begin and end the letter in the accepted, formal way. Write between 250 and 350 words.

# 21.2 Tissue engineering

### Text 21.2.1 Ears and noses could be grown in lab

**Below** Sam Clompus with his new-grown right ear.

**British scientists have developed a process to grow ears and noses in a laboratory by turning stem cells from body fat into living cartilage, through tissue engineering**

Lifelike ears and noses could be grown in a laboratory and transplanted into humans using a technique developed by British scientists.

Researchers from Great Ormond Street Hospital and University College London have become the first to turn stem cells from body fat in the abdomen of children into living cartilage, through tissue engineering.

This ground-breaking procedure could help young patients who are born with debilitating facial abnormalities, such as 'microtia', where the outer ear is underdeveloped, or those who require reconstructive surgery after an accident.

Experts believe it could ultimately be utilised in many other types of transplant surgery, to help reduce the risk of the body rejecting a replacement organ.

Currently, when facial features of children with severe birth defects need to be rebuilt, surgeons have to take cartilage from other parts of the body, such as the ribs, which is an invasive and painful procedure.

Then they fashion the shape of a nose or an ear by hand, before placing this 'scaffold' under the skin of a patient.

However, using the new technique, doctors would simply be able to 'grow' a new ear or nose from scratch that would ultimately be biologically indistinguishable from the real thing.

To achieve the breakthrough, researchers took stem cells from a child's abdominal fat and then combined them with a polymer 'nano-scaffold' – almost a microscopic netting.

They then managed to manipulate this composite in a laboratory so that human cartilage tissue grew into the tiny holes within the polymer.

## 21 Repairing the body

The technique could now be used to help treat a number of conditions. For patients with 'microtia' for example, the stem cells that make the cartilage tissue could be placed in a mould so that it grew into the shape of an ear.

This new approach could also allow children to have facial reconstructive surgery earlier. At the moment surgeons have to wait until the child's ribs have grown enough to provide sufficient cartilage for reconstructing the ear. But Dr Ferretti said: "Our goal is that over time the synthetic component of the grafted ear would disappear and the grafted tissue will continue to grow with the child."

For patients like Sam Clompus, 15, of Bristol, who suffers from 'microtia', it would mean that one simpler operation could have restored his ear. Sam was born with just a nub where his right outer ear should have been.

"Growing up, at times he was self-conscious," said mother Sue, 50, a senior lecturer in nursing.

"Lots of people used to stare at him which made him feel uncomfortable. Most of his childhood he had longer hair to cover it but when he went to secondary school he wanted his hair short so then it was more noticeable.

"His schools have always been supportive, he was just known as the kid with the funny little ear, and everyone got on with it.

"When he was younger they offered Sam a prosthetic ear but we thought that was a bit too Frankenstein.

"We had looked at other options over the past few years. At first we were quite reticent because as a family we believe that you shouldn't change you appearance to fit in with what is considered normal."

Around 7,000 people are affected by 'microtia' in Britain but tens of thousands of babies are born with other kinds of facial abnormalities each year. And it could help people who have suffered accidents or trauma.

Sam's surgery was carried out by Mr Bulstrode at Great Ormond Street Hospital and Sam is 'delighted' with his new ear.

But the procedure would be far less invasive using the new technique.

"At the moment it is quite gruelling, particularly where they go in and take out the rib cartilage," added Sue.

"That is a big operation and he was sore for quite a while after that. So the new stem cells technique would mean that a fairly large part of the procedure would not be necessary, which would be a good thing."

Last year scientists at Massachusetts General Hospital in Boston proved it was possible to grow a human-like ear using animal tissue.

Previously the researchers had grown an artificial ear, the size of a baby's, on a mouse.

http://www.telegraph.co.uk/science/science-news/10670157/Ears-and-noses-could-be-grown-in-lab.html

### General comprehension

1. Two types of tissue engineering are described in the text: the old method and the new method. What is the difference between the two methods?
2. Which method was used to give Sam a new ear – the old or the new method? How do you know this? Give two quotations from the text that justify your answer.
3. For what medical condition is the word 'microtia' used?
4. Sam Clompus was given a new ear. In the part of the text that describes Sam's family's attitude to the operation, which word means that they were not eager to have the operation carried out at first?

### Text handling

What phrases in the text do these words refer to?
1. it (line 17)
2. which (line 25)
3. they (line 38)
4. it (line 46)

### Interactive oral activity

In groups of two or three, one of you will describe the picture. Discuss your reactions to the picture and also the implications that this development has for patients. Consider the possible future developments in growing 'spare parts' for repairing bodies.

Be prepared to share the ideas and thoughts you have with the other groups in the class.

## 21.3 Xenotransplantation

Text 21.3.1 Xenotransplantation – an option for organ transplants?

### What is xenotransplantation

Xenotransplantation is the name given to the transplantation of cells, tissue or organs from one species to another, for example from pigs to humans or from apes to humans.

It may seem a very modern idea, but experts in transplantation have discussed the possibilities since the beginning of the twentieth century. In fact, in the 1960s there were attempts to transplant chimpanzee kidneys to humans. There was a general consensus that chimpanzees were the animals closest to humans, a belief that has since been replaced by knowledge from research that indicates pigs might have the most resemblance to humans – as an examination of the genetic composition of pigs reveals.

Today there is a severe shortage of organs, for example human kidneys, for transplantation. Many thousands more people are waiting for a kidney donation than there are donors. As the number of donors is small, there is a significant waiting time for patients hoping for a transplant.

# 21 Repairing the body

The use of animals to relieve the demand for organs might provide patients waiting for an organ with a solution if the transplants were successful. There would also be the advantage that animal organs are not as susceptible to viruses as human organs are.

### Why is xenotransplantation a great controversy?

Despite the benefits that animal organs offer the medical world, there are ethical problems. For example:

- Is it acceptable to transplant animal organs into humans and to use animals only to harvest their organs? Do animals have rights?
- Could organs carry infectious agents that scientists are not yet aware of?

These are questions that remain to be answered.

## General comprehension

1. How long has xenotransplantation been under discussion among surgeons?
2. According to the text, are all animals equally suitable for xenotransplantation?
3. What two facts are mentioned in the text to support the idea of using organs from a different species for human transplants?

## Text handling

Which of the words given (a–c) best fits the meaning of the word from the text?

1. consensus
    a) permission
    b) agreement
    c) questionnaire

2. resemblance
    a) identity
    b) possession
    c) similarity

3. severe
    a) critical
    b) strict
    c) uncomfortable

4. significant
    a) increasing
    b) meaningful
    c) considerable

5. susceptible
    a) easily affected
    b) well-known
    c) protected

6. harvest
    a) produce
    b) gather
    c) sell

## Zoom in on grammar

**'May' and 'might'**

We use *may* and *might* to say that something is possible; when the words are used in this way there is no important difference between *may* and *might*. Examples from the text:

   It *may* seem a very modern idea.

   Pigs *might* have the most resemblance to humans.

There is also a negative form of the words:

   Pig hearts *might not* be accepted by the human body.

   Patents *may not* like the idea of having a pig heart.

Only *might not* is contracted in spoken English: Pig hearts *mightn't* be accepted..

## Text 21.3.2 *Pig-Heart Boy* by Malorie Blackman

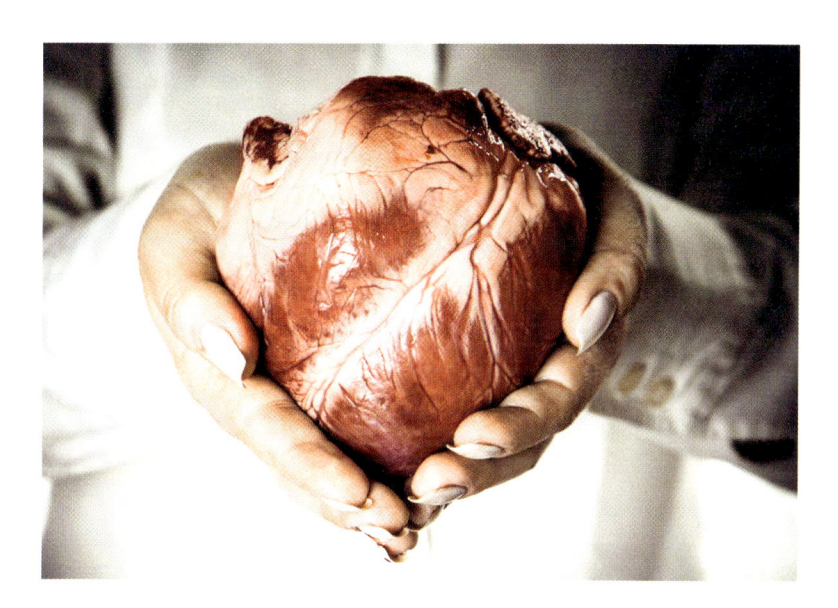

Cameron is 13 years old and very ill. If he does not get a new heart, he will die. But there are no human hearts available. Dr Bryce, a pioneering surgeon, can help. He can give Cameron a new heart – a pig's heart. Cameron wants to live, and he is a fighter, so he agrees to have this dangerous operation. But is this the right decision?

I stared at the pink pig, who totally ignored us, her snout in the food trough that lined one side of her small sty. I would have stayed longer to watch her but Dr Bryce swept on.

'And here she is! Our star – Trudy! Trudy is one of the fourth generation of pigs that have key human characteristics to some of their hormones. We truly believe that Trudy is as close as we've come to having a viable heart for transplantation into a human being.'

Well Cameron – this is it. Keep your own heart and count every beat in case it's your last. Or have a heart transplant. Simple.

I watched as the huge pig came whiffling up to us. Trudy looked straight at me. I looked back at her. She was going to die so that I could live. I told myself that pigs die every day to make bacon and pork pies and chops and sausages. This wasn't any different – except for the fact that I'd seen the pig first.

She was going to die so that I could live. Wasn't that a fair exchange?

So why did I feel so… guilty? More than guilty, I felt horrible – almost like a murderer. I told myself not to be so stupid. Trudy was just a pig. Just a pig… The words sounded like an excuse in my head.

# 21 Repairing the body

Just a pig…

People always used that argument when they wanted to use and abuse animals – or even other people. Part of the excuse used to justify slavery was that we black people were 'less than human'. And the Nazis said the same things about Jewish people. Like Mum said, it was such a convenient excuse. If other people and animals were different but equal, then you had to treat them with the same respect that you wanted for yourself. Different but 'less than' was an entirely different proposition. To some people, animals were 'less than' human in the same way that tables and chairs were 'less than' human.

It all boiled down to what I believed. And the trouble was, I did believe that animals had rights – just the same as we humans. So what was I doing here? I had the answer to that one. I was trying to save my own life. And what did that make me? Someone who was the biggest hypocrite in the world, or just someone who was desperate?

*Pig-Heart Boy by Malorie Blackman, ISBN 978-3-12-578023-1, Ernst Klett Publications, www.klett.de/ www.lektueren.com, blurb; pp. 63–4*

### General comprehension

1. The vocabulary referring to parts of an animal is often different from words referring to the parts of humans. What word in the text refers to Trudy's nose? And what is the verb that describes how she breathes through her nose?
2. 'Just a pig' – which word could replace 'just' in this phrase?
3. According to the text, name two historical events which in the past were justified by people using the phrase 'less than human'.
4. Identify the place in the excerpt where the reader learns that Cameron is black.

### Interactive oral activity

In groups, prepare to debate the 'for and against' of xenotransplantation. First decide who will speak in favour of xenotransplantation and who will be against. Then prepare some arguments to use in the discussion. Use phrases for agreeing and disagreeing, raising a new point or interrupting a speaker politely.

## Written work

Imagine you are Cameron and are waiting to have your operation to receive Trudy's heart. It is the evening before the operation. Write your diary entry to reflect your feelings: your hopes and fears for the future.

Write between 250 and 300 words.

## 21.4 The gift of life

### Text 21.4.1 Be an organ donor

`http://www.kidney.org/transplantation/beadonor.cfm`

Many people who need transplants of organs and tissues cannot get them because of a shortage of donations. Of the 118,000 Americans currently on the waiting list for a lifesaving organ transplant, more than 96,000 need a kidney, but fewer than 17,000 people receive one each year. Every day 13 people die waiting for a kidney. Organ and tissue donation helps others by giving them a second chance at life.

#### ♥ Deceased donation

Identifying yourself as an organ and/or tissue donor is simple. Simply visit the Donate Life America website at www.donatelife.net and choose your state of residence to join your state's online registry for donation. You can also declare your intentions on your driver's license.

Signing up online through your state registry or on your driver's license is a good first step in designating your wishes about donation, but letting your family or other loved ones know about your decision is vitally important. Family members are often asked to give consent for a loved one's donation, so it's important that they know your wishes.

#### ♥ Living donation

You can also consider being a living kidney donor. Living donation takes place when a living person donates an organ or part of an organ to someone in need of a transplant. The donor is most often a close family member, such as a parent, child, brother or sister. A donor can also be a more distant family member, spouse, friend or co-worker. Non-directed donors – those who donate anonymously and do not know their recipients – are also becoming more common.

*http://www.kidney.org/transplantation/beadonor.cfm*

### General comprehension

1. In your own words, explain the difference between 'deceased' and 'living' donation.
2. Make a list of organs you think could be donated by a living donor. Make a similar list for organs that could be donated by a person after their death. You may need to do some research to complete this task.
3. In the final paragraph, what do you think 'spouse' means?
4. What adjective would be used to describe a donation by a person who did not want his name to be known?
5. Which word could be used as a synonym for 'vitally' as it is used in the text?

### Individual oral activity

In small groups, discuss the issue of becoming an organ donor. Would you be willing to carry an organ donor card and donate your organs if you died unexpectedly? Think about the arguments that are used both for and against this.

Be prepared to share your ideas with the class.

# 21 Repairing the body

## Text 21.4.2 Illegal trade in organs

### An organ is sold every hour, WHO warns: Brutal black market on the rise again thanks to diseases of affluence

The U.N. public health body estimates that 10,000 organs are now traded every year, with figures soaring off the back of a huge rise in black market kidney transplants.

Wealthy patients are paying up to £128,500 for a kidney to gangs, often in China, India and Pakistan, who harvest the organs from desperate people for as little as £3,200.

Eastern Europe also has a huge market for illegal organ donation and last month the Salvation Army revealed it had rescued a woman brought to the UK to have her organs harvested.

With kidneys believed to make up 75 per cent of the black market in organs, experts believe the rise of diseases of affluence – like diabetes, high blood pressure and heart problems – is spurring the trade.

The disparity of wealth between rich countries and poor also means there is no shortage of willing customers who can pay a premium – and desperate sellers who need the cash.

Dr Luc Noel, a WHO official, told *The Guardian*: 'The stakes are so big, the profit that can be made so huge, that the temptation is out there.'

The WHO does not know how many of the 106,879 known transplant operations in 2010 were performed with illegally harvested organs, but Dr Noel believes the figure could be as high as 10 per cent.

A lack of law enforcement in some countries, and an inadequate legal framework in others meant that the traffickers urging poor people to part with an organ have it too easy, said Dr Noel.

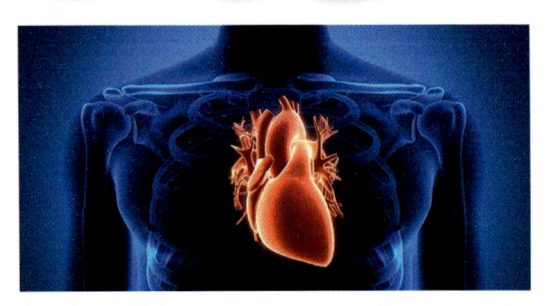

A medical source with knowledge of the situation in China told *The Guardian* anonymously that rich foreigners mainly from the Middle East and Asia are the usual customers.

'While commercial transplantation is now forbidden by law in China, that's difficult to enforce; there's been a resurgence here in the last two or three years,' he said.

He added that some of China's military hospitals are even believed to be carrying out the operations. Jim Feehally, professor of renal medicine at University Hospitals of Leicester NHS Trust, said that the key issue was one of exploitation, with poor donors often left with no medical care to recover from the brutal operations.

'The people who gain are the rich transplant patients who can afford to buy a kidney, the doctors and hospital administrators, and the middlemen, the traffickers,' he said. 'It's absolutely wrong, morally wrong.'

http://www.dailymail.co.uk/health/article-2150932/An-organ-sold-hour-WHO-warns-Brutal-black-market-ris

### General comprehension

1. What reason is suggested in the text for the increasing illegal trade in human organs?
2. What is a synonym for 'affluence'?
3. What are the three 'diseases of affluence' mentioned in the text?
4. Does the WHO (World Health Organization) know how many of the operations carried out in 2010 used organs that had been obtained legally? Which sentence justifies your answer?
5. Why is it relatively easy in some countries to operate a black market in organs?

## Text handling

Of the statements A to J, tick the five that are true according to the text; one has been done as an example.

- **A** Diseases linked to a wealthy lifestyle are the cause of the increase in the illegal trade in human organs.
- **B** 24 organs are sold every hour.
- **C** Kidneys are the organs most frequently traded on the black market. ✔
- **D** Donors on the black market give their organs willingly because they are in need of money.
- **E** It is not easy to find poor people who will donate an organ because of the strict laws.
- **F** There are many rich customers willing to pay for organs sold on the black market.
- **G** The chance to make a big profit makes criminals take the risk of getting caught.
- **H** There have been fewer transplants done in China in the last two or three years.
- **I** The profits to be made in organ sales are extremely high.
- **J** The fact that organs save lives makes all transplantation morally acceptable.

## Written work

You have been asked to speak to the student body at your school about the world-wide illegal trade in organs. You feel that one part of the solution could be to increase the number of people who are willing to become organ donors in the event of their death. You want to encourage the students at your school who are over the age of 16 to consider becoming organ donors. Write the text of your speech.

Write between 350 and 400 words.

## Exam practice

# Exercises

### Written assignment 1: Essay title (HL)

The illegal trade in organs is becoming an increasing problem. Write an essay explaining why this is the case and make suggestions how the problem could be solved. Write between 250 and 400 words.

### Written assignment 2: Personal response (HL)

Give a personal response to the following stimulus and justify it. Choose any text type you have studied in class. Write between 150 and 250 words.

> 'Any sufficiently advanced technology is indistinguishable from magic.'
>
> *Arthur C. Clarke, British science-fiction writer*

### Written assignment 3: Essay title (SL)

You feel strongly that everyone should agree to donate their organs after they die. Write an article on this subject for your school magazine. Write between 250 and 400 words.

# 22 Technology and mankind

**Opposite** Car assembly by robot welding in Germany – how does this affect society?

## Objectives
- To practise time conjunctions
- To review verbs and nouns with prefixes
- To discuss the effect technology has on our lives
- To consider the importance of robots in our lives

# 22.1 Technology and mankind

Text 22.1.1 How texting stops us walking tall

**Texting on a mobile phone forces the body into a hunched position which can lead to poor posture and balance and make walking around dangerous, academics say**

By Sarah Knapton,
Science Correspondent
7.00AM GMT Jan 23 2014

It has taken millions of years of evolution for humans to walk upright but it appears texting could be undoing our natural posture. Hunching over to type or read a text message causes people to hunch, swerve, slow down and lose their balance, a study suggests.

Researchers asked 26 volunteers to walk at a comfortable pace without a phone then monitored them as they read or text or typed a message. A computer which tracked the body's movements revealed that texting altered the posture and changed the way people walked. Hunched over with the heads down, texters were less able to walk in a straight line and more likely to topple off balance.

Dr Siobhan Schabrun from the University of Queensland said: "Texting, and to a lesser extent reading, on your mobile phone affects your ability to walk and balance. This may impact the safety of people who text and walk at the same time." Most people adopt a forward-and-down head position while they text. Holding your head in such a posture can add up to 30 pounds of extra weight to the upper vertebrae which can pull the spine out of alignment.

Physiotherapists have previously dubbed the pain experienced from hunching over a mobile phone as 'text neck' which can put strain on the muscles in the neck and shoulders. A previous study by San Francisco State University discovered that 83 percent of subjects reported some hand and neck pain during texting — but also displayed other signs of tension, like holding their breath and increased heart rates.

*http://www.telegraph.co.uk/science/science-news/10590561/Descent-of-man-how-texting-stops-us-walking-tall.html*

# 22 Technology and mankind

**Above** Communication in the 21st century.

## General comprehension

1. What effect is texting having on our posture?
2. Which four verbs does the author use to describe what may happen when people are hunching over to type or read a text message?
3. How did researchers discover the extent of the problem?
4. Describe the possible dangers of texting while walking, in your own words.
5. What is the effect of bending the head while texting?
6. What is 'text neck'?
7. What other physical symptoms have been reported by people when texting?
8. Do you text while walking? What side effects have you noticed?

## Text handling

1. Identify the subjects of these sentences.
   a) Hunching over to type or read a text message causes people to hunch, swerve, slow down and lose their balance, a study suggests.
   b) A computer which tracked the body's movements revealed that texting altered the posture and changed the way people walked.
   c) Hunched over with the heads down, texters were less able to walk in a straight line and more likely to topple off balance.
   d) A previous study by San Francisco State University discovered that 83 percent of subjects reported some hand and neck pain during texting.

2. Match the vocabulary to the nearest meaning according to the way the words are used in the text.

| I | to hunch | A | give something or someone a particular name |
| II | to swerve | B | how we stand, sit, etc. |
| III | posture | C | process of gradual change over many generations |
| IV | evolution | D | raise shoulders, lower head and lean forward |
| V | undoing | E | downfall / failure |
| VI | to topple | F | suddenly change direction |
| VII | alignment | G | tumble / become unstable |
| VIII | to dub | H | correct position |

## Zoom in on grammar

**Describing how two events occur at the same time effectively**

Look at these two sentences from the text:

> Researchers asked 26 volunteers to walk at a comfortable pace without a phone then monitored them *as* they read or typed a message.

> Most people adopt a forward-and-down head position *while* they text.

*When*, *while* and *as* are conjunctions which are used to describe more than one event occurring at one time. There is a difference in their use: as you can see in the examples above, both *as* and *while* describe actions which take place over a short period – in contrast, *when* is used to describe one action occurring and interrupting an action which was already continuing:

> I was walking along *when* suddenly I tripped.

## Grammar in context

**Describing how two events occur at the same time effectively**

Choose *when*, *as* or *while* to put in the following sentences:

1. The boy was reading a book _____ his mother was making dinner.
2. The boy was riding his bicycle _____ suddenly a dog ran in front of him.
3. The girl talked continuously _____ she sent text messages on her phone.
4. _____ she was texting, a new SMS arrived.

368

### Zoom in on grammar

**Prefixes: un-**

The prefixes *un-*, *im-* or *in-* can be added to the beginning of adjectives, adverbs and nouns to form words that have the opposite meaning. Let's focus on *un-* first.

conscious – *unconscious* / happy – *unhappy* / happiness – *unhappiness* / fit – *unfit* / important – *unimportant* / diminished – *undiminished* / likely – *unlikely* / natural – *unnatural*

The prefix *un-* can be added to the beginning of a verb that describes a process to form another verb that describes the reverse of that process. For example, in the text:

... it appears texting could be *undoing* our natural posture.

### Grammar in context

**Prefixes: un-**

Make sentences with the following pairs of words; an example is provided.

**Example:** The thought of having a holiday from school made the students very *happy*, but then they remembered the test scheduled for the next day and they felt *unhappy*.

1. conscious – unconscious
2. important – unimportant
3. likely – unlikely
4. reliable – unreliable

## Written work (HL)

> 'When a distinguished but elderly scientist states that something is possible, he is almost certainly right. When he states that something is impossible, he is very probably wrong.'
>
> Arthur C. Clarke, British science-fiction writer

Give a personal response to the stimulus and justify it. Choose the text type which is most effective for your message. Write between 150 and 250 words.

## Text 22.1.2 The effects of technology on children

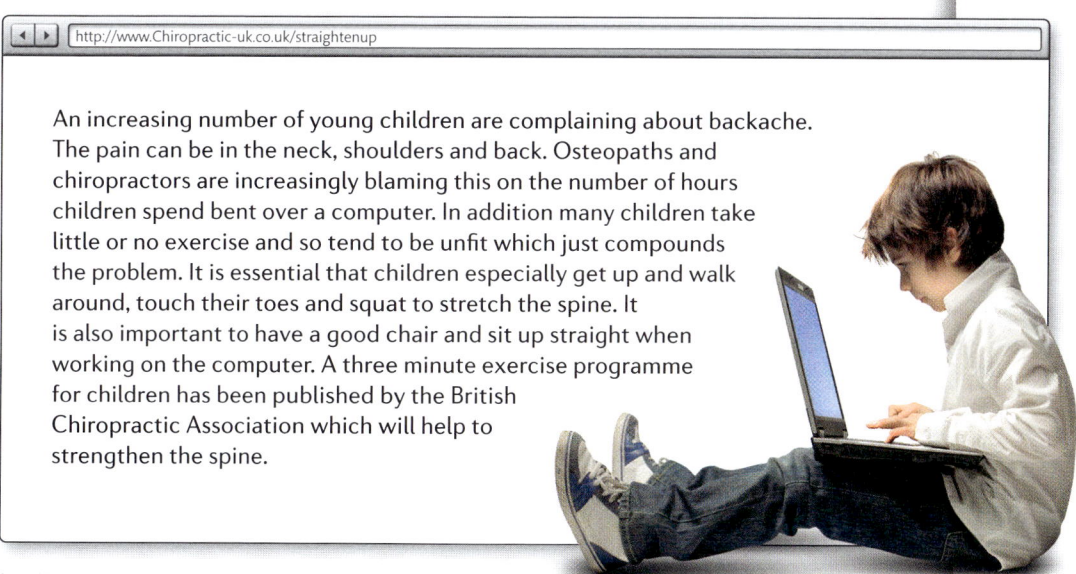

http://www.Chiropractic-uk.co.uk/straightenup

An increasing number of young children are complaining about backache. The pain can be in the neck, shoulders and back. Osteopaths and chiropractors are increasingly blaming this on the number of hours children spend bent over a computer. In addition many children take little or no exercise and so tend to be unfit which just compounds the problem. It is essential that children especially get up and walk around, touch their toes and squat to stretch the spine. It is also important to have a good chair and sit up straight when working on the computer. A three minute exercise programme for children has been published by the British Chiropractic Association which will help to strengthen the spine.

http://www.Chiropractic-uk.co.uk/straightenup

# 22 Technology and mankind

Below are more tips for students.

## Ergonomic tips for students who use notebook computers

### Notebook screen
Elevate your notebook computer monitor using a riser and position it directly in front of you, at about an arm's length away. The top third of the screen should be at or slightly below eye level. This will help to decrease visual discomfort, which will decrease worker fatigue and increase productivity. Position the notebook screen perpendicular to the window, if there is one. This will help to avoid glare on the screen and as a result reduce visual discomfort.

### Keyboard
Use an external keyboard, and make sure the keys do not stick or need excessive force to operate. Position your external keyboard at elbow height. Do not use a wrist rest. Research suggests that using a wrist rest doubles the pressure inside the carpal tunnel because the floor of the carpal tunnel is a more flexible ligament that transmits external pressures directly into the carpal tunnel. Place your arms and elbows close to your body when typing and maintain your wrists in a neutral position.

### Mouse
Use an external mouse instead of the touchpad. Make sure the mouse is at the same level as the keyboard and kept close to the keyboard.

### Desk
Keep your desk area clear so that your mouse can move freely and your notebook computer and keyboard are placed at comfortable positions.

### Chair
Sit in a chair with lower back support, armrests, and an adjustable seat depth and height. This will give you a more comfortable posture that fits your body in relation to your desk. When seated, your knees should be at an angle greater than 90° and the bottoms of your feet should reach the floor or footrest.

### Floor/Bed
When sitting on your bed or floor, use pillows, blankets, or rolled towels to provide support for your back and arms. Add or adjust lighting without producing glare.

### Rest breaks
Take a 30-second rest break every 20 minutes.

http://blogs.bu.edu/kjacobs/files/2010/02/TipSheetforStudentsUpdated.pdf

## General comprehension

1. What is thought to be the reason an increasing number of children complain of backache?
2. Who identified the cause of this problem?
3. What effect does lack of fitness have on this problem?
4. Which of the key tips listed do you practise?
5. Do you have other suggestions for taking care of your spine while working on the computer?

## Text handling

1. Find words in the text which could be meaningfully replaced by the following terms. They are in the order they appear in the text.
    a) lift up
    b) diminish
    c) tiredness
    d) vertical
    e) shine
    f) lessen
    g) too much
    h) supple

2. Identify to whom or what the underlined words refer.

    Elevate your notebook computer monitor using a riser and position <u>it</u> directly in front of you, at about an arm's length away. The top third of the screen should be at or slightly below eye level. <u>This</u> will help to decrease visual discomfort, <u>which</u> will decrease worker fatigue and increase productivity. Position the notebook screen perpendicular to the window, if there is <u>one</u>. <u>This</u> will help to avoid glare on the screen and as a result reduce visual discomfort.

## Zoom in on grammar

### Prefixes: im-

The prefix *im-* can be added to the beginning of adjectives, adverbs and nouns to form words that have the opposite meaning. For example:

   possible – *impossible* / mature – *immature* / measurable – *immeasurable* / balance – *imbalance*

## Grammar in context

### Prefixes: im-

Make sentences with the following pairs of words; an example is provided.

**Example:** It is *possible* to remove ink from a T-shirt, but paint is *impossible* to remove.

1. mobile – immobile
2. polite – impolite
3. movable – immovable
4. patient – impatient
5. permanent – impermanent

## 22.2 Robots

Text 22.2.1 Robots in the home: What might they do?

### Robots in the home

Robots are coming, but what does this mean to ordinary folks? First of all, don't believe all the hype. Lots of hobbyists and small ventures would have you believe that robots are already here, capable of a wide variety of interactions, including health care and monitoring medication compliance, security monitoring, education, errands, and entertainment. Robots are, of course, used in manufacturing, in search and rescue missions, and in the military. But when we get away from industry and the military and discuss machines that are reasonably priced, most of these so-called applications are more imagination than reality, with unreliable mechanisms barely able to get through demonstrations.

For everyday home applications, the use of robots is restricted to entertainment, vacuum cleaners, and lawn mowers. Note, however, that the definition of "robot" varies widely, often being used for anything mobile, even though controlled by a human. Personally, I would classify intelligent home appliances as robots: my coffee maker, microwave oven, dishwasher, and clothes washer and dryer have more intelligence and actuators than robot vacuum cleaners — and they are also a lot more expensive. But they don't move around the room, which for many people disqualifies them from the label of "robot."

Given that any successful product for the home must be affordable, reliable, safe, and usable by everyday people, what might a home robot do? And what would it look like? In the home, form probably will follow function. A kitchen robot might be built into the counter space, with dishwasher, pantry, coffee maker, and cooking units all arranged so that they can communicate with one another and pass items readily back and forth. An entertainment robot might take on a humanoid appearance (as in Wow Wee's Robosapien), or animal-like (as in Sony's Aibo). And robots that vacuum or mow lawns will look like, well, vacuum cleaners and lawn mowers.

Making robots work well is incredibly difficult. Their sensory apparatus is limited because

**Above** Robot vacuum cleaner.

sensors are expensive and interpretation (especially common-sense knowledge) is still more suited for research than deployment. Robotic arms are expensive to build and not very reliable. This limits the range of possibilities: Mowing and vacuuming? Sure. Sorting laundry? Hard, but doable. Picking up dirty items around the home? Doubtful. How about assistants for the elderly or those who need medical supervision? This is a booming area of exploration, but I am sceptical. Today's devices are not reliable, versatile, or intelligent enough — not yet, anyway. Moreover, the social aspects of the interaction are far more complex than the technical ones, something the technology-driven enthusiasts typically fail to recognize.

Three likely directions for the future are entertainment, home appliances, and education. We can start with today's existing devices and slowly add on intelligence, manipulative ability, and function. Start small and build. The market for robots that entertain by being cute and cuddly is already well established. The second generation of vacuum cleaners is smarter than the first. Sony's dog gets smarter and less expensive with each new version. We don't yet think of washing machines, microwave ovens, and coffee makers as robots, but why not? They don't move around the house, but they are getting better and smarter every year. And when the coffee maker is connected to the pantry and dishwasher, that will be a home robot worthy of the name: same for the coupling of sorting, washing, drying, and storing clothes.

Education is a powerful possibility. There is already a solid basis of educational devices that aid learning. Today's robots can read aloud in engaging voices. They can be cute and lovable — witness the responses to the multiple quasi-intelligent animals on the toy market. A robot could very well interact with a child, offering educational benefits as well. Why not have the robot help the child learn the alphabet, teach reading, vocabulary, pronunciation, basic arithmetic, maybe basic reasoning? Why not music and art, geography and history? And why restrict it to children? Adults can be willing and active learners.

Now this is a direction worthy of exploration: robot as teacher. Not to replace school, not to replace human contact and interaction, but to supplement them. The beauty here is that these tasks are well within the abilities of today's devices. They don't require much mobility nor sophisticated manipulators. Many technologists dream of implementing Neil Stephenson's children's tutor in his novel *The Diamond Age: Or, a Young Lady's Illustrated Primer*. Why not? Here is a worthy challenge.

**Above** Wow Wee's 'Robosapien'.

http://www.jnd.org/dn.mss/robots_in_the_home_.html © Donald A. Norman. All rights reserved.

## General comprehension

1 Why do people not count coffee makers and dishwashers as robots?
2 What does the author think the home robot should be able to do in the kitchen?
3 Why is it difficult to make robots work well?
4 What does the author think is wrong with today's devices?
5 How would you define a robot?

## Text handling

Put these words from the text into the appropriate sentences.

**worthy / booming / reliable / engaging / versatile / supplement / restricted**

1 The need for more helpers for the elderly makes this a _____ area to be explored.
2 The children love listening to the robot as it has an _____ voice.
3 Studying with robots could be a valuable _____ to children's learning.
4 Studying with robots should not be _____ to children.
5 A robot in the household must be safe and _____.
6 Today's robots need to be developed so that they become more _____.
7 Developing robots to support learning is a _____ project.

## 22 Technology and mankind

### Text 22.2.2 Caring machines

Twenty-five years ago the Japanese calculated that demography was working against them – there would not be enough young Japanese to take care of their aging generation. They decided that instead of having foreigners take care of the elderly, they would build robots to do the job. While some of the robots designed for the aging population of Japan have an instrumental focus – they give baths and dispense medication – others are expressly designed as companions.

The Japanese robot Wandakum, developed in the late 1990s, is a fuzzy koala that responds to being petted by purring, singing and speaking a few phrases. After a year-long pilot project that provided the "creature" to nursing home residents, one seventy-four-year-old Japanese participant said of it "When I looked into his large brown eyes, I fell in love after years of being quite lonely… I swore to protect and care for the little animal." Encouraged by such experiments, Japanese researchers began to look to artificial companionship as a remedy for the indignities and isolation of age. With similar logic, robots were imagined for the dependencies of childhood. Children and seniors: the most vulnerable first.

**Right** An Aibo doll computer.

*Alone Together* by Sherry Turkle. Basic Books, pp. 105–6

### General comprehension

True or false? Justify your answer with a relevant brief quotation from the text.
1 The Japanese have built robots to look after their elderly instead of having foreigners do the job.
2 The robots are designed only to be companions.
3 The robots look like animals but cannot communicate.
4 Now the Japanese are planning to use robots to care for children.
5 Children and the elderly were chosen as they are the weakest members of society.

### Written work (HL)

'It was once said that the moral test of government is how that government treats those who are in the dawn of life, the children; those who are in the twilight of life, the elderly; and those who are in the shadows of life, the sick, the needy and the handicapped.'

*Hubert H. Humphrey, 38th Vice-President of the United States*

Give a personal response to the stimulus and justify it. Choose any text type you have studied. Write between 150 and 250 words.

### Exam hints

Remember to plan your writing first so that it is well organised and the reader can follow your arguments.
- What do you want to say?
- Do you agree with the quote or do you have other ideas?
- Which text type will you use and who will be your audience? .

## Text 22.2.3 Agriculture shock: How robot farmers will take over our fields

**Monday Sep 23 2013 6:00 am**

The term "robot" may conjure up images of humanoid-looking automatons, but not only is modern science nowhere near making such devices commercially viable, they're largely unnecessary. Practical robots still have much more in common with a car factory assembly line than they do with The Terminator. "The robot's role is to do the repetitive tasks, that's what they're good at", said David Gardner, chief executive of the Royal Agricultural Society of England (RASE). "The actual task itself could be quite complicated, like milking a cow, but if it's just being done repeatedly all the time and it basically sits within one paradigm, there's the opportunity to use a robot to do it."

Each country has its own peculiar farming issues and in Britain it's the robotic milker which has become *de rigueur* for many farms, with more mobile machines slower to catch on. "It's a very sophisticated robot," said Gardner. "It actually removes each teat cup one at a time, rather than removing all four at once – which potentially reduces mastitis. The cups are steamed between each cow, so again there's an advantage in terms of spreading infection." He added: "Robots tend to do a better job than humans. Whilst they can break down, they don't get tired, they don't get sloppy. They do the same job to the same standard every time. The interesting thing about the milking robot is that it has tended to be taken up by family farms where they are looking to get away from having to milk cows twice a day. They still want to keep cows but they don't want to milk them twice a day."

Even on a smaller farm this is still likely to have an impact on jobs, but according to Gardner one of the contributing reasons to the increased popularity of robots in farming is the fear that soon employers won't be able to get enough willing labour.

"Very large parts of the industry are already reliant on Eastern Europe, things like picking fruit and harvesting vegetables," he said. "The use of robots, inevitability, will have an impact on jobs, but it will probably create some higher quality jobs too."

But back in Britain, fruit harvesters are likely to be the next major market, with the replacement of combine harvesters still a low priority for British farmers. "The robotic fruit harvester I saw didn't touch the strawberry itself, it touched the little green stem that the strawberry hangs on," said Gardner. "So you've got not finger bruising. So, like the robotic milker, they do a better job consistently, all the time."

Other robots such as the British-made weeder are also becoming more common. But there are some jobs on the farm a robot is never likely to take over. "There's maintenance and service jobs, that kind of thing", said Gardner. "And lambing sheep. Can you imagine a robot lambing sheep? I don't think so."

Gardner's own prediction is that fruit harvesters will become ubiquitous within five years and that within 20 years almost all farms will have a robot of some sort. Prof Corke agrees with this time frame. "Young people are not going into farming," he said. "As a planet, we need to produce a whole lot more food than we're producing now, so we need to get more productivity out of the land, but there are less and less people wanting to work the land. This often happens with robots, in that they're being sucked into jobs that people are vacating. It's not that robots are pushing people out, there's a vacuum and robots are being sucked in."

http://metro.co.uk/2013/09/23/robot-farming-4055079/

**Below** How a robotic orange harvester might look.

# 22 Technology and mankind

## General comprehension

1. Which kind of task do robots do most successfully?
2. In what ways do robots do a better job than humans?
3. What is the main reason robots have become more popular on farms?
4. What is the effect on people's jobs?
5. Why is the robotic fruit harvester particularly effective?
6. Why do you think young people are not going into farming?
7. What problem does the world face?
8. Are the robots to blame for people losing their jobs in farming?

## Text handling

Match the vocabulary to the nearest meanings according to the text.

| | | | | | | | |
|---|---|---|---|---|---|---|---|
| 1 | viable | 7 | low priority | A | dependent on | G | fashionable |
| 2 | paradigm | 8 | prediction | B | possibly | H | forecast |
| 3 | de rigueur | 9 | ubiquitous | C | undoubtedly | I | seems to be everywhere |
| 4 | potentially | 10 | vacuum | D | unimportant | J | space |
| 5 | reliant on | | | E | feasible | | |
| 6 | inevitably | | | F | pattern | | |

## Zoom in on grammar

**Prefixes: in-**

The prefix *in-* can be put in front of some verbs, adverbs, nouns, etc. to make the opposite meaning.

consistent – *in*consistent / accessible – *in*accessible / ability – *in*ability

## Grammar in context

**Prefixes: in-**

Make sentences with the following pairs of words; an example is provided.

**Example:** Marion's work is *consistent*: she concentrates well, always does her work carefully and neatly and gets the right answers on a regular basis.

On the other hand, Elizabeth's work is *inconsistent*: she rarely concentrates, often chats in class and produces work which is sometimes very good but can also be quite poor.

1. secure – insecure
2. edible – inedible
3. formal – informal

## Interactive oral activity

Choose one of the pictures below and study it carefully. Imagine you are the representative of the company and you need to convince a farmer of the amazing benefits this product could bring. The text does not give much detailed information, so you can be imaginative and add more ideas that will help to sell the product. Work in pairs: one person plays the role of the sales representative and the other the farmer, and then swap.

**Rosphere** *Creator: Technical University of Madrid (UPM)*, **Spain**
It looks like a hamster ball and, in terms of locomotion, it works like a hamster ball. The Rosphere (Robotic Sphere) is the research project of a four-man team in Spain and is designed to work on uneven or unstable (i.e. sandy) terrain. Because of its small size, the Rosphere is not used to tend crops directly, but instead to monitor them: keeping a check on soil conditions and warning a farmer of the need to water or spray.

**Merlin Robotic Milker** *Creator: Fullwood*, **Britain**
Not the sort of contraption that's likely to be leading a robot invasion of Earth - it can't move. Nevertheless, this is the robot that is the most common on British farms, and it is also made there. As well as making life easier for the farmer, it allows the cow to wander into the unit whenever it wants.

**Orange Harvester** *Creator: Vision Robotics*, **USA**
One of the few robotic farmers to at least look vaguely like something out of Star Wars, the Orange Harvester is still under development. However, it's a glimpse of the sort of device that may become common as fruit pickers. Stereoscopic cameras at the end of its front arms create a 3D image of the entire tree, complete with the position and size of the oranges. This information is then passed to the harvesting arms behind, which do the picking.

## Exam practice

# Exercises

### Written assignment 1: Essay title (HL)

Write a speech to be given to younger students in school outlining the proper and appropriate use of technology in school.

### Written assignment 2: Personal response (HL)

Give a personal response to the following stimulus and justify it. Choose any text type that you have studied in class. Write between 150 and 250 words.

'It is the greatest truth of our age: Information is not knowledge.'

*Caleb Carr, American novelist and military historian*

### Written assignment 3: Essay title (SL)

Write a set of guidelines for elementary students who are to use the internet.

# 23 Written Assignment: Higher Level

## Introduction to the Written Assignment: Higher Level

The Written Assignment counts for 20% of the final grade in English B Higher Level.

Students must produce a piece of creative writing based on a work of literature that they have read in class as part of the course. The literary work must be in English and should not be a translation of a work in another language. The piece of writing must be 500–600 words in length plus a 150–250-word rationale.

The objectives of the Written Assignment are listed below.

- To provide the student with the chance to reflect upon and develop further understanding of the works read in class.
- To develop their receptive and productive skills to a higher degree.
- To produce an appropriate text in the selected text type.
- To organise writing purposefully and coherently.
- To extend language skills.
- To demonstrate intercultural understanding through reflection on the assignment.

## Completing the Written Assignment: Higher Level

Below are a number of points to remember.

- The piece of writing you produce must be a development of the ideas presented in the rationale.
- The language must be carefully chosen for your text – is it appropriate to the type of text you have chosen? Would the character speak in this way and use this vocabulary?
- What you write must be connected to the literary text and the characters in it.
- Your teacher may talk to you and advise you but is not allowed to correct the written assignment at any point during the process.

## Rationale: Higher Level

Students must write a 150–250-word rationale introducing the assignment. The rationale must include the following.

- A brief introduction to the literary text used. It is important to include the title and author of the text. In one or two sentences describe the main theme of the novel.
- An explanation of how the task is linked to the literary text. For example, the character and/or part of the story to be focused on.
- An explanation of the aim of the chosen genre. This will explain why you have chosen this part of the story for the written assignment and why it best fulfils the intended aim.
- An explanation of how you intend to achieve your aims. This will include choice of text type, the audience, the register and style.

Here are three examples of how the Written Assignment can be chosen, based on the literary work.

## *The Book Thief* by Markus Zusak

A novel set in the Second World War. It is about human relationships and the ability of books to feed the soul.

> Narrated by Death, Markus Zusak's groundbreaking new novel is the story of Liesel Meminger, a young foster girl living outside of Munich in Nazi Germany. Liesel scratches out a meagre existence for herself by stealing, when she discovers something she can't resist – books. Soon she is stealing books from Nazi book burnings, the mayor's wife's library, wherever they are to be found.
>
> With the help of her accordion-playing foster father, Liesel learns to read and shares her stolen books with her neighbours during bombing raids, as well as with the Jewish man hidden in her basement.
>
> The Book Thief by Markus Zusak, Borzoi Books – Random House Children's Books, Toronto, ISBN: 0-375-83100-2, front cover blurb

How this novel could be used for the Written Assignment:

| Source | Task | Text type | Rationale |
| --- | --- | --- | --- |
| Novel: *The Book Thief* by Markus Zusak | Examine the thoughts of the mayor's wife about her dead son after she sees Liesel steal a book that has not completely burnt from the pile of books burnt in the market square by the Nazis. | Diary entry | A summary of the literary text, an introduction to the character and her thoughts as expressed in the story. The rationale will explain how the piece of writing will explore the mayor's wife's feelings about the book burnings and her memories of reading with her son. In the story they are not explored, only briefly mentioned. |

## *Unique* by Alison Allen-Gray

A science-fiction novel set in the present that explores the possibilities of genetic engineering and the ethical consequences.

> *I turned the last page and felt myself go hot all over. I was staring at the face of a young man… It was my face looking at me. A few years older, but my face. But it couldn't be!*
>
> When Dominic finds the photograph in his grandad's loft, at first he can't believe what he is seeing. How can it be possible? How can there be someone else looking so like him? And then it begins to dawn on him that this must be his brother. But why has he never been told that he had a brother? Why has it been kept a secret? And what happened to him?
>
> When his parents refuse to tell him anything, Dominic decides to find out the truth for himself. But when he starts his search, Dominic uncovers a horrifying secret and unleashes a chain of events that will have far-reaching and disastrous consequences for everyone involved…
>
> Unique by Alison Allen-Gray. Oxford University Press 'Rollercoasters', ISBN: 978 0 19 832633 5, front cover blurb

# 23 Written Assignment: Higher Level

How this novel could be used for the Written Assignment:

| Source | Task | Text type | Rationale |
|---|---|---|---|
| Novel: *Unique* by Alison Allen-Gray | Write a letter that Dominic could have received after the death of Imogen. Imogen wrote it to him before she died, explaining her motives in participating in the cloning experiment and how her feelings changed when she met Dominic. | Letter | The rationale will offer a summary of *Unique*, introduce the character of Imogen and describe her involvement in the story. The rationale will state the aim of the letter, which will be to develop ideas about the realities of the ethical dilemma Imogen is confronted with when she meets the living Dominic. It will be written in the style of Imogen's speech in the novel. |

## *About a Boy* by Nick Hornby

The novel is set in the present and explores human relationships.

> Will is thirty-six but behaves like a teenager. He's single, rich and cool. He has no responsibilities – no job, no family, no worries. Marcus is twelve and very different from the average teenager. He has just moved to London with his divorced Mum, Fiona, and is having problems adapting to his new life and his new school. Fiona is depressed and heading for a breakdown. Will and Marcus meet by chance the day that Fiona tries to kill herself. She recovers, but Marcus is worried that she will try again, leaving him on his own. He turns to Will for help. Although Will runs away from this responsibility at first, he realises he can help Marcus, not with his suicidal mother, but by teaching him how to be a 'normal' kid who wears the right trainers and listens to the right music. Will and Marcus change each other's lives forever. Marcus teaches Will to grow up and accept responsibility, whereas Will teaches Marcus to live in today's world.
>
> Blurb from Penguin Active Reading Teacher Support Programme, Pearson Education 2008, About a Boy by Nick Hornby. Penguin.

How this novel could be used for the Written Assignment:

| Source | Task | Text type | Rationale |
|---|---|---|---|
| Novel: *About a Boy* by Nick Hornby | Write a dialogue between Will and a journalist at Christmas time at the end of the story. Will explains why he does not need to work (because of royalties from a Christmas song his father wrote) and reflects on the need to have goals in life and to be involved positively with other people. | An interview for a magazine for teenagers and young people | The rationale will offer a summary of *About a Boy* and the character of Will. The aim of the interview will be to give Will an opportunity to reflect on the change he has gone through and how he has become aware that people in society need other people to survive. The chosen register and language will reflect those of the novel. The rationale will explain who the audience is. |

# Written assignment (HL) practice

Now practise the written assignment. Read the following short story.

## *We Walked on Water* by Eliza Robertson

Land of the misty giants: cedar, alder, Ponderosa pine. Cascade Mountains pushing out green like grass through a garlic press. The veg here is fungal. Jungle. All of it is rainforest: fern-webbed paths and moss like armpit hair, the exclusion of 70 per cent of the sky. You see the tallest trees in the first half of the drive – between home and Hope, Hope and Allison Pass. I'm the kid at the back of the bus with a packet of apple-rings, slouched in his trackpants over two velour seats. I could have cycled: Chilliwack to Penticton, 285K, a hundred clicks longer than the route in the race. But it's best not to overdo it. Rest well, race well. Taper time now.

Aunt Bea will meet me at the terminal, in her plaid-patched skirts, smelling of patchouli. She'll drive her Volvo from Nelson, kayak on the roof-rack when she rolls into the lot. Last year we 'made a week of it'. Our parents browsed bookshops and beadshops; Aunt Bea sat on the beach and sliced watermelon. Liv and I trained in the lake. We raced between the Peach and the Riverboat, and sometimes I let her win. Once she almost won for real, but I grabbed her heels and yanked her under. She kicked me in the hip and I let go. Asshole, she said. She splashed water into my eyes and swam to the shore to practise handstands.

When you train, numbers are everything. Kilojoules in and out, pounds per inch, the speed and duration of mass in motion. Zeros and ones, like a computer. Liv understood how to be a computer better than I did, though I think I've caught on. Our nutrition plans were similar: four to six small meals. Fistful of protein; fistful of starch; two fistfuls of colour. We ate space food. Sports gels in squeeze tubes: Accelerade, Perpetuem. She dipped salted pretzels into cottage cheese. I drank non-fat chocolate milk.

What worried Mom was the swim scrum: one lake, no lanes. Anthem ends and the start horn blares. 2600 participants wade into the water, identical in our neoprene and brightly coloured swim caps. It feels baptismal, sacrificial. We drop row on row into a tangle of legs and windmilling arms. Stay out of trouble, Liv, Mom said. Stay out of trouble. People assume she got held down. 5'4, 105 pounds: easy to front-crawl over. But that wasn't it. She stayed near to me. The first leg, 1600 metres lakeshore to Last House, I kept her in sight. In the scrum, you move as a group: a collective consciousness. Sometimes you let yourself be carried. You slip over bodies like spawning salmon, which Liv and I actually tried once. Salmon run 2005, Vedder River. We in our swim skins and matching caps. We let the current steer us. Watched their shadows through our goggles, how darkness darted over algaed stones. Their hook jaws and flared teeth, port-stain scales, how they tumbled over each other and over our ankles. The flick of their fins.

Last year, the swim made me woozy for the rest of the race. 3.8 kilometres, one breath per stroke cycle. Rhythm is key. Beats per minute, strokes per metre. Your heart, your lungs, your metronome. The left is my poor side. I breathed on my left for the first half of the course and on my right for the second. You learn how to swim slippery, with

# 23   Written Assignment: Higher Level

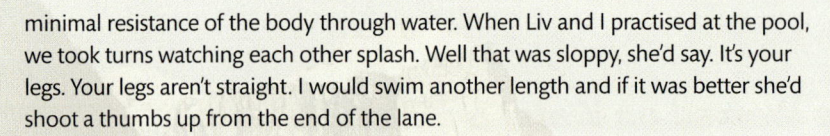

minimal resistance of the body through water. When Liv and I practised at the pool, we took turns watching each other splash. Well that was sloppy, she'd say. It's your legs. Your legs aren't straight. I would swim another length and if it was better she'd shoot a thumbs up from the end of the lane.

Sometimes they wired separate music into the underwater speakers. You'd hear Top 40 on deck, but in the competition lane they played Beethoven. The lake is a different music – the calm hum of underwater ear pressure. In the race, you follow that hum to the shore, then find your landlegs, where your feet start and the wet sand ends. I remember juddering through the time chute – hands on my back, guiding me to the change tents. They unzip the wetsuit for you, spray you with sunscreen while you call for your glasses. I searched for Liv when I ran to the bike racks, but the ladies' tent was crowded and she always took longer to change. Some athletes would pause at the nutrient station. They peeled their bananas and PowerBar wrappers. I kept my bike calories in a single bottle. Accelerade + CarboPro. Energy gels to top up.

Tonight, Aunt Bea and I will eat spaghetti. I used to make fun of Liv when she measured, but this weekend I packed her food scales. 400 grams whole wheat spaghetti, crushed tomatoes, extra-lean turkey. After dinner, we'll drive the bike course. Follow the lakes: Skaha to Vaseux, Vaseux to Osoyoos. Penticton – Oliver – Keremeos, 180 kilometres. Every twenty-five clicks, I'll get out and cycle. That's how you notice the camber, the incline of road when the street appears flat. Never mind the mountain passes. The highest altitude comes near the end: 2500 feet. Aunt Bea will drive slow beside me. She will play Creedence Clearwater on tape. When she brakes for me to haul in the bike, she'll sing *I like the way you walk, I like the way you talk, oh, Susie Q*. Tomorrow we'll drive the run route. We did this last year but I don't like surprises. We all have our rituals. On raceday, Liv used to eat sun. We have this skylight in our kitchen; from May to September the light floods in. She'd stand below the glass with a bowl of white yogurt until the sun reeled off her spoon. I watched from the hall, sometimes. You could pinpoint each moment the glare made her blink. But on Ironman Sunday you eat breakfast before sun-up. Check-in's at five; we set the radio for four. She aimed for toast and peanut butter, but couldn't keep it down. Raceday nerves – I heard her retch in the shower. But ask any competitor: on raceday you go liquid. Mothers said it in the fifties. Don't eat and swim. A girl eats careful and it's a disorder; her brother eats careful and he's an athlete. We shared the same BMI.

This is the first time I've taken the Greyhound. Last year, our parents drove. Liv asked for lunch in Princeton because it was the only town with a Booster Juice. Booster Juice stamps the nutrition label on every drink, so you know you're getting thirty grams of protein with your 500 calories of Bananas-a-Whey. I wanted Dairy Queen. A Butterfinger blizzard layered twice with hot fudge.

That's obscene, said Liv.

I have a craving.

That's over 100 grams of sugar. For a medium.

Well.

Look at you. You'll make yourself sick. That's like six bananas.

How many bananas before you grow tits?

She didn't speak after that. She inserted her earbuds and frowned out the window. You knew Liv was upset if you saw a glimmer of sweat above her eyebrows, or on her cheekbones. And sometimes she left her mouth open after she spoke, like she couldn't quite catch her breath. But then I might poke her shoulder with my eyelids flipped inside-out, and she would smack the back of my head.

Long QT syndrome, the medical examiner had said. Arrhythmia. Mutated sodium channels, reduced flow of potassium: the medspeak never sounded severe enough. This year, Mom forbade me from competing. She said, 'I forbid you.' We fought when I registered in October, a few days before Halloween. We were carving pumpkins. She shoved hers off the counter with the heel of her palm.

Dad won't come this year either. He says it's because of work, but he's not contracted for Sundays. Last year, they ate at Thomasina's, a bakery with oven-hot scones and rounds of sourdough that steam from the centre when you pry them in half. We all shared a booth. Liv and I plugged into our iPods and frosty wax cups. Mom and Dad staring out the window, buttering their scones.

The tallest building in Princeton is the visitor information centre. My bus will wait there thirty minutes, and I might treat myself to a Strawberry Slam. Sometimes I wonder about the diets of other animals. How millennia of worms and woodbugs might contribute to the bone density of birds. The musculature of flight, lean protein for air-friendly pectorals. Versus penguins, who swim and eat squid. We've lost weight since we were apes; we've become more aerodynamic. I wish we had wings. Though the run rules say, no form of locomotion other than running, walking or crawling. Liv cut that line from the athlete guide and pasted it into her journal. It was funnier before the bike-to-run transition. The weight of your muscles, the downward propulsion, your blood and your breath pumping into the pavement.

Last year I made it to dusk. To the chicken broth and Coca Cola. The coke fizz went down like static electricity, like the charge from a balloon you rub in your hair and stick to the wall. The volunteers distributed the broth in warm paper cups. You would ease into a jog and graze fingers with the kid in a mint volunteer shirt as he handed you the cup. It tasted like the most nourishing thing you'd had all day and you held the liquid in your cheeks and nodded at the kid, who had Down's syndrome, and he grabbed another cup from the table and fired you an A-OK sign.

At one point near Skaha Estates, I stopped running at the top of a hill and waited forty-five seconds to spot Liv. I thought she must be ahead of me. She was a stronger runner. I thought maybe she slipped in front when I used the toilet at the bike-to-run. But then I saw Dad's Ford Escape at the turnaround on Christie Beach, his cheeks slanted and white through the windshield. Athletes crowded the special needs table, ghosted the nutrient station with their neon bottles of Gatorade. I stalked off the road and walked straight to the car. He shifted his eyes to me through the window, and for a moment neither of us moved. He flicked a switch at the wheel and the passenger door unlocked. I opened the door and climbed into the front seat and his palm clapped my shoulder. His eyes squinted into mine, and then he turned the ignition. I noticed there were two small Tim Horton's coffees in the cup-holders. He drove off the course, on the other side of Skaha Lake, and it wasn't until we were halfway to Kaleden that he pointed to the cup nearest me and said, that one's yours.

# 23 Written Assignment: Higher Level

Eliza Robertson is a Canadian writer and one of the four winners of the 2013 Commonwealth Short Story prize.

> A premature ventricular contraction is medspeak for your heart skipping a beat. The contraction is initiated by your heart ventricles rather than the sinoatrial node. You can listen to high-pitched recordings on Wikipedia. It sounds like bagpipes. *Tempo rubato* is Italian for stolen time. Rhythmic freedom. The expressive speeding up and slowing down of a piece of music. Chopin played steady with his left hand, timed to the metronome, while his right hand weaved in and around the beat like a ferret inside a chest of drawers. Your left is your clock. Your timekeeper. Liv played 'Chopsticks' with her toes. Tilted onto her tail bone, the stool pushed back, half a grapefruit between her palms. She sucked the juice through a straw, and I waited for her to flick her chin and fire the pulp at me. I remember her in screenshots. Like she's in motion, but my mind can only capture single frames. That's how I imagine her in the lake. Involuntarily, when my mind slips in flashes. Liv with her jaw gaping, gasping in water. Liv with a thin wrist braced to her thorax. Liv with her eyes bulged like a fish. When I imagine my sister, I do not see Ophelia. Her heart's seized and she's choking in lake and I wonder at what point she knew.
>
> I read once that grief is like waiting. Waiting to sleep. Waiting to wake up. Waiting for Act III, the plot twist. Like when you drop a twig into the stream and it never emerges on the other side of the bridge. Tonight in Penticton, I might take out Bea's kayak. Go for a paddle. Liv and I rowed the swim course last year, with a Thermos of hot chocolate and a box of Ritz crackers, our boom box, the Beach Boys and six D batteries. We paddled into that warm darkness, the blue hour of bats. How they screeched and swooped over the dry-patched Summerland hills. Liv laid her oar across the cockpit coaming and shut her eyes. I continued to row. Motel neon glowed from the lakeshore, and we slipped past their spears of reflected light.
>
> http://www.granta.com/New-Writing/We-Walked-on-Water

## Written work (HL)

- Decide what kind of creative writing response you want to make. What is your goal in the writing you have chosen to do?
- Choose a text type. How will you present your ideas? Who will be 'the audience'?
- Plan your writing. Decide on the register and tone of your writing – keeping in mind the characters in the story.
- Write the rationale (150–250 words). Include the author and title of your chosen piece of literature and be careful to include all the relevant information as mentioned in 'the rationale' on pages 378–9.
- Write the text (500–600 words).

## Written Assignment: Receptive and written productive skills (HL)

### Criterion A: Rationale and task

- How well does the student use the rationale and the task in order to accomplish the assignment?

- How clearly has the task been introduced in the rationale?

- How successfully does the task achieve the aim(s) stated in the rationale?

- How appropriate is the choice of the text type to the task?

**Note:** 'Creative piece of writing' refers to the fact that a formal (literary) essay is not an acceptable text type for the written assignment; however, artistic merit is not assessed.

| Mark | Level descriptor |
|---|---|
| 0 | The work does not reach a standard described by the descriptors below. |
| 1–2 | **The student uses the rationale and the task in a limited way and may have partially accomplished the assignment.** <br> There is an introduction but there is very little explanation of how the task is connected to the literary work(s). <br> The student has barely explained what his or her aims are. <br> The task is not a creative piece of writing and is not connected to the literary work(s). <br> The chosen text type is inappropriate to the audience and purpose stated in the rationale. |
| 3–4 | **The student uses the rationale and the task in order to accomplish the assignment to a certain extent.** <br> The student has sometimes explained how the task is connected to the literary work(s). <br> The student has explained what his or her aims are but not how he or she intends to achieve them. <br> The task is creative but not connected to the literary text(s). <br> The chosen text type is not completely appropriate to the audience and aim(s) stated in the rationale, and is applied inconsistently throughout the task. |
| 5–6 | **The student uses the rationale and the task adequately in order to accomplish the assignment.** <br> The student has explained how the task is connected to the literary text(s). <br> The student has explained what his or her aims are and how he or she intends to achieve them. <br> The task is creative but sometimes connected to the literary work(s). <br> The chosen text type is not completely appropriate to the audience and purpose stated in the rationale, but is applied consistently throughout the task. |
| 7–8 | **The student uses the rationale and the task well in order to accomplish the assignment.** <br> The student has clearly explained how the task is connected to the literary text(s). <br> The student has clearly explained what his or her aims are and how he or she intends to achieve them. <br> The task is a creative piece of writing and generally connected to the literary work(s). <br> The chosen text type is appropriate to the audience and purpose stated in the rationale, and is applied throughout the task. |
| 9–10 | **The student uses the rationale and the task effectively in order to accomplish the assignment.** <br> The student has clearly and fully explained how the task is connected to the literary text(s). <br> The student has clearly explained what his or her aims are and how he or she intends to achieve them. <br> The task is a creative piece of writing and consistently connected to the literary work(s). <br> The chosen text type is appropriate to the audience and purpose stated in the rationale, and is applied consistently throughout the task. |

## Criterion B: Organization and development

- How effectively are ideas organized and developed?

**Note:** Criterion B is applied to the task only.

| Marks | Level descriptor |
|---|---|
| 0 | The work does not reach a standard described by the descriptors below. |
| 1–2 | The organization and development of ideas is mostly ineffective. |
| 3–4 | Ideas are organized and developed mostly effectively. |
| 5–6 | Ideas are organized and developed effectively. |

# 23 Written Assignment: Higher Level

### Criterion C: Language

- How appropriately and effectively does the student use language in relation to the task?

**Note:** Criterion C is applied to the task only.

| Mark | Level descriptor |
|---|---|
| 0 | The work does not reach a standard described by the descriptors below. |
| 1–2 | **The use of language is mostly limited.**<br>Vocabulary is limited or is generally inappropriate to the task.<br>Simple sentence structures are rarely clear.<br>The rhetorical devices are not used, or are used inappropriately. |
| 3–4 | **The use of language is generally adequate.**<br>Vocabulary shows range but is sometimes used inappropriately to the task.<br>Simple sentence structures are clear but no complex structures have been attempted.<br>There is limited use of appropriate rhetorical devices. |
| 5–6 | **The use of language is appropriate and is generally effective.**<br>Vocabulary shows range and is mostly appropriate to the task.<br>Simple sentence structures are clear but there are errors in complex structures.<br>The rhetorical devices are used appropriately. |
| 7–8 | **The use of language is appropriate and effective.**<br>Vocabulary shows good range and is consistently used appropriately to the task.<br>Complex sentence structures are clear and effective.<br>The rhetorical devices are varied and used effectively. |

*Taken from* Language B guide © International Baccalaureate Organization 2011, pp. 46–49

# 24 Written Assignment: Standard Level

## Introduction to the Written Assignment: Standard Level

The Written Assignment counts for 20% of the final grade in English B Standard Level.

It is based on an inter-textual reading followed by a written task of 300–400 words plus a 150–200-word rationale based on the core topics.

## Completing the Written Assignment: Standard Level

### Requirements from 2015 onwards

The assessment of the task emphasises content and organisation over format. The student should demonstrate understanding of the subject matter of the written assignment, as well as the ability to organise and use the information from the sources.

The student should:

- demonstrate understanding of the core topic
- organise the information from the sources in a manner appropriate to the text
- use the information from the sources to form a new text without copying
- use language appropriate to the text type and purpose.

*Taken from* Language B guide © International Baccalaureate Organization 2011, p. 34

For the Written Assignment task you must find your own topic and materials and discuss them with the teacher.

In this section, you will find two sets of three articles linked by a common theme for practice. Read all three articles carefully. The task is to produce a piece of writing of between 300 and 400 words in response, in any of the text types studied. This task involves inter-textual reading – that means understanding the articles and being able to synthesise the points made in each into one piece of writing. You must also write a rationale which explains why you chose to write your particular response. You should read each text very carefully and make notes of the main points which interest you. These could be in the form of a Venn diagram or a chart with three columns.

- Are some ideas common across the texts?
- Or are the ideas very different?
- Which points of view do they present?
- Which standpoint do the authors take?
- What is your opinion after reading the texts?

After making notes, think about what point you want to make.

- What do you want to say?
- What is your message? Who are you addressing?
- Do you want to share the information or do you want to discuss it?
- Do you want to focus on one or two main issues?

Decide on your goal.

When you have decided on what you want to say, think about whom you are talking to

# 24 Written Assignment: Standard Level

or writing for and how you want to convey the message. So, the key ideas are:

- Content: What is your goal?
- Text type: How will you write it?
- Register and tone: Who is it for?

Then begin to draft your writing.

## The rationale

In addition to the text, you need to write a rationale. The rationale will explain what your goal is and how your choice of text type and audience help you achieve your goal. The rationale should be 150–200 words.

## Written Assignment (SL) practice (I)

### Text: Climate change

### Prince Charles: climate change is the greatest challenge facing humanity

By Emily Gosden
12:01AM BST September 22 2014

Tackling global warming is the biggest challenge facing the world today, Prince Charles has said, urging governments to act on climate change before it is too late. After months in which the crises in the Middle East and Ukraine have dominated the political agenda, the Prince of Wales will call on world leaders to turn their attentions to "the battle against climate change".

"Even in a world full of daunting perils and crises, it is hard to imagine anything that poses a greater challenge and opportunity for humanity," he will say. His comments come in an address to political and business leaders in New York ahead of major international climate change talks, convened by UN secretary general Ban Ki-moon.

David Cameron and Barack Obama are among world leaders expected to attend the summit, at which Mr Ban has urged countries to make bold pledges for cutting their greenhouse gas emissions. The Prince, who has long been an outspoken campaigner on climate change, will make clear his frustration that more has not been done to tackle global warming, despite clear warnings from UN scientists of the potentially catastrophic risks it poses.

In a pre-recorded video address, the Prince shakes his head as he says: "We are running out of time – how many times have I found myself saying this over recent years?" His comments come in his capacity as patron of the Prince of Wales's Corporate Leaders Group, a group of businesses calling for action on climate change. The warning comes as new research shows global emissions of carbon dioxide – the bigger contributor to global warming – are on track to hit a new record high of 40 billion tonnes in 2014, about 2.5 per cent higher than last year.

The report by the Global Carbon Project, backed by the Tyndall Centre for Climate Change Research at the University of East Anglia, highlights the growing improbability of the world cutting its emissions back to the level scientists say is necessary to avert the most severe effects of global warming.

Scientists believe temperature increases of more than 2°C above pre-industrial levels would have a devastating effect. To stand a chance of limiting warming to that level, historical and future carbon dioxide emissions must stay within a finite budget of 3,200 billion tonnes. Two-thirds of this quota has been used up already and if emissions continue at their current rate the remainder will be used up in just 30 years, the report warns. Global emissions need to be cut by more than 5 per cent each year, the report finds.

Yet most countries are yet to commit to cutting emissions at anything like the scale required. The extent to which different countries should cut their respective emissions will be a key focus of the talks. The report shows that while the UK cut its emissions last year, China, the USA and India all increased theirs.

Prof Corinne Le Quéré, director of the Tyndall Centre at UEA, said: "We are nowhere near the commitments necessary to stay below 2°C of climate change, a level that will be already challenging to manage for most countries around the world, even for rich nations."

In his video, Prince Charles says the world cannot "delay, regroup, prevaricate or wait for more and better information" and warns that tackling global warming will require "an unprecedented transformation of our communities, societies and lifestyles". He calls for renewable energy – such as wind farms and solar panels – to be "vastly scaled up. Taking action on climate change is neither inherently bad for business nor against economic interests. It is, in fact, the only rational choice," he will say.

"We simply have to win the battle against climate change to secure our future, and the future of our children and grandchildren. I fear there is not a moment to lose."

http://www.telegraph.co.uk/news/uknews/prince-charles/11110457/Prince-Charles-climate-change-is-the-greatest-challenge-facing-humanity.html

## Text: Renewable energy

# Over £200 million boost for renewables

Press release
Department of Energy & Climate Change, Thursday July 24 2014.

Renewable energy projects to compete for a budget of over £200 million a year, as part of reforms to the electricity market.

From October, renewable energy projects will compete for a budget of over £200 million a year, as part of the government's reforms to the electricity market, Energy and Climate Change Secretary Ed Davey announced today.

The funding is for the first allocation round for the new Contracts for Difference, which provide long-term certainty and reduce risk for investors. The government's reforms to the electricity market will reduce emissions from the power sector much more cheaply than through existing policies – around 6% (£41) lower on the average domestic electricity bill up to 2030.

Mr Davey said that renewable energy projects would have to bid competitively for the contracts, ensuring that new, clean electricity generation would be built at the lowest possible cost to energy consumers.

We are signalling now that at least a further £50 million is planned for an auction round in 2015, with a total of around £1 billion potentially available later for further projects, including Carbon Capture and Storage, up to 2020–21.

Mr Davey said:

"Our plan is powering growth and jobs as we build clean, secure electricity infrastructure for the future. By radically reforming the electricity markets, we're making sure that decarbonising the power sector will come at the lowest possible cost to consumers.

"Average annual investment in renewables has doubled since 2010 – with a record breaking £8 billion worth in 2013.

"These projects will create green jobs and green growth, reduce our reliance on foreign-controlled volatile energy markets and make sure billpayers get the best possible deal.

"We're building a secure, low-carbon electricity system that will be the powerhouse of the British economy, supporting up to 250,000 jobs by 2020."

The funding is managed by the Levy Control Framework, which caps the cost to consumers of renewable energy policies.

The new system is designed to bring more competition and encourage private sector investment in low-carbon electricity generation. The budget

# 24 Written Assignment: Standard Level

estimate comes after the European Commission confirmed yesterday that the Contracts for Difference, Capacity Market schemes, and five offshore wind projects supported by early Contracts for Difference, are in line with its rules on state aid.

The CfD budget will be split between up to three technology groups – one for more established technologies, like onshore wind and solar, and one for less established technologies like offshore wind, and one for biomass conversions.

Within each group, contracts will be allocated competitively - putting the UK in the forefront of driving down the costs of supporting renewable technologies and delivering better value for consumers.

The reforms build on the UK's status as one of the most attractive places to invest in energy globally, supporting economic growth and creating jobs.

https://www.gov.uk/government/news/over-200-million-boost-for-renewables

## Text: Causes of and solutions to global warming

The "pause" in global warming may last another decade before surface temperatures start rising again, according to scientists who say heat is being stored in the depths of the Atlantic and Southern Oceans.

Global average surface temperatures rose rapidly from the 1970s but have been relatively stable since the late 1990s, in a trend that has been seized upon by climate sceptics who question the science of man-made warming.

Climate change scientists have proposed more than a dozen theories to explain the "hiatus", which they say is a "distraction" from the widespread consensus on global warming.

A new study, published in the journal *Science*, suggests that a natural cycle of ocean currents has caused the phenomenon by drawing heat from shallow waters down almost a mile into the depths of the Atlantic and Southern Oceans. The cycle naturally produces periods of roughly 30 years in which heat is stored near the surface of the Atlantic Ocean, leading to warmer temperatures, followed by roughly 30 years in which it is stored in the depths, causing cooler surface temperatures, it suggests. Rising surface temperatures in the last three decades of the 20th century were roughly half caused by man-made global warming and half by the ocean currents keeping more heat near the surface, it finds.

When the ocean cycle reversed around the turn of the century, drawing heat down into the depths, this served to counteract the effects of man-made global warming. "When the internal variability that is responsible for the current hiatus switches sign, as it inevitably will, another episode of accelerated global warming should ensue," the study concludes.

Prof Ka-Kit Tung of the University of Washington, one of the report's authors, said: "Historically the cool period lasted 20 to 35 years. The current period already lasted 15 years, so roughly there [are] 10 more years to go." But he said that other impacts of climate change could upset the cycle, which is caused by variation in the salinity of the water as denser, saltier water sinks. Prof Tung said the study's findings were a surprise because previous studies had suggested it was the Pacific Ocean that was "the culprit for hiding heat".

"The data are quite convincing and they show otherwise," he said.

Prof Piers Forster, professor of climate change at the University of Leeds, said the paper was "another a nail in the coffin of the idea that the hiatus is evidence that our projections of long term climate change need revising down".

"Variability in the ocean will not affect long-term climate trends but may mean we have a period of accelerated warming to look forward to," he said.

Prof Richard Allan, professor of climate science at the University of Reading, said: "Although it is human nature to seek a single cause for notable events, in reality the complexity of the climate system means that there is not one simple explanation for a decade of unusual climatic conditions."

http://www.telegraph.co.uk/earth/environment/climatechange/11049540/Global-warming-pause-may-last-for-another-decade-scientists-suggest.html

### The task

These three articles are all about global warming and are related to the core topic Global Issues. When you have read the articles very carefully and made your notes, begin to think about your aim and how your choice of text type and audience will help you achieve it.

From the wide variety of text types you have studied, choose the one to suit your aim most effectively.

For example:
- If you want to share the information you have gained with your peers, you could write a speech to be given in assembly.
- If you want to share the information with students, teachers and parents, you could write an article for the school newspaper.
- If you want to make your voice heard in protest, you could write a formal letter to a local councillor or a newspaper.
- Or you could choose to write an email, an essay, an official report, a flyer or a set of guidelines.

The text type you choose should help you reach your goal and you should be able to explain how and why this is so in the rationale.

## Written Assignment (SL) practice (II)

Below are three articles linked by another common theme for practice. Read all three articles very carefully. The task is to produce a piece of writing of between 300 and 400 words in response, in any of the text types studied, as well as a rationale which explains why you chose to write your particular response.

### Text: Shared interests are the key to friendships

Researchers found that having enthusiasms and hobbies formed a strong bond but when we change those interests we change our friends. Scientists studied Facebook style sites to try and unlock the secrets of real life friendship and sometimes it could be as simple as having the same favourite X Factor contestant. Millions of people are members of online social networks such as Facebook, or Twitter, where they join 'groups' according to their likes, or hobbies. This phenomenon leads to friends being grouped more and more by cliques, and led academics to analyse the social butterfly effect – how we change friends throughout our lives.

During the study, researchers built a computer model of a real social network.

They discovered that throughout society we often form cliques and circles of friends with common interests, such as politics, music, religion, sport or the same profession. Even if friendships are fleeting, we gravitate to those who enjoy the same things we do or support the same football team. Scientists from the University of Southampton, Royal Holloway, University of London, and the Institute of Zoology at London Zoo came to the conclusion that people go from clique to clique as their interests change, usually forming a tight knit of friends.

The study is published in the *Journal of the Royal Society* Interface.

Dr Sebastian Funk, from the Institute of Zoology, said: "We changed the model so that individuals tended to form links with similar others and we saw the cliques start to form."

The researchers then went on to look at what happens when peoples' interests change, for example they take up a new hobby. Dr Funk said: "It was fascinating to see how the cliques could form without any one person organising everything. We saw individuals moving from one clique to another. Over time some cliques disappeared while new ones were established. It was interesting to see that new cliques tended to either fail very quickly or grow and persist for a much longer time, with very few in between."

*http://www.telegraph.co.uk/science/science-news/8171136/Shared-interests-key-to-friendship.html*

# 24 Written Assignment: Standard Level

## Text: How Facebook makes you distrusting and miserable

**NEW RESEARCH finds that exposure to homophobic, racist or misogynistic content on social networks including Facebook 'may threaten subjective well-being'**

New research finds that social networks including Facebook "may threaten subjective well-being" by eroding a user's trust in the rest of society with exposure to homophobic, racist or misogynistic content.

Scientists from the Sapienza University of Rome and the Institut National de la Statistique et des Études Économiques du Grand-Duché du Luxembourg explored survey data from 50,000 people in 24,000 Italian households which looked at internet and social network use, as well as self-reported levels of happiness and self-esteem. They found that social networks increased the risk of being exposed to "offensive behaviours and hate speech", which could have a harmful effect on people's mental well-being.

"In online discussions with unknown others, individuals more easily indulge in aggressive and disrespectful behaviours. Online networks also are a fertile ground for spreading harmful, offensive, or controversial contents often lying at the verge between free speech and hate speech," they said.

This hateful content can reduce the reader's trust in others, and therefore have a detrimental effect on their own well-being – social trust has been shown to be one of the strongest predictors of self-reported happiness in previous studies.

The results add weight to previous research which found that social networks can decrease people's happiness and general satisfaction with their lives. For two weeks a group of 82 people were sent text messages five times a day and asked to reply explaining how they felt that moment, and also how satisfied they were with their lives overall.

What the researchers found was that using Facebook tended to lower the results for both questions. "The more people used Facebook at one time point, the worse they felt the next time we text-messaged them; the more they used Facebook over two-weeks, the more their life satisfaction levels declined over time," said the paper.

"On the surface, Facebook provides an invaluable resource for fulfilling the basic human need for social connection," said Ethan Kross, a social psychologist who led the work at the University of Michigan. "But rather than enhance well-being, we found that Facebook use predicts the opposite result – it undermines it."

Currently Facebook has over a billion users, 500 million of whom interact with the social network every day through the website or apps.

*http://www.telegraph.co.uk/technology/facebook/11067618/How-Facebook-makes-you-distrusting-and-miserable.html*

Text: Facebook friends are virtual, finds Oxford University study

**Facebook might give us the ability to have thousands of friends but it does nothing to expand how many we keep in real life, an Oxford University study has found** By Stephen Adams

11:16AM GMT January 24 2010

Humans appear incapable of maintaining more than about 150 active relationships, according to Robin Dunbar, a professor of evolutionary anthropology. He arrived at that figure – coined 'Dunbar's number' – in the 1990s. Recent study into how social networking sites affect Dunbar's number indicates that that advances in technology have not been matched by changes in mental capacity.

When he looked at how people use sites like Facebook, Bebo and MySpace, he found that those with lots of 'friends' only interact with a relatively small proportion of them.

"The interesting thing is that you can have 1,500 friends but when you actually look at traffic on sites, you see people maintain the same inner circle of around 150 people that we observe in the real world," he told *The Sunday Times*.

While "people obviously like the kudos of having hundreds of friends" the reality was that their social circle was unlikely to be bigger than anybody else's.

His earlier research claimed that people limit the number of real relationships they have in complex societies, because the part of our brains that cope with language and personal interaction cannot deal with any more.

*http://www.telegraph.co.uk/technology/news/7066454/Facebook-friends-are-virtual-finds-Oxford-University-study.html*

# 24 Written Assignment: Standard Level

## The task

These three articles are all about Facebook and Facebook friends and are related to the core topic Social Relationships. When you have read the articles very carefully and made your notes, begin to think about your aim and how your choice of text type and audience will help you achieve it.

From the wide variety text types you have studied, choose the one to suit your aim most effectively.

For example:

- If you want to share the information you have gained with your peers, you could write a speech to be given in assembly.
- If you want to share the information with students, teachers and parents, you could write an article for the school newspaper.
- If you want to make your voice heard in protest, you could write a blog.
- Or you could choose to write an email, an essay, an official report, a flyer or a set of guidelines.

The text type you choose should help you reach your goal and you should be able to explain how and why this is so in the rationale.

## A final note

In the Written Assessment you will choose three or four texts based on one core topic to write your own text. You will find selections of texts based on core topics in other chapters of this book, which could also be used for practice.

## Written Assignment: Receptive and written productive skills (SL)

### Criterion A: Rationale and task

- How well does the student use the rationale and the task in order to accomplish the assignment?
  - How clearly has the task been introduced in the rationale?
  - How successfully does the task address the subject and aim(s) stated in the rationale?
  - How appropriate is the choice of the text type to the task?

| Mark | Level descriptor |
| --- | --- |
| 0 | The work does not reach a standard described by the descriptors below. |
| 1–2 | **The student uses the rationale and the task in a limited way and may have partially accomplished the assignment.**<br>There is little reference to the source in the rationale.<br>The student has barely explained what his or her aims are.<br>The subject is hardly relevant to the chosen sources and not addressed in the task.<br>The chosen text type is inappropriate to the audience and aim(s) stated in the rationale. |

| Mark | Level descriptor |
|---|---|
| 3–4 | **The student uses the rationale and the task in order to accomplish the assignment to a certain extent.**<br>There is some reference to some of the sources in the rationale.<br>The student has explained what his or her aims are but not how he or she intends to achieve them.<br>The subject stated in the rationale is partially relevant to the chosen sources or not addressed throughout the task.<br>The chosen text type is not completely appropriate to the audience and aim(s) stated in the rationale, and is applied inconsistently throughout the task. |
| 5–6 | **The student uses the rationale and the task adequately in order to accomplish the assignment.**<br>All sources have been referred to but not necessarily described in the rationale.<br>The student has explained what his or her aims are and how he or she intends to achieve them.<br>The subject stated in the rationale is generally relevant to the chosen sources and addressed throughout the task.<br>The chosen text type is not completely appropriate to the audience and purpose stated in the rationale, but is applied consistently throughout the task. |
| 7–8 | **The student uses the rationale and the task well in order to accomplish the assignment.**<br>All sources have been described in the rationale.<br>The student has clearly explained what his or her aims are and how he or she intends to achieve them.<br>The subject stated in the ratioale is relevant to the chosen sources and addressed throughout the task.<br>The chosen text type is appropriate to the audience and purpose stated in the rationale, and is applied throughout the task. |
| 9–10 | **The student uses the rationale and the task effectively in order to accomplish the assignment.**<br>All sources have been fully described in the rationale.<br>The student has clearly explained what his or her aims are and how he or she intends to achieve them.<br>The subject stated in the rationale is focused, relevant to the chosen sources and consistently addressed throughout the task.<br>The chosen text type is appropriate to the audience and purpose stated in the rationale, and is applied consistently throughout the task. |

## Criterion B: Organization and development

- How well are ideas organized and developed?

**Note:** Criterion B is applied to the task only.

| Marks | Level descriptor |
|---|---|
| 0 | The work does not reach a standard described by the descriptors below. |
| 1–2 | The organization and development of ideas is mostly ineffective. |
| 3–4 | Ideas are organized and developed mostly effectively. |
| 5–6 | Ideas are organized and developed effectively. |

## Criterion C: Language

- How appropriately and effectively does the student use language in relation to the task?

**Note:** Criterion C is applied to the task only.

# 24 Written Assignment: Standard Level

| Mark | Level descriptor |
|---|---|
| 0 | The work does not reach a standard described by the descriptors below. |
| 1–2 | **The use of language is mostly limited.**<br>Vocabulary is limited or is generally inappropriate to the task.<br>Simple sentence structures are rarely clear.<br>The rhetorical devices are not used, or are used inappropriately. |
| 3–4 | **The use of language is generally adequate.**<br>Vocabulary shows range but is sometimes used inappropriately to the task.<br>Simple sentence structures are clear but no complex structures have been attempted.<br>There is limited use of appropriate rhetorical devices. |
| 5–6 | **The use of language is appropriate and is generally effective.**<br>Vocabulary shows range and is mostly appropriate to the task.<br>Simple sentence structures are clear but there are errors in complex structures.<br>The rhetorical devices are used appropriately. |
| 7–8 | **The use of language is appropriate and effective.**<br>Vocabulary shows good range and is consistently used appropriately to the task.<br>Complex sentence structures are clear and effective.<br>The rhetorical devices are varied and used effectively. |

*Taken from* Language B guide © *International Baccalaureate Organization 2011, pp. 36–38*

# Theory of Knowledge

## Objectives
- To acquire and practise the language of TOK
- To practise expressing opinions and discussing themes orally and in writing

## What is Theory of Knowledge all about?

The Theory of Knowledge (TOK) course is an element of the Diploma Programme which is very different from the other classes you will take. In TOK you learn to ask more questions, to question what you think you know or what you are told and to ponder more on things.

Oral participation and oral presentations are an important part of the course, and this is often challenging for students who are not native speakers of English or who have not yet reached bilingual proficiency. This chapter will help you to become familiar with the vocabulary of TOK and the kinds of thinking and questioning you will need to do in your TOK classes. There are also opportunities for you to discuss the topics in the English B class, which should make you feel more confident in discussions in the mainstream TOK class.

Written work is also important in TOK and the final major assessment is an essay. Take every opportunity offered in this chapter to practise your writing skills for TOK. It is a good idea to keep a reflection journal where you make notes about ideas and arguments which interest you or are new and different from your own thoughts. This journal will be a record of your thoughts during the course and may be a source of inspiration for the final essay.

### Interactive oral activity

Discussion topic: Who are you?

What do you know? How do you know what you know?

Why do you think the way you do?

Think about yourself for a moment – how would you describe yourself to someone who doesn't know you?

You would probably begin with the facts (name, date of birth, etc.) and some impressions of your physical appearance. But why do you think the way you do? Who or what influences you? What are your beliefs? How do you know when you are right?

## How do we know anything? Introduction to the Ways of Knowing and Knowledge Claims

### Interactive oral activity

What can you see above? What is it? How do you know? Describe each picture carefully to your partner.

How do you know the chair is a chair?
Can you prove it?

What about the pipe? Is it a pipe?

Do you know this from experience or previous knowledge?
To what extent is perception involved?

## The Ways of Knowing

This is a term you will hear often and it is important that you fully understand it. In TOK classes we talk about eight Ways of Knowing.

While you are reading about the Ways of Knowing, be aware and consider carefully which of them are important in each of the subjects you are studying at school. In TOK classes and discussions we refer to the subjects studied in school as the Areas of Knowledge.

Some Ways of Knowing are easier to understand than others.

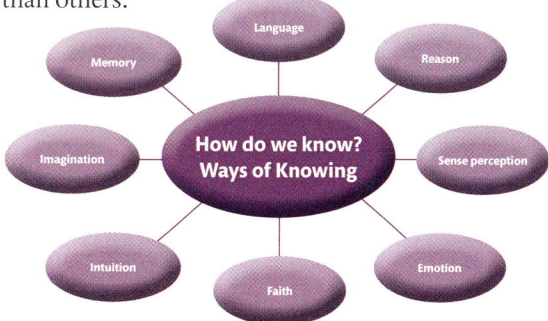

## Language

We speak different languages and have different ways of expressing ideas, with different vocabularies and sometimes also different writing systems.

- Our language is closely connected to our identity. What does your language mean to you? Discuss this with a partner who has a different mother tongue.
- Are there some expressions or ideas which can be expressed in your own language which cannot be expressed in English? Can we express ideas without words?
- Does our language influence our thinking? The Sapir-Whorf hypothesis, developed by two American linguists, suggests that language does influence the way we think. You could research this hypothesis for more information.

Many questions in TOK begin with the phrase 'To what extent' – for example, we could ask:

*To what extent does our language influence our thinking?*

This question does not allow a yes /no answer; we have to explore and discuss the question, and look at the question from different perspectives.

### Written work (HL)
**Personal response**

'The limits of my language are the limits of my mind. All I know is what I have words for.'
*Ludwig Wittgenstein, Austrian-British philosopher*

This Language B, Paper 2-style exercise can also help you form your ideas about the role of language as a Way of Knowing. Write between 150 and 250 words. Remember to justify your arguments.

## Sense perception

This includes all of our human senses – sight, smell, touch, hearing, taste. However, we know that often we interpret things differently from others. We enjoy different tastes, different smells or sounds. If two people saw an accident in the street, they might each interpret and understand it differently, although they actually saw the same event.

But can we trust our senses to tell us the truth? What is the truth?

If we see a picture such as the one above, our eyes tell us one thing, but our reason tells us something different.

## The effect of culture on perception

### Written work

Now look carefully at the picture opposite and then write about 100 words to describe what you see.

Share your writing with others in your group. Look to see if there are any differences in the way you each describe the scene. Could these differences be based on your culture?

Theory of Knowledge

398

### Interactive oral activity

Read the quote below and discuss it with your partner. Do you agree? Can you think of examples which illustrate the quote?

> 'No man ever looks at the world with pristine eyes. He sees it edited by a definite set of customs and institutions and ways of thinking.'
>
> Ruth Benedict, American anthropologist

After the discussion, write a personal reflection about the quote.

### Interactive oral activity

In small groups, think about an event at school which the whole class has recently shared, perhaps an assembly or a concert.

When you have all agreed on an event, each person should write about 100 words describing the event.

Then share your writing with others in your class.

You were all at the same event – are the descriptions all the same? What kinds of differences can you identify? Why are there differences?

What kinds of differences are there between us that make our perceptions differ? Relate this to the quote above.

# Reason

Reason means rationality, being logical and figuring things out.

N.B. *It doesn't mean giving a reason for something.*

In TOK, if we give a reason for something, we justify it. You have come across this term in Language B and other subject areas.

In TOK we talk about:

- Inductive reasoning – this begins with particular observations and data collections, which can be repeated to reach general conclusions. For example, if a large number of people complete a survey, the results can be used to identify general patterns.
- Deductive reasoning – this moves from general observations to the particular, so that we identify a generality and then try to use that example to support a particular concept.

When making an argument based on reason, be careful not to make sweeping statements, i.e. universal generalisations.

For example: *All IB students study hard.*

This kind of statement can be disproved very easily – how?

Also beware of statements which include *all, no one, everyone, everywhere, never, always*, etc., as these can also be disproved easily. Be thoughtful in discussions and writing.

399

### Interactive oral activity

With a partner, read these statements and contradict them.

- All girls wear make-up.
- Everyone has read *Oliver Twist*.
- No one is interested in the news.
- You never listen to me.

Were the statements easy to contradict? Why?

## Syllogisms

We often use a sequence of ideas to express and prove an argument in a logical form called a syllogism. The ideas are called 'premises'. The first premise is a major premise, which is a universal, general statement. This can be positive, using 'all', or negative, using 'no', and it is followed by the second premise, which is a general statement related to the first statement. If the steps are logical and correct, the syllogism is said to be 'valid'; if not, it is 'invalid'.

| Example 1 | | |
|---|---|---|
| Premise 1 | All IBDP students study TOK | (true) |
| Premise 2 | Tracy is an IBDP student | (true) |
| Conclusion | Tracy studies TOK | this syllogism is valid |

| Example 2 | | |
|---|---|---|
| Premise 1 | All dogs have four legs | (true) |
| Premise 2 | My cat has four legs | (true – but not relevant) |
| Conclusion | My cat is a dog | this syllogism is invalid – but why? |

A valid syllogism states:

*All A are B*

*C is A*

*Therefore C is B*

## Emotion

Emotion is related to our feelings. Individually, identify the emotions shown in the pictures and write a caption for each one.

When everyone has finished, share your results in a small group. Did you all agree? Why not?

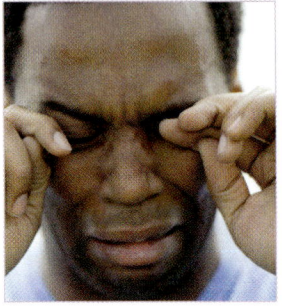

A range of emotions.

### Interactive oral activity

How are emotions related to the Areas of Knowledge? Discuss in your group to what extent different Areas of Knowledge are influenced by emotions. Be ready to report back to the class.

## Memory

To what extent can we rely on our memories? To what extent is memory related to perception and the other Ways of Knowing? How important is memory to you as a student?

Much of our knowledge today is based on the collective memories of past and present generations. These are shared in a variety of records: written, oral, visual, etc. Which Areas of Knowledge rely most on shared memories?

## Imagination

'I am enough of an artist to draw freely on my imagination. Imagination is more important than knowledge. Knowledge is limited. Imagination encircles the world.'

*Albert Einstein, German physicist*

'I dream my painting, then I paint my dream.'

*Vincent van Gogh, Dutch post-impressionist artist*

### Interactive oral activity

How important is imagination in the Areas of Knowledge? Discuss in your group the various subjects you study and the role of imagination in them.

## Intuition

What is intuition? Intuition is a way of knowing which does not have any logical reasons. We just 'feel' that something is so. The role of intuition can vary greatly between cultures. How is it regarded in your culture? Is it important?

'It is through science that we prove, but through intuition that we discover.'

*Henri Poincaré, French mathematician, scientist and philosopher*

## Faith

Faith involves accepting ideas without any proof, which might convince people who do not share the faith. The dictionary definition of faith states:

faith (n): a strong feeling of trust or confidence in someone or something

*Longman Dictionary of Contemporary English 6*
ISBN: 9781447954194

A particular religion such as Christianity or Islam is also referred to as 'a faith'.

We can also have faith in someone or something without it being a religious belief. Maybe you have faith in a friend who has promised to do something for you. You have no proof that they will do it or that it will be a success – but you have faith that they will try. In PE class when you do gymnastics on a high bar, you have faith that your teacher will help you.

Faith has a different role in different cultures of the world. Who or what do you have faith in?

### Interactive oral activity

Think about your culture and the role faith plays. Share your thoughts with a partner.

Discuss what is happening here with a partner.

What kind of knowledge do these people possess?

## Knowledge and Knowledge Claims

*Knowledge is knowing a tomato is a fruit. Wisdom is not putting it in a fruit salad.*

People have different kinds of knowledge: a Chinese farmer will have different knowledge from a New York banker; a sales assistant in a grocery store will have different knowledge from a florist; a science professor will have different knowledge from a history professor; a mother will have different knowledge from a grandmother.

**Personal knowledge** is knowing how to do something, and knowledge gained through personal experience. These can be expressed by saying 'I know how to…' or 'I know that…'

**Shared knowledge** is knowledge gained from a larger community, family, friends and teachers, but also from history.

Often personal knowledge and shared knowledge merge, or we gain new knowledge through experience and reflection.

What role do you think social network sites play in sharing knowledge?

Which kinds of knowledge are the people in the pictures using? Which Ways of Knowing do they demonstrate?

A Knowledge Claim is a statement made about something we know, or say we know. It can be presented as true but may not really be true; it can be an assertion that something is true when it is actually an opinion or belief.

Knowledge Claims can be based on observation, personal and shared, on values, on definitions, on predictions based on previous experience, etc.

*I know that my foot is sore.*

*I know that the weather is awful today.*

*I know that fish and chips taste wonderful.*

*I know that a square has four equal sides.*

*I know that one day I will be rich.*

## Written work

Write some Knowledge Claims of your own; include some from your Areas of Knowledge.

## Truth tests

It is important to be able to justify a Knowledge Claim; for this we need supporting evidence, or even proof.

To explore Knowledge Claims we can use the three Truth Tests – although these do not always present conclusive results, they do help us think about the truth.

## The Coherence Test

Does this fit in or is it consistent with what I already know or what others have shown? Check by doing some research and thinking around the claim.

## The Correspondence Test

Does this claim fit in or correspond to what I can see or observe myself? Go and look!

## The Pragmatism Test

Does this work? Is it practical?

Try the three tests for each of the following statements and see how helpful they are.

1 This book was printed in China.

2 The best way to study is standing on your head.

3 There are no butterflies left in the world.

4 The weather is getting worse because people have stopped believing in a god.

So far, you have started to learn about the nature of TOK: Ways of Knowing, Knowledge Claims and Truth Tests. Use this knowledge in your subject classes and look for examples of how the Ways of Knowing are used and examples of Knowledge Claims and Truth Tests and how they are applied and in which subject areas.

## Ethics

Another important Area of Knowledge in TOK is ethics.

Ethics is all about:

- what is right or wrong
- how you learnt what is right or wrong
- what makes a good person
- how to make good decisions
- how we should live.

When discussing and debating these themes, remember to take other people's perspectives into consideration.

One popular activity in discussions about ethics is described below. Read this paragraph and then talk the problem through in your class.

- What would your action be? Why?
- What would you not do? Why?

Discuss the problem in your group and try to reach a decision. Share your answers with the class before reading on.

## Text: An ethical dilemma: Teetering on the footbridge

Tuesday, June 27 2006

By Wray Herbert

Imagine that you are the operator of a San Francisco cable car. One day, the car's brakes go out, and you're careering down Powell Street at an untoward speed. Ahead you see five students, crossing the track on their way home from class. There is no way to stop the car or warn the students. The only way to avoid killing all five is to throw a switch and turn onto another track. But if you do that you will run over and kill another student who is straggling behind the group. What do you do?

403

This is a slightly embellished version of what philosophers call the "trolley dilemma," which is used to explore how people reason about morally ambiguous situations. The scenario is often used together with another, the so-called "footbridge dilemma." In this case, a runaway trolley is again heading toward five innocent victims. But you're no longer the driver. You and a fat man are standing on a footbridge overlooking the track, and you realize that the only way you can spare the five students is to push the fat man off the bridge, on to the track below. Push or no push?

Nevermind that even a very fat man would probably not stop a runaway trolley car. That's not the point. Focus on the two dilemmas, which are fundamentally the same. In each, you can sacrifice one life to save five. Yet people react very differently to the two situations. People automatically see the logic in the trolley dilemma, and almost all opt for the utilitarian solution. But given the footbridge dilemma, most are morally repulsed by the idea of pushing the fat man off the bridge. They won't do it. This seeming inconsistency has baffled both philosophers and psychologists for years.

Why does the human brain process these two dilemmas so differently? Why does our reason fail us on the footbridge? Northeastern University psychologists Piercarlo Valdesolo and David DeSteno are among the scientists who have been studying moral judgments in the laboratory, and they are coming to believe that moral reasoning is not as, well, reasonable as we like to think. Indeed, what we do in the name of morality may be more emotional than rational. According to the theory, humans operate according to certain "rules of thumb." These are automatic, knee-jerk assessments, and they are very powerful, requiring a lot of mental work to overcome. Much of the time they are helpful, in routine everyday matters, but we also fall back on them in situations of uncertainty—or moral ambiguity. And they sometimes fool the more rational mind.

That's what happens on the footbridge, say Valdesolo and DeSteno. Apparently one rule of thumb, emotionally powerful, says we don't push people off bridges. Perhaps it's the tactile nature of the act that makes it seem more like murder than saving lives. Whatever the source of the feeling, it's strong enough to prevent what's arguably the more reasonable (and moral) action: Keeping five students from perishing. There is experimental evidence for this: The rare few who do opt to sacrifice the fat man clearly struggle with the choice. They take much longer to decide, as if they had to free themselves from the tug of the quicker intuitive impulse.

Valdesolo and DeSteno wondered: If our emotions are so influential in our moral judgments, might it be possible to determine people's actions by manipulating their emotions? The short answer, as they report in the June issue of *Psychological Science*, is yes. The scientists presented research subjects with the two classical dilemmas, but before they did, they primed their emotions with completely irrelevant materials. One group watched a video clip of a Saturday Night Live skit, while another watched part of a short documentary about a Spanish village.

Funny as the Spanish village was, it was no competition for the Not-Ready-For-Prime-Time-Players, so the first group headed into the dilemmas feeling much more upbeat. And this uplifted mood trumped the negative feelings tied to the fat man falling. The participants were more likely to choose the practical, logical course of action on the footbridge, and what's more, the longer they took the more likely they were to choose the greatest good for the greatest number. The mood manipulation did not affect choices in the trolley dilemma, which makes sense since this scenario was not as ambiguous to begin with.

None of this answers the fundamental question: Are you a better person if you murder one person to spare five? That's for ascended masters. But you probably are a more humble person now, knowing just how easily your most profound judgments and actions can be shaped by others.

To learn more about human nature, go to www.pearsonhotlinks.com, enter the title or ISBN of this book and click on Chapter 25.

http://www.psychologicalscience.org/onlyhuman/2006/06/teetering-on-footbridge.cfm

### Text handling

1. Did you recognise Ways of Knowing in the text?
2. Make a list of new vocabulary which may be useful in your TOK classes.

# Index

## A

'a lot of'/'lots of'   204
Aarons, Celine   181
*About a Boy* (Nick Hornby)   80
abstract nouns   80, 175, 271
action verbs   65
active sentences   5, 284
adjectives
   adjective–noun   80
   comparatives   334
   im- prefix   371
   modifiers   254
   superlatives   322, 334
   the + adjective   23
adventure sports   287–9, 296–7, 300–3
adventure tourism   303
adverbs of frequency   288–9
advertising   144–59, 198
   changing consumption habits   157
   child-specific advertising   152–5, 198
   junk food advertising   152–5
   persuasive language   149–51
   social media marketing   157
   strategies and effects of   147–9, 156–7
   television advertising   134, 153, 196
'affect'/'effect'   203
affective conditioning   147, 148, 149
Afghanistan   77, 78
afternoon tea   351
agar-agar   228
agriculture
   food waste   3, 4
   greenhouse gas emissions   215, 217
   insect farming   219
   livestock farming   215, 217
   robots in farming   375–6, 377
   seaweed harvesting   228–9
   slave or child labour   44, 45
   water usage   11, 215
Alcott, Louisa May   94

*Alice in Wonderland* (Lewis Carroll)   317, 349
Allen-Gray, Alison   379
alternative energy *see* renewable energy
alternative food sources
   edible insects   214–21
   seaweed   228–9
   vegetarian food   222–7
Amateur Swimming Association   238
American Dietetic Association (ADA)   227
American English   4, 44, 129, 130
American Psychological Association   295
ancestral languages   136–8
Anglo-Saxon dialects   129, 133, 255
animal rights   226, 362
'any'/'some'   132
apostrophes   209, 311
Aristotle   79
Ashworth, Jenn   86
assimilation   136
Austen, Jane   93
Australia
   Australian English   129
   home schooling   118–19
   undocumented immigration   70–3

## B

Bacha Khan   76
Bahamas, customs and traditions   346–8
Ban Ki-moon   75, 388
Bangladesh   41, 43, 54
Bank of England   93
Banksy   264, 265
Belgium   307
Bell, Alexander Graham   67, 195
Benedict, Ruth   399
biomass conversion   390
black cats, superstition and   335
Blackman, Malorie   361–2
blogs (writing practice)   5–6, 10, 23, 45, 73, 138, 267, 353
   tips   6, 46

Bluetooth   184
Blyton, Enid   86
boating   309
body image   246–7
body mass index (BMI)   235
body repair technologies   354–65
   illegal trade in human organs   364–5
   limb transplants   354–7
   organ donors   363
   tissue engineering   357–9
   xenotransplantation   359–62
Bond, James   182
book reviews, writing   53
*The Book Thief* (Markus Zusak)   379
Botox 247
Boudicca 93
Bowler, Gerry   330, 331
Boyle, T.C.   60–1
Brazil, Angela   85, 87
breakfasts   234
Brick Lane, London   178, 263–5
Britain
   'bad girl' fiction   85–6
   bank notes   93
   bungee jumping   300–2
   childcare   125
   children and swimming abilities   237–9
   Commonwealth   338–40
   cultural diversity   250–67, 280–1
   customs and traditions   321–4, 349–52
   cyberbullying   210–11
   education   85, 86, 95–6
   ethnic minority population   255
   families   109–11
   food sharing   20–3
   gender equality gap   307
   junk food marketing   153
   Manchester   256–61
   mobile phone use   177–8, 180, 181, 182
   National Curriculum   238
   organ transplants   355–7
   renewable energy   389
   robots in farming   375, 377

405

# Index

school sports activities   244
sport, participation in   244, 305, 321–2
suffrage movement   85, 86
Thames, River   317–21
tissue engineering   357–9
undocumented immigration   59, 63–4
volunteering   305
wind energy industry   28–9, 31–2, 36–7
women in traditional male occupations   98–104
see also English language; London
British Broadcasting Corporation   196
British English   129–30
see also English language
Broughton, John   109, 111
Broughton, Paul   109–10, 111
Brown, Gordon   75
Buck, Pearl   94
Bullokar, William   134
bungee jumping   287, 288, 300–3
Burns, Robert   342
'but'   220
butchers   103–4

## C

cab drivers   100–1
Cahill, Mark   355–6
calcium   235
calories   153, 224, 234, 235
Cambodia   219
Cameron, David   388
Canada
 Canadian English   130
 junk food marketing   153
car mechanics   101–2
Carbon Capture and Storage   389
carbon dioxide emissions   3, 388
Caribbean culture   266
carpal tunnel syndrome   370
Carr, Caleb   377
Carroll, Lewis   317, 349
Carter, Larry   224–5, 226
Catherine of Braganza   350–1
Caxton, William   133, 134
celebrations   274, 283
 Carnival   266–7

Christmas   330–2, 341, 342
 Junkanoo   346–7
 New Year   341–3, 344
cell phones see mobile phones
cereal crops   3
Ceylon see Sri Lanka
Chabris, Chris   149–50
Chang, Jung   69
Chappe, Claude   195
Charlemagne   267
Charles, Prince of Wales   32, 388–9
cheap clothing   41–2, 54
Chicken Tikka Massala   281
childcare   109, 110, 125–7
 nurseries   125
children
 advertising and   152–5, 198
 child labour   41, 44, 45, 46, 63, 64, 78
 childhood obesity   152, 153
 cyberbullying   210–13
 mobile phones and   115, 206–8
 swimming abilities   237–9
 technology, physical effects of   369
 see also childcare; education; families
China   130
 illegal organ donation   364
 Peking opera   273
cholesterol   235
Christianity   401
Christmas customs and traditions   330–2, 342
 Santa Claus   330–1
 Twelve Days of Christmas   341
Churchill, Winston   93
Clarke, Arthur C.   369
clauses
 dependent clauses   117
 –ing clauses   135
 independent clauses   117
 noun clauses   242, 316
Clegg, Nick   177–8
climate change   3, 388–9
 causes and solutions   390
climbing   292
Cohen, Randy   145
Cold Light (Jenn Ashworth)   86
collective memories   400

collectivism   270
colloquial expressions   112
 see also idiomatic language
Colombia   217
colonialism   129, 136, 339, 344
Columbus, Christopher   346
Commonwealth   130, 338–40
customs and traditions   341–8
 member countries   340
Commonwealth Games   339
comparative adjectives   334
complex sentences   9, 90–1, 117
computers   44
 cyberbullying   205–6, 210–13
 ergonomics and   370
 Flat Classroom project   172–5
 global collaborative learning experiences   172–5
 Hole-in-the-Wall project, India   170–1
 laptops in the classroom   161–3, 161–7, 164–9
 One Laptop Per Child (OLPC) project, Rwanda   168–9
Constantine, Emperor   330
Cook, Robin   280–2
Cooper, Martin   180
countable and uncountable nouns   200
creative writing   378
creativity, action and service (CAS)   xii, 242
Croker, Charlie   139–40
Cronogue, Joel   109–10, 111
crossword puzzles   134, 311–12
 cryptic clues   312
crowd funding   184, 185
cultural diversity   250–67, 280–1
 Britain   250–67
 cultural challenges   275–80
 national cuisines   272–4
 political view of   280–2
 Singapore   282–4
 World Day for Cultural Diversity for Dialogue and Development   274–5
culture   268–70
 cultural amnesia   58
 cultural bias   271
 cultural differences   269–70

406

cultural practices, protection of 272–3
Hofstde Dimension of National Culture 269–70
Maori culture 327–9
perception, effect on 398
see also cultural diversity; customs and traditions
Curie, Marie 94
Curran, Colleen 86
curry 255, 259, 260, 264
Curry Mile, Manchester 259–61
customs and traditions 326–53
Bahamas 346–8
Britain 349–52
Christmas 330–2
Commonwealth countries 341–8
Hogmany 341–3
Maori culture 327–9
Sri Lanka 344–5
superstitions 334–7
Valentine's Day 332–4
see also culture
cyberbullying 05–6, 211–13, 392
Cybersexism (Laurie Penny) 85

## D

dairy foods 235
Dangerous Sports Club 287
Dante Alighieri 345
Darwin, Charles 93
Davey, Ed 389
Davies, William Henry 306
debates 39, 168, 362
Democratic Republic of the Congo 44
Denmark 25
dependent clauses 117
Desai, Kishwar 81–3
'despite' 90–1
'despite'/'in spite of' 245
DeSteno, David 404
diary writing (writing practice) 10, 19, 66, 84, 88, 127, 152, 180, 344, 362
Dickens, Charles 196, 317
dietary fibre 223, 234
direct speech 33, 163, 169
Douglass, Frederick 46–9
Doyle, Sir Arthur Conan 317

Doyle, Ryan 298–300
drought 11, 17
'during'/'while' 91
Dyar, Harrison 195
Dyhouse, Carol 85

## E

eating disorders 246
eco-protein see insect protein
edible insects 214–21
Edict of Nantes 262
Edinburgh, Philip, Duke of 31–3
education 74–91, 160–75
fear of failure 95, 96, 113
fictional accounts 85, 86
Flat Classroom project 172–5
girls 78, 82, 83, 84, 89, 95–6, 113
global collaborative learning experiences 172–5
home schooling 118–20
language learning and self-confidence 95–6, 97
Minimally Invasive Education 170
National Curriculum (UK) 238
peer-to-peer learning 172–5
social learning 174
the struggle for 75–9
team sports and educational performance, connection between 243–5
technology in education 160–75
transformative power of 88, 89
Egyptians, ancient 335
Einstein, Albert 401
electricity
lack of access to 35
mini- and off-grid solutions 35
wind-generated 25–34
Eliot, George 93
Elizabeth II, Queen 339
emails (writing practice) 10, 91, 135, 190, 197, 203, 226, 229, 292, 303, 348, 353
exam hints 348
emergency food assistance 7
Emerson, Ralph Waldo 325
emotion 400
energy
energy poverty 34–6, 169
see also electricity; renewable energy

English language 128–41, 255
American English 44, 129, 130
British English 129–30
English as a second language 133
global language 129–30
grammar guides, early 134
history of the English language 133–5
idiomatic language 252, 300
informal English 265
mis-translated English 139–41
English Project 133
entomophagy 214–21
ergonomics 370
Esperanto 141–3
ethical issues
advertising 148
cheap clothing 41–2, 54
energy poverty 34–5, 36
food shortages 6–9, 20–3
food waste 3–5
slave labour 40–55
water scarcity 10–12, 13, 14
xenotransplantation 359–62
ethics 403–4
ethical dilemmas 403–4
see also ethical issues
ethnic food 255
Evans, Mary Anne (George Eliot) 93
expressions of quantity 352
extreme sports see adventure sports
Extreme Sports Channel 287–8

## F

Facebook 157, 391, 392, 393
facial reconstructive surgery 357, 358
fad diets 234, 235
Fagan, Jenni 86
faith 401
families 108–27
childcare 109, 110, 125–7
fatherhood 109–12
grandparents 120–4
helicopter parents 113–14, 115–16
home schooling 118–20
parental role models 116
social media and 206–8
FareShare 20

407

# Index

farmer–buyer agreements   4
farming *see* agriculture
fast food industry
   junk food advertising   152–5
   self-regulation   154
fatherhood   109–12
fats   234, 235
femininity   270
fertilizers   3
'fewer'/'fewest'   308
Fincher, Jonathan   185
first conditional   114–15
first-footers   342
fishing   309, 318, 324
   stilt fishing   345
Flat Classroom project   172–5
flavonoids   223
fluid intake   234
flyers   62, 95
   tips   62
Flynn, Gillian   86
food
   afternoon tea   351
   alternative food sources   214–29
   cultural importance of   272–4, 283
   edible insects   214–16
   ethnic food   255
   food banks and food parcels   20
   food sharing   20–3
   food stamps   7
   healthy eating for teenagers   234–6
   junk food advertising   152–5
   school vending machines   154
   shortages   6–9
   vegetarian and vegan food   222–7
food value chain   3
food waste   3–5
   reducing   3, 4, 20–1
FoodCycle   20
'footbridge dilemma'   404
fossil fuels   25–6, 27, 28
*Foxfire* (Joyce Carol Oates)   86
France
   French cuisine   272–3
   gender equality gap   307
   Lascaux cave paintings   287
free running   298–300
freshwater   10, 11

Freud, Sigmund   67
Friedman, Thomas   173
friendships
   'Dunbar's number'   393
   social butterfly effect   391
   social media and   391–3
fruit harvesters, robotic   375, 376, 377
Fry, Elizabeth   93
future tense   258

## G

gambling   324
Gandhi, Mahatma   76, 285
Gardner, David   375, 376
Garn, Howard   314
Garrison, William Lloyd   47
gender equality gap   81, 82, 105, 307
gender roles   85, 105
'Generation Y'   231
Germany   307
gerund   193, 233
gerund clauses   237
Gilbert and George   262
Gillard, Katie   98–9
*Girl Trouble* (Carol Dyhouse)   85
girls
   'bad girl' fiction   85–6
   education   78, 82, 83, 84, 89, 95–6, 113
Gladstone, William Ewart   349
Global English   129
global issues
   climate change   3, 388–90
   food shortages   6–9
   food waste   3–5
   slave labour   40–55
   undocumented migration   56–73
   water scarcity   10–12, 13, 14
   wind energy   24–34, 389, 390
global warming   3, 27, 388–9
   causes and solutions 3   90
golf   324
*Gone Girl* (Gillian Flynn)   86
Good Samaritan law   21
graffiti art   264, 265
Grahame, Kenneth   317
grammar
   'a lot of'/'lots of'   204
   adverbs of frequency   288–9

   'affect'/'effect'   203
   'any'/'some'   132
   apostrophes   209
   'but'   220
   'despite'   90–1
   'despite'/'in spite of'   245
   direct speech   33, 163, 169
   'during'/'while'   91
   expressions of quantity   352
   'fewer'/'fewest'   308
   gerund   193, 233
   gerund clauses   237
   idiomatic language   252, 300
   imperative   124, 179
   indirect (reported) speech   33, 112, 163, 169
   'less'/'least'   308
   'look forward to'   356
   'many'/'much'   204
   'may'/'might'   360
   'more'/'most'   308
   'must'/'have to'   30
   'ought to'   62
   passive voice   183
   the possessive   209, 311
   present participle   233
   reference pronouns   23, 82, 114
   'should'   62
   'since'   202–3
   'since'/'for'   172
   'stop'   43
   'tell'/'say'   112
   'the more..., the more...'   83
   time, expressions of   172
   'to be able to'/'unable to'   239–40
   'too'/'not... either'   343–4
   'used to'   226
   'used to'/'get used to'   186
   'would'   50
   *see also* adjectives; clauses; nouns; prefixes; sentence structure; verbs
grandparents   120–4
greenhouse gases   3, 27, 215, 217, 388
greetings cards   333
Grey, Elisha   195
group discussions, organising   55, 59, 131, 200
Guide Dogs for the Blind   290

## H

Hackett, A.J. 302–3
Hampton Court 318
Harbottle, Charlotte 103–4
Hargadon, Steve 174
Harris, Robert 315
Hart, John 134
hate speech 392
health
   body repair technologies 359–65
   teenage health 230–49
   *see also* sport
health and safety legislation 54
helicopter parents 113–14, 115–16
*The Help* (Kathryn Stockett) 52–3
Henry V, king of England 134
Hindi language 136, 137
Hofstde Dimension of National Culture 269–70
Hogmany 341–3
Holbein, Hans 66
Hole-in-the-Wall project, India 170–1
home, working from 188
homelessness 6–8
Hornby, Nick 380
horseshoes, lucky 336
HOT Watch 184–6
*Huckleberry Finn* (Mark Twain) 206
Huguenots 262
Huhne, Chris 31
Humphrey, Hubert H. 374
hunger *see* food shortages

## I

–*ing* clauses 135
idiomatic language 252, 300
illegal immigrants 56–73
*im-* prefix 371
imagination 401
immigration 57
   animosity towards 57, 59
   assimilation 136
   illegal immigrants 281
   language loss 136–7
   positive aspects of 66–9, 70, 267
   undocumented 56–73
   well-known immigrants 66–9
   *see also* cultural diversity
immunosuppressant drugs 355–6

imperative 124, 179
*in-* prefix 376
inattention blindness 178
independent clauses 117
India
   child labour 78
   Hole-in-the-Wall project 170–1
   Indian cuisine 255, 259, 260, 264, 281
   Indian English 130
indirect speech 33, 112, 163, 169
individualism 270
industrial accidents 41, 54
Industrial Revolution 195, 257
industrialization 25, 105
information overload 149
insect protein 215, 216, 217, 219
instant messaging 207
interactive oral
   exam hints 156
   *see also* oral practice
International Energy Agency (IEA) 34
International English 129
International Women's Day 105–7, 307
interview practice 69, 138, 183, 256
intuition, role of 401
"invisible gorilla" study 150
iPhones 182
   *see also* mobile phones
*Iqbal* (Francesco d'Adamo) 46
Ireland, emigration from 58, 68, 262
iron, sources of 234
Islam 401
Italy 307

## J

Japan 130
   alternative food sources 217
   robotics 372
   seaweed harvesting 228
Jerome, Jerome K. 317
Jewish people 67, 262, 362
Jinnah, Muhammad Ali 76, 87
Jones, Claudia 266
junk food advertising 152–5
Junkanoo 346–7

## K

Kagame, Paul 168
Kahlo, Frida 94
Kahn, Philippe 181
Kandyan Dance 345
kelp harvesting 228
Kennedy, John F. 68
Kenya, water and sanitation projects 17–19
Kickstarter 185
kidney donors 363, 364
Killiecrankie, Battle of 301
King, Martin Luther 76
knowledge 402
   knowledge claims 402
   personal knowledge 402
   shared knowledge 402
'the knowledge' (London cab drivers) 100
Kulkarni, Arjun 197–9

## L

lacto-ovo vegetarianism 226
ladders, superstitions and 335
Lake, Caroline 101–2
landfills 3, 4
language 128–43
   ancestral languages 136–8
   Esperanto 141–3
   and identity 398
   language loss 136–7
   multi-lingual households 256–7
   persuasive 149–51
   Sapir-Whorf hypothesis 398
   *see also* English language
Laos 217
laptops in the classroom 161–3, 164–9
Lascaux cave paintings, France 287
leaflets and flyers 62, 95, 186, 265, 303
leisure 286–325
   active leisure 317–25
   activities around the world 321–5
   characteristics of 305
   free activities 311–15
   gender differences in 307
   hidden costs of 308–10
   mental challenges 311–14
   reading novels 314–15

# Index

volunteering 305
*see also* sport
'less'/'least' 308
letter writing 16, 325, 334, 357
   formal 30–1, 43, 229
   to newspapers 34, 43
Lewis, C.S. 349
Liberia 44
libraries
   library fines 309
   use of 134, 305
lifeboat crew 99–100
limb transplants 354–7
   hand transplants 355–6
   immunosuppressant drugs 355–6
   organ rejection 356, 357
Lincoln, Abraham 47
litter fines 309
*Little Women* (Louisa May Alcott) 94
livestock farming 215, 217
London 261–7, 281
   black cabs 100–1
   Brick Lane 178, 263–5
   Notting Hill Carnival 266–7
   Spitalfields 261–2
London Marathon 290
London Olympics 243
long distance running *see* marathons
'look forward to' 356
*Lost in Translation* (Charlie Croker) 139–41
low-carb diets 235
Lucas, Bill 133

## M
Maasai people 18
macrobiotic diets 226–7
magazine articles (writing practice) 12, 117, 143, 149, 221, 267, 325, 353, 365
   tips 12
Magna Carta 318
Manchester, UK 256–61
Mandela, Nelson 76, 89, 91
'many'/'much' 204
Maori culture 327–9
Marathon, Battle of 287
marathons 287, 290
Marconi, Guglielmo 195
marine conservation 36–7

martial arts 299
Martin, Danielle 218–19
masculinity 270
mass media 195–200
   constructive use of 199
   impact on the young 198–9
   *see also* radio; social media; telephones; television
'may'/'might' 360
MEDEC (Maasai Environmental Development Consortium) 18, 19
'melting pot' 58, 252, 283
memory 400
   collective memories 400
men
   childcare duties 109, 110
   fatherhood 109–12
methane emissions 3, 4
Mexico 217, 219
microtia 357, 358
migration 57
   motivations 57
   *see also* immigration
migratory birds 27
'Millennials' 231
Minimally Invasive Education 170
minimum wage 57
Mitra, Dr. Sugata 170–1
mobile phones 44, 115, 176–93
   camera phones 181
   future capabilities 190–1
   history of 180–3
   HOT Watch 184–6
   masts 182
   newspaper readers 145
   parenting issues 115, 206–8
   phantom calls 182
   safety issues 178, 181
   social etiquette 177–8
   and stress overload 187–9
   texting 177, 178, 181, 207, 231–3, 233, 367–8
   theft of 181
modal verbs 149, 236–7
Moore, Clement Clarke 331
moral reasoning 404
morally ambiguous situations 404
More, Gordon 294
'more'/'most' 308

Morse, Samuel 195
Morse code 195
mother tongue 136–8
multiculturalism *see* cultural diversity
museum and gallery visiting 305
'must'/'have to' 30

## N
*Narrative of the Life of Frederick Douglass, an American Slave* 47, 48–9
National Curriculum (UK) 238
*National Geographic* 11
national identity 281
Native Americans 136
Nazis 67, 362
negative sentences 132
Netherlands 25, 217
neuroscience 314–15
New Year 341–3, 344
New Zealand
   Maori culture and tattoos 327–9
   New Zealand English 129
   sports and leisure 302–3, 323–5
newspapers 196
   headlines 36
   newspaper websites 145
Nicholas, St. 330–1
Nigeria 78
   Nigerian English 30
'The Night Before Christmas' (Clement Clarke Moore) 331
NIIT (Learning Solutions Corporation) 170, 171
Nokia 181
Norse language 133–4
Notting Hill Carnival, London 266–7
nouns
   abstract nouns 80, 175, 271
   adjective–noun 80
   countable and uncountable nouns 200
   noun clauses 242, 316
   noun phrases 282
   verb–noun 80
novels, reading 314–15
number games 314
nurseries 125
nutrition
   education 232

healthy 234–5
*see also* food
nutritional deficiencies 227, 235

## O

Oates, Joyce Carol 86
Obama, Barack 88, 89, 388
Obama, Michelle 88, 89
obesity 246, 249
Olympic Games 287, 297
One Laptop Per Child (OLPC) project, Rwanda 168–9
*The Opening of the Unreasonable Writing of our Inglish Toung* (John Hart) 134
oral practice
  book discussions 316
  debates 39, 168, 362
  group discussions 27, 36, 43, 55, 59, 70, 76, 79, 84, 105, 124, 131, 143, 159, 174, 179, 190, 200, 227, 236, 245, 275, 320, 332, 343, 359, 363
  interviews 69, 138, 183, 256
  options themes 263, 289, 323, 329, 341, 353
  presentations 10, 28, 46, 62, 95, 169–70, 260, 325
  role playing 69, 165, 209, 256, 377
  speeches, delivering 275
  two-person discussions 156, 179, 209, 216, 302
organ transplants
  illegal trade in human organs 364–5
  organ donors 363–5
  xenotransplantation 359–62
Organisation for Economic Co-operation (OECD) 34, 307
'ought to' 62
Oxford and Cambridge Boat Race 319–20
Oyster cards 190

## P

paintball 288, 293–5
Pakistan 77
*Pamphlet for Grammar* 134
*The Panopticon* (Jenni Fagan) 86
Papworth, Neil 181

parkour 298–300
Pashtuns 77
passive sentences 5, 284
passive verbs 258–9
passive voice 183
past continuous tense 65, 258
past simple tense 183, 258, 329
patriarchy 105
Peer, Rachel Martin 100–1
Penny, Laurie 85
people trafficking 63, 64, 281
perception 248
  effect of culture on 398
Perskyi, Constantin 195
pesci-vegetarianism 227
pesticides 3, 216
phrasal verbs 155
phytonutrients 223
*Pig-Heart Boy* (Malorie Blackman) 361–2
Pink, Dan 173
plagiarism 164, 165
Plato 79
poetry 251–2, 306–7, 319–20, 331
Poincaré, Henri 401
pollution 11
*Pompeii* (Robert Harris) 315
positive sentences 132
the possessive 209, 311
poverty
  energy poverty 34–6, 169
  food poverty 20–3
  United States 7
Power Distance 270
prefixes
  *im-* 371
  *in-* 376
  *un-* 369
premises 400
prepositional verbs 189
prepositions 111
  'despite'/'in spite of' 245
present continuous tense 183, 258
present participle 233
present perfect continuous tense 104
present perfect tense 202, 329
present simple tense 183, 258
presentations 10, 28, 46, 62, 95, 169–70, 260, 325

*Pride and Prejudice* (Jane Austen) 93
Primark 41–2
pronouns, reference 23, 82, 114
Protestant Reformation 331, 342
pump storage schemes 32
puns 36

## Q

questions
  'any' 132
  rhetorical questions 97, 275
  'some' 132

## R

radio, invention of 195
Raffles, Sir Stamford 283
rainwater harvesting 17, 18–19
rationality 399
  deductive reasoning 399
  inductive reasoning 399
  moral reasoning 404
Rec Ball 293
recipe writing 273
The Recuyell of the Historyes of Troye 134
reference pronouns 23, 82, 114
Reid, Melanie 246–7
religions 401
renewable energy
  solar power 27, 389
  wind power 24–34, 389, 390
Rentokil 220–1
reported speech 33, 112, 163, 169
reporting verbs 169
resources, squandering 3
  *see also* food waste
rhetorical questions 97, 275
Richard the Lionheart, king of England 280
RNLI (Royal National Lifeboat Institution) 99
Robertson, Eliza 381–4
robots 372–7
  agricultural applications 375–6, 377
  artificial companionship 374
  educational applications 373
  home applications 372
role playing 69, 165, 209, 256, 377
Rosphere (Robotic Sphere) 377

# Index

rugby   324
running   289–91
Rwanda
   energy poverty   35
   school computers   168–9
Ryan's Well Foundation   13–16, 17, 18

## S

salt, superstitions and   335
Samburu Project   17
Samhain   341
Santa Claus   330–1
Sapir-Whorf hypothesis   398
saturated fat   234, 235
Saturnalia   331, 341
schools
   adventure sports activities   288
   community projects   13
   school vending machines   154
   *see also* education
science and technology
   body repair technologies   354–65
   mobile phones   44, 115, 176–93
   technology in education   160–75
Scotland
   bungee jumping   300–2
   customs and traditions   341–4
   surfing   321–2
Scrabble   313
seaweed harvesting   228–9
self-esteem   243
semaphore   195
Senegal   88
sense perception   398
sentence structure   80–1, 83, 117, 348
   active sentences   5, 284
   complex sentences   9, 90–1, 117
   negative sentences   132
   passive sentences   5, 284
   positive sentences   132
   zero conditional   146
   *see also* clauses
Shakespeare, William   133
*Sharp Objects* (Gillian Flynn)   86
Shatner, William   142
'should'   62
Silverstein, Robert Alan   51
Simons, Daniel   149–50

'since'   202–3
'since'/'for'   172
Singapore, cultural diversity in   282–4
slave labour   40–55, 347, 362
   child labour   41, 44, 46, 63, 64, 78
   products of labour abuse   44–5
smartphones   177, 181, 184
   activities   145
smartwatch   184–6
sneezing, superstition and   335
social learning   174
social media   201–13
   advertising and marketing   157
   cyberbullying   205–6, 210–13
   educational networking   174
   family issues   206–8
   friendships and   391–3
   knowledge sharing   402
   personal information, protecting   205
   personal wellbeing, impacts on   392–3
   positive impacts   201–3
social relationships
   English language   128–41, 255
   women achievers   92–107
   *see also* education; social media
Soemmering, Samuel   195
solar power   27, 389
South Africa   88
   alternative food sources   217
   education deficit   88
   South African English   129
South Korea   130
Spain
   flamenco   273
   robotics   377
Sparkes, David   238
speech writing   51, 58, 96, 97, 120, 204, 223, 249, 365, 377
   main principles   79
   rhetorical questions   97
   tips   97
speedball   293–4
spirulina   228
Spitalfields, London   261–2
sport
   adventure sports   287–9, 296–7, 300–3

Commonwealth Games   339
motivation   289–91
Olympic Games   287, 297
optimal amount of   240–2
prehistoric times   287
protective benefits of   241
team sports and educational performance   243–5
teenagers and   237–42
therapeutic benefits of   295
Sri Lanka, customs and traditions   344–5
state verbs   65
steel bands   266, 267
stem cells   357
'stereotypes game'   274
stilt fishing   345
stock market   6
Stockett, Kathryn   52
'stop'   43
Strauss, Levi   68
stress, work-related   187–9
sub-Saharan Africa   3
   education deficit   88–9
   education initiatives   168–9
   energy poverty   34–5, 36, 169
   water and sanitation projects   13–19
Sudoku   314
suffrage movement   85, 86, 105, 107
sugars   234, 235
superlative adjectives   322, 334
supermarkets, and food sharing   20–1
superstitions   334–7
supply chain   3, 4
surfing   321–2
SUS laws   252, 253
swimming   237–9, 305
Sydney Harbour Bridge Climb   291–2
syllogisms   400

## T

T-charts   167, 204
tablets   145, 162
Tactical-Milsom paintball   293
Taliban   76, 77
Tanzania   88
tattoos   327–8, 329

tea 349–52
team sports, and educational performance 243–5
technology and mankind 366–70
   effects on children 369
   ergonomics 370
   robots 372–5
   texting, posture and 367–8
technology in education 160–75
   Flat Classroom project 172–5
   Hole-in-the-Wall project, India 170–1
   laptops in the classroom 161–3, 164–7
   One Laptop Per Child (OLPC) project, Rwanda 168–9
teenage health 230–49
   body image 246–7
   healthy eating 234–6
   sport 237–42
   texting health messages 231–3
telegraphy 195
telephones
   invention of 67, 195
   *see also* mobile phones
television
   advertising 134, 153, 196
   first colour television 196
   invention of 195
   licences 309
   viewership 145
'tell'/'say' 112
Teresa, Mother 76, 94
terrorism 57, 78
'text neck' 367
textile workers 41, 54, 68, 257, 262
texting 177, 178, 181, 207, 233
   health messages 231–3
   posture and 367–8
Thailand 217
Thames Barrier 320–1
Thames, River 317–21
Thatcher, Margaret 93
'the more…, the more…' 83
Theory of Knowledge (TOK) 43, 397–404
   ethics 403–4
   knowledge and knowledge claims 402
   Truth Tests 402–3

Ways of Knowing 397–401
third conditional 248
*Three Men in a Boat* (Jerome K. Jerome) 317
time, expressions of 172, 202
time management 188, 244
tissue engineering 357–9
'to be able to'/'unable to' 239–40
*To Kill a Mockingbird* (Harper Lee) 314, 315
Tolstoy, Leo 142
'too'/'not… either' 343–4
toponyms 134
*The Tortilla Curtain* (T.C. Boyle) 60–1
toxic waste 27
Trades Union Congress (TUC) 4
Trafficking Victims Protection Reauthorization Acts 45
Tricking (martial arts) 299
'trolley dilemma' 404
truck drivers 98–9
Truth Tests 402–3
   Coherence Test 403
   Correspondence Test 403
   Pragmatism Test 403
Twain, Mark 206
Twelve Days of Christmas 341
Twitter 157, 233, 391

## U
Uganda
   energy poverty 35
   water and sanitation projects 12, 13
umbrellas, superstitions and 335
*un-* prefix 369
uncertainty avoidance 270
unemployment 6, 7
UNESCO 89, 272–3
*Unique* (Alison Allen-Gray) 379–80
United Nations 75
   Food and Agriculture Organization (FAO) 217
   Millennium Development Goals 34
United States
   alternative food sources 217
   American English 129, 130
   'bad girl' fiction 86
   childhood obesity 152, 153

   food waste 4
   foreign aid 89
   gender equality gap 307
   homelessness and hunger 6–8
   immigrant language loss 136, 137
   junk food marketing 152–4
   mobile phone use 178, 180, 207
   poverty 7
   racism 136–7
   robots in farming 377
   slavery 46–7, 48–9
   undocumented immigration 57–8, 60–1
   vegetarianism 226, 227
   white-water rafting 296–7
universal generalisations 399
Unsworth, Cathi 86
'used to' 226
'used to'/'get used to' 186
Ustinov, Peter 142

## V
vaccines 35
Valdesolo, Piercarlo 404
Valentine's Day 332–4, 341
van Asch, Henry 302–3
van der Bergh, Adriaan 161–2
van Gogh, Vincent 401
veganism 226, 227
vegetarian food 222–7
   calorie content 222
   changing to 224–5
   dietary fibre 223
   economic option 226
   phytonutrients 223
   semi-vegetarian diets 226–7
   vitamins 222–3
verb–noun 80
verbs
   action verbs 65
   active verbs 258
   first conditional 114–15
   future tense 258
   imperative 124, 179
   modal verbs 149, 236–7
   passive verbs 258–9
   past continuous tense 65, 258
   past simple tense 183, 258, 329
   phrasal verbs 155
   prepositional verbs 189

# Index

present continuous tense   183, 258
present perfect continuous tense   104
present perfect tense   202, 329
present simple tense   183, 258
reporting verbs   169
state verbs   65
third conditional   248
zero conditional   146, 311
veteran homelessness   7
Victoria, Queen   351
video games, violence and   294–5
Vikings   341
vitamins and minerals   222–3, 234
volunteering   305

## W

Washington Fellowship for Young African Leaders   89
water
  conservation   11, 13
  food production and   11, 215
  Ryan's Well Foundation   13–16, 17, 18
  water and sanitation projects   13–19
  water scarcity   10–12, 13, 14
*We Walked on Water* (Eliza Robertson)   381–4
weight
  management   235
  obesity   152, 153, 246, 249
*Weirdo* (Cathi Unsworth)   86
whales and dolphins   36–7
white-water rafting   296–7
wholegrain foods   234
*Whores on the Hill* (Colleen Curran)   86
*Wild Swans* (Jung Chang)   69
Wilkins, Fran   99–100
Wilson, Harold   142
wind energy   27
  history of   25–6
  wind turbines   25, 26, 27, 28, 29
  wind farms   24–39, 389, 390
    anti-wind farm lobby   31–2
    benefits   27
    costs   28–9
    disadvantages   27, 31–2, 37
    offshore   32, 37, 390
    subsidies   31, 32
*The Wind in the Willows* (Kenneth Grahame)   317
windmills   25
Windsor Castle   318
wingsuit flying   288
winter solstice   341
Wise, Ernie   180
*Witness the Night* (Kishwar Desai)   81–3
women
  female achievers   92–107
  International Women's Day   105–7
  social inequalities   81, 82, 105
  suffragettes   85, 86, 105, 107
  in traditional male occupations   98–105
  violence against   81
  women's rights   78
  *see also* girls
woodsball   293
word games   134, 311–13
work
  time management   188
  unemployment   6, 7
  workplace stress   187–9
World Day for Cultural Diversity for Dialogue and Development   274–5
World Energy Outlook (WEO)   34
World English   129
Worsley, Jenyth   319
'would'   50
writing practice
  blogs   5–6, 23, 45–6, 73, 138, 267, 353
  book reviews   53
  diary writing   10, 19, 66, 84, 88, 127, 152, 180, 344, 362
  emails   10, 91, 135, 190, 197, 203, 226, 229, 292, 303, 348, 353
  formal proposals   107, 156, 165
  guidelines, preparing sets of   180, 204, 275, 377
  leaflets and flyers   62, 95, 186, 265, 303
  letters   16, 30–1, 34, 43, 229, 325, 334, 357
  magazine articles   12, 117, 143, 149, 221, 267, 325, 353, 365
  personal response tasks   16, 51, 81, 87, 91, 107, 159, 196–7, 233, 249, 267, 285, 303, 325, 345, 353, 365, 369, 377, 398
  recipe writing   273
  speech writing   51, 58, 96, 97, 120, 204, 223, 249, 365, 377
  summaries   297
written assignment: higher level   378–86
  key points   378
  language use   386
  objectives   378
  organization and development   385
  rationale   378, 384–5
  receptive and written productive skills   384–5
written assignment: standard level   387–96
  language use   396
  organization and development   395
  rationale   388
  receptive and written productive skills   394–5
  requirements   387–8
Wynne, Arthur   311

## X

xenotransplantation   359–62

## Y

York   133–4
Young African Women's Leaders Forum   89
Yousafzai, Malala   75–9, 81, 84

## Z

Zamenhof, Lazar   141–2
Zephaniah, Benjamin   251–4
zero conditional   146, 311
Zusak, Marcus   379
Zworykin, Vladimir   196